LIVE AS LONG AS YOU DARE!

A Journey to Gain Healthy, Vibrant Years

by Leonard W. Heflich

Printed in the United States of America

ISBN: Softcover   978-1-63871-525-2
        eBook   978-1-63871-523-8

Republished by: PageTurner Press and Media LLC
Publication Date: 09/02/2021

To order copies of this book, contact:

PageTurner Press and Media
Phone: 1-888-447-9651
info@pageturner.us
www.pageturner.us

Live as Long as You Dare!

A Journey to Gain Healthy, Vibrant Years

Second Edition

Leonard W. Heflich

November 10, 2019

Preface

This book is about living. If you want to live a longer, healthier life, this book is for you. You can be of any age to benefit. Age is only a number, and often a state of mind, neither of which should limit our expectations. Daring to live a longer, healthier, more vibrant life, regardless of our current age, is the first step in making it happen. Age is an artificial barrier that we must dare to break through.

If you are twenty, in forty short years, you will be sixty. What condition do you want to be in when you get there? Nurturing and developing your healthy practices now, will enable you to arrive in great condition, ready for another fifty or more active years. And the best part, is that we don't have to wait to enjoy the benefits. The changes that we are able to make in diet and lifestyle today will produce benefits that we can enjoy now.

If you are sixty, why not dare to live for another fifty years, or longer? It will take active steps to make this happen. Most people incorrectly believe that their health is what it is and cannot be changed. We believe that some people have good genes and are healthy, while others suffer and live in a diminished state for uncontrollable or unavoidable reasons.

The fact is that our genes account for only a small part of our health. Practices and attitude are more instrumental than we think. Attitude plays an important role in this book and in our journey. The first mistake we usually make is accepting our health as it is. The second mistake is not doing something about it. And often, the third mistake is taking drugs to 'correct' it. We don't want to go there. We want to take active responsibility for our health, learn as much as we can about practices and technology that can help us, and adopt a healthy routine that will nurture and develop our health, so that we can live longer, healthier lives. It is not an accident or good luck. We must dare and then do it.

When I talk about taking steps to maintain our health, I am assuming that you have the capacity to be healthy. If you were healthy at some point in your life, but have lost it in some ways, there is hope that you can stop the further progression of disease and perhaps even take steps to reverse it, in order to restore your healthy state. I am not talking about diseases for which a cure doesn't currently exist, but rather about preventable diseases, such as heart disease, hypertension, diabetes, obesity and many forms of cancer. These diseases have a common set of root causes, and are avoidable, if we are aware of and make the necessary changes in our behavior and lifestyle. This is the route we want to take. I realize that we are not accustomed to thinking of these diseases as being preventable, because we are not aware of the common causes. We can change this. The prize is large, while the cost and risk are low. We will want to learn as much as we can about our particular health issues and identify the root causes. Then we will take steps to eliminate or reverse them.

> For every complex problem, there is an answer that is clear, simple
> and wrong.
> -H. L. Mencken

Much of this book is based on my own personal journey to learn how to take care of myself. As I write this, I am sixty-six years of age (notice that I didn't say old!), basically healthy, with occasional aches and pains, but have discovered during my research for this book that I was well on my way to becoming diabetic and hypertensive, like too many people today. Writing this book helped me to realize these facts about my own body, even though no one, including my own doctor, had warned me. I have read, experimented, observed, theorized and learned how to improve my own health, making significant improvements in blood glucose control and blood pressure in less than a year. I am stronger and feel better than I have in decades. I will share what I have learned, and hope that you can benefit by making similar changes and improvements in your health.

There isn't just one change; there are dozens, perhaps hundreds of changes, each of which makes a tiny impact, but when combined and directed towards our vision, add up to make a powerful change. It helps when dealing with a big, intractable problem, like aging, to break it up into small, bite-sized pieces that we can manage. Then as we find a solution to each little piece, we make that change part of our routine. We can commit to making one change a week, for example, so as not to overwhelm ourselves with change. You will be amazed after a year of effort how much progress you can make. Our goal is to get off of the death spiral, where we gradually gain weight, lose muscle tone, and lose control of blood glucose and blood pressure. The result is that we reduce activity only to experience a further deterioration of capability in a declining spiral. Wait a second – isn't that what happens during aging? Yes and no. Yes, if we stay on the death spiral. No, if we choose to reverse it by losing weight, doing more, building muscle, improving blood glucose and blood pressure control. The result then can be that we are able to do more, while enhancing bodily capabilities in an ever-improving virtuous cycle. This is where we want to be!

You have to apply yourself each day to becoming a little better. By applying yourself to the task of becoming a little better each day over a period of time, you will become a lot better.
-UCLA Basketball Coach John Wooden

Before I started writing this book, I spent a lot of time educating myself about the existing published studies. There are literally thousands of journal articles and several $500 books to invest in. What amazed me is that the answers to most of my questions were already studied and published. Some were published over ten years ago. And yet, I had not seen the results of these studies reported or reviewed anywhere, and I consider myself to be a well-informed person. After all, this was my career. Even worse, friends and family members were not aware of the results of these studies or how they could help themselves by incorporating the learning into their own lives.

I am not a Doctor or even a Nutritionist. I am a problem solver. I have spent my forty-plus-year career as a chemist and a food scientist, studying the relationship between diet and health. It is the kind of complex, multi-factored problem that I love to work on. There are many pieces to the puzzle, which often do not fit neatly together, and many of the 'facts' we have are incomplete or even wrong. Butter is bad; butter is good. Coconut oil is demonized as a poison, then is vindicated by real research and ultimately becomes a health food and cure! We're told that eggs and cholesterol are clogging our arteries, so we stop eating eggs and take drugs to reduce cholesterol, only to learn that our bodies make more cholesterol than we can ever eat and the low-fat diet we went on was the real root cause of our imbalanced blood chemistry. And on and on. Need I say more? We will discuss what we know, what we don't know and what we can theorize based on what is observable, even if we don't fully understand it. If there is a conflict between what I say and what you hear from your doctor, I suggest that you discuss it with your doctor, and if that doesn't resolve the difference, then follow your doctor's advice. Doctors are starting to learn more about the microbiome and the impact of diet and lifestyle on health. Let's look forward to the day when doctors will prescribe a high-fiber diet for hypertension relief instead of a drug. The suggestions I make in this book are based on what is published in the scientific literature and on my own personal experience. Use this as a starting point for your own investigation into what will work best for you.

> The doctor of the future will no longer treat the human frame with drugs, but rather will cure and prevent disease with nutrition.
> - Thomas A. Edison

My plan for this book is to describe a journey from where we find ourselves now to where we want to be. In order to get 'there' we will need to take many steps. There will be uncertainty and the need for us to ask questions, be observant and learn. We will need to consider where the 'there' is that we would like to arrive at someday. The good news is that the possibilities are expanding rapidly and will accelerate in the near future. I suggest that it is better to think and act expansively and not confine ourselves to a diminished future, limited by drugs, restrictive diets and low expectations. I won't tell you what to eat but focus on how to eat. I will not discuss drugs or medical procedures. I am not a fan of restrictive diets, as avoiding groups of foods can be unhealthy by depriving us of beneficial nutrients, and the evidence supporting the benefits or possible harm is weak at best and will take at least thirty years for the science to be done. History shows that prognostication from incomplete data is how we got into this mess in the first place. I'm not going there.

We will examine the forces that drive us, and present enough science to enable us to better manage our diets in order to achieve a healthy body weight. We will talk about diabetes and related diseases and consider what is causing these. We will collect souvenirs along our journey and these will become the hundreds of little changes that we make in our lives in order to maintain or even build our strength. Like any good journey, it will change us. It will make us aware of new possibilities and open us to new ways. Let the journey begin.

An interesting piece of trivia is that my family emigrated to the US in 1854 from Darmstadt, Germany. 'Darm' means 'intestine' in German, so Darmstadt is intestine city. Ironic perhaps that the intestine has become the focal point and root cause of my investigation into staying healthy. Like the saying that all roads lead to Rome, all of our health issues lead back to the intestines. We all live in Darmstadt!

> Our food should be our medicine and our medicine should be our food.
> - Hippocrates

I hope that this book is informative and compelling enough to motivate you to dare to live a longer and healthier life and give you some ideas on how to do it.

Dedication

I dedicate this book in honor of, and to the loving memory of, my best friend, Leonard E. Burger Jr. He struggled his entire life with obesity, eventually succumbing to diabetes and heart failure. He had a very big heart, but not big enough to deal with obesity and diabetes.

I am saddened not just with the loss of my friend, but with the reasons why. Why did he die? Who or what killed him? Did he unknowingly allow it to happen? In a sense, we all share his fate, because we do not, or seemingly cannot change the path we are on. On the other hand, much of the advice that we have been given over the past thirty years, from well-intentioned but misinformed activists, media and experts, was wrong and often harmful to our health. This has put most of us unknowingly on the wrong path. Only recently, for example, we have learned how wrong it was to reduce fat, while unavoidably increasing sugar consumption. My friend died from bad nutritional advice. In a way, this is a murder mystery, and we are all characters and potential victims in the story. We choose our role in this story.

I have had to accept the heavy burden that although I can help myself, I may not be able to help others, including my best friend, without their desire. His journey is over. Ours is just beginning. I sincerely hope that this book gives you some information that will allow you to help yourself to live a healthy, vibrant, extended life for as many years as you want. For as long as you dare.

Acknowledgements

Many people have helped inspire me to write this book, some by their good example, and some by not so good! By people who have spent their careers working to improve our understanding of aging and nutrition. By people who love me and support me.

Thank you especially to my mentors, coaches and supporters:

Leonard E. Burger Jr.

William H. Knightly

Dale Kuhn

Dr. Otto Siegel

Carolina Maria Brose

Vianet Galan Mendez

Marilyn Ann Heflich

Lynda, Adrienne and Brian

CHAPTER 1

Life Extension – The Launching Pad for the Journey

The concept of life extension is relatively new. Jim Strole and Bernadeane Brown started talking about it in 1968 when they cofounded the Coalition for Radical Life Extension. They have pioneered the shocking concept that death is not inevitable. We die because we either allow it or actually want it. Perhaps you have had the experience of being with a person when they were dying. The mind may give up, but the body wants to live, fighting up until the last breath. The opposite also happens, where the person gives up and mentally chooses to die, especially when they have lost a beloved spouse. We are raised in a culture where death is considered to be a part of life. That may be a healthy way to cope with death, but not a good way to extend life. If we want to extend our healthy lives, we must start by believing that it is possible, and then dare to do so. Jim and Bernadeane turn the tables on aging and death by challenging the culture of death. If death is not inevitable, and we can take active steps to extend our lives, would we take them? Given the rapid advance of technologies that already exist with many more powerful ones to come soon, maybe we should do what we can now so that when those powerful new technologies become available, we can still be alive enough to benefit. We may actually be the first generation to dare to live as long as we want. Read Jim and Bernadeane's book, *Living Without Death: The Experience of Physical Immortality*[1]. It will shock you and inspire you to start the journey to extend your healthy life.

Modern-day western medicine has done a great job of extending our unhealthy lives, largely by treating the symptoms of disease after it is too late to prevent it. This may be better than dying or suffering, as people did before modern medicine, but since the drugs treat symptoms, not the root cause, we may feel better, but not get better. The side effects and interactions are often worse than the disease itself. This is not where we want to be. We want to extend our healthy lives with cure not care. To do this, we must identify and eliminate the causes that underlie the illness so that further treatment is not required. This is where we want to be. Healthy living for an extended period of time, without drugs or disease. We can do this if we listen and support our bodies' natural, healthy mechanisms. We have ignored or confounded these mechanisms with stress, antibiotics, lack of exercise, poor diets, lack of sleep and relaxation, lack of exposure to the sun, lack of exposure to nature, etc. – in essence, bad practices and bad attitudes.

If you are depressed, you are living in the past.
If you are anxious, you are living in the future.
If you are at peace, you are living in the present.
-Lao Tzu

There's not much sense in extending our life if we are only gaining additional years of debilitating illness. The goal of extending our lives requires that we are healthy enough to enjoy an active and vibrant life. Being healthy doesn't only mean the absence of disease, but being fit and able physically, mentally, emotionally and spiritually. Achieving all those dimensions of health will keep us busy. Being healthy is table stakes in life extension. But it won't happen just by wishing or even daring. We must do it.

In nature, there are neither rewards nor punishments--there are consequences.
-Robert Green Ingersoll

The Technology of Life Extension

There has been a lot of activity in the development of life extension technologies over the past 30 years. Some of these technologies are powerful and ready to be implemented now. Others with tremendous potential are still in the experimental stages and will take another ten years or more before being ready for the market. We can learn about these technologies and avail ourselves of the ones that are ready and relevant to our personal needs. Failing to do so could be a huge opportunity missed. There is no single technology or solution that will successfully extend our healthy lives. There are many different technologies, each targeted on a different cause of aging, that together can synergistically combine to give us an extended healthy life. We will address some of these technologies later in the book. Others are beyond the scope of this book, such as: stem cells, telomerase, bioactive peptides, Growth Differentiating Factor, and hormonal balance. If you really want to keep up with the latest technologies and advances in life extension, attend the annual RAAD Festival (Revolution Against Aging and Death), organized by the Coalition for Radical Life Extension, held each year in September.

What Is Aging?

Aging is considered to be a natural and normal process of programmed senescence and loss of function that happens to living things. If we look around the animal kingdom, we find that most animals exhibit aging and death and therefore, we consider it to be 'normal'. However, there are cells in our body that do not age, meaning they show no evidence of senescence or decrease in function with time. These cells are in our reproductive system. There are animals that do not age as well. Flatworms, Planaria, bacteria, yeast and fungi do not age. They continue to divide and live without limit, or until something else eats them! Cancer cells also do not age.

Aging, therefore, is not universal. And perhaps not even inevitable. Our goal is to identify and understand the root causes of aging so that we can take steps to slow them down, stop them or even reverse them.2 Aging is a complex and intractable problem, which is made more obscure by misinformation, lack of information and a plethora of cultural traditions that prepare us for death instead of life.

We live in a culture of the past, defined around the concepts of aging and death. The way we talk, the words we use, the way we think, the way we plan, are all derived from a culture of death. We are forced to 'retire' from work, when many of us actually don't want to stop working.

We make a 'last will and testament' to plan for what happens to our assets when we die. We live our lives according to rules that were designed to control our behavior in this life so that we achieve reward in the next life. We move into fifty-five plus communities to be isolated from other 'old' people, trying to enjoy our diminished existence while waiting to die. Our bodily functions deteriorate but our doctor tells us that this is 'normal' for our age, rather than considering a proactive approach such as hormone replacement therapy, or changes in lifestyle that could stop or reverse the loss. We become diabetic, overweight, hypertensive, hypercholesteremic and our doctor prescribes drugs with life-threatening or mind-numbing side effects, instead of helping us make changes in our behavior that could have the same result without the negative side effects. We become 'senior citizens'. We dress like 'old' people. We get defined and define ourselves as 'old'. Aging is inevitable; the calendar relentlessly marks the passage of days and years. But getting old and dying are not the inevitable results of aging. We actually plan and choose to get old and die. It's the way it's supposed to be, so why fight it? We fight it because we can and because we want to live.

Personally, I don't want to live forever. I believe that the day will come when I will decide that I have had enough and it's time to move on. However, in the meantime I want to make my life as full of meaning and value as I can manage. I want to savor every minute like a gourmand who slowly chews and explores the flavor, texture, aroma and nuance of every mouthful. But at the same time, pack every minute with meaningful activities and accomplishments. The opportunities to explore, learn, experience and do, today are greater than ever before in history. What an exciting and wonderful time to be alive!

Let us endeavor so to live so that when we come to die even the undertaker will be sorry.
-Mark Twain

Ernest Becker in his masterwork, *The Denial of Death*[3], points out that "the idea of death, the fear of it, haunts the human animal like nothing else; it is a mainspring of human activity – activity designed largely to avoid the fatality of death, to overcome it by denying in some way that it is the final destiny for man." He later states, "There are 'healthy-minded' persons who maintain that fear of death is not a natural thing for man, that we are not born with it." Our culture and our behaviors are deeply rooted in death, based on the belief that the 'healthiest' way to deal with the reality of the death of our loved ones and eventually of ourselves, is to consider death to be a natural part of life. If we can believe that our dead friends and family members are actually not 'dead' but merely have transitioned to a different state, we can avoid some of the anxiety of missing them. We can deny death, accept it as our destiny, or live without placing artificial limits on what is possible, while neither denying nor accepting death. We choose life instead of death.

When was the last time you saw a squirrel that was unable to climb a tree? Or had to ask a buddy to crack open an acorn for them? You know, I cannot do that anymore? Squirrels live about 18 years, according to Wikipedia, which is a long time for a little critter. They are active and continue to do squirrely things until the day they die. We also want to keep doing squirrely things until the day we die!

There are many factors that combine together to cause what we observe as aging, including:

- Immune system decline of function and eventual failure

- Hypertension (inability to maintain healthy blood pressure)

- Diabetes (inability to control blood glucose)

- Decline in the ability to heal

- Failure to thrive (loss of the will to live)

- Accumulation of damage from oxidative stress

- Circulatory failure (heart disease, arterial blockage, hardening of the arteries)

- Loss of muscle quantity and tone

- Dropping hormone levels and imbalance

- Dropping levels of bioactive peptides

- Slowing metabolism that results in weight gain and obesity

- Loss of mental acuity and ultimately dementia

We cannot deny that these factors are real and cause real decline in bodily function over time with eventual death. The questions we need to consider are: Are these factors normal? Are they inevitable? Do we have to accept these declines in bodily function or can we do something about them? We cannot stop aging, but perhaps we can avoid getting old. There are technologies available and steps we can take now to extend our healthy lifespan. Declining or inclining capabilities? We have more control and influence than we think. In Appendix 7, I have listed 100 little changes you can make to improve your health and longevity.

Disease and the Metabolic Syndrome

There is an epidemic of disease that has been raging for the past thirty years globally and continues to worsen. The diseases include: diabetes, hypertension, depression, heart disease, obesity, stroke, cancer, food allergies, autoimmune diseases and PCOS (polycystic ovary syndrome).[4] The worst part is that almost all of us, regardless of age, are on the path to contracting these diseases. We call it the progression of old age, as if the consequences were expected and inevitable. But even young people are on the path and already are experiencing health issues in spite of being in 'good' shape. Most of us are in denial and choose to ignore the early warnings until the disease state is reached and drugs are prescribed.

We diagnose and treat these diseases in isolation as if they were not connected, but we now know that they are connected. Gerald Reaven, in 1988, called it the Metabolic Syndrome, by proposing a common set of causes that connect these seemingly unconnected diseases. The picture that is emerging shows that these diseases are linked to an underlying set of common causes. It is complicated and difficult to explain or even imagine and will take decades for the complete scientific evidence to emerge.

How did we get into this mess in the first place? Basically, it all started in 1985 with a Denver millionaire named Phil Sokolof, who became the first successful food activist. Mr. Sokolof had a heart attack and asked his doctor why it happened and what he could do about it. His doctor explained that it was due to a diet high in saturated fats. Phil did some reading about it and discovered that many of his favorite foods were high in saturated fats, but even worse, the saturated fats were often from imported tropical oils like palm and coconut. Sokolof took out full-page ads in the major newspapers, accusing food companies of killing Americans to save a few pennies on the ingredient cost by using cheap, imported tropical oils that were high in saturated fats, when they could be using domestically produced soybean oil that was healthier, instead.

The food companies immediately reacted by replacing the tropical oils with partially hydrogenated soybean oil. This was low in saturated fats; however, the partial hydrogenation process that was used to process the oil to make it functional and stable also produced trans fatty acids. No one knew what the health impact of these would be at the time. Ironically, years later when the research was done, we discovered that the trans fats actually caused heart disease, while the saturated fats they replaced, did not. In any case, tropical oils came out of our diet and trans fats went in. At the same time, it was concluded that fat, not just saturated fat, was the cause of heart disease, so we went on a low-fat craze. Products were reformulated to remove or reduce fat, with the unfortunate result of increasing sugar. Low-fat diets became popular. In hindsight, we did everything possible wrong.

The production of trans fats via partial hydrogenation has since been banned and removed from our diet, and fats in general, saturated fats specifically, have been shown not to cause heart disease. The result is that butter, cocoa butter, coconut oil and palm oil are now considered healthy and are back in out diet. The real culprit all along was sugar, and by reducing fat and increasing sugar in our diet, we made things worse and started a huge upswing in obesity and the diseases of the Metabolic Syndrome. Good intentions and overzealous extrapolation of data resulted in disease and death for millions of people. We made a lot of mistakes, and we still have a lot to learn. We now know that high amounts of sugar in the diet is part of the problem, but let's avoid the temptation to think it's that simple. We need to be careful not to demonize sugar, gluten, carrots, or any other food or group of foods, as we demonized fat and saturated fats in the past, as we could unwittingly create the next wave of disease.

Where am I to go now that I've gone too far?
-Golden Earring, 'When the Bullet Hits the Bone'

The diseases of the Metabolic Syndrome are related and stem from similar causes. We don't have to accept them and can take active steps to prevent them, allowing us to live longer, healthier lives without these diseases.

Vision

We want to have a personal mission and vision to guide us on our journey to a longer, healthier life. Having no mission or vision is like walking in the woods, with trees and hills all around blocking our view. We have a difficult time deciding in which direction to walk. We are lost. A vision is like having a compass that always points north, to our vision. It allows us to walk towards our vision even though we cannot see it. When we have a personal mission and vision, everything else falls into place. We have a framework, a reference, a context within which to make decisions and operate. Making decisions, even big ones, gets easier and we make better decisions, ones that are aligned with our vision.

In order to support our daring goal of living longer, healthier lives, we are going to do something that we probably have never done before. In fact, it is something that very few people have done before or needed to do. Because the technology and practices supporting healthy life extension are advancing so rapidly, there are many people alive today, even those currently in their sixties and eighties, who are likely to live productive lives for another fifty years or more. We will need a vision in order to make that happen. Only Toyota has a fifty-year vision!

Yesterday I was clever, so I wanted to change the world.
Today I am wise, so I am changing myself.
-Rumi (13th century Persian poet)

9

To help us define our vision, let's start with a question that is radical and new: Would we live our life differently today, if we knew that we had fifty or one hundred more healthy, active years to live? I think we would. In fact, it almost doesn't matter how long we actually live. Having a vision to live longer will change the way we behave today. We may be more inclined to tackle that big project or take a long trip or do something 'crazy' that we wouldn't consider doing if our expected horizon was shorter. *Why bother, I'll be dead in ten years?* What a terrible way to limit our potential. Most people currently in their sixties and eighties, consider that they have at best a ten- or twenty-year horizon ahead, with the last ten likely spent going to doctors, taking lots of pills and not feeling like doing very much. This is not the horizon that I am talking about. I'm talking about energetic and active years, where we are healthy and vibrant enough to do what we want to do and enjoy it. Leave the walker and cane at home – we will not need them!

If I knew I was going to live this long, I'd have taken better care of myself!
- Mickey Mantle

What will we look like when we arrive at our visionary goal? Will we be diminished in health and vibrancy or will we maintain our activity level? Is it actually possible for us to be better and stronger than we are today? If our health doesn't limit our physical and mental activities, what kind of goals will we set?

"Would you tell me please, which way I ought to go from here?"
"That depends a good deal on where you want to get to" said the Cat.
"I don't much care where" said Alice.
"Then it doesn't matter which way you go" said the Cat.
"So long as I get somewhere" Alice added as an explanation.
"Oh, you're sure to do that", said the Cat, "if only you walk long enough."
-From Lewis Carroll's Alice's Adventures in Wonderland

Our vision doesn't need to be very detailed, and it doesn't need to describe a destination or even a specific goal. We may surprise ourselves and get to the destination sooner than we planned or even worse, when we get there we may not know what to do next. Maybe when we get there we won't be ready to die! Life is best considered to be a journey and not a destination. Our vision should describe the journey we want to take. Envisioning a journey that is robust enough to guide us for the next fifty or one hundred years is truly a new adventure. We are among the first to attempt to do this, therefore we will be pioneers cutting a new path and developing new tools. The good news is that since no one knows how to do this, we can have some fun and make it up as we go. Let's get together in one hundred years to compare notes. Pretty heady and exciting stuff!

A personal vision can guide us towards a desired, healthy future state. Why vision small? We want to dare to aim high. We want to live our lives with intent and intensity. The intent comes from our vision. The intensity comes from our commitment to the vision. We want to create a BHAG – a Big Hairy Audacious Goal as described beautifully in *Built to Last: Successful Habits of Visionary Companies* written by <u>Jim Collins</u> and <u>Jerry I. Porras</u>[5]. Making the vision big, audacious and a little scary (that's the hairy part!), makes it interesting, challenging and worth our extra effort to achieve. Visioning small is a waste of time and effort. Visioning big will inspire us and those around us to dare to do big things.

> "The size of your dreams must always exceed your capacity to achieve them.
> If your dreams do not scare you, they are not big enough."
> -Ellen Johnson Sirleaf

A vision is the most powerful way to direct long-term behavior. It is a compass that keeps us heading in the right direction, even if we are occasionally derailed from our path by the stuff that life throws at us. We have no way of knowing what challenges will confront us in the future, but with a vision, we will not lose our way. We will always know which way to go and what choices to make, enabling us to make the little and big decisions along the way. A good choice is one that is aligned with and helps us get closer to our vision. Other choices that are not aligned with our vision will slow us down, dilute our efforts and drain our vital energy.

Where there is no vision, the people perish.
-Tao Te Ching

A vision also helps us stay focused on the future, not the past. The past was great, and it is gone. The only time that anything ever happens is now. We want to drive our 'now' based on where we want to be tomorrow and in the future. If every step we take brings us closer to our vision, and we keep at it for some time, we will eventually get there.

Yesterday is gone.
Tomorrow has not yet come.
We only have today.
Let us begin.
-Agnes Gonxha Bojax (Mother Theresa)

Without a vision, we are not only lost, but we are listless too. We don't know where to go and we don't know what to do. This is a recipe for disaster. We will lose interest in life and lose our love of life. Once this happens, it is a short distance to giving up. It's time to consider what we want to do (present) versus what we have to do (past), and what we will need to do in order to be successful (future). Limits are a thing of our past. We want to live in the moment, every single one of them for the next fifty or one hundred years, as Eckert Tolle describes in his seminal book, *The Power of Now*[6]. And we want to make each moment count and be valuable. Fifty years sounds like a long time, but to put it into perspective, it is only 18,250 days. That is a small finite number!

The search for happiness is one of the chief sources of unhappiness.
-Eric Hoffer

Purpose and Play

Consider two seemingly mutually exclusive concepts: purpose and play. We need a purpose to our lives in order to motivate us and excite us. And that is where the play comes in. Play is fun and fun is good. Play brings in the excitement. We want to devote our lives to some purpose that is meaningful to us, and also have some fun while doing it. Play is the grease on our gears and bearings. Without play we get grumpy and tired and eventually fail. Like a motor running without oil, it gets harder and harder all the time to do what we used to do easily. There just seems to be more friction, more obstacles in our way every day. That hill we used to climb has gotten a lot bigger lately. We have less and less tolerance for distractions and difficulties. This is not where we want to be. We want to live our lives with intent and intensity. Intent is having a purpose and a reason to live. Intensity is the energy we put into living so that we get the satisfying and meaningful experiences we seek.

Dr. Stuart Brown has written a serious and playful book on exactly that subject: *"Play: How It Shapes the Brain, Opens the Imagination, and Invigorates the Soul"*[7]. In the book, he shows the importance of play in the development of young animals, including humans. Actually, especially in humans, because we have a more extended adolescent period than any other animal. Play is the method used by all animals to develop their brains and social skills. But play is important for other activities as well, including social interaction, bonding, mating, friendship, building trust and work. Play is so important that animals are willing to risk their lives in order to play. Dr. Brown describes how baby mountain goats play by jumping from rock to rock, but occasionally they slip and fall to their death. Their playing allows them to learn how to jump to safety when a predator is chasing them, a very useful skill. There is a cost to this learning and they are willing to pay it.

Play is not just for kids (Ha!). Adults need to play too. In fact, Dr. Brown shows that adults need play almost as much as adolescents, for different reasons. Adult play is less focused on developing social skills than on creating and maintaining social ties. A relationship without sufficient play becomes stale and stiff. The interactions become rote and joyless. A little teasing and friendly banter between people reduces tension and creates social bonds. People who play every day are happier. They find the joy in life. They create and share their joy for life with those they interact with. These are great people to have around and we want them as friends. Play keeps them and us young. If we want to extend our healthy lives, we must play every day.

Play puts joy into our work and our purpose. This is not drudgery; it is fun and exciting. We want to achieve our vision because it is meaningful, but more than that, we want to work on achieving our vision because it is fun and we make it fun. The key is making it fun. Making it fun doesn't happen by accident. We must do so on purpose! See how purpose and play fit together nicely?

A great way to give work a purpose is by doing work that contributes to some greater good. Helping others can be very satisfying. Applying a special skill or experience that we have to solve a problem, teach, write or create can be rewarding, especially if appreciated. Most schools and universities gladly accept knowledgeable people as guest lecturers or aides. I find that there is no shortage of work when you are not looking to get paid! My pay comes from their appreciation for my experience. Of course, this is a benefit that I enjoy after having worked for many decades. Young people are very smart and open to learning but may lack the real-world experience to put what they learn in school into a useful context. This is where an experienced person can contribute.

Some people have hobbies to keep them busy. There is nothing wrong with this, unless there is no goal or vision to give the work a purpose. Without a vision to drive the hobby, there is no purpose, except to keep busy. We may be able to motivate ourselves for a while, but eventually we will lose interest and the work will become drudgery. Work that has meaning can get us out of bed in the morning. It can sustain us when there are difficulties. Challenges become hills to climb instead of mountains that block our way. Many people have a strong need to create. Hobbies can be an effective outlet to express our creativity and satisfy this need. A nice painting or

14

photograph is a great gift, or looks great hanging on the wall, giving us satisfaction every time we walk past. I hang up everything on the walls of my office and elsewhere! The joy I get from seeing those theatre tickets from a play we saw is better than leaving them sit overlooked in a drawer. Going to that play was a pleasant experience that I want to remember often. You will probably agree that creating and remembering good experiences is more satisfying than buying a new gadget. The novelty of the gadget often wears out before the batteries, but the joy from a good experience lasts forever.

A vision and a purpose make what could be 'work' into 'satisfying fun'. People who enjoy what they do and have fun doing it, will never really work another day in their lives! Good work keeps us mentally and physically active, not just busy. The older I get, the more I realize the value of good work, motivated by a vision. I like to say that the most optimistic thing we can say every day is, 'We have work to do'. When the day comes that we have no work to do, that will be a bad day indeed. It is similar to eating, and we will talk a great deal about diet in the coming chapters. I do not live to eat, but rather eat to live. Similarly, I don't live to work, but rather work to live. Attitude!

A vision without a task is but a dream.
A task without a vision is drudgery.
A vision with a task is the hope of the world.
-Anonymous, Circa 1730

What Is Possible?

When considering our vision, we will need to consider what is possible and what is impossible, and then push the limits. First, let's consider the factors that drive our definition of the impossible:

- Where do our limits and constraints come from?

- Are we inhibited by feelings or fears?

- Do we have physical, mental or emotional limitations?

- Are we worried about failing or ridicule?

- What scares us the most about failing?

- What concerns us most about how other people think of us?

Now, let's flip it and consider the factors that drive our definition of the possible:

- Have we really thought about what is possible in our life?

- What motivates us and drives us to excel?

- What is there that we cannot do today, but if we could, it would change everything?

- What is the worst that can happen?

- How is that working for you?

- What is the best that can happen?

If the worst that can happen is failure, and we can handle it, then the worst is not so bad. Elon Musk, founder of Tesla, Solar City and Space-X is not afraid to aim very big and fail. He knows that even if one or more of his projects failed, he would still survive. But he is not planning for failure. He is planning and hiring the best people to assure success. For people like this, failure is not an option. They will have a plan B and C ready just in case plan A flounders. With just a little luck and common sense, we won't be eaten by a lion or end up in prison! We can do better than that.

> The greater danger for most of us,
> is not that we aim too high and fail,
> But that we aim too low and succeed.
> - Michelangelo

Be suspicious when an 'expert' says that something is impossible! An expert is often limited by their vast but still finite experience. Their experience blinds them to the possibilities and opportunities. Francis Fukuyama famously predicted the 'end of history' in his

1989 essay, proclaiming that the cold war was over and liberal democracy had been established as the model for the future. There have actually been volumes more history written since then, in spite of his prediction and lots more to come. What expert could have predicted in 1947 when Bell Lab scientists Bardeen, Brattain and Shockley invented the transistor, that it would replace vacuum tubes and eventually reduce the size of the device from several inches to less than five nanometers that is standard in 2017 and continuing to shrink as this is written. It was not possible to see that far ahead and therefore, an expert at the time would likely have said that it was impossible to make a device as small as is routinely done today.

An expert can only stand on the hill that he or she is on. Standing on top of the hill gives them a better view than anyone else, but all that they can see is the next hill. When the next hill is climbed, it is possible to see further, but again, only to the subsequent hill. By successively climbing hill after hill, eventually we arrived where we are today. It took persistence, commitment and guts to continue climbing technological hill after hill to get to where we are today. But there is no other way. This is the power of vision. To see beyond many hills to a distant, unseen but desirable future state. The vision gives us the faith to keep on climbing hills. Taking the challenge one manageable step at a time, but always in the direction of our vision, so we don't get lost.

The reasonable man adapts himself to the world; the unreasonable one persists in trying to adapt the world to himself.

Therefore; all progress depends on the unreasonable man.
- George Bernard Shaw

The world today is bursting with opportunities. The rate of change in almost every industry is faster than ever and still increasing. Where there is change, there is opportunity. When the ground is stable, it is impossible to move large objects like buildings. But when the earth is moving, as in an earthquake, even large buildings and mountains move. Today, the foundations of our society exist in a perpetual earthquake. The ground they are built on is now soft and moveable. Changes that would have been impossible to consider a few decades ago are happening today and can only be made to happen by people with vision and purpose.

> The journey of one thousand miles, begins with a single step.
> -Lao Tzu

Attitude

I already told you that attitude was going to play a big role in this book. Having a positive attitude about life and our current situation is going to be critical to our future success. If we have a positive attitude, we can weather the difficulties and occasional failures. We can endure some hardships, especially if those events are the result of efforts towards achieving our vision. A positive attitude can also mean that we take a bad situation and change it for the better. We don't just put up with failure or pain; we actually do something about them. In order to be happy and successful, we need optimism and pessimism in the proper balance. Without optimism, we become bitter. Without pessimism, we become fools.[8]

> The pessimist sees the difficulty in every opportunity;
> the optimist, the opportunity in every difficulty.
> -Winston Churchill

Attitude can impact our behavior and health, both negatively and positively. Some people in clinical research studies get well, believing that they are getting a breakthrough medicine, even though they are in the control group getting sugar pills. This is the placebo effect. The opposite effect is called the nocebo effect. People feel worse or get ill, believing that a drug or treatment will harm them, even though the treatment is harmless or they haven't received the treatment.[9] If we believe that we will get sick when we fly on an airplane, because we read it somewhere, we are more likely to get sick. People can make themselves feel better or worse, depending on their expectations and attitude.[10] If we want to extend our healthy lifespans, we will need a positive attitude. We want to take advantage of the placebo effect and avoid the nocebo.

Don't die before you're dead
-title of book by Russian poet, Yevgeny Yevtushenko,

Why do people choose to die before they are dead? This is the power of attitude. My friend Tom Pickard told me a powerful story about his father, who was suffering from heart disease. He was a big, strong, physically active man, but heart disease was wearing him down. This was before modern medicine found ways to address the symptoms of heart disease. One day, he told Tom that he realized that he couldn't win this fight. He gave up mentally and within a few weeks he died of a heart attack.

Giving up may not literally mean giving up. I have friends who have retired and when I ask them what they are planning to do in retirement, they answer proudly, 'Nothing'! Or they end up spending too much time watching TV. This is not healthy and is just another way of giving up. If we want to extend our healthy lives, we need a purpose driven by a vision. We need something to do and a reason to do it. Don't die before you're dead, unless you want to.

Ability is what you are capable of doing.
Motivation determines what you do.
Attitude determines how well you do it.
- Lou Holtz

One more thing that we will need to consider all through the rest of this book is the concept of life force. Our life force is what drives us to live every day. If we are really serious about extending our healthy lives for twenty, fifty, one hundred, or more years, we will need to have a strong life force. The first step is to be aware of our life force and how it depends on our attitude. Then we must learn how to nurture our attitude and life force in order to develop and make them even stronger.

Let him that would move the world, first move himself.
- Socrates

What We Don't Want!

Paradoxically, it's easier to identify what we don't want in the future than what we want. Therefore, in the exercise that follows, we will identify some of the places and situations where we don't want to be on our vision date. We will then turn these around to help us identify the places we would like to be and what we need to do in order to get there. It's easier to envision from the negative perspective, but always better to act from the positive. Why is that? Our culture is based on avoidance. Eight of the Ten Commandments are written as 'Thou Shalt Nots'. Only keeping the Sabbath and honoring your parents are written as a 'Thou Shalt'. We probably got the same message from our parents. Even laws and regulations are written predominantly from the perspective of what is illegal as opposed to what is desired. The Declaration of Independence, by the way, is a strikingly wonderful exception to this rule!

Of course, some behaviors carry such a heavy penalty that avoidance is the only practical way to manage them. Smoking cigarettes, addictive drugs and murder are best avoided at all cost. Staying out of jail and not being broke might be worth avoiding as well. We need to educate ourselves and take the appropriate steps to avoid what we don't want while working to get what we do want. Ignorance is no defense when it comes to regulations and laws, so we will need to be aware of these. Money is nice but it is not everything and should not be a goal in itself. I advise people that their vision should never be to make money. Making money is a result of achieving our vision, not our vision. Usually, if we are good at something and practice constructive behaviors such as sharing, collaborating, aspiring, growing, thinking, partnering, etc., the money will come as a natural consequence of our success. On the other hand, if we focus on making money at the expense of these other activities, we will either fail or be miserably rich. Not where we want to be.

Based on our culture and upbringing, which are largely based on the avoidance of sin as opposed to the commission of virtue, it's no wonder that we find it easier to envision avoidance behaviors. We will use this cultural bias to help us identify what we don't want in our vision and then flip them around to identify the positive things we want, as it is more effective to motivate behavior in a positive fashion. A vision based on avoidance does a good job of describing what not to do, but not a very good job of describing what to do. We want to focus on what to do. Lastly, striving for the good things we want to do, leaves space for some of the bad things we will want to do! Strict avoidance behavior leaves no room for a little bad to leaven the good. After all, we are not angels and really don't want to be.

I've learned from years of work in consumer research that most people cannot identify what they want, but they have no problem describing what they don't want! We can easily come up with the usual silly answer – I want to be rich, good-looking, healthy, married to a person half my age, in a beach house, without a care in the world, with no demands, etc., etc. That does sound pretty good, but it's not realistic and I don't know about you, but I would need something to do. I need a challenge and a purpose. Perfection is not happiness; it is death. Let's try a different approach.

That which can be foreseen can be prevented.
-Charles Mayo

Once we have identified and eliminated the places where we don't want to be, then what is left should be places where we would like to be. Maybe not a specific place but a bunch of acceptable places. That could be a good way to start. Let's make a big list of places and situations we don't want to be in on our vision date, and then we are going to turn those around to define the places we want to be. The rest of this book will then be devoted to figuring out how we can get into those places. We will need to work at it and even change some things in our lives. But the point is, with some directed effort led by our vision, we **can** make changes and take the steps that will **enable** us to get where we want to be! Not only can we do this, but also if we want to extend our healthy lives, we must do this.

Here is a list of some places we don't want to be on our vision date in the future:

- Dead

- In jail

- Broke

21

- In the hospital or in a nursing home

- Alone

- Cancerous

- Obese

- Suffering from inflammation

- Diabetic

- Down with stroke or heart disease

- Hypertensive

- Addicted

- Miserable

- Demented

- Depressed

- Unable to do the things we enjoy

- Suicidal, or at least willing to die

That's a good list to start with. Perhaps your list would be different. Let's turn each of these around in order to define **what we will do** to achieve **what we do want**.

- Living a healthy, vibrant life (that covers a lot of them!)

- Free and able to do what we want

- Active and physically capable of doing what we want

- Healthy blood pressure (not hypertensive)

- Healthy blood glucose (not diabetic)

- Positive attitude

The list of what we want is shorter, because each one encompasses many of the 'don't wants'. Notice that good-looking, rich and famous are not on my list! Maybe they will be on yours. Let's get started. We have work to do!

Action

Life is what we make of it. The universe is full of energy, change and possibility. But the universe is silent. It is nonjudgmental and unforgiving. It does not take sides, nor condemn action. It is supportive, giving us all we need to develop and grow, if we choose to do so. It is a giver of life and energy. But if anything is going to happen, we must make it happen. And before we can make it happen, we must dare to do it. Assess the situation, identify the opportunities, how we can contribute, changes we can make, what is possible, what is seemingly impossible, then decide, commit and go.

Part of extending our healthy lives is to enjoy the healthy life we have. These are mutually generating feelings. If we are healthy and vibrant, we are more capable of enjoying life. If we enjoy our life, we are more likely to be healthy and vibrant and take the steps needed to stay there. It is a virtuous cycle. We want to be here!

Unless people believe that they can produce desired effects and forestall
undesired ones by their actions, they have little incentive to act.
-Albert Bandura (Psychologist)

There are so many ways to enjoy our lives and to share that enjoyment with others. Sharing our joy doesn't diminish but rather enhances it. Purposeful work, contributing, collaborating, volunteering and teaching are great ways to enjoy life and share it. And there are others too like eating great food, traveling, or just plain relaxing. We can create great experiences for ourselves and our loved ones by traveling or by having parties. We have had an annual BBQ party at our house for the past 40 years. It has become a tradition that we all look forward to and is one of the best things we ever did. So many of our friends say – "We need to do this too". But then – you know – the kitchen needs to be painted, or the rug in the den needs to be replaced first. The result is they never have the party!

I know that we will have the party in July, so if the kitchen needs painting, I had better do it in January. Or if it doesn't happen, no one will notice that it needs painting except me – so let's have the party!

To find the meaning of life, ask 'what gives meaning to my life?'
-Me

We need other people. We need to be part of a community in order to be healthy and extend our healthy life. Teaching and mentoring others are great ways to give back. Exposure to young people can keep us young too. We are all part of the matrix of life and need to stay connected to other people. I have always had several mentors. These were people who I respected and trusted enough to share personal problems with. They were able to help me see a different perspective on my problems. They gave me confidence that I was on the right track or guidance when I wasn't. These are the people who support us in times of need. We need mentors and to be mentors to others. We want to continue to learn and grow.

Creativity is a special gift that all of us get in some measure. The need to create is strong in many of us. Part of enjoying life is allowing our creative juices to flow as they will. We all have talents, but we cannot expect to sit down at an easel and paint a picture without study or practice. We need to take some steps to enable our talent to develop and mature. Many people discover and develop their latent talent when they are older and wiser. Grandma Moses is a famous example, not starting to paint until she was seventy-eight years old. Tony Bennett has also become an accomplished painter after a remarkable career as a singer. There are lots of ways to express our creativity. One that I particularly like is finding new ways to enhance my health, strength and life force. Writing this book has been a result of that search and I hope you find it worthwhile and creative!

Life is a gift. Think about it. Why are we alive? Is there a reason or a purpose for our life? Can a universe with over two trillion galaxies be an accident? Can we be an accident? We can attempt to answer these questions or avoid them, like most of us do, because we cannot answer them or because we might not like the answer. But these questions are there. We can enjoy them and allow the answers we identify enrich our lives.

Hope

Human beings live on hope. Without hope we are lost and empty. Hope gives us the push we need to get over the occasional rough spot in life. It keeps our attitude positive in spite of challenges or crises that befall us. We cannot control everything in our lives, so bad things will happen to us, regardless of our preparations or plans. That is not pessimism; it is reality. Bad things sometimes happen to good people, but we cannot allow those bad things derail us from our vision and goals. We need hope to bridge the gap and bring us to a new level beyond the crisis du jour.

He who has a why to live for can bear almost any how.
-Nietzsche

Hope keeps us emotionally whole and allows us to function even when it looks futile. We stay the course towards our vision and goals, confident that the crisis will pass eventually and we will get to fight another day. But hope is not enough. We still must persist and work towards our vision and goals. Continue to nurture and develop your health even when you don't feel like it. Stay the course in spite of a temporary illness or a pulled muscle. You may need to adjust or find some new practices to help you get over this challenge. This is one way in which we grow. We pull a muscle or aggravate a joint doing what we thought was a good activity. We need to assess what happened, why it happened, what we can do now to repair it, and what we can do differently in the future so that it doesn't happen again. Maybe we should wear a supportive brace on our knee in the future when we do strenuous work involving the knee. Maybe we need to do more strength-building exercises with our knees to protect them from injury in the future.

Hope tells me that there is a solution, if only I can find it. Hope tells me to persist and not accept a diminished level of activity or vibrancy. Once we stop doing something, because 'we cannot do it anymore', it is lost. This is how we get old. We stop hoping and accept a diminished physical, mental or spiritual state, which then defines us going forward. We don't want to go there!

Summary of Life Extension

As Yogi Berra once said, "The future ain't what it used to be." Our future doesn't have to be the future that previous generations had to accept, or even the one that we thought we had to accept. We have a unique opportunity to create a different kind of future, not just longer, but healthier and more active. Technology is part of it, but attitude and desire are also necessary elements. The pieces of a huge puzzle are falling into place, allowing us to envision a different kind of future. A future that is worth daring to create.

CHAPTER 2

Life Force

Our life force is our will to live. Life is not an accident; it is highly intentional. Look around and wherever we look, there is evidence of the power of the life force. I love to garden and I collect seeds wherever I go. I have acorns from Oak trees in many different places. I've noticed something interesting when I plant them. Most of them will germinate and start to grow. Some sprout vigorously and take off for the sky like rockets. Others are more tentative and grow slowly. And some, sprout and then stop, as if they changed their mind. I realize that seeds are highly variable, and this is what drives natural selection. The vigorous seeds grow and pass on their genes to future generations. The tentative ones fail and wither away. We are no different. Some people are born with a powerful life force. These people are the doers. They are vibrant and seemingly up all the time. They attack life with vigor and good humor and are usually the most successful among us. If we want to extend our lives, we will need to take some lessons from these people in order to nurture and build our life force.

Our life force emanates from every cell in our body. It is not localized in any particular organ or part of our body. The collective force from all our cells combines to create our life force. Some people call the life force an aura or energy field. These are describing the same thing. We want to be aware of our life force and then take steps to actively nurture and develop it. There are programs designed to help visualize it. Bob Monroe Associates has some excellent meditation programs to do this[11]. Our life force doesn't exist only inside of us; there are several other significant forces around us that contribute to it as well.

> I know, your Honor, that every atom of life in all this universe is bound up together.
> I know that a pebble cannot be thrown into the ocean without disturbing every drop of water in the sea. I know that every life is inextricably mixed and woven with every other life. I know that every influence, conscious and unconscious, acts and reacts on every living organism, and that no one can fix the blame.
>
> – Clarence Darrow

The following graphic identifies some of the elements of our life force and our connection to the earth, moon and sun. There is also a force emitted by the surrounding universe, but I couldn't fit the more than two trillion galaxies we now know to exist on the page. We will have to imagine those!

Let's start at the bottom and work our way up the tree. The Tree of Life has roots, and around the roots are the grounding activities that we need in order to nurture our life force. Like the roots of a tree that gather life-giving moisture and minerals from the soil, and anchor it to the earth, we gather energy and stability from the Earth Force via our roots. To be fully alive and experience life in a meaningful way, we need strong roots to nurture and support us. There are many roots, starting with the love we receive and share with others. We take in spiritual nutrients from others by partnering, sharing and touch. The ultimate form of this kind of sharing is intimacy, which occurs on physical, mental and spiritual levels. Physical intimacy does not necessarily mean sex, but certainly sexual intimacy involves intense physical sharing, partnering and touch. Mental intimacy is achieved when we can share our deep, innermost thoughts with another person, without fear of judgment or criticism. Spiritual intimacy is the highest level, achieved through deep love and mutual understanding. Fortunate people, who experience this level of intimacy will not agree on everything, but they allow each other the space to express their individuality in the context of a stable and supportive partnership. Like Adam and Eve, still in the Garden of Eden, naked before each other, they do not feel exposed, trusting each other enough to share their bodies and thoughts without fear of criticism or judgment. They are like atoms in a molecule, each contributing their own uniqueness, but bonded together to create a new material. Sodium and chlorine, for example are two highly reactive, and totally different chemicals. But when bonded together, these atoms create sodium chloride or salt, a stable molecule that is benign and necessary for life.

In order to be physically, emotionally, mentally and spiritually healthy, we need to experience intimacy with at least one other person. It may not be fair to expect one person to be able to give us everything we need. Therefore, we need a variety of people in our lives, each contributing a piece of the intimacy that we crave. The sum of these relationships is love. We cannot live without love in our lives – love of life, love of ourselves, love of others and love from others. If we are not experiencing enough of these grounding activities, then our life force is diminished, and we may be unstable.

A strong gust of wind, in the form of a severe challenge, could knock us down. Or when there is a drought, we could wither and weaken.

In order to have positive relationships, we need to build trust with other people. We need to have contact with people whom we trust enough to share, partner and develop intimacy. These acts are risky and we must expose our inner self in order to develop intimacy. If we are closed up and unable to trust, we cannot develop intimacy. Conversely, we need people who trust us so that they feel free to open up to us. These grounding activities enhance our life force by giving us energy. We get physical energy from interacting with people that we love and trust. We mutually stimulate each other to do things and be active. I often don't much feel like taking a hike by myself, although I have done it. It's far more fun to plan and take a hike with other people. We challenge them and they challenge us. We get emotional energy from others. We talk and question and tease a little. This healthy banter raises our energy level and our mood. If I'm in a bad mood, for whatever reason, I call or text my friend and she knows exactly what I need to hear to get me going again. We get mental energy from others in the form of ideas or questions. These ideas expand our horizons and help us to change and improve. There is so much going on today all around us; it is impossible and undesirable for us to try to keep up with it all. I tap into the experience of my friends, who have different interests than I do, which enables them to discover new ideas that I would never find. New ideas keep us mentally fresh and challenged. Finally, we get spiritual energy from others. When we are together, we can share our life force up close with a touch, a handshake or best of all, a hug. Hugs are a great way to share our energy with each other. We both gain and neither lose.

Did you know that we can build our life force by doing simple activities that create joy in our lives? When was the last time you skipped? Skipping is unlike walking or running. It is an expression of the joy of life. Skipping can enliven us and lift our mood, enhancing our life force. Simple acts like this can nurture and develop our life force. And imagine if someone sees us skipping! They may think that we are crazy, but they cannot help but share in the joy and life force we are expressing!

Only that day dawns to which we are awake.
-Henry David Thoreau

The roots of the Tree of Life are grounded in the earth and derive sustenance and energy from the earth. We can enhance our life force by tapping into the earth force. We are part of the earth. The earth is alive. It is not some chunk of dead rock floating in space. Some people call this Gaia, recognizing that the earth itself is a living organism. We are one small part of the life force on earth. All around us, there are life forms, many we have never even discovered and certainly are unaware of. We dig a well one mile deep and find bacteria there. The earth is literally alive. All of these life forms emit life energy. Even inside of us and all over our bodies there are over ten trillion bacterial cells without which we could not survive. We are only beginning to understand the nature of our microbiome and its impact on our health. There is tremendous energy in all of these life forms and in the living earth. We are part of the earth and our bodies absorb energy from the earth. We can enhance this effect by being aware of it and practicing Chi Gong, where we feel the energy from the earth entering our body through our feet, progressing through each organ and body part, until it reaches the top of our head and then cycles back again to our feet, building and building. This is a powerful exercise to do every morning and if we do it right, we will energize our body and strengthen our life force.

We can enhance our attitude via meditation, thinking and reflection. Reflection on our successes and mistakes can be fun and help us to improve, as long as we don't dwell in the past. These activities focus our mental energies inward so that we can understand ourselves. We need to pay attention to our body and our mind in order to assess our condition and discover what we need. Then we need to take active steps to care for ourselves in order to keep well and improve.

Stress is one of the most destructive forces in our lives. The world, and our personal world, are changing constantly and not always in ways that we like. Other people, even those that we love, impose their will on us and cause us distress. We can feel the stress of change in our mind and in our bodies. Some of us are able to absorb the stress and not worry or seem to care. This could be positive, or they might be hiding the impact, even from themselves, allowing the stress to build inside. Others fret and allow the stress to wash over them like a wave, knocking them off their feet. The best approach is to be aware of the stress, consider our options to deal with it in a positive manner, and then move on, not burying it, but defining and keeping it outside. Meditation and reflection are positive ways to deal with stress, while maintaining a positive attitude. We need to be like a duck – the wave might wash over us, but we maintain our balance and it doesn't make us wet.

You may want to add some other grounding activities that are important to you. I was going to add shopping! Hobbies, travel, partying, exercising, running, hiking, bowling, fishing, golfing and many other activities can be part of our earth force. Recognize which ones are most important to you personally and take active steps to enjoy and develop these.

In the leaves of the Tree of Life, I have placed the expressive activities that define us as people and allow us to enjoy life. With these activities, we enhance our life force and make life worth living by constantly growing, improving, changing and healing, just like a tree. Without these activities, we will die. These come from our vision, which drives us to aspire, dare and strive based on our purpose. We are curious, listen and learn by observing. We sing, dance, and skip with the joy of life, because it is in us and we express it in everything we do. Finally, we give to others by sharing.

On the trunk of the Tree of Life, I have placed 'Love for Others' and 'Love of Life'. These are the forces that convert our grounding behaviors into life energy. If we do not love ourselves, other people and life itself, our life force will be weak, and we will die. Loving life means loving what we do and caring about it. It means loving ourselves enough to do what is necessary to take care of ourselves even when sometimes those behaviors are difficult. Loving life means loving the people we interact with, always searching for new people to bring into our lives and sometimes eliminating those who are not interested in living. The power and vitality of their life forces will combine with ours to enhance or detract. Love of Life means loving everything about life, wanting to be alive and actively living in a vibrant, positive manner.

The moon emanates a force too, which is especially powerful for women. The menstrual cycle is only one easily observable and powerful impact of the moon force on our bodies. The moon impacts the weather, the seasons and of course the tides of the ocean. All life on earth is in tune with the rhythm and energy of the moon. The full moon is known to cause behavioral changes in humans. Call centers staff up on full moons, knowing that the influx of calls will increase. The moon has a special pull on water, and thus the tidal effect. We are also composed mostly of water and this water feels the force and ebbing attraction of the moon.

The sun emanates tremendous energy that we can easily see and feel. Sunlight contains infrared radiation in addition to UV and visible light. The infrared is particularly healing for our bodies because it penetrates several inches below the skin to reach and energize internal organs. We should try to get ten to fifteen minutes of direct sunlight onto as much of our body as we can manage every day. The idea that sunlight causes cancer, or that we need to wear sunblock whenever we are in the sun, is incorrect. Sunburn, which is damage caused by excessive exposure to UV radiation, causes cancer. A few minutes of direct exposure to the sun without sunblock will not cause cancer and has beneficial healing properties. It also produces Vitamin D.

The earth and the moon are so intimately connected, that the rotation of the moon exactly coincides with its orbit around the earth. The moon rotates on its axis once every twenty-four hours, exactly as the earth. This is why we always see the same side of the moon. By the way – the same is true for the earth and the sun. The orbit of the earth around the sun exactly coincides with the rotation of the earth. This is why at noon the sun is at its highest point in the sky every day of the year. If this were not true, then at noon on December 21st the sun would be high in the sky, and on June 21st at noon our time, it would be middle of the night. The sun, earth and moon are intimately connected. There is value in appreciating that we are part of this highly interconnected system.

Finally, there is Universe energy. The most powerful telescope built by man, Hubble, has seen two trillion galaxies, each with several hundred million stars. We don't know how many galaxies are actually in the universe, but if we can count two trillion, the real number is far larger, perhaps ten or one hundred trillion. That is beyond our most expansive imagination. If the earth, moon and sun emit so much energy, can you even imagine how much energy comes from ten trillion galaxies? Perhaps it is also beyond our imagination to realize that we are part of that universe. We are not a mistake or an accident. Compare the universe outside of us with the universe inside of us. There are about one hundred trillion cells in our body, the universe inside of us. There are perhaps one hundred trillion galaxies in the universe outside of us. We have as much complexity inside of our body as exists in the universe outside. That is a remarkable concept. We are a tiny but complex part of the universe. And you have difficulty loving yourself?

> Beloved, I pray that you may prosper in all things and be in health, just as your soul prospers.
> -2 John 1:2

These forces from the earth, moon, sun and universe seem remote and even mythical. We have a difficult time feeling them directly. Our awareness of them is low and needs to be developed. Let me tell you about a real impact these forces have on our body. Dr. Thomas Cowan has written an outstanding book on the heart and circulation system, *Human Heart, Cosmic Heart*[12]. The ancient

Greeks thought that there was a special force in our bodies that made blood flow. In 1628, an English physician named William Harvey published a treatise on the circulatory system where he showed that the heart was the motive force behind blood flow in the body, not some inherent force in the body. He used science to dispel the ancient theory and this has been the conventional wisdom ever since. However, Dr. Cowan, following the work of Rudolf Steiner, showed that it is impossible for the heart to pump blood through some three thousand miles of veins, arteries and capillaries in the human body. Clearly, the heart does pump blood, but the pumping force generated by the heart is insufficient to the task. There must be some other force that works with the heart to enable blood to flow as it does. He studied trees and found that the tiny tubules in a tree carry sap from the roots to the top of a tree several hundred feet up. And trees do not have a heart or any other pumping organ. The sap just flows. Capillary action and osmotic pressure contribute to the force but are not sufficient.

Cowan proposes that the force that pumps sap in a tree and blood in our capillaries is the same force. It is due to an electrical charge that is created inside the capillary. Water in the blood that is next to the capillary wall is charged and has a different structure than ordinary water. He calls it structured water, because it is more highly structured, it is viscous and has the curious ability to force normal, unstructured water, of which blood is composed, to flow. The electrical charge in the structured water is responsible for the flow of blood in capillaries. This pumps blood back to the heart to enable the heart to do its job. Without the capillary capability, there is no blood flow. Where does the electrical charge that drives the capillary pumping action come from? It comes from external sources of electrical energy – the earth's magnetic field and sunlight are the two most important. Therefore, it is electrical energy from the earth and the sun that provides the motive force to pump blood through our bodies. Our bodies also generate electrical energy, so we can survive for some time without exposure to the sun or earth energy, but at some point, we need to 'recharge'. We generate electrical charge by metabolizing glucose, which comes from a plant that produced it via photosynthesis, which is sun energy. No matter how we look at it, we are running on sun and earth energy.

You might wonder, where does God fit into this model? That is a personal decision. We all define God differently, if we believe in the existence of one at all. It seems to me that if our belief in God helps fill in some of the gaps in our belief system, then that is good and healthy. It's interesting to note how we behave when we are confronted with a crisis in our lives. Do we get depressed or despair of the situation? Do we come together with friends and family for support and get it? Do we internalize the issue and act as if nothing happened only to suffer from it for years? Do we cry or get angry? Do we pray and put our faith in God? A crisis in our lives can be a severe challenge to our life force and can derail us from progress towards our vision. If faith in God helps us, that is good and powerful healing. On the other hand, if our belief in God is excessively restricting our freedom to live our life due to avoidance rules, then it could be a liability. And don't forget the guilt driven by religion. Carrying around the guilt for our sins for the rest of our lives can be crippling. The Catholic Church got this one right – confess, take absolution, accept forgiveness and move on, without guilt.

The child whispered, "God, speak to me."
And a meadow lark sang.
The child did not hear.
So, the child yelled, "God, speak to me."
And the thunder rolled across the sky
But the child did not listen.
The child looked around and said,
"God let me see you" and a star shone brightly.
But the child did not notice.
And, the child shouted,
"God show me a miracle."
And a life was born, but the child did not know.
So, the child cried out in despair,
"Touch me God and let me know you are here."
Whereupon, God reached down and touched the child.

Where do you think we come from? From the earth is the simple, obvious answer. Where does the earth come from? The higher-level elements such as oxygen, nitrogen, sulfur, iron, zinc, magnesium, calcium, iodine, carbon, and sodium required tremendous energy to form from elemental hydrogen. The only place where there is sufficient energy to produce these elements is in a star. Life is not possible without these elements and they all came from a star that existed billions of years before the earth. The star produced these elements, died and exploded, spreading these elements out into space. Eventually, the matter ejected by this dying star, cooled and coalesced due to gravity into our solar system and earth. We are made of these elements.

There is uncertainty as to where the water that defines our planet came from. Some was retained inside the rock mantle that formed as the earth cooled, to be released later by weathering and fracturing of the rocks. The rest almost surely arrived on earth from asteroids – snowballs from space. In either case, the water came from the stars. Therefore, we are made from asteroids from space, and the cooling matter from stars. It is no exaggeration to say that we are made from the stars![13]

Our life force is anti-entropy. Entropy is death. Entropy is the natural and unavoidable direction of the universe away from order, towards increasing disorder. Entropy is thought to be the clock of the universe, always pointing in the same direction, and never reversing. Heat flows from a warm substance to a cold one, never the other way around.[14] An ordered state tends to move to a more disordered state over time (my desk is a good example!). Human activity can reverse entropy for a while, but eventually it catches up. We can build a wall, but eventually it will fall down. Life is the force that builds walls and opposes entropy. A cell takes disordered molecules and puts them together to produce a highly ordered and functional cell wall.

An organism combines many different kinds of cells, each with a specific function, into a highly ordered and functional structure such as the human body. The fact that these highly ordered collections of cells produce a life force and a living animal is still miraculous to us because we don't understand it, but thousands of different kinds of animals perform this miracle every day.

Women are the source of the life force among humans. Women are more in touch with the earth and moon than men. They are the only ones who can create life and give a newborn child a life force of its own. They draw on energy from the universe, sun, moon and the earth. Most religions have at least one female deity or member to connect with the female life force. Even the male-centric Catholic Church reveres the Blessed Virgin Mary and many prominent female saints, such as Joan of Arc and Mother Theresa. Men can also tap into these external sources, but most of a man's life force comes from the women in his life – his mother, his wife and friends. Men seek the company of vibrant women, with strong life forces for this reason.

We are a twig on the tree of life. We are derived from the earth, sun and stars. We cannot exist without the life-giving energy from the earth and sun. We are a tiny speck existing on a tiny speck in a tiny section of the universe, and yet, we are a part of it just as sure as it is a part of us. It is a worthy goal to be aware of these energy forces and how to tap into them to enhance our own life force. If we want to extend our healthy lives, we will need all the life force we can get!

I love the Vince Lombardi quote:
"Winning isn't everything but losing is nothing!"
And paraphrase it for our purposes as:
Living longer isn't everything but dying is nothing!

Be Nice to Yourself!

If we are going to successfully extend our healthy lives, we will need to be nice to ourselves! I hope that you love yourself. We will have a difficult time loving others, or loving life, if we don't love ourselves. We are all we have. We are not perfect, but we can improve, if we want to. We are going to need every part of our body working together in order to live a healthy, extended life. Therefore, we need to appreciate all of our parts and all of our characteristics, including the imperfections. In fact, especially our imperfections, as these define us as a person just as much as our strengths. We need to cherish who we are and be grateful for what we are.

Loving ourselves in balance with our love of others and of life isn't narcissistic. Dr. Otto Siegel[15] calls this "Extreme Self Care", because if it's going to help, we need to get good at it and take our self-care to a new, extreme level. This is about changing our lifestyle in order to change our lives. It is extreme, in that it will take a lot of effort and persistence to care for ourselves in ways that we have never done before. No one knows us better than we do. No one can feel what we feel or interpret what we are feeling to find the sometimes-hidden meaning. Doctors try to help us but often apply the same treatment to different people experiencing a common set of symptoms. Perhaps this is adequate, but it is not extreme. We need to get involved, observe, ask questions, read, experiment and learn how to take care of ourselves. Push the limits. Don't accept the standard. Go to the extremes to find a better way. Extending our healthy, vibrant lives will happen by intent, not by good genes or good fortune.

There are so many ways to be good to ourselves, to increase our joy and love of life. Being good to ourselves makes life worth extending. We will have to work hard to successfully extend our healthy lives, and to achieve our vision and goals. Why do all that if there is no reward? Life itself is a reward. Health is a reward. Doing activities that we enjoy with people we love is the icing on the cake.

A hot tub, sauna or a warm shower is a great way to relax not only our muscles, but also mentally. I have a routine of stretches and yoga exercises that I do twice a day in the hot tub and shower. The warmth loosens up stiff muscles, making the stretches more effective and less likely to cause damage. Put some Epsom salt in the water to make it even better. There is a lot of evidence that frequent use of a hot tub or sauna prevents hypertension and improves circulation. It's also great for sore muscles after a workout or after overdoing the yardwork.[16]

Go get a massage! Do it on a schedule with the same person and you and they can learn what and where to focus. Myofascial therapy and chiropractic are two other ways to push and shove muscles and bones back where they are supposed to be to alleviate pressure on nerves and joints. They are very different therapies and useful for different issues. I hurt my knees by hyperextending them and spent two years in pain. Just before accepting that the next step was an MRI and probable surgery, a friend suggested that I try myofascial therapy instead. There is a myofascial therapist a mile from my house, so I went. Caran Kalish pushed and shoved my knee and the tissues surrounding it for six sessions and the pain disappeared. I work my knees hard with yard work every day. I can work with pain and did, but it's so much nicer when they don't hurt! I am now a believer in myofascial therapy and suggest that you add it to your toolkit. Keeping ourselves well and in good condition is a project that we need to take seriously and get good at.

Making time to exercise is one of the best ways to be nice to ourselves. See the section in Chapter 7 on Exercise.

Having a hobby is a wonderful way to be nice to ourselves, doing something that we love to do. The activity, if aligned with our vision, can be motivating, rewarding, and an outlet for our need to create. And when we accomplish something, it brings great satisfaction, especially if we can share it with another person.

We will need to balance the good work we must do to extend our healthy lives and accomplish our vision and goals, with time to relax and enjoy it. Find ways to relax that are enjoyable to you and the people you spend time with. Reading is one of my favorite ways to relax and I like to read on a range of subjects. Listening to music is also very relaxing. Taking a walk, especially barefoot in the grass, is great. Have a party with friends, even if it's just two or three people. Make it special and laugh a lot!

Eating and drinking well is a good way to be nice to ourselves. Of course, we have to be careful not to eat too much, but we can eat well in quality and variety without exceeding our limits on quantity. And once a week, we can allow ourselves to go beyond the limits, as long as we make up for it in the next few days.

All things in moderation, especially moderation.
-Ralph Waldo Emerson

Incorporating essential oils into our daily routine is a luxurious way to be nice to ourselves. We can aspirate lavender into the air. It smells great, it relaxes us and supports our parasympathetic nervous system. It helps us sleep better and deeper. Coriander oil makes a luxurious foot massage and eliminates fungal infections. It's great fun experimenting with different combinations of oils like rosemary, clary sage, honeysuckle, patchouli, geranium, tea tree, lemon grass, thyme, eucalyptus, and many more. There are lots of great books on the subject.[17]

Another way to be nice to yourself is to always have something to look forward to. Plan a trip or a party a few months away. When it's done, plan another. Having something to look forward to focuses us on the future, which is where we want to be focused. We don't want to dwell or live in the past. The past was great and it's done. Let's look forward to an even greater future.

Whenever I do a task, I think of a way of rewarding myself, if I've been a good boy and gotten it done! The reward can be small like a cup of coffee or a beer, but it focuses my efforts and helps me persist to get it done so that I can enjoy the reward. *Zen and the Art of Motorcycle Maintenance: An Inquiry into Values* by Robert M. Pirsig[18] is a fascinating book about the human condition, and a little about motorcycles. He talks about the importance of getting up the gumption to do a task before setting out to do it and what happens when the ten-minute job that we expected, turns out to be two hours. Simple rewards can give us the gumption we need to get the job done in spite of setbacks and extra difficulties we didn't anticipate.

If we are going to live longer, healthier lives, we will need the gumption to do so. Gumption is an attitude that comes from our vision. We need to visualize our future and then develop a plan and actions around the vision in order to make it a reality. Henry Ford said, "Whether you think you can, or you can't – you're right." If we want to live for another fifty years or longer, the first step is to think that we can. If we think that we cannot, then we are already defeated. Thinking that we can will enable us to find the steps we need to take to make it happen, and then actually do it. Try visualizing your longer, healthier life and see how it changes your attitude. Creating that vision and using it to guide our actions is a powerful way to make it a reality.

> For it is in giving that we receive.
> -St. Francis of Assisi

Lastly, one of the best ways to be nice to ourselves is by being nice to others. Maybe that sounds a bit selfish, and if you like we can have a side discussion on whether any human activity can be purely altruistic! However, it really feels nice to give to others, especially when they appreciate it. It is a win-win. Teaching, sharing our hobbies, even simply showing interest in another person are ways to give.

> We make a living by what we get,
> we make a life by what we give.
> -Sir Winston Churchill

Existence and Exploration

Daring to live longer will put us on a journey of exploration and discovery that starts with ourselves. We have so much to learn about ourselves. We send probes into space to take pictures and gather samples from distant planets, but we know so little about the bacteria that colonize our intestines. Do we really know ourselves? What do we see when we look in the mirror? Actually, even that is wrong, as it is a reversed image of us. This is why many of us don't like photographs of ourselves, as they are a true image of us, and not a match for what we think is us – what we see in the mirror.

Are we comfortable with ourselves? We are who we are and cannot change dramatically. The first step in self-discovery is to accept what we find there.

The next step in exploration and discovery regards others. Do we really know the people with whom we live and interact? Are we interested enough in them to ask them probing questions? What do they like? What are their goals? What is their vision? These are questions that we usually don't ask. We get stuck in small talk about the weather, sports and politics and never get around to asking them how they feel about life. We don't really know the people around us. If we are going to successfully extend our healthy lives, we need other people that we know deeply. We need to know their vision and goals and they need to know ours. Sharing our visions is a powerful way to create positive, enduring partnerships, where we support each other to success.

Finally, we need to explore the universe around us. We are a solitary person, on a tiny planet, in a small solar system, that is part of an unremarkable galaxy, in a huge universe of over two trillion galaxies. And we think we are special? Well, actually, we are special. Among all of those galaxies, it's only reasonable to conclude that there must be other planets like earth that could support life. Life is such a powerful force; it is hard to imagine that earth is unique and alone among over two trillion galaxies. However, when we do find life on another planet, it is likely to be different from us. We may not be able to physically or even optically explore the vastness of the universe, but we can imagine the extent and power it generates. We are a part of the universe. We can explore ways to bring the energy that it emits into our bodies to enhance our life force and health.

In many ways, we are explorers on a mission to discover how we can extend our healthy lives. The word 'discover' is appropriate, as much of what we need already exists inside of our bodies or in the world around us, and our mission is to find these techniques, materials, activities and forces. We are among the first in history to take on this quest, so we should be prepared to make mistakes and for inevitable surprises. This is exciting and can be a purpose in itself. This is where we want to be!

Learning and Self-Development

If we are going to live another vibrant fifty or one hundred years, we will need to continue to learn and grow. The world is changing at an accelerating pace. We can choose to keep up or fall behind. Falling behind is one reason why people choose to die. They can no longer relate to the world around them. Often, their friends and family members have passed on, leaving them alone. They don't recognize the world anymore. They cannot understand how to use new devices and technology. They become more and more isolated and cut off from society. We don't want to go there. We want to keep up with the world as it changes. This means keeping up with technology as it develops, keeping up with our communities as they inevitably change and grow, and keeping current with the bigger world around us in terms of politics and programs. It means keeping up with our friends and having a network of people we can talk to and socialize with. We do not want to become isolated or alone in any sense.

We have to learn how to learn. Learning is a skill just like any other. If we practice it, we can get better at it. There are so many opportunities to learn today and many are available for free. Coursera is an online service that offers university level courses on almost any topic to anyone. The cost is minimal or free if you choose. The key to learning is to ask questions, to be curious. When we stop being curious, it means that we know everything we want to know or just don't care. This is death. Learning is challenge. Learning is growth. Learning is life. We choose life.

I know of no more encouraging fact than the unquestionable ability of man to elevate his life by conscious endeavor.
-Henry Thoreau

We can focus our learning on improving what we already know a lot about. This could be one of our hobbies, special talents or work skills. For example, let's assume we are good at woodworking, we can find some books or courses on woodworking that will take us beyond what we already know. We can buy a new tool that we've always wanted or teach a course on woodworking. The best way to learn is to teach! The other option is to learn something new. Learn a language, how to paint, play piano, etc. There are lots of wonderful skills we can develop that will bring joy to us and the people we know. A friend of mine has a German heritage, and in his eighties, he decided to learn how to play accordion to accompany him when he sings at the annual family Oktoberfest. Al is the hit of the party.

The illiterate of the future will not be those who cannot read, but those who cannot learn.
-Alvin Toffler

Volunteering

Volunteering is an interesting and effective way to collaborate with other people and to share our experience and joy with others. The concept of volunteerism largely originated from one very influential person – Benjamin Franklin. Ben wrote a beautiful little autobiography that I highly recommend to you[9]. An interesting bit of trivia is that he wrote the original in French while he was in France cajoling Louis to support the American Revolution. In the book, he chronicles his lifelong efforts on self-improvement. He was a printer, a writer, a political activist, a humorist, a statesman, an ambassador, a signer of the Declaration of Independence, a scientist, an inventor and a community organizer. In addition, he pioneered the creation of free public libraries, volunteer fire departments, local community hospitals, local universities, and more.

Volunteerism has become a unique and important part of American culture. We often don't wait for government to solve a problem; we organize and find a way to get the job done. This is very Ben Franklin! We can build upon this pillar of our society by using our leadership skills and experience to organize a group to tackle some problem in the community. It is a great way to contribute and give back. It is a great way to share our expertise and love for our community. If we want to extend our healthy lives, we need a powerful life force that enables us and makes us want to live intensely and intentionally. Volunteering can help us to do that.

Developing Our Life Force

We know so little about life. We are ignorant about the existence of life elsewhere in the universe and yet cannot imagine that in the vastness we are the only planet to manifest life. We are only slightly more informed about life on our own planet. We are just starting to appreciate the life that exists on and inside of our own bodies. We observe that life is everywhere on our planet and body. We wonder how life started. What was the spark that took simple elements and pushed them to defy the inevitable, grinding advance of entropy to increase order? This force is the life force, and it is incredibly powerful. We have this force inside of us and all around us. We can build our awareness of this force, develop it, nurture it and ultimately use it to improve our lives and health.

CHAPTER 3

Nutrition Basics

Extending our healthy lives will require that we understand some basic facts about nutrition and the impact that diet has on our health. Human nutrition is a complex and developing science. Food and diet depend on many factors including the availability of food, economics, seasonality, personal preference, culture, religion, social interaction, and much more. Studies on the impact of diet, therefore, have a lot of variation to contend with. We talk about the Mediterranean Diet and attribute the apparent health benefits enjoyed by its practitioners to olive oil and red wine. These are likely part of the story, but stress, smaller portions, socializing, activity level and other factors are not to be overlooked.

Performing controlled studies on human nutrition is notoriously difficult as people are uncontrollable and often don't pay much attention to what they eat. In addition, the impact of diet on health often takes several decades to become measurable. The best nutrition studies, such as NHANES and The China Study, involve over five thousand people and monitor their diet and health over many years. There are some problems with these studies as well to be aware of. The data collected is usually analyzed via statistical correlation, a technique that finds trends and associations in the data. Unfortunately, correlation does not indicate causality, so a positive result must be further studied to determine the true root cause of the apparent association. A famous example was the finding that coffee consumption correlated positively with heart disease. The initial conclusion was that people who drank more than three cups of coffee a day were at greater risk of developing heart disease. We now know that coffee, due to its high antioxidant content, is actually protective against heart disease and other health issues. It took twenty years for the research to be done that finally vindicated coffee, and now coffee is considered to be healthy. The mistake was caused by the presence of other underlying root causes that were not included in the study. It was eventually discovered that people who drank more than three cups of coffee per day had different lifestyles than the non-coffee drinkers, and those behaviors were the true cause of heart disease, not the coffee.

Let's start with some basics on nutrition to set the stage for discussions about diet and disease.

Calorie-Containing Nutrients:

There are only three kinds of calorie-containing nutrients – carbs, protein and fat. The unavoidable consequence of this is that if we want to reduce one, we will increase the others. Low-fat diets unavoidably increase the amount of protein and carbohydrates. There is nothing else to replace the fat we remove! This is one reason, for example, why low-fat diets don't work and are unhealthy long term. Low-carb diets suffer from the same problem. A reasonable balance of the three types of nutrients is critical to digestion and good nutrition. We cannot be healthy without these three basic nutrients, in proper balance.

Proteins:

Proteins are polymers of amino acids. There are twenty-one amino acids in the proteins that constitute the human body. Eight of these are essential, meaning that our bodies are not capable of producing them. Our bodies also have no way to store protein, so eating a high protein meal today does us little good tomorrow. Any protein we ingest, that is in excess of what our bodies need today, will be converted into urea and excreted in our urine. Eating protein is a daily requirement. If we do not eat the right amounts of the right amino acids, we will not have the amino acids that we need and the body will scavenge the amino acids needed for repair by breaking down muscle, resulting in muscle loss. In a sense, using muscle as a source of necessary amino acids is a sort of 'storage' mechanism, but not one that we want to utilize. The easiest way to get a good balance of proteins is to eat a variety of different foods. Restrictive diets can make this difficult.

Some protein sources are naturally balanced according to what our bodies need. Egg protein, for example, contains the most perfect balance of amino acids of any protein source. Milk, meats, fish and soy are also well balanced to our needs. Other protein sources such as rice, beans, wheat and corn contain a less perfect balance of amino acids. The balance of amino acids is expressed as a number called the Protein Efficiency Ratio (PER). Egg protein, with a perfect balance of amino acids for human nutrition, has a PER of 1.0. Wheat has a PER of 0.86, meaning that it is 86% efficient. We need to consume 1/0.86 or 1.16 grams of wheat protein to get the same benefit as 1 gram of egg protein. We can and should eat different kinds of foods with different protein efficiency ratios so that the deficiency in one food is compensated for by the excess in another. A classic example is eating beans and rice together. Rice is low in lysine, a required amino acid, while beans are high enough in lysine to compensate for the shortage, when the two are consumed together. It's not that one protein source is good and another bad, but rather that some are more efficient than others and combining different kinds can compensate for the imbalance. In the case of rice and beans, the result is that the body gets the amino acids it needs in proper balance from a diet that contains both protein sources.

Basically, protein is the building block of muscle, and there is a minimum level of protein intake required to repair and build muscle. Too little protein can result in the body breaking down muscle to liberate the required protein. We don't want this to happen. Too much protein in the diet results in high uric acid content in the urine. This could be a benign consequence, unless we also have poor circulation in the extremities of the body like toes and fingers, in which case the uric acid could form tiny, sharp crystals in the tissues, causing gout, which is very painful. The Dietary Reference Intake (DRI) for protein is 0.36 grams of protein per pound of body weight or 54 grams for a 150-pound adult. Bodybuilders increase their protein intake up to 1 gram per pound of body weight in order to build muscle, or 225 grams for our 150-pound adult. As you can see, recommendations range from 54 grams up to 225 grams per day for a 150-pound adult. That is a wide range. Increasing protein in the diet also allows us to decrease fat and carb intake to moderate levels, which is a good direction to go, especially when we are trying to lose weight, reduce body fat, reduce stored intracellular fat, and reduce fat stored in the liver, with the goal of increasing insulin sensitivity. Twenty percent of calories from protein in a 2,000-calorie daily diet is 100 grams of protein. This is a reasonable target.

Fats:

Fats are used to build the walls of our cells. Fat is a required nutrient, meaning we would die if we stopped consuming fat. In addition, our bodies are not able to produce all of the kinds of fat that we need. For example, our brains are high in omega-3 fats, and since we are not able to produce certain required omega-3 fats, a shortage will have a serious impact on our health. Some of the less severe consequences of eating too little fat include dry skin and hair falling out. Fats contain 9 calories per gram, which is more than double the caloric content of protein and carbs at 4 calories per gram. Protein and carbs are almost never eaten dry. Most protein and carb-containing foods have over a fifty percent water content, which increases the weight of the food and decreases the caloric content, whereas fat absorbs no water and is often eaten as is, such as in butter or olive oil. Therefore, in order to control caloric intake, we want to be careful with how much fat we eat. A moderate and reasonable goal when trying to reduce or avoid excess stored body fat is for fats and oils to comprise about twenty percent of our caloric intake, which is 45 grams per day of a 2,000-calorie diet.

Carbohydrates:

Last and not least, carbohydrates are composed of sugar molecules linked together in different ways and in different patterns. Sugar, starch, cellulose and dietary fibers are carbs. Some carbs can be broken down into sugar, while others cannot, passing into the intestines largely intact. There are many different kinds of sugars. The most common sugars are glucose and fructose. Glucose is found in corn syrup and in sucrose. Fructose is found in fruits and in sucrose. Sucrose is a disaccharide, composed of two sugar molecules linked together, one glucose and one fructose molecule, making it half glucose and half fructose. Sucrose is found in cane and beet sugar and is what we know as 'table sugar'.

Glucose is the fuel that our bodies burn, and carbs are the only energy source we can metabolize directly to produce glucose. Protein and fats must be converted into glucose in order to provide energy. The basal requirement for a human is approximately 2500 total calories per day. A bit of trivia is that this is equivalent to approximately 75 watts of electricity – so we burn about as much energy as a 75-watt incandescent light bulb! (or 5 – 15 watt LED bulbs).

Fructose cannot be metabolized directly by the cells in the body and must first be converted into glucose. This happens in the liver, where there are enzymes to make this happen. Oddly, there is no good mechanism in the body to control the conversion of fructose into glucose, versus storage as glycogen or fat, as there is for glucose. The result is that a substantial percentage of the fructose we consume is converted into glycogen and fat, specifically very low density lipoproteins (VLDL).[19] [20] You probably have heard of LDL and HDL, which are fatty components in our blood. HDL is protective and LDL is destructive to arteries and veins. VLDL is even more damaging than LDL. This is how diets high in fructose are thought to contribute to heart disease. Fructose is in sucrose, high fructose corn syrup (HFCS) and fruit sugar. HFCS is 55% fructose and 45% glucose, similar to sucrose. The sugar in apples, oranges, bananas, berries, etc. is almost pure fructose. Apples, oranges or a banana contain 20-25 grams of sugar per fruit, mostly as fructose. The body can handle this amount of fructose safely. It is only when daily consumption of fructose goes higher than about 75 grams that there are issues with VLDLs. Don't forget that fructose is coming into your diet from several sources, including fruit, sucrose and high fructose corn syrup. Plain corn syrup is pure glucose and not an issue. It is the best and most healthy sugar to consume.

Starch is a polymer of glucose molecules. The process to break down starch into glucose begins in our mouths. Saliva contains amylase enzymes that immediately begin breaking down starch into glucose. In fact, if you keep a starchy food in your mouth, you will notice that it becomes sweeter with time. This is due to the breakdown of starch occurring in your mouth. Interestingly, trees are also made of glucose, but the glucose molecules in cellulose are linked together differently than in starch. Our intestines do not contain the enzyme necessary to digest cellulose and therefore we cannot eat trees. Termites live on wood but actually the bacteria in their guts digest the cellulose! Read a wonderful account of sugar production in plants in *Lab Girl* by Hope Jahren[21]. Think about it – trees are actually giant candy canes!

If you are keeping track of the calorie targets we've set for protein and fat, both at 20% of caloric intake, then you already know that our target for carbs will be the remainder, 60% of caloric intake. This represents 1200 calories of our 2,000-calorie daily intake. At 4 calories per gram, this translates to 300 grams of carbs daily. This sounds like a lot but remember that carbs are the fuel that run our body. The quantity of carbs consumed should be in balance with activity level. If you live a sedentary lifestyle, then you want to keep carbohydrate intake near the basal level of 300-350 grams per day. If you are a marathon runner, you need to eat more carbohydrates, or you will literally starve to death. The American Council on Exercise estimates that a 180-pound man will burn 17 calories per minute while running, so during a 3-hour marathon, a runner will burn 3060 calories or 765 grams of carbohydrates! This is more than ten times the normal daily basal requirement for a sedentary person of about 1.4 calories per minute. Getting this amount of energy from protein or fat will put tremendous strain on the liver and could cause ketosis, a dangerous imbalance of blood pH. Please see the section on exercise in Chapter 7 for more details.

Everything you see, I owe to spaghetti.
-Sophia Loren

When we ingest more carb calories than we need, the excess is converted into glycogen and fat, to be stored in anticipation of a time when we will need the extra calories. If that day never comes, meaning we eat multiple times a day, always taking in as many or more calories than we need, the fat just accumulates. We need to give our bodies an opportunity to remove some of the stored fat or we will become diabetic, overweight and eventually obese. Excess storage of fat in the liver and muscles blocks insulin receptor sites, one of the causes of insulin resistance and diabetes. Chronic over-nutrition is a common cause of diabetes and the Metabolic Syndrome[22].

Non-Caloric Nutrients:

Non-calorie-containing nutrients include: vitamins, minerals, antioxidants, non-nutritive sweeteners and non-digestible fibers. Many non-caloric nutrients are required and we will literally die if we do not consume an adequate amount. We are all aware, for example, of the result of Vitamin C deficiency – scurvy – a severely debilitating condition. We are less aware of what can happen if we have a deficient intake of zinc or Vitamin E, because the results may be less obvious or debilitating but still can have a significant impact on our health.

When we eat a variety of different foods, we are more likely to get a balance of vitamins and minerals in our diet. This is one of the risks of the restrictive diets, where certain foods or classes of foods are excluded from the diet. Those foods contain nutrients that are beneficial and by restricting what we eat, it becomes more difficult to get an adequate amount of the required nutrients. The resulting imbalance is likely more harmful than the small benefit gained from excluding these foods.

Dietary Fibers

Dietary fibers are carbohydrates of a special kind – these fibers are not digested in the stomach allowing them to pass intact into the intestines, where there are bacteria with the ability to digest them. There are many kinds of dietary fibers, some soluble in water and some insoluble. All fibers are beneficial to human digestion and health by feeding intestinal bacteria and by increasing the viscosity of food in the intestine, slowing absorption of nutrients across the intestinal wall. Different fibers feed different bacteria, so eating foods with a wide variety of fibers promotes both the quantity and diversity of our microbiome.

Some functional dietary fibers and where to find them include:

- Inulin: found in wheat, chicory root and artichokes. Inulin is a soluble fiber and can cause a laxative effect and flatulence at high levels, especially if your microbiome is not capable. Taking Beano ® can help.

- Benefiber ® is a soluble fiber from corn dextrin. It has no flavor and dissolves in water, making it convenient to take. Since it is soluble, it presents the potential issue of causing flatulence. Again, Beano ® may help.

- Polydextrose: produced by fermentation. As the name suggests, it is a polymer of glucose. Use polydextrose cautiously at first, as it can produce a laxative effect and flatulence.

- Beta Glucan: found in oat bran, barley bran and yeast cell walls. This is the one of the best fibers to take, because not only is it good food for your bacteria, but also it improves insulin sensitivity, and it acts as an immune modulator, meaning it enhances immune function when too low and moderates it when too high[23]. Recommended intake of beta glucan is 0.5 to 1 gram per day, easily gotten from oat bran cereal.

- Cellulose: found in wood fiber, cottonseed fiber, oat fiber, soy fiber and wheat fiber.

- Pectin: found in fruits especially in the skin of apples, oranges and grapefruit.

- Psyllium husk: the husk from a psyllium seed. It is over 80% fiber, comes in a flake or powder form, has a pleasant, grainy flavor and easily mixes in water. Just don't try to bake with it – it absorbs so much water that it will ruin the texture of a batter or dough! I find psyllium to be one of the easiest fibers to incorporate into my diet, with lots of benefits and minimal digestive distress.

- Sunfiber ® is partially hydrolyzed guar gum. It is still an insoluble fiber, but easily disperses in water. It is easy on the digestive system, easy to use and has no flavor. Since it is insoluble, it avoids the problems of causing laxation and flatulence that exist with soluble fibers.

- Wheat bran: found in whole wheat products.

- Resistant starch: found in baked products. I find it to be one of the easiest fibers to incorporate into my diet, with minimal negative impact.

- Gums: there are many kinds of gums used in food including: agar, acacia, guar, xanthan and carrageenan. Gums are often fibers, meaning they are not digested until the bacteria get to them in our intestines.

Adding a meaningful amount of fiber to your diet will require a coordinated effort involving several different food types. Beans have one of the highest fiber contents of any food at 7.5 grams per 100 grams. Whole grain products like whole wheat bread contain about 6 grams of fiber per 100 grams. Vegetables like asparagus, kale, collards, brussels sprouts, or broccoli contain about 2.5 grams of fiber per 100 grams. Oat bran, walnuts, cocoa powder, and cinnamon are beneficial sources. Supplements like psyllium are easy to take and contain a lot of fiber.

Start out low and increase your fiber intake slowly. Too much fiber, especially one that your digestive system is not capable of handling, can cause significant intestinal distress, including bloating, flatulence, sour stool, diarrhea, and anal leakage. Not a pretty picture. Go slowly and if you experience distress, stop and try a different fiber. I find the easiest to handle are psyllium, resistant starch (in bread), oat bran, wheat bran, cellulose, hydrolyzed guar (Sunfiber ®) and pectin. Beano® is a dietary supplement that contains enzymes to help digest fiber and can prevent flatulence and bloating. This can be especially useful when you will be eating some new foods, for example when traveling. I find that taking it for a few days is often enough. And once your microbiome catches up, you won't need it until the next change in diet.

Most of us, today, are not ingesting sufficient amounts of dietary fiber to keep our intestinal bacteria healthy. The University of Arizona Cooperative Extension estimates that Americans consume about 11 grams of fiber per day, less than half of the 25 gram Recommended Daily Value set by the government for adults and children older than age four. The USDA Dietary Guidelines for Americans published in 2015 increased the recommended intake to 32 grams per day. I have seen recommendations ranging up to 100 grams per day. From my observations on my own diet, the magic number is 50 grams per day. There are many reasons why we under-consume fiber. Most people avoid eating foods or parts of foods that are high in fiber. When we eat an apple or potato, we often remove the skin, which is where most of the fiber is located. The same is true of an orange or grapefruit. Admittedly, eating the peel of an orange is a bit difficult, but that is where most of the pectin and fiber are located. There is no fiber in meat, fish, eggs or any animal product. Only plants can make sugar and fiber. The fact remains that it is difficult to eat a diet with 50 grams of dietary fiber per day. There simply don't exist enough foods that are convenient to eat with sufficient fiber content to make it possible. We need to work on this.

Dietary fiber in the diet has many benefits including:

- Feeding the bacteria in our intestines.

- Increasing the number and diversity of bacteria in the intestine, allowing them to colonize and form a layer of live bacterial cells on the surface of the intestine.

- Creating a layer of mucous to coat the inside of the intestine.

- Improving the balance of bacteria in the intestines.

- Producing short chain fatty acids as a waste product of bacterial growth, reducing the pH of the intestine wall, making it more resistant to pathogenic infection.

- Reducing the permeability of the intestinal wall, preventing leaky gut syndrome which allows undigested food to enter the bloodstream where it can cause an allergic or immune response.

- Increasing the viscosity of food inside the intestine, slowing down absorption of glucose into the blood stream, reducing the size of glucose spikes, improving blood glucose control, putting less stress on the glucose control system, preventing beta cell fatigue, preventing insulin resistance and eventually diabetes.

- Producing short chain fatty acids that are absorbed into the bloodstream, improving the circulation of high melting point fatty materials such as LDL, VLDL, saturated fats and cholesterol, reducing the risk of heart disease.

- Reducing blood pressure.

When we increase the amount of fiber in our diet, magical things start to happen. Things like losing weight and body fat, or improvements in blood chemistry, better control of blood glucose, reduced morning blood glucose fasting level, and a reduction in blood pressure.[24] It is best to measure and keep track of your blood glucose and blood pressure as you move to increase fiber in your diet, to enable you to learn how to manage the change well. Blood glucose levels below 75 for extended periods can make you dizzy or faint. And blood pressure, if it drops too low, can also be an issue. We want these changes to happen but need to give our bodies time to adjust and manage properly. Measure and track.

We urgently need to get dietary fiber back into our diets at sufficient levels to solve the diseases of the Metabolic Syndrome, including diabetes.

Glycemic Index

The Glycemic Index (GI) is a measure of how the level of glucose in our bloodstream changes after eating a specific amount (usually 100 grams) of a food. It is a measure of how quickly the food is digested and absorbed into the bloodstream. Foods that are composed of high levels of sugar, or starch that is readily converted into glucose, are quickly absorbed directly into the bloodstream. The result is a rapid and sharp rise in blood glucose and insulin level in response. Pure sucrose is used to calibrate the scale; it has a GI of 100. Carbs that are complex take more time to break down to release the sugars, and have GI values that are lower. Fiber, for example, is digested slowly in the intestines and has a GI of near zero. The concept behind using the GI value in deciding what to eat is to avoid foods with high GI and eat more foods with low GI values, in order to limit the extent to which blood glucose rises after eating a meal. This is a good goal, as this will make it easier for the body to manage and avoid unhealthy, high levels of blood glucose. As usual, it is more complicated than that and foods cannot be effectively reduced to a number.

There are some problems with the GI value, starting with the way GI is determined. 100 grams of a pure foods is fed to people who have been fasting overnight. The test is to monitor how high their blood glucose level rises after eating 100 grams of the pure food. We seldom eat pure foods in isolation. The presence of other foods in the meal will change the way that the carbs in the food break down and therefore the GI of the food. Some other factors that will also have an impact are: fat content, how much is eaten, protein, fiber, how much water is taken with the food, how well we chew it, the temperature of the food, the condition of our digestive system, how ripe a fruit or vegetable is, and many others. This makes GI, by itself, an unreliable indicator.

The GI can help us identify which foods contain higher levels of readily digestible starches or free sugars that can be absorbed quickly into the bloodstream, potentially causing a spike in blood glucose levels. Eating these foods along with other foods, especially those that have low GI, will slow down the release and absorption of sugar and can reduce the glucose spike. Fats in the meal will slow down the digestion of starches. For example, butter on bread or toast will slow down the release of sugars and reduce the GI. Fiber in the diet will slow down absorption of sugar in the intestines. GI is a simple model for how quickly a food is converted into sugar, but in most cases, it is too simple.

Glycemic Load expands the concept of GI to take into account how much food is eaten and what foods are eaten in a meal to estimate the total glycemic response of the meal. This is better, but still there are lots of variables that are not accounted for. The best advice is to consider GI as a guide when selecting foods to eat but keep in mind the limitations.

In general, foods that are high in GI will cause a larger spike in blood glucose. However, it is more complicated than that. We can turn the complication around into an advantage, by learning how our body reacts to various combinations of foods. A great way to learn which foods or meals to avoid and which ones to eat more often, is to test our blood glucose. We can make a game of it, seeing who can design the meal with the lowest or no impact on blood glucose. Here is how the game is played:

1. Select a meal, where we combine different foods, with the purpose of minimizing the blood glucose spike.

2. Wait without eating anything for at least three hours, so that our blood glucose is at baseline. Measure it. Let's say we get 103.

3. Eat a reasonable amount of the meal. The amount we eat will impact the effect, usually more food causes a higher blood glucose spike. The idea here is to assess the impact of food as we would eat it and in the amount that we would normally eat. In the standard GI test, 100 grams of a food are consumed, but we usually don't eat foods alone, so it will be more natural and meaningful for us to prepare and eat the food as we normally would. For example: if we want to test how our body reacts to whole grain rice, cook it up as we normally would and then add the other ingredients that we want, such as salt, butter, olive oil, meat, veggies, etc., and eat the combination as a meal.

4. Test blood glucose fifteen minutes after eating, and then every fifteen minutes until blood glucose returns to baseline.

5. In some cases, the level will spike up quickly and then drop again quickly, going down below the baseline, even plunging below 80. These are the foods we want to avoid or at least eat less of.

6. In other cases, the level will rise slowly and then just as slowly go back down to baseline. These are foods that our body can tolerate. We can include these in our diet in moderation.

7. In other cases, the level will not change at all. It just stays flat with no rise or decline. These are foods that our bodies can manage easily. We want to eat these more often.

8. Then for fun, try mixing the foods to create meals and see how it works. The goal is to design meals that have minimal impact on your blood glucose levels. This will reduce the stress on the blood glucose control system and allow our body to rest and recover from the barrage of glucose spikes experienced in the past.

9. Foods eaten alone will usually spike blood glucose more than when eaten in combination, especially if the other foods do not spike it. This is why the glycemic index is not very useful. Fats and oils, proteins and fiber are good for this. Rice is a good test example, as it is high in carbs and not high enough in protein, fiber or fat to moderate the digestion and rapid absorption of sugar into the bloodstream. Therefore, eating rice can spike our blood glucose to unhealthy levels. We can avoid eating rice or find a way to eat it in a way that allows our body to process it safely. First, eat less. It is much easier for our body to deal with a few tablespoons of any food than a heaping portion. And, eat it with other foods that contain fat, fiber and protein. Putting butter or oil on the rice will help. Mixing in some chia seeds or pine nuts will add protein, fat and fiber. Get in the habit of adding nuts to recipes, as they are high in protein, fiber and fat, and will moderate glucose absorption, in addition to other health benefits. All good.[25]

10. Drinking while eating will usually spike blood glucose more quickly, therefore avoid drinking a lot during a meal. Wait thirty minutes, then drink that beer, or sip it slowly while eating. Wine is fine during a meal, as the amount of liquid is low.

11. Making the food more viscous will decrease the rate of sugar absorption. We can do this by drinking a psyllium shake with a food that is high in carbs. The recipe is in Appendix 6. We can add chia seeds to a food to add viscosity and fat. That will slow the absorption of sugar. I drink a psyllium shake before eating a few fresh peaches from a tree in my yard and my blood glucose barely budges. Drinking a psyllium shake before eating a meal can also be a good practice, with several benefits: It will increase the viscosity of the food, slowing sugar absorption; it will feed the bacteria in the intestines; and it will fill us up a bit, allowing us to eat less. All good.

Some foods have little or no impact on blood glucose and are useful to eat alone or in combination with the high glycemic index foods to help moderate the absorption of sugar into the bloodstream. Some good examples include:

- Sunflower seeds

- Nuts – especially pistachio nuts because they are high in fiber

- Psyllium shakes

- Chia seeds

- Protein shakes (keep the sugar below 5 grams)

- Chocolate (85% cocoa or higher)

- Artichoke hearts (a cup is only 114 calories and has 14 grams of fiber, mostly inulin)

- Beer – in fact most alcoholic drinks that are low in sugar and consumed in moderation will have no impact

And remember that eating more of any food will result in a higher spike in blood glucose. Just eating less of that food will reduce the spike.

I suggested making it a game. The game we want to play is figuring out how to incorporate the foods we love or want in our diet, in a manner that allows our bodies to competently manage blood glucose levels. For example, oat bran cereal has more beta glucan than any other food. I want it in my diet, but it is also high in carbs and will spike blood glucose levels if eaten alone. Combining oat bran with other ingredients can reduce the GI and the blood glucose spike. Cocoa and cinnamon are reported to improve control of blood glucose – let's add those. Fat will slow down the absorption of the sugars into the bloodstream – let's add some. Viscosity will help slow down the absorption of sugar – let's add chia seeds. And so on, until we find a way to make it possible to eat oat bran and not worry about blood glucose. See the recipe in Appendix 4. This is a game we play for keeps – for our life. Game on!

Supplements

A combination of different foods will usually provide a mix of nutrients to meet our needs. The exceptions to this are Vitamin E, Vitamin C and magnesium. I said that there wasn't a pill that will help you to extend your healthy life. I lied a little. There are actually several pills that you should consider taking to improve your health.

Supplements are a controversial subject, but until we find foods that we will eat enough of to provide the benefits we are looking for, supplements are worth taking. One benefit of a supplement is that it has been standardized to deliver a specific amount of a nutrient or active ingredient. We don't have that kind of control over the foods we eat. Foods vary in freshness, cooking methods, amount consumed, absorption rate, etc. Nutrients and active ingredients may not be active or bioavailable in the food we eat. Turmeric is a good example. Turmeric spice contains the active ingredient curcumin, but the bioavailability varies greatly. The supplement is processed to assure that the curcumin is bioavailable and absorbable by the body. The supplement is usually validated, reliable and convenient – check them out to confirm.

Here are some supplements for you to consider taking every day:

- Vitamin D – Most of us are deficient in Vitamin D because we don't get enough exposure to the sun. Vitamin D has been found to be very important in preventing cancer. I take 6,000 IU twice a day. Next time you have a blood test, ask for Vitamin D to be included so that you can assess if you are getting enough. You want to be at the top end of the 30-100 ng/ml range that the medical profession identifies as 'normal'. And keep in mind that the FDA Recommended Daily Value is based on disease prevention, meaning the amount you need to take so that you don't develop a disease due to insufficient intake. We don't want to be there. We want to take an adequate amount for optimal health and, of course, disease prevention. That is a much higher amount. Vitamin D is not toxic until there is a very high intake, in the range of 40,000 to 100,000 IU, per day, according to the Mayo Clinic, so the risk of overconsumption is very low.

- Curcumin – select a bioactive form either in pill or liquid liposomal dispersion. It is a powerful antioxidant and helps to reduce inflammation. This has to be one of the best finds for life extension ever. There are no known negative side effects to curcumin. The impact is all good. It is also called turmeric spice. Using the spice in cooking is great for flavor, fiber and antioxidants, but the absorption of the antioxidant from the spice is limited, which is why it's important to get the bioactive form.

- Antioxidants – necessary to combat oxidative stress. Antioxidants react with free radicals in the body to protect against damage due to oxidation. There are many kinds of free radicals and many kinds of antioxidants. There is a benefit to ingesting many different kinds of antioxidants as opposed to overloading on just one or a few. Grapeseed extract is a good one. Dr. Life is marketing an herbal blend that is more active than typical antioxidants[4]. The most powerful antioxidant is Carbon 60, or C60. It is especially effective due to its small size at penetrating cell membranes, even inside of mitochondria, where most of the damaging free radicals are produced as a natural byproduct of respiration. The soluble form produced by Fuller Life C60 is the most biologically active and effective. Antioxidants also reduce inflammation. You can include some good antioxidants such as turmeric, nuts, wheat bran, cinnamon and cocoa in your cooking. These are also good sources of dietary fiber.

- Charcoal powder – This is a very finely ground powdered, activated, pure charcoal. It has a tremendous surface area because the particles are so small, making it highly active for absorbing toxins from food in the intestines. All food contains toxins, most of them naturally occurring in the plant as a defense mechanism against being eaten. We and the plants have been playing a game of one-ups-man-ship forever. They create a new toxin; we develop an antidote or way to detoxify it. Our body is very good at this but wouldn't complain if we gave it a little help. Charcoal powder is a way to help. It doesn't take much – about a gram or two a day is plenty. Don't get scared, as it will turn your poop a deep, elegant black color. That's about all you will notice. But it will help improve your intestinal function and intestinal microbiome. It is in the All-In Biome Balance ™ Bagel. Eating one of these bagels each day will give you plenty of charcoal. Or you can add it to your psyllium shake or even oat bran cereal if you are daring. Avoid charcoal if you are taking a chemotherapy drug such as methotrexate, as the charcoal will absorb the drug, reducing the effectiveness of the treatment.

- Melatonin – a good antioxidant to reduce inflammation and a great sleep aid. Even if you are sleeping adequately, you will notice a difference. Take ten to twenty-five mg of melatonin right before going to sleep.

- Multivitamin – just to be sure that you're not missing anything important.

- Omega-3 fish oil – the only good source of required Eicosapentanaenoic acid (0.25 grams per day), which we need for our brain. The other required fats are linoleic acid (10 grams a day required, which we can get from 1 tablespoon of walnut or grapeseed oil) and linolenic acid (2 grams a day required, which we can get from a teaspoon of flaxseed oil). Our bodies cannot make these oils and also cannot store them, so it is important that they are part of our diet. We can make flaxseed or grapeseed oil part of our diet every day by using these oils on salads or in our cooking. Fish oils are more difficult due to their extreme sensitivity to oxidation. And you probably don't want to eat salmon or fish every day. The krill oil supplement is the best fish oil.

- Collagen (types I, II and III) – necessary for healthy joints, skin, nails and intestines. We don't get enough collagen in the meat we eat today, because we eat almost exclusively muscle meats, avoiding cartilage and organ meats, which are high in collagen. When you start taking collagen daily, you will be amazed at the impact on your skin and nails. These are the most visible places where collagen is important. Your intestines are also composed of collagen protein, so as your nails improve, your intestines are also improving. That is where we want to be.

- Prebiotic beneficial bacteria – The jury is still out on the benefits of prebiotic bacteria. The best ones are spore-based such as Thrive® as they survive stomach acids and become active in the intestine, where needed. However, introducing a large quantity of any bacteria can cause imbalance, which is not beneficial. Several studies have shown that we are better off feeding the bacteria we have, rather than adding more underfed bacteria into our intestines. The foods we eat today are too sterile. Most have been treated with an antimicrobial spray or processed to reduce or eliminate pathogenic bacteria. That sounds like a good thing, as it prevents illness due to contaminated food. However, these treatments also reduce or eliminate the good bacteria that our digestive system needs to function properly. I personally think that FDA is on the wrong path, trying to make food sterile. Food is not sterile, is not meant to be sterile and will never be sterile unless we kill everything. That will not be good for anyone. Rather, we need to propagate and nurture a healthy bacterial microbiome in our intestines in order to enhance our immune systems and protect ourselves from the few pathogenic bacteria we are going to ingest, regardless of how hard FDA tries to prevent it. If we don't have enough bacteria in our intestines because we don't feed them properly, then pathogenic bacteria will find a hospitable environment and cause illness. There is a constant battle going on in our intestines between different kinds of bacteria. We want to develop a healthy quantity and balance of bacteria that make the intestines inhospitable to pathogenic bacteria. Feed your bacteria fiber.

- Psyllium fiber – Two tablespoons in a glass of water once a day works wonders for our digestive system, not to mention the good it does for our bathroom visits! We don't get enough fiber in the foods we eat. We tend to avoid high fiber foods such as kale, collards, wheat bran, oat bran, etc. The result is that the bacteria in our intestines are undernourished. This means that the quantity and quality of the bacteria in our intestines is suboptimal. Getting bacteria into our intestines is only half the fight. Once there, we must feed them to keep them healthy. When the bacteria are there and fed well on dietary fiber, they produce short chain fatty acids as a waste product (yes, we are talking about their poop!). These are predominantly propionic acid and butyric acid and have many health benefits.[26] They reduce the pH in the vicinity of the intestinal wall where the bacteria are colonizing. This protects the intestinal wall from invasion by pathogenic or illness-causing bacteria, which cannot tolerate the low pH. And these short chain fatty acids are absorbed into the bloodstream where they help keep fats and cholesterol moving and not clogging.

- Magnesium – If you experience leg cramps, especially common at night, you may be deficient in magnesium. Magnesium can be taken as a pill, a spray or even as an Epsom salt soak.

- Mushrooms – We are only beginning to learn about the existence and benefits of fungi. Fungi are far more prevalent and impactful than we thought. Read a book by a real expert on the subject: Paul Stamets' book, *Growing Gourmet and Medicinal Mushrooms*[27]. Detoxification, glucose control and cancer prevention are just a few of the potential benefits.

> Hypochondria is the only disease I haven't got.
> -Anonymous

CHAPTER 4

The Digestion Process

Digestion is the process of breaking down the food we eat into a form that is capable of being absorbed across the intestinal wall into the bloodstream, delivering the nutrients to our organs and cells. Digestion begins in the mouth, where the food is masticated to reduce the size of the pieces. Mastication makes it possible for us to swallow the food, increases the available surface area and mixes the food with water and amylase enzymes supplied by saliva in our mouths. After swallowing, the food is delivered via the esophagus into the stomach, where the food is mixed with more enzymes and acid. Enzymes are specialized proteins, some of which are present in the foods we eat, others are secreted into our stomachs, and still more are produced by bacteria in our digestive system. These enzymes include amylases that break down starch into sugar, lipases that break down fats and oils into fatty acids and glycerin, and proteases that break down protein into amino acids. Lysozyme is a very powerful enzyme present inside the cells of the food we eat that is released when the cells are ruptured during the digestion process. These enzymes include those that can break down dietary fibers, bran and even to some extent cellulose. Bacteria in the human gut can only partially digest cellulose fiber and therefore, for us, cellulose is not an efficient food source.

Intestines

Most of the work of digestion and absorption of food occurs in the intestines. It is a complex and fascinating structure that winds through our belly, measuring over thirty feet in length. It is flexible and irregular in shape, but essentially it is a pipe through which food materials travel. Partially digested food comes in one end, from the stomach and travels through the small intestine until it is passed into the large intestine. It takes one to three days for the food to complete the journey. As the food moves along, the enzymes and acid from the mouth and stomach are augmented by enzymes excreted by bacteria that colonize the walls of the intestine. These bacteria, collectively, are called our microbiome. Our microbiome not only influences how we digest food, but also when it is unbalanced, has negative impacts on the entire body that include obesity, the diseases of the Metabolic Syndrome, how our bodies look and even how we behave.

A fascinating article on the importance of our humble gut bacteria is "Feeding the brain and nurturing the mind: Linking nutrition and the gut microbiota to brain development", by Manu S. Goyal, et. al.[28, 29] We will discuss the microbiome in more detail and how our failure to keep it healthy leads to disease.

In the small intestine, fibers are broken down allowing the sugar and small chain fatty acids produced to be absorbed into the bloodstream. The fiber in plant-based materials serves as a food source for the bacteria. When we don't eat enough fiber, these bacteria are undernourished, underactive and will cause damage by consuming the mucosal wall of the intestine, resulting in a leaky gut that allows undigested food materials to pass into the bloodstream, with many bad consequences. The microbiome in our intestines can be changed by what we eat, both in quantity and balance. If we change our diet by eating a food we haven't eaten in a while, the microbiome may not be capable of providing the right enzymes to digest this food and the result can be some intestinal distress. For example, if a person who has been eating a vegetarian diet for some time eats meat, they may experience some digestive distress, as their microbiome will respond negatively to the new food. Another example is found in people who remove gluten from their diets for some time and then eat a slice of bread. They feel some distress and conclude that the gluten is really bad for them, when their microbiome is reacting badly to a food it hasn't seen in a while and for which it is not prepared. Similarly, eating a big serving of beans, when you haven't eaten beans on a regular basis, will result in severe flatulence and discomfort. The problem isn't the beans, but rather that your microbiome was unprepared for the quantity or type of beans you ingested.

It is critically important to our health that sugars in food are absorbed slowly, giving the body time to metabolize the glucose, to properly process and store the excess as glycogen and to safely convert fructose into glucose. These factors, plus the fact that the glucose is entering the blood slowly, reduce the amount of glucose in the blood at a given time and decrease the size of the spike in blood glucose level. Remember that the main cause of diabetes and failure to control blood glucose is the repeated presence of high levels of glucose that stress and damage the control system. Sugar absorption through the intestinal wall and into the bloodstream is mediated by several factors. The first line of defense against rapid sugar absorption is having sufficient bacteria in the intestines. The bacteria colonize the surface of the intestinal wall, forming an additional layer that traps mucous and acts as a barrier to slow down the absorption of glucose.[30]

Another factor that slows down the absorption of glucose into the bloodstream, and is critical in the prevention of diabetes, is the presence of fiber in food. Not only does the fiber feed the intestinal bacteria, but also it absorbs water and increases the viscosity of the food material as it passes through the intestine. This slows down the absorption of glucose through the intestinal wall into the bloodstream. It gives the bacteria in the intestine more time to ferment the glucose and convert it into good materials like short chain fatty acids. As important as low sugar consumption is in preventing diabetes and the other diseases of the Metabolic Syndrome, the real underlying cause is insufficient dietary fiber. This lack of dietary fiber has depleted the microbiome in our intestines, resulting in leaky intestines that allow undigested proteins to enter the bloodstream, causing autoimmune diseases. Low fiber levels in the intestines allow sugar to enter the bloodstream rapidly causing damaging blood glucose spikes, result in a lack of short chain fatty acids, which make the intestine more susceptible to pathogenic bacterial infections, and if that isn't enough, the lack of short chain fatty acids in our blood results in poor ability to manage high melting point fatty materials, resulting in circulatory damage and heart disease. Returning dietary fiber to the diet is one of the key steps to resolving all of these diseases.

We must feed the bacteria inside our intestines so that they produce a healthy, complex mucosal layer. Fiber is the main 'food' for intestinal bacteria. There are some other materials that are particularly beneficial such as L-Glutamine and Zinc Carnosine. These materials have been found to be beneficial to repairing and maintaining a healthy mucosal layer. When the mucosal layer is intact, proteins bind to the mucous and are held there until fully digested into amino acids and dipeptides that are small enough to pass through the healthy wall. The intact mucous layer is a barrier that prevents undigested protein from getting into the bloodstream where it can sensitize the immune system. Please observe that these factors are interconnected and reinforcing. We want to turn this around by building the mucosal layer, which will bind to proteins, allow the proteins to be fully digested, keep undigested proteins inside the intestines until fully digested into amino acids and only allow fully digested amino acids and dipeptides into the bloodstream.

L-Glutamine is an amino acid. You can buy it as a supplement. Research shows that a daily intake of 1 to 5 grams is beneficial to repairing and maintaining the mucosal layer[31]. I'm a chemist, so I cannot help but point out that this material, that has been found beneficial to intestinal health, is the main amino acid in wheat gluten. When wheat gluten is properly digested into amino acids, it cannot cause a sensitivity and in fact is beneficial. This digestion takes place in the mucosal layer of the intestine where the polypeptide protein is bound and held until safely broken down. Glutamine is the most abundant amino acid in human blood. It is considered to be a conditionally required amino acid, meaning our bodies can make it from other materials, but dietary intake is beneficial. And, to shock you even more, the sodium salt of this amino acid is called monosodium glutamate. Yes – MSG. I love chemistry!

Zinc carnosine is a patented supplement that has been found to promote intestinal health and repair[32] [33]. Zinc is a nutritionally important mineral, to us and to our intestinal bacteria. Carnosine is a dipeptide that has been found to promote intestinal health and repair. The combination is especially effective. My personal experience with this material is that it is effective and has a noticeable and beneficial impact on digestion by improving the integrity of the mucosal layer. This has many benefits, including preventing leaky gut syndrome, assuring digestion of proteins, protecting the intestinal wall from being damaged or irritated by food, and coating the contents as they pass through with a lubricating layer of mucous. This last benefit is one that you will observe every time you go to the bathroom. Later in this book, I talk about the perfect poop. Perhaps not a subject for polite discussion, but when you experience it you will understand the benefit!

I have personally suffered for the past 15 years with acid reflux. I learned how to manage it by reducing sugar and carbohydrate intake and taking over-the-counter meds as needed. However, since increasing dietary fiber levels to 40 to 50 grams per day, I no longer have acid reflux and haven't taken any medication for it in the last two years. I still keep sugar and carbohydrates under control but have noticed that even when I occasionally stray and eat cake or a big portion of rice or beans, there is no reflux. Thanks, microbiome!

When we consider our intestines, we can see how the three factors of diet, activity and microbiome are connected. Diet comprises what we put into the digestive system, how much and when. Activity effects the muscles that push and squeeze the food materials while in the digestive system, resulting in mixing, size reduction, residence time, water removal and many other benefits. A lack of sufficient physical activity results in poor digestion. Humans were designed to walk and be far more active than we are today. Our intestines suffer because of our inactivity and poor abdominal muscle tone. We don't need to be professional athletes, or have a 'six-pack' abdomen, but rather just keep active to help out our intestines. The intestinal microbiome digests food and keeps the intestinal wall healthy and efficient at keeping undigested food inside the intestine where it belongs and not in the bloodstream where it can cause severe damage. Resolving the Metabolic Syndrome requires restoring balance to these three. And remember that I'm a 'Darm' Mann (from Darmstadt – intestine city) and so are you!

Microbiome

The bacteria in or on our body are collectively called the microbiome. The intestines are home to thousands of different kinds of bacteria, but so are the skin, mouth, lungs, vagina and all other surfaces that come into contact with the outside world. These bacteria protect us from the outside world and provide many other benefits. The skin is easy to see, but our inner 'skin', the intestines are not so easy to see or even be aware of. It is estimated that there are up to one hundred trillion bacteria making up our microbiome, weighing about five pounds. There is a natural balance of the types and number of bacteria that is a result of what we feed them and how we treat them. When the balance of bacteria in the intestines is compromised, some types of bacteria can get out of control, while others may be depleted. It is not so much that some bacteria are good and others are bad, excepting pathogenic bacteria of course, but many different types are required in proper balance for good health. The balance can be altered by taking antibiotics, eating foods with powerful emulsifiers, eating too much sugar, eating too little fiber, eating a restricted diet, and more. These bacteria protect the intestine from pathogenic microorganisms and determine how the intestines digest the foods we eat. Everyone's microbiome is unique because we are unique: our environmental exposure from birth onwards, what we eat, how we eat, when we eat, how much we eat, activity, exposure to antibiotics, use of antibacterial soaps, hygienic habits, and many more factors influence and create our unique microbiome.

Plants produce a class of proteins called lectins that are anti-nutritive factors, designed to discourage insects and animals from eating the plant. There are hundreds of such proteins in almost all plants, especially in the seeds[34]. Beans, especially soybeans and fava beans, contain trypsin inhibitor, as an example, that prevents digestion of the bean proteins. An animal or insect that eats the raw bean will have severe digestive distress. This includes humans. The good news is that cooking denatures and detoxifies most of the lectin, so we have learned to cook beans. Wheat gluten is another lectin protein. After cooking, the second line of defense against these proteins is in our intestine. The lectin proteins bind to the mucous in the intestine. The bacteria in the mucous produce enzymes that can break down the lectins, turning them into harmless amino acids. When the mucous layer and the bacteria in it are in good condition and balance, we are protected from the lectin proteins produced by plants. And cooking helps too!

Leaky Gut Syndrome

The wall of the intestine is partially porous, in order to allow only digested food material to pass through and enter into the bloodstream. The wall consists of a several layers: a cell membrane, live bacteria and a coating of mucous, that together produce a barrier that prevents undigested particles of food from passing through. When the layer of colonizing bacteria and mucous is damaged or missing, the wall of the intestine allows partially digested food to pass into the bloodstream. This is called leaky gut syndrome. These partially digested food materials include fats or oils (as opposed to fatty acids), polypeptides (as opposed to amino acids and dipeptides) or multi-unit starches (as opposed to sugar), don't belong in our bloodstream and will cause problems there. The purpose of digestion is to break down food into fatty acids, sugar and amino acids.

When undigested fats or oils enter the bloodstream, the result is irritation to the walls of the arteries, which causes a defense response where a layer of protective plaque is applied on the artery lining. As this process repeats itself, the successive layers of plaque accumulate to eventually block the artery – causing arterial failure and heart disease. Note that the root cause of plaque buildup is not that we ate fat, the wrong kind of fat or even too much fat. The root cause is the presence of undigested fats and oils in the bloodstream, where they do not belong.

Polypeptides that enter the bloodstream will be detected by the immune systems as foreign objects to be attacked and removed. When this response is severe, it can result in an allergic or autoimmune reaction. The foreign polypeptide may have the same amino acid sequence as a polypeptide that is present somewhere else in our bodies, for example the cartilage in our joints. When our immune system is sensitized to attack this particular polypeptide by partially digested food that gets into our bloodstream, the same immune response can result in an attack on the cartilage in our joints. The immune system cannot differentiate between the foreign material and the material that is present in our body, so it attacks the material in our body as well. This is possibly how arthritis and other autoimmune diseases like scleroderma and allergies may be caused. Again, please note that the root cause of these diseases is not that we ate protein, the wrong kind of protein or even too much protein, but the presence of undigested protein in the bloodstream, where it doesn't belong. The leaky gut is the issue that we must correct via diet and exercise.

The intestinal wall is literally the 'skin' inside our bodies, and like the skin that covers the outside of our bodies, it acts as a barrier between the outside world and our inner organs. It is a critical function of the intestinal wall to protect the body from exposure to potentially harmful material. The size of the molecule determines which pass through the intestinal wall and which are retained inside the intestine for further digestion. With the intestines located inside of our bodies, it may be difficult to see them as a barrier to the outside world, but all of the food and water that we ingest from the outside world must pass through our intestines in order to enter the body. The intestine acts as a screen, keeping potentially harmful materials out of the body, while allowing beneficial nutrients into the body. Differentiating between the good and the bad is not so easy. We depend on a healthy intestine to do that and suffer when the intestine is unhealthy.

Recent research on diets that are deficient in dietary fiber confirm not only the benefits of fiber on the health of the bacteria in our intestines, but also go far further. A study by a group at the Luxembourg Institute of Health led by Mahesh S. Desai[35] has found that when the diet is deficient in fiber, the bacteria in our intestines are deprived of nutrients and instead metabolize the mucous layer inside the intestine wall. The title of their paper says it all: "A Dietary Fiber-Deprived Gut Microbiota Degrades the Colonic Mucous Barrier and Enhances Pathogen Susceptibility". This degradation by the starved bacteria, creates holes in the mucous layer, causing a leaky gut. This is a shocking and critical finding with huge health consequences related to all the diseases of the Metabolic Syndrome. This is the smoking gun that we have been looking for.

When we don't have enough fiber in our diet, the bacteria that colonize the intestinal wall do not have sufficient food and instead digest the mucosal layer itself, making holes in the layer. This is very bad and the cause of a long list of negative health impacts, including:

- The mucosal layer protects the wall of the intestine from damage due to irritating materials in the food. When the intestinal wall is exposed, the acids and enzymes that digest the food will also attack the intestinal wall. And, it's a fact that even 'natural' food contains toxins and irritants. Do you like hot sauce or spices? When the intestine is unprotected, these materials can cause irritation, inflammation and damage. The result can be colitis or irritable bowel syndrome (IBS).

- The mucosal layer provides a home for bacteria. When they are fed adequate amounts of fiber, these bacteria produce small chain fatty acids like acetic acid, butyric acid and propionic acid that decrease the pH of the mucosal layer, which makes it inhospitable to pathogenic bacteria like Listeria, Salmonella and E. coli. Viral particles in the food will have a more difficult time attaching to the wall of the intestine when the mucosal layer is intact. The result of a compromised mucosal layer is that we get sick more often.

- The mucous lining the healthy intestine is a lubricant, allowing food material inside to flow easily as it digests. This lubrication will also be beneficial when it's time for the fully digested and dewatered material to exit the body.

- The bacteria in the intestine produce vitamins that are released into the digesting food and absorbed through the intestinal wall and into the bloodstream. The bacteria in the intestine literally feed us. When our diet contains too little fiber, the bacteria starve, their number or balance are compromised, and we starve!

- The mucosal layer slows down the rate of absorption of nutrients into the bloodstream. The result, when the layer is intact, is that nutrients are absorbed slowly over a longer period of time than when the layer is missing or compromised. Slow absorption allows the systems of the body that manage nutrients, like glucose, more time to respond. When glucose from a meal is absorbed too quickly, the result is a sharp spike in blood glucose level that in turn spikes insulin. Too much insulin production causes the liver, brain and muscles to become insulin resistant, eventually causing diabetes. Too much insulin production causes the beta cells in the pancreas to eventually fatigue and fail to produce sufficient insulin, eventually resulting in diabetes. Moderating the rate of absorption of nutrients, especially glucose across the intestinal wall, is critical to preventing diabetes.

- The mucosal layer with embedded bacteria binds and breaks down natural toxins in food such as lectins, protecting us from the harmful effects of these anti-nutritive proteins.

- The holes in the mucosal layer create a leaky gut. The intestinal wall is a barrier between the undigested food inside the intestine and the bloodstream. Food is supposed to be digested inside the intestine and absorbed across the intestinal wall only when broken down into simple sugars, amino acids and fatty acids. When undigested or partially digested protein polypeptides are able to pass through the leaky gut into the bloodstream, the immune system detects them as foreign materials, is sensitized, produces antibodies and destroys the foreign protein. This is how the immune system operates. The problem is when the sequence of amino acids in the foreign food protein happens to match the amino acid sequence of a tissue inside the body, the immune system cannot tell the difference. The sensitized immune system will search out proteins with that specific amino acid sequence wherever they may be in the body. If that protein is in the knuckles or joints, the result is arthritis. If in the skin, the result is scleroderma or psoriasis. If the protein is in the beta cells of the pancreas that produce insulin, the result is type I diabetes.

- Our bodies are a holism – all parts connected, all parts contributing, all parts important. A leaky gut is the first step in a chain of harmful events that leads to diabetes, getting sick more often from the flu and food poisoning, obesity, allergic reactions to food, autoimmune diseases, intestinal disorders like IBS and colitis, high blood pressure, heart disease, cancer and more. Fixing our intestines should be our number one priority.

Unfortunately, there are many ways to damage the healthy intestinal wall:

- Taking antibiotics kills the bacteria that colonize and coat the surface of the wall, with numerous bad consequences. We should only take antibiotics when necessary to fight an infection. Afterwards, we need to pay special attention to restoring the bacteria in our intestines. In the next section, please read on how to do that.

- Eating a diet that is low in dietary fiber fails to provide the food that the bacteria need to live and grow in sufficient number.

- Eating a diet that is high in sugar changes the balance of bacteria in the intestine, allowing some to proliferate, while others decline. The balance of many different kinds of bacteria is beneficial to digestion, nutrition, the immune system, resistance to infection and much more.

- Eating a diet that contains strong emulsifying agents. Emulsifiers are materials that stabilize tiny droplets of fats and oils that can then be suspended in water, forming a stable emulsion. Many foods are emulsified and there are many kinds of emulsifiers. There are natural emulsifiers including milk proteins, egg lecithin, soybean lecithin. These are strong enough to form stable food emulsions like ice cream and milk, but not strong enough to act as detergents. There are synthetic emulsifiers, such as polysorbates and Tweens, that are much stronger and are able to act as detergents. This is an important difference, because the detergent action of synthetic emulsifiers is capable of damaging the cell wall of bacteria. Plants and animals have cell walls based on cellulose and lipoproteins, respectively. This is why detergents do not harm our skin or plants. But bacterial cell walls are mostly made of fat and can be disrupted by a detergent. This is how soaps and detergents clean our dirty hands and also act as sanitizers, killing bacteria. This is all good for hands, dishes and kitchen counter tops. The problem comes when these strong emulsifiers are in food inside of our intestines, where they can disrupt the cell walls of bacteria, causing damage to our microbiome.

There are ways for us to maintain or recover the healthy intestine, especially:

- Eating foods that contain fiber, such as beans, whole grains, vegetables, fruits, spices and chocolate. Only plants can make fiber. We must feed our bacteria with fiber to keep them healthy. Indigestible fibers pass through our stomach and enter the intestine undigested. The bacteria in the intestine digest the fibers and excrete small chain fatty acids as their waste product. Perfect! These fatty acids, mostly butyric acid and propionic acid, reduce the pH of the intestinal wall, making it inhospitable to pathogenic bacteria and are absorbed directly into the bloodstream, where they clean arteries.

- The 2015 USDA Dietary Guidelines for Americans recommends 33 and 38 grams per day of dietary fiber for women and men respectively. There is insufficient evidence to claim with certainty that this is enough fiber. I have found that for me, 50 grams a day is a good target level. You may have to learn how much is right for you individually. Start low and increase the level of fiber in your diet SLOWLY. If you eat too much fiber, your intestines will rebel, and you will not be a happy camper. By adding fiber and slowly increasing the amount in your diet, you give the bacteria in your intestines time to adapt to quantity and type. Too much, too fast will overburden the ability of the bacteria to digest the fiber and cause distress including bloating, flatulence, and even pain. It has taken decades to train our digestive system to be what it is. Don't expect it to change overnight. Retraining the system will take several months.

- Take probiotics in moderation. Probiotics are concentrated doses of live bacteria. About 99% of the live bacteria that we ingest will be killed in our stomach, but a pill that contains ten billion live bacteria can still deliver one hundred million live cells into the intestines. The best probiotics contain spores, which survive the stomach and enter the intestines intact ready to grow. Some are now advising against taking probiotics, claiming that we really don't know which bacteria are beneficial and we could create an imbalance, actually making things worse. We already have the bacteria that we need in our intestines, just not in the right quantity or balance, because of poor diet. Fixing the diet will enhance the quantity and allow the balance to correct itself. That is a compelling argument.

- Eat foods that are fermented. These include yogurt (unsweetened), kefir, kombucha, sour kraut, fermented vegetables, and unpasteurized beer. The food we eat is too clean and free of bacteria. Even the lettuce we buy today has been ozone treated to reduce the risk of pathogenic bacteria. This is fine, except the good bacteria go the same way as the bad – dead. We benefit from a constant influx of good bacteria into our guts to keep the good guys in control and the bad ones under control. Even if the live bacteria in the yogurt or sauerkraut are mostly killed in the stomach, we still benefit from all the healthy fermentation byproducts such as short chain fatty acids. Eating fermented foods will favor the growth of good bacteria in the intestine and help reestablish or maintain the proper balance.

- Exercise!!! Our intestines need strong abdominal muscles to move the digesting food and waste products through in a reasonable time. The motion of the exercise helps too. Walking is great. Stomach crunches and sit-ups are ideal.

- Avoid antibiotics as much as possible. Avoid foods that contain synthetic emulsifiers and polyols.

There are some other diseases such as autism and schizophrenia that are now also hypothesized to be caused by the leaky condition of the gut. Dr. Natasha Campbell-McBride has written a book called *Gut Psychology Syndrome: Natural Treatment for Autism, Dyspraxia, A.D.D., Dyslexia, Depression, Schizophrenia* [36] in which she describes the horrible gut condition of people with these diseases and the work she has done to reverse it. We can learn a lot from her work and apply it to our own quest for a healthy intestine. If we want to extend our healthy life, we will need to learn.

The road to health is paved with good intestines!
–Dr. Sherry A. Rogers

In: Yafa, Stephen. "Grain of Truth." Penguin Publishing Group, 2015-04-13. iBooks.

We have a lot to learn about our microbiome and the condition of our intestines. What we do know is that we have done a poor job of caring for our intestines through the use of antibiotics, poor diet and lack of exercise. If we want to extend our healthy lives, we need to learn how to nurture and care for our intestines and cure our leaky gut.

Toilet Paper

Did you ever wonder why we are the only animal on the planet that needs to clean themselves after defecating? Do you think cavemen and women walked around with toilet paper or maybe they used leaves? Not likely. Actually, we would not need to use toilet paper either, if our digestive systems were working properly. The answer is once again a combination of diet, activity and the microbiome.

It starts with what we eat. The component of food that is most responsible for our need to use toilet paper is fiber. Fiber absorbs water in the intestine and acts as a bulking agent in the stool, increasing water-binding capacity, increasing mass and providing structure. All good features, but the real reason that fiber is so beneficial is that it feeds our microbiome, which acts as a trap for mucous, a slippery, viscous fluid that is an effective lubricant. It is in saliva to lubricate food to help it pass cleanly and painlessly down the esophagus. It is also inside our intestines as a lubricant to help the food materials move along easily as they digest and transform from food particles to stool. Lubrication aids in the efficient movement, prevents constipation, prevents damage to the intestinal wall and reduces residence time in the digestive system. All good things.

The mucous that is present in a healthy gut due to the healthy bacterial layer has another benefit. It coats the surface of the stool as it passes through the intestine. When the stool exits through the anus, this layer of mucous acts as a lubricant so that the stool exits cleanly and easily. Another clue is, how long do you spend on the toilet? When the stool is properly formed, and lubricated by mucous, it shouldn't take more than thirty seconds to do our business.

The stool is squeezed by the muscles in the abdominal wall, which is why activity is also important. Strong abdominal muscles, which are the result of exercise and activity can properly squeeze the intestines to form the stool, remove water and coat it with mucous. Weak abdominal muscles cannot do the job and the food and stool move slowly and inefficiently through the intestine, causing excessive residence time, excessive amounts of waste in the intestines, bloating, flatulence, pain and constipation. The best exercise for good intestinal function is the sit-up. Do at least ten sit-ups per day. Activity such as walking also keeps the food moving properly while it is in the intestines. If you are constipated or bloated, instead of taking medicine, consider activity level and, of course, fiber intake.

Do you know where bad breath comes from? It often comes from what we eat, of course, but mostly it comes from our intestines. When our intestines are out of balance, we will notice it in our breath. There is research being done now to assess a person's health based on an analysis of their breath. This can work because the aromatic compounds in the breath come from other parts of the body, especially the intestines.

To summarize; when we have the following issues, there is an imbalance in our diet which is causing an imbalance in our intestinal microbiome, probably too little fiber or too much sugar, or both:

- Poop is smelly

- Poop sinks in water (it should float)

- Poop is sticky or tarry, making cleanup difficult

- Pooping hurts

- Poop is sour, maybe even burning or irritating your behind

- Poop is hard as a rock

- Pooping is explosive with lots of gas

- Poop is loose and not formed into units

- Poop is liquid and watery

These issues are not normal and we should not live with them. Something is wrong and we can fix it. The fix involves several factors:

- Exercise, especially walking and sit-ups

- Adequate insoluble fiber in the diet (excessive soluble fibers can cause the opposite effect)

- Good nutrition for gut bacteria – L-Glutamine and Zinc Carnosine

- Adequate hydration

- Reduce sugar intake

- Avoid undigestible materials like sugar alcohols

- Cook your food to make it more digestible and to kill pathogenic bacteria

- Eat foods that bind like green bananas, bread and rice

The benefits to good pooping go far beyond the intestines. I hope this discussion wasn't too graphic, but it really is a serious issue and a good clue about the health of our intestines, the balance or lack of balance in our diet, activity and microbiome. And, nothing feels as good as a good you know what!

CHAPTER 5

Constructing a Diet

Dieting and Weight Management

First, let's differentiate between diet and dieting. Our diet is the sum of all the food and meals we eat. We all have a diet that is uniquely our own, based on the multitude of decisions we make every day about the food we eat. Our diet can be consistent or inconsistent depending on the choices we make. In contrast, 'Dieting' is the popular notion of modifying our diet to achieve some dietary goal, usually weight loss or health improvement. Dieting is often unsuccessful or only successful in the short term. We may achieve our weight reduction goal in the short term by dieting, but after the dieting is over, if we return to our original diet, then we should expect to go back to our original weight. This should be obvious, but most people see dieting only as a short-term practice to achieve a goal. This is faulty thinking. Unless we change our diet for the long term, we should not expect success from dieting. This is why our diet needs to be part of our lifestyle. If we are overweight or overeating, then we need to modify our diet and incorporate the changes into our lifestyle for long-term success. We need to manage our diet and get beyond 'dieting'!

It is easier to change a man's religion than to change his diet.
-Margaret Mead

Portion control is the most important part of controlling our diet. When it comes to eating, size does matter! Most of us have no concept of what one hundred grams of avocado looks like. There are studies that show that people eat more when their plates are larger – so maybe it will help if we use a smaller plate. The best investment we can make (besides this book of course!) is to spend $50 on a small digital scale. There are some very nice units available in any good cooking supply store that will weigh up to 2000 grams. Use it to calibrate your eye by weighing the ingredients or components of your meals. This will help you to manage how much you eat and develop a diet that fits your personal preferences while achieving your dietary goals. Any food can be incorporated into a healthy diet with the proper portion control and balance with other foods.

As we have already discovered, taking in more calories than we need on a chronic basis over years, is the primary underlying root cause of the Metabolic Syndrome. We need to get control of how much we eat if we are going to be successful. Food very often becomes a surrogate for boredom and an antidote for stress. In addition, we eat by the clock and eat what is put before us, or what we think is appropriate. Buffets are often the worst because if people are allowed to eat all they want, most will eat more. We need to be aware of how much we are eating, pay attention and then choose thoughtfully, not in a reactionary or emotional manner. Eating is important business.

There are differing views on the frequency and timing of eating. Our bodies produce insulin in order to metabolize and control glucose, but insulin also regulates fat metabolism. Basically, our bodies only metabolize glucose when insulin levels are high and only metabolize fat when insulin levels are low. Insulin acts as a switch – high for sugar, low for fat. We want to design our diet so that our bodies are able to efficiently process the foods we eat while avoiding excessive blood glucose spikes that can lead to diabetes.

Have you ever watched a wild animal, like a deer or groundhog, eat? Unfortunately, I get that opportunity too often as my desk overlooks the backyard, so I helplessly watch these critters graze on my trees, bushes and flower gardens! The interesting thing is that they eat a variety of plants, and do not gorge themselves on just one, even when that one plant is available in surfeit. I have a long hedge of Wisteria, so in the spring there are a lot of tender Wisteria shoots available, and the deer stop and eat some. They could stand there all day and eat themselves full on just the Wisteria, if they chose to. But they don't. They eat a few here and a few there and then move on to the next tasty plants, which are usually my Purple Cone Flowers or Shasta Daisies! I believe they eat in this manner, not out of compassion for the plants, or me, but rather to get a variety of plants into their diet for nutritional purposes. In addition, almost all plants contain anti-nutritive ingredients or natural toxins designed to protect the plant from being eaten, and by eating a small amount of many different plants, the deer can avoid consuming a toxic overload of the anti-nutritive factor from any one plant. We can benefit by learning from the deer and doing the same. The concepts of balance and variety are critical to diet. Ideally, we want our diet to provide a good balance of protein, carbs, fats, vitamins and minerals in proportion to what our bodies need, and the best way to do this is by consuming a wide variety of foods.

There are some excellent apps that make it easy to calculate and keep track of what we eat and the nutrients contained. One that I use is called 'Bitesnap'; it allows us to take a photo of our food, identify the food, the quantity and calculate the nutritional content. If it fails, you can search for it or even add it. It is convenient, powerful and fun to use.

Food and Comfort

Who can deny the pleasure of eating a well-prepared meal with quality ingredients that complement in flavor, aroma, texture and appearance? Having enough to eat is satisfying and pleasurable as well. Food is a major source of pleasure in our lives. Food is at the bottom of Maslow's pyramid of needs. It is a basic need, but much more. We celebrate victories and holidays with food. We console ourselves with food after funerals. We use food to celebrate religious ceremonies. Food is an integral part of the human social fabric. Food defines us as peoples and as cultures. We eat to console ourselves, often when we are bored or upset. There is no food to compare with what our own mothers served us when growing up. We can remember the flavor, texture and aroma of food for the rest of our lives and often are nostalgic for foods we ate when young or on a special occasion. We call foods that are warm or pleasurable 'comfort foods'. Warm stews for dinner on a cold winter night or a refreshingly cold borsht on a hot summer day are good examples.

What is the sense of denying ourselves the comfort of foods that are so much a part of our lives? I jokingly suggest to my friends that a chocolate covered donut (Entenmann's® of course!) is health food. Yes, it is high in fat and sugar. But eating it is an experience that can make us happy, if we can just relax and enjoy it. The texture and flavor are wonderful. And since being happy makes us healthy, it is therefore a health food! I am, of course, saying this with some levity, but eating a chocolate covered donut is pleasurable. If we adjust our diet for the fat and sugar we ingest, we can suffer no long- or short-term negative consequences. Eating such a donut every day of our lives might be excessive, but once a week certainly won't kill us, especially if we balance our overall diet to appropriately compensate. There are no good or bad foods, only bad diets. If we balance our diets, we can even eat a chocolate covered donut without harm. I don't want to be lying on my deathbed bemoaning the fact that I unnecessarily denied myself the joy of eating a few donuts in my lifetime! Let's learn how to balance our diets, so we can eat the foods we love, even if some food guru says that they are unhealthy.

Designing a Recipe

It is useful, when selecting the ingredients to include in a recipe, to consider that each ingredient plays a different role in producing the desired nutrition, flavor, aroma and texture. There are three basic categories of ingredients: those that are characterizing, those that are complementary and those that contribute. This is just as true for nutrition as for flavor, texture and aroma.

Characterizing ingredients are the main players that dominate the recipe in nutrition, flavor, aroma or texture, or possibly all four. These are the ingredients that define the recipe. We want them to be obvious and define the character of the recipe. For example, when we eat a steak, we want to taste, smell and feel the texture of the steak. Adding another ingredient to a steak that is stronger in flavor or aroma would detract from the steak. We can add complementary or contributing ingredients like pepper, salt, mushrooms, blue cheese, onions or even a savory steak sauce, but not another dominant ingredient like ketchup!

Complementary ingredients are side players that are strong enough to be detected in flavor, aroma or texture, but complement the characterizing ingredient. Adding ripe, sliced pears or even pine nuts to a salad, complement the flavor and texture of the leafy green we are using, especially if the leafy part of the salad is something bitter like endive, radicchio or arugula. The sweetness of the pear and the nuttiness of the pine nuts complement the bitter flavor of the endive. These flavors are obvious and add to the complexity of the salad in a pleasant manner without detracting from the flavor of the characterizing ingredient. Complementary ingredients are excellent for boosting the antioxidant and fiber content of a recipe. Some versatile ingredients that can help you to do this effectively include: cinnamon, cocoa powder, ginger root fresh or powder, clove powder, turmeric, chia seeds, pine nuts, pistachio nuts, pecans, blueberries, dried cranberries and balsamic vinegar.

Contributing ingredients are background players that enhance but are not noticeable in flavor, aroma or texture. They do not stick out above the other ingredients, but rather add additional background notes. These can be strongly flavored ingredients that are used at a low enough level so as not to be obvious, but only enhance. For example, dried ginger powder is a great enhancer that contributes a bright, spicy note to a salad or soup. When used at a low level, the flavor of ginger itself is not characterizing or obvious, but still contributes flavor and beneficial antioxidants. Vanilla is another great example of a contributing flavor that we use liberally in baking, beverages and desserts, because it is a wonderful enhancing flavor. At high, characterizing levels, vanilla becomes bitter and chemical tasting. Even in vanilla ice cream, the vanilla note is at best complementing the sweet dairy notes. The quintessential example of a recipe with contributing notes is Coca Cola. The recipe for Coca Cola, of course, is a top secret, but it is well known that the ingredients include cinnamon, coca bean and vanilla among others. These ingredients are difficult to define in the flavor of Coke, because they are perfectly balanced and blended so that no single note sticks out to be characterizing. All the flavors present in Coke are contributing so that we cannot detect the individual ingredients, but all contribute to creating the iconic flavor of Coke. The point is to learn how to add contributing ingredients to your recipes to enhance nutrition, flavor, texture and aroma.

It is important to use good ingredients. Good does not mean expensive; it means in good condition as appropriate to what we are trying to achieve. An example is choosing the right degree of ripeness in a pear. If we are using it in a pie, we want the pear to be firm and crispy so that it stands up to the baking. If we are using pears in a salad, we probably want a riper and softer pear, where the sweet flavor and soft texture of the pear blend in nicely with the salad. Or maybe, we want a firm, crispy pear that we can slice very thin so that it blends in with the lettuce better. The condition of the ingredient is important to consider. Using, limp, rubbery broccoli can never be good, and no amount of kitchen wizardry will improve it. We can ruin a good ingredient with improper technique, but rarely, can good technique recover a poor ingredient. Consider the condition of the ingredient and what effects of flavor, texture and aroma we are trying to achieve with it.

Don't be afraid to experiment. Sometimes the pears are too firm, or we don't have all the ingredients that we need but have some others that may substitute. Adjust as appropriate and aim for a good final result in spite of the challenges. Who knows, we might like it better!

What does all this have to do with good nutrition and diet? Our goal is to change the way we eat in order to change our lives. Living a longer, healthier, vibrant life will require that we get the diet piece right, not only because of the nutrients it delivers, but also because of the enjoyment we get from eating. In order to be sustainable as a set of changes that we make and keep for the rest of our lives, the changes need to fit our lifestyle and be enjoyable. We have learned over and over again that people will stay on an inconvenient or unenjoyable diet for a limited period of time and then go back to what they enjoy. Our goal is to change what we know and make it our new normal. We will still deviate occasionally, but when we come back, this new and improved diet is what we will come back to. We will incorporate new ingredients into our existing diet and add some new meals. The result will be a change we can live with and enjoy. It will consistently deliver moderate levels of carbs, protein and fat; with high fiber and antioxidants. It will make us look and feel better. It will make us want to live longer, because we are feeling better. It will prevent the diseases of the Metabolic

Syndrome. We don't want to go there. Remember, we don't want care; we want cure. Now, that is a vision!

Constructing a Meal

We should think about each meal, the components in it and how each contributes to the total nutrition of the meal. A meal is constructed from individual foods that we select for nutrition, flavor and pure enjoyment. Eating can be fun, satisfying and nutritional all at the same time. The idea is to combine foods that allow us to achieve a nutritional balance of calories, fats, protein, carbs, sugar, fiber, ORAC, omega-3s, etc. It's really not rocket science, or even very complicated. If we learn how to eat a balanced diet, composed of many different foods, and add some new, functional ingredients to our potpourri, we can get there!

First, let's discuss a little background information on the approach we will take. Recent topics of discussion in nutrition circles include the concepts of nutrient density and satiety. The suggestion is to consume highly nutrient dense foods. What this means is to select foods that are high in good nutrients like protein, fats, moderate in carbs and low in sugar. Satiety is the feeling of fullness we get from eating a food. Foods vary in the degree to which they make our bellies feel full. If we eat foods that are high in satiety, the idea is that we will eat less. Sometimes that doesn't work so well, enabling overeating. On the other hand, eating low nutrient density foods will allow us to eat more, and feel satisfied while keeping caloric intake low. Satiety and nutrient density are both interesting technical concepts but may be difficult to implement in our daily dietary choice, so let's consider a simpler approach.

It takes about 500 to 600 grams of food to make our bellies feel satisfied. Notice that I didn't say stuffed! We don't want to overeat. Too much of a good thing is not a good thing. We want to select foods that provide the nutrients our bodies need in the right balance, without too many calories. The table below shows reasonable target values for the grams of food, calories, grams of carbs, grams of protein and grams of fat in a meal, depending on whether we are eating two or three meals a day.

The FDA Nutrition Facts Panel that is required on all food products sold in the US, is based on a 2,000 daily caloric intake. The amount of calories you personally need to consume depends on many factors, but especially your activity level. You need to adjust your personal daily caloric intake based on your unique needs. The best way to decide if you are getting the right amount of calories is to watch the scale! The scale doesn't lie.

Assuming we will eat 2 meals a day, good targets to aim for in a meal are:

2 Meals/Day	Total Grams*	Calories	Carbs Grams	Protein Grams	Fat Grams
Lunch	500	750	100	40	20
Dinner	750	1250	200	60	25
Total	1250	2000	300	100	45

*Total Grams includes water – most foods as consumed are over 50% water

If we are eating 3 meals a day, the totals stay the same, just distributed differently. This is why it's better to eat 2 meals a day. When we eat three meals, it's difficult to avoid overeating.

3 Meals/Day	Total Grams	Calories	Carbs Grams	Protein Grams	Fat Grams
Breakfast	150	300	40	15	10
Lunch	350	500	60	25	15
Dinner	750	1200	200	60	20
Total	1250	2000	300	100	45

*Total Grams includes water – most foods as consumed are over 50% water

The following table compares two meal choices. One is a McDonalds® meal and the other is our Special Salad (the recipe is in Appendix 1).

	Weight (grams)	Calories	Total Fat (grams)	Saturated Fat (grams)	Total Carbs (grams)	Omega-3 (grams)	Sugar (grams)	Fiber (grams)	ORAC (umol TE)	Protein (grams)	Cholesterol (mg)
McDonalds Double Quarter Poundter w/Cheese, Medium Fries and Medium Coke	488	1290	58	22	145	Low	68	7	? Low	51	165
Special Salad	508	681	52	6	53	3	18	23	12,382	7	0

This simple table has only two meals in it for easy comparison – a McDonalds® meal comprised of a Double Quarter Pounder® with cheese, medium fries and a medium Coke®, compared to our special salad. Let's consider these two alternative meals as options for lunch or dinner. Both will fill you up with about 500 grams of food. But that's where the similarities end! The calories of the special salad are half, total fat is about the same, but the quality of the fat is totally different, saturated fat is reduced by over 4X, carbs are reduced by 3X, the salad provides over half of your required omega-3 versus almost none, fiber is over triple, ORAC is off the charts and cholesterol is zero for the salad. Change the Coke® for a Diet Coke® or water and the sugar and carbs in the McDonalds® meal drop by 45 grams along with 180 calories. The only way the McDonalds® meal beats our special salad is in protein – providing over 7 times the protein. But we can design breakfast and lunch to provide plenty of protein.

This comparison points out the differences between an indulgent McDonalds® meal and a mixed salad. And just for the record, I occasionally eat at McDonalds®, and the Double Quarter Pounder® is my favorite! As long as we balance the calories and fat over the next few days, we can eat a McDonalds® meal without any harm. When I come home after a few weeks in a country in Asia that I won't mention at the risk of offending someone, the first thing I do when I get off the plane is head to a McDonalds® for this meal.

It recalibrates me. When you need a McDonalds® hit, go for it, and as a steady diet, go with the special salad!

The next step is to design other meal choices that meet our nutritional needs and are fun and fit our lifestyle. The goal is to minimize carb intake in the morning to extend our nighttime fast until lunch, or even better to eat two meals a day and skip breakfast. At lunch and dinner, we need to increase the carbs to support our metabolic needs. If we are mostly sedentary that day, keep the carbs at around 250 grams total for lunch and dinner. If you are active physically, then feel free to increase carbs as needed. It's hard to estimate the amount of carbs that each person needs, since there are so many factors involved. This is why it's important that we know our own body. The most effective way for us to assess if we are on balance with carb intake is to look at our body. Are we carrying around excess baggage in belly or leg fat? If yes, then reduce carb intake, and use a scale to assess progress. If not, then maintain what you are doing. If we are too skinny and don't have enough body fat, then increase carb intake. Carbs are the gas pedal that we use to control speed.

Transforming Ordinary into Extraordinary!

The goal is to take ordinary meals and transform them into extraordinary meals that meet our nutritional, cultural and lifestyle needs. We want to learn how to substitute ingredients as needed to cope with availability, economics, personal preference or just for the sake of variety. Have some fun with it!

Let's start with a breakfast meal – oat bran. Oat bran is a good choice, as it is high in beta glucan fiber, moderate in carbs, very low in sugar, inexpensive, widely available, tastes good and can be modified to our taste. I prefer a coarsely milled oat bran cereal, as I like the texture better and it cooks up with less lumps than the finely milled varieties.

How can we transform an oat bran breakfast from ordinary to extraordinary?

- First, let's start with our oat bran cereal – 40 grams (3 tablespoons dry)

- Add 13 grams (1 tablespoon) of Chia seeds. This adds omega-3 fat, increases the fiber even more, adds antioxidants and adds an interesting texture of the seeds.

- For good antioxidants, let's add 7.4 grams (1 tablespoon) cocoa powder, and 6 grams (1 teaspoon) of ground cinnamon. If you are really adventurous, a gram (1/3 teaspoon) of ginger powder and a dash of ground cloves will spice it up. These add flavor too. The cloves are strongly flavored, and it may take some getting used to, but after eating it a few times, you will like it better. The antioxidant content of cloves is very high, even higher than cinnamon or ginger. Cinnamon is amazingly versatile. You can add a small amount to a dish like this and it is noticeable but not overpowering, and adds a very pleasant, spicy and floral note. Ginger is also amazing, as it incorporates well into a dish like this. You will not even notice that it is there. The only evidence of its presence is the slightly hot (picante) note and a brightness of flavor that is unique to ginger and very pleasant. Cocoa powder is mild in flavor and easy to incorporate into many different recipes.

- Good oils are still missing in this dish. Except for the Chia seeds, everything we have added so far is low in fat of any kind. So, let's add 45 grams (3 tablespoons of walnut oil). Walnut oil has a pleasant nutty flavor and is a healthy oil with a low melting point.

- Add 200 grams of water (7 ounces) and stir. I like to microwave it in 45-second increments until it is rising like a cake, stirring in between each. If you don't like microwave ovens, then boil the water first and add it to the oat bran and chia seeds.

- Lastly, I like to add a little milk or even half and half cream to help cool it off a bit and to improve the flavor and texture. I typically add 45 grams (3 tablespoons). The amount of saturated fat this adds is not worth mentioning. This is optional.

- See Appendix 4 for the full recipe, and nutritional values.

That's it! Simple enough and we have transformed this meal by adding a significant amount of antioxidants, good oils, increased the fiber, made the texture more interesting and given it some interesting flavor. That is one way to transform an ordinary meal into an extraordinary one! Notice that we didn't add any kind of sugar. We could add a little sugar, but with some taste-bud training, we can skip the sugar, especially by adding spices. The benefit is we can keep the sugar content of this meal very low and since it is typically a breakfast meal, we can keep our blood glucose level low and allow our bodies to remain in fat metabolism until lunch. Since we haven't eaten anything since dinner last night, this allows us to extend the period of fat metabolism from eight hours to at least twelve hours. And since we are active in the morning, our bodies will need calories and we want those to be fat calories taken from the fat stores in our body. It's time to take some of that fat we deposited in the past out of the bank. All good!

Designing a Diet

Here is a list of a few of the nutritional factors that we need to be aware of when designing a meal or a diet:

- How many grams the meal delivers. Grams matter because this determines how satisfied we will feel after eating. This is why eating a bowl of soup, as is customary in European cuisine, is a great strategy to partially fill the belly with a great tasting soup that is mostly water and contains very few calories. We don't want to starve or be hungry all the time. On the other hand, we need to get accustomed to eating less and not eating until we are full. Remember, overeating is one of the main causes of the Metabolic Syndrome and diabetes.

- How many meals a day we plan to eat. If we can get down to two meals a day, it makes it easier to plan satisfying meals. Avoiding snacking in between meals helps too, as this can add significant calories that we are unlikely to compensate for when we eat the meals. Drinking sugar-free liquids or water any time helps avoid snacking. I find sparkling water to be more satisfying than plain.

- How many calories the meal or diet delivers. Calories matter! For a sedentary lifestyle, depending on body size (not fat), aim for 2,000 total per day. If you are more active, increase the carbs, keeping protein and fat the same. Be careful not to overestimate how many calories you are burning during exercise and work. The human body is remarkably efficient. The best gauge of your need for more carbs is to watch the scale. If you are losing weight and don't want to, then increase carbs. If you are losing weight and need to, don't increase the carbs! Water contains no calories, so drinking more water or sugar-free liquids is an easy way to increase intake without adding calories. There is conflicting evidence on whether artificially sweetened beverages cause an impact on blood glucose – small amounts are unlikely to cause any harm.[37]

- How much protein the meal provides (protein quality is important too, but beyond the scope of this book to consider). Typically, we aim for twenty percent of calories from protein. Protein contains about 4 calories per gram, so a good daily target is 100 grams of protein each day.

- How much fat, saturated fat, monounsaturated fat, polyunsaturated fat, omega-3 fatty acids, omega-6 fatty acids and cholesterol the meal or diet delivers. Typically, we aim for twenty to forty percent of calories from fats and oils. These contain about 9 calories per gram, so a good daily target is 45 grams of fats and oils per day.

- How much carbohydrates, sugar and dietary fiber the meal or diet delivers. Typically, aim for sixty percent of calories from carbs. Keep sugar as low as possible. Carbs contain about 4 calories per gram, so a good daily target is 300 grams of total carbs per day.

- How much vitamins (folate, niacin, pyridoxine (B6), pantothenic acid, riboflavin, Vitamin A, Vitamin C, Vitamin D, Vitamin E and Vitamin K) the meal or diet delivers.

- How much minerals (calcium, sodium, potassium, phosphorus, copper, iron, magnesium, manganese, selenium and zinc) the meal or diet delivers.

- How much antioxidants the meal or diet provides. ORAC is the measure of the quantity of antioxidants in a food. Recommendations on how much antioxidants to consume vary greatly. 5000 um TE/day is a good minimum, but I have seen recommendations up to 5 times that. The science is lacking to establish a good target, but there is some consensus that 25,000 Units per day is good. There is some evidence that too much antioxidants can cause harm as well.[38]

- Lastly, don't obsess too much with the numbers. A few grams either way or even a hundred calories don't matter much. The bigger variable by far is your activity level. Aim to be close to the targets until you can calibrate your eyes and you start to get some feedback from your scale!

The trick is to find foods that complement each other to provide the necessary nutrients in a reasonable balance while managing caloric intake. Learning how to do this with foods that we can afford, that are available where we shop, that we like to eat and that allow us to mix it up for variety so we're not eating the same foods every day is a fun challenge! This is why we must be passionate and be willing to invest the time to become somewhat of an expert in what we eat.

Let's start by looking at some real foods and break down their nutritional content. I've selected some common foods from each category for simplicity. From this, we can get an idea of how to build a diet. There is a lot of help available on apps and websites, including the outstanding USDA Nutrition Database, which is comprehensive and free.

USDA Handbook No. 8 and SR-21 Nutrition Values for Foods

Shrt Desc	Grams of Food per 100 Calories	Percent Water	Calories Per 100 grams of Food	Grams Protein per 100 Grams of Food	Grams Fat per 100 Grams of Food	Grams Carbs per 100 Grams of Food	Grams sugar per 100 Grams of Food	Grams fiber per 100 Grams of Food	ORAC umTE/100 gms
ASPARAGUS,RAW	500	93.22	20	2.2	0.12	3.88	0	2.1	3017
COLLARDS,CKD,BLD,DRND,WO/SALT	385	91.8	26	2.1	0.4	4.9	0.4	2.8	1200
KALE,RAW	357	91.2	28	1.9	0.4	5.63	1.3	2	1770
ARUGULA,RAW	286	90.35	35	0.64	0.13	8.24	2.1	2.9	1900
BROCCOLI,RAW	286	89.25	35	2.38	0.41	7.18	1.7	3.3	1590
CARROTS,RAW	286	90.17	35	0.76	0.18	8.22	1.4	3	1215
OAT BRAN, COOKED	250	84	40	3.21	0.86	11.44	1.7	2.6	2183
APPLES,RAW,WITH SKIN	192	85.56	52	0.26	0.17	13.81	16	2.4	3000
CORN,SWT,YEL,RAW	116	76	86	3.2	1.2	19	3.2	2.7	728
BANANAS,RAW	112	74.91	89	1.09	0.33	22.84	12.2	2.6	879
FISH, SALMON,ATLANTIC,WILD,RAW	85	72	117	18.28	4.32	0	0	0	30
EGG,WHL,RAW,FRSH	70	76.15	143	12.56	9.51	0.72	0.8	0	20
AVOCADOS,RAW,ALL COMM VAR	63	73.23	160	2	14.66	8.53	0.7	6.7	1933
FISH, SALMON,ATLANTIC,FARMED,RAW	49	64.75	206	22.1	12.35	0	0	0	30
BEEF, COMP OF RTL CUTS,LN&FAT,1/8"FAT,CHOIC,CKD	45	63.03	223	18.87	15.75	0	0	0	795
WHOLE WHEAT BREAD, COMMERCIAL	40	38	247	13	3.3	41.3	5.6	6.8	1421
CHEESE, SWISS	26	37.12	380	26.93	27.8	5.38	1.3	0	697
NUTS, PISTACHIO NUTS,DRY RSTD,W/SALT	22	4.5	446	18.55	19.4	53.75	0	18.4	7675
COOKIES, CHOCOLATE CHIP, MADE W BUTTER	18	3	548	6.45	32.3	61.3	35.5	3.2	8750
PEANUTS,ALL TYPES,DRY-ROASTED,W/SALT	18	6.39	570	26.15	49.6	15.82	4.2	9.5	3166
NUTS, WALNUTS,BLACK,DRIED	15	4.07	654	15.23	65.21	13.71	1.1	6.7	13541
PECANS	14	1.12	710	9.5	74.27	13.55	4	9.4	17940
BUTTER, WITH SALT	14	15.87	717	0.85	81.11	0.06	0.1	0	730

Column 2 – Grams of Food per 100 Calories

I've sorted these foods by the Caloric content, with the lowest first and increasing from there. The first column shows how many grams of the food it takes to contain 100 calories.

- The first food on the list is asparagus with 500 grams required to deliver 100 calories. That is a lot of asparagus! Why is it so low in calories? First, notice that it is 93 percent water. It is also very low in fat (0.12%), has no measurable sugar, has 2.1% fiber and a respectable ORAC value of 3017.

- Most veggies are low in calories, and here I have included arugula, kale, broccoli and carrots, which are high in water content (over 90%), are low in fat (less than 0.4%), low in sugar (less than 2%), moderate in fiber (2-3%) and good sources of antioxidants (1200-3000 ORAC). Carrots get a bad rap for containing sugar. This is nonsense, as carrots have no more sugar than any other vegetable, and the little sugar they contain is well worth it considering the benefits of low calories, good fiber, good antioxidants, Vitamin A (16,705 IU/100 gm), potassium (320 mg/100 gm), not to mention great flavor, texture and crunch. Foods that are high in water content naturally contain less calories and the bulk helps to fill up our bellies, making us feel satisfied sooner. All good things.

- Next, we get to grains, fruits, fish, meats and whole wheat bread. These foods are moderate in caloric content, due to the high-water content, (60-90%) as eaten. We don't eat grains raw, thank God! When grains like oat bran are cooked, they absorb a lot of water that adds bulk and keeps calories low. Grains and the foods made from them, like whole wheat bread, are great sources of complex carbs, fiber and protein, with moderate caloric content, good ORAC values and low in sugar.

- The high caloric value foods include cheese, nuts, cookies and finally butter. Dried cheeses are higher in calories because the moisture content is low. Unaged cheeses like cottage cheese or mozzarella are higher in water content and lower in calories. Nuts are low in water content and high in fat, giving them high caloric values. And butter is mostly fat (80%), making it high in calories. But that doesn't make it bad! It only means that we should consume it in moderation, with awareness of the calories it brings. But it also brings great flavor, texture, moderates sugar absorption and provides butyric acid, which is good for our brains![28]

Please note that these are all 'Good' foods! By being aware of the tradeoffs of water content, calories, and beneficial nutrients, we can construct a balanced and nutritious diet that contains all of these foods and many others.

Column 5 – Grams of Protein per 100 Grams of Food

This column is not sorted, so protein levels vary by food. A few important points to notice:

- Veggies and fruits are low in protein (0.26-2.38%)

- Grains are moderate in protein content (3.21%)

- Eggs are moderately high in protein content (12%)

- Meats and fish are high in protein (18-22%)

- Nuts and whole wheat bread are high in protein (10-26%)

- Cheese (dried) is very high in protein (26.83%)

We need to include these foods in our diet to get the protein we need.

Column 6 – Grams of Fat per 100 Grams of Food

The fat content of foods varies widely from:

- Very low in veggies and fruits (0.12-0.41%), with the exception of avocados at 14.66%

- Moderate in whole wheat bread, eggs, meat and fish (3.3 -15%)

- High in dried cheese (27%)

- Very high in nuts (50-74%), with the exception of pistachio nuts at 19.4%.

- Butter, fats and oils are almost 100% fat.

Don't be afraid of fat. All the hype about saturated fats being bad for us has finally been proven wrong, as long as our diet also contains adequate amounts of the low melting point oils that we get from nuts and fish. **Fat doesn't cause heart disease. Fat doesn't cause heart disease.** I said it twice, and put it in bold type, because the opposite has been drummed into our heads for the past 30 years. We have been given bad advice. Very bad, because if we eat less fat, then we must eat more carbs (usually sugar) and protein. The protein is generally not an issue, but the higher carbs and sugar certainly are. And fat helps reduce the blood glucose spike caused by eating high carb foods. Fat is good! Fat will help us avoid diabetes. And can I say it again? **Fat doesn't cause heart disease!** Even trans fats are no longer a risk, as the partial hydrogenation process that produced them has been banned, and the naturally occurring trans fats in meat and butter aren't a risk.

My dear friend Bill Knightly was a fat chemist (he wasn't fat, but what he studied was!). He presciently told me years ago that the issue with fat and heart disease was melting point. Saturated fats have higher melting points than monounsaturated and polyunsaturated fats. Coconut oil melts at 75 to 85 degrees F, butter melts at 80 to 92 degrees F, and Cocoa butter melts at 93 to 98 degrees F. These are all below or close to body temperature, so shouldn't be a problem in the body – and they are not a problem. Some common trans fats have melting points of 150 degrees F, much higher than body temperature, and that was part of the problem. But cholesterol, which our bodies produce at the rate of about 4 grams a day, has a melting point of 250 degrees F – much higher than body temperature. As long as we have sufficient lower melting point fatty acids in our bloodstream to keep cholesterol moving, there is no problem. This is why the advice to reduce fat intake, including even good fats like olive oil, nut oils and fish oil, was so bad. And remember those short chain fatty acids that our intestinal bacteria make when they are happy and fed properly – acetic acid, butyric acid and propionic acid? Those also help prevent cholesterol and other high melting point fats from causing heart disease. Are you ready to kiss your intestinal bacteria yet?! And besides all that, fat is a required nutrient, so we want fat in our diet for lots of reasons.

Column 7, 8 and 9 – Grams of Carbs, Sugar and Fiber per 100 Grams of Food

The carb value in column 7 is total carbs, which includes the complex carbs, sugar and fiber, as these are all carbs. We need to separate these in order to minimize the sugar in our diet, get a moderate amount of complex carbs and increase fiber as much as possible.

- Meat, fish, eggs, and all animal products have no or very low carbs. This sounds good, but they also have no fiber. In a balanced diet, this is not a problem, as we can select other foods to contribute the fiber we need.

- Vegetables are low in carbs (3.9 to 8.2%), very low in sugar (0 to 2.1%) and contain a significant amount of fiber (2 to 3.3%). Even carrots, at 8% total carbs, contain only 1.4% sugar and deliver 3% fiber.

- Fermented products like hard cheeses and yogurt will be low in sugar, unless it is being added (read the label) as fermentation digests the sugar.

- Fruits and corn are moderate in carbs at 11.4 to 22.8%, have 12.2 to 16% sugar and 2.4 to 2.6% fiber.

- Nuts are moderate in carbs, low in sugar and high in fiber.

- Baked goods are high in carbs (41.3 to 61.3%), mostly complex carbs that take time to digest and absorb. Even 'Evil' White bread has over two grams of fiber per 100 grams – about the same as broccoli and kale. Whole wheat bread is low in sugar at 5.6% and high in fiber at 6.8%. Most of the carbs are complex carbs, such as starch, that take time to digest, slowing the release of glucose. No surprise, ordinary chocolate chip cookies are high in sugar (35.5%). Not mine – by the way! More about that later.

Column 10 – ORAC per 100 Grams of Food

ORAC stands for the Oxidation Radical Absorbance Capacity and is reported in μmole TE per 100 grams. This is a measure of the oxidative capacity of the food. μmole means micro moles, and TE stands for Trolox Equivalent, which is a type of vitamin E, used as a standard in the analysis. Suffice it to say that antioxidants are a good thing in the diet, preventing chronic inflammation of tissues and damage to the body from free radicals, which are highly reactive chemicals formed by contact with oxygen. Believe it or not, oxygen is actually poisonous to life. Early life was strictly anaerobic, meaning free from oxygen. Life had to find a way to deal with oxygen, when it started building up in the early atmosphere, and the solution was to harness it to enhance energy production in the cell, while controlling it with antioxidants to prevent harm.[39] Good for us that plants produce a lot of antioxidants to protect themselves and us from the negative effects of oxygen.

- Meat, fish, eggs and most animal products are low in antioxidants with ORAC values ranging from 20 in eggs to 795 in beef and butter.

- Vegetables contain moderate amounts of antioxidants (1200 to 3017 ORAC). This includes peanuts, which, of course, are actually a legume. Grains are also moderate and whole wheat bread contains 1421 ORAC.

- The real stars of antioxidants are the nuts and dark colored fruits such as blueberries and raspberries. Even chocolate chip cookies deliver 8750 ORAC due to the cocoa in the chocolate chips. Cocoa, cinnamon, turmeric, ginger and cloves are the most potent antioxidant foods. Nuts are particularly great in the diet, as they are high in ORAC, high in low melting point fats, high in fiber and very low in sugar. All good.

The interpretation of the ORAC value of foods has come under question in recent years. The problem is that the issue of antioxidants is more complicated than a single value can portray. There is no doubt that antioxidants are necessary and beneficial in the diet. There is also evidence that having a wide variety of antioxidants in the diet is beneficial. The real controversy comes when trying to assess adequate versus optimal intake. The purpose of antioxidants is to neutralize charged molecules called free radicals. Free radicals are highly reactive and cause damage to proteins, carbohydrates, fats and even DNA, which can result in aging, disease and cancer. The body has intricate systems to maintain a balance between free radicals and antioxidants to control them, but there are many environmental factors that increase free radical exposure as well as factors that decrease the body's production of antioxidants. Air pollution, cosmic radiation during high altitude travel, sunburn, and intense exercise are a few of the factors that increase free radicals in the body. Dr. AS Naidu has written a fascinating and comprehensive book on oxidation chemistry in life called *Redox Life*, in which he describes the highly choreographed dance between oxygen, free radicals and antioxidants[40].

Most of us think that a good meal, and therefore diet, is composed of a piece of meat or fish in the center of the plate, some carbs like potatoes, rice or pasta, and then to garnish the plate with a vegetable like corn or peas. This is backwards thinking. Instead, we should place the vegetables at the center of the plate, but not corn or peas please, as these are too high in carbs. Start with a healthy portion of vegetables that are moderate in carbs, low in calories and sugar and high in fiber and antioxidants, such as asparagus, broccoli, broccoli rabe, Brussels sprouts, kale, cabbage, or collards. Then add a carb but choose one that is high in fiber and low in sugar, such as whole wheat bread served with butter, olive oil or just balsamic vinegar for dipping. Finally, add a small piece of meat or fish for protein. The idea is to increase antioxidants in the diet.

When I was growing up, we were told, like in the Pink Floyd song "Another Brick in the Wall", that we had to eat the meat. For us today, this is also backwards thinking. There is nothing wrong with eating meat, from a nutritional perspective, ethics and environmental sustainability notwithstanding. However, the point is that we would get more fiber and antioxidants, if we ate less meat and more veggies. We would also do better to start the meal with soup and vegetables. This approach will allow us to eat a satisfying meal, while keeping calories low, sugar low, protein moderate, carbs moderate, fiber high, and antioxidants high. Serving a bowl of broth soup (not a cream-based soup or bisque) before the meal is even better. Eat bone broth or chicken stock with some leafy green vegetables like arugula, endive or escarole. It couldn't be much easier, and it tastes great.

Getting Fiber into Our Diet

If we are going to make a real change in the health of our intestinal microbiome, we need to increase our daily fiber intake to fifty grams. Most people on a western diet are getting around eleven grams per day. We literally don't know how to go from eleven to fifty. We need to learn how to get that much fiber and make the changes in our daily diet to put it there and keep it there, every day, for the rest of our lives.

Let's consider the options. I'm going to focus on foods and recipes that deliver at least ten grams of fiber per serving or meal. We must do this!

- First, we can eat green vegetables that are high in fiber. The Special Salad recipe in Appendix 1 delivers a whopping 19 grams of fiber. Not so bad for one meal, already 40% of our goal. We can eat asparagus, broccoli, broccoli rabe, Brussels sprouts, kale, Swiss chard, collards – all contain 2-3 grams of fiber per 100 grams serving. That is part of the problem. To get ten grams of fiber, we have to eat a pound of green vegetables. That's too much. We need to do better.

- Whole wheat and whole grain breads are one of the highest in fiber of any food at 6.8% (6.8 grams of fiber per 100 grams of bread). Even white bread has 2.3% fiber. People who go gluten-free or keto lose most of the fiber in their diet, to the detriment of their microbiome. How about whole wheat bread with a bean pate like the one in Appendix 8? It tastes great, is easy to make, contains no animal products and has 7.6 grams of fiber when served with a slice of toasted whole wheat bread. Double the amount and it's a light meal for one person. Make it fun and healthy!

- We can eat oat bran cereal. A cup of cooked oat bran delivers about 3 grams of fiber. It is mostly beta glucan, which is one of the best fibers we can eat, because it does more than just feed our microbiome. This is good, but not going to get us to 50 grams. We can boost the fiber by adding cinnamon powder, cocoa powder and chia seeds. Cinnamon is about 50% fiber, while cocoa powder and chia seeds are about 33% fiber. A tablespoon of cocoa powder weighs about 7.4 grams and delivers 2.4 grams of fiber. A teaspoon of cinnamon powder weights about 6 grams and delivers 3 grams of fiber. A tablespoon of chia seeds weighs about 13 grams and delivers 4 grams of fiber. Adding a tablespoon of cocoa powder, a tablespoon of chia seeds and a teaspoon of cinnamon powder to our three tablespoons of dry oat bran cereal in a cup of water will not only make it taste a lot better, but also increase the fiber per serving from three grams up to 12.4 grams. We are now in the ballpark!

- There are now several good tasting high-fiber cereals that deliver up to 16 grams of fiber per serving. This is a good addition to our diet, as it gets us almost a third of the way towards our goal of 50 grams per day. And best of all, it can fit our lifestyle without any sacrifices. One of them is called "Poop Like a Champion ™" – no need to say any more than that!

- There are some excellent pasta products made from chickpeas or lentils that deliver 15 grams of fiber per serving with no noticeable impact on flavor or texture.

- Beans have one of the highest fiber contents of any food at 5 to 8%. Incorporate beans into your recipes. Put them in salads, mixed with veggies, make a pate spread or refry them Mexican style (awesome!). Beans can be difficult to digest until you can train your microbiome. Beano® really helps. And having sufficient fiber in your diet will help too.

- We can eat nuts. Most nuts have about 10% fiber, so to get 10 grams of fiber we need to eat 100 grams. That is possible but delivers a lot of calories (600 to 700). Pistachios are 18% fiber, so we only need to eat 55 grams and that will have 245 calories. Now we're in the ballpark. 55 grams of shelled pistachio nuts are about 1/3 cup by volume or 4 good handfuls.

- Psyllium husk fiber is convenient, as it is almost pure fiber, has no flavor and is easy on the digestive system. It comes in two forms – whole flake and powder. Nutritionally, they are the same, but the powder form absorbs water voraciously and quickly, forming a strong gel. The whole flake form will also absorb a lot of water, but it does so more slowly, making it possible to mix it into a cup of water and drink it down before it turns into a gel. Twelve grams of whole flake or powdered psyllium husk will deliver 10 grams of fiber.

I fast until 11 AM, with only coffee before that, have a psyllium shake at 11 AM and eat pistachio nuts or a few pieces of bitter unsweetened chocolate at 4 PM. This gives me lots of fiber, no sugar, very few calories and I'm not hungry until dinner time, enabling me to achieve a 22-hour fast once a week. Watch your blood glucose level – mine doesn't budge after the psyllium shake. See Appendix 6 for an improved recipe.

- Soluble fiber ingredients are easy to incorporate in the foods we already eat and drink because they dissolve and add no texture or flavor. These include polydextrose, inulin, and Benefiber ®. Use these cautiously at first, as they can cause laxation or flatulence if your microbiome is not up to speed.

- Sunfiber® is an insoluble fiber that disperses in water with no flavor and minimal viscosity, making it easy to use. Since it is insoluble, it doesn't exhibit the flatulence or laxation effect, making it a convenient and effective way to add fiber to the foods and drinks you consume every day. Two tablespoons of Sunfiber weighs about 10 grams and easily disperses in a 4 oz. glass of water.

- Chocolate is a great food to incorporate as an ingredient and for snacking in order to increase fiber and antioxidants. Slowly train your taste buds to accept chocolate with higher and higher levels of cocoa and therefore, more fiber and less sugar. The 60% and 85% cocoa chocolates contain about ten % fiber, and the bitter or unsweetened chocolate contains about sixteen % fiber.

- It is important that we have access to foods we like to eat and also deliver fiber, and that is why I have developed a chocolate cookie recipe that delivers ten grams of fiber per 50-gram cookie with only five grams of sugar. It is low in sugar and tastes great. I eat one for dessert after dinner when I feel the need. The recipe contains allullose, which is a sugar that is absorbed by the body but has one tenth the calories of sucrose or other sugars. It comes as a fine powder, looks like sugar, is about 70% as sweet as sucrose and is available online. This sugar doesn't cause intestinal distress like the sugar alcohols. It is not an intense sweetener, so you use it like sucrose in recipes. It can replace sucrose in a cookie recipe, for example, as I have done. It is called the 'keto sugar' because it doesn't spike blood glucose and isn't metabolized like a sugar. This is one way to create foods that we like to eat and deliver the fiber we need. One of these cookies will provide 10 grams of fiber – that is probably double what you eat now in a whole day. This is a game changer. And I would rather eat a great tasting cookie than drink a slimy psyllium goo. But that's just me! You can bake these cookies yourself, using the recipe in Appendix 3, or they are available from The Biome Bakery ™ at www. biomebaking.com. These cookies have been formulated on purpose to moderate the absorption of sugar and to have a minimal impact on blood glucose.

- Another easy food to incorporate into our everyday diet and lifestyle is a bagel. For that purpose, I have also developed a bagel made with whole wheat flour that delivers 16 grams of total fiber, one gram as beta glucan, 25 mg of lutein antioxidant, 10 grams of flaxseed meal to provide essential fatty acids (linoleic and linolenic), while having less than one gram of sugar. Most of the fiber is resistant wheat starch which is easy on the digestive system. It also contains activated charcoal powder, which has been shown to protect the intestinal bacteria by absorbing toxic materials that are present in food. I think they are great! The available carbs are only 25 grams per bagel (about half a normal bagel), which is low enough to fit into a keto diet, while providing much needed fiber. I also have a Pumpernickel Whole Wheat variety, in case you don't like charcoal! These are also available from The Biome Bakery ™ at www.biomebaking.com.

- Experiment and learn how to incorporate fiber into your own recipes. The easiest ingredients to do this are probably already in your pantry! The point is that a little extra fiber here and there adds up to real numbers. This can be fun, taste great and make you a better cook. Here are some examples:

  - Cocoa powder: 33% fiber and very high in ORAC – can be sprinkled on or added to almost any recipe and it tastes great. A tablespoon adds 2.4 grams of fiber. Unsweetened chocolate is also great for fiber at sixteen %. A 20-gram piece of unsweetened chocolate gives you over 3 grams of fiber and almost no sugar. A great snack. And once you get used to eating it without sugar, you will cringe at how sweet regular chocolate is.

  - Cinnamon powder: 50% fiber and very high in ORAC – can be sprinkled on or added to almost any recipe and it tastes great. A teaspoon adds 3 grams of fiber. Limit total daily consumption to 2 teaspoons per day. I find cinnamon powder to irritate my stomach, so I use cocoa instead.

  - Sprinkle a few nuts on almost anything – salads, veggies, even pasta! Nuts are around 10% fiber, so 20 grams of nuts, which is a handful, will add 2 grams of fiber. Walnuts, pine nuts, pecans, almonds, cashews, etc. are all good. Pistachio nuts are best due to having lower fat, lower calories and higher fiber content than the other nuts.

  - Chia seeds: 33% fiber and high in omega-3 fatty acids. Chia seeds can be sprinkled on almost any recipe – salads, veggies, mashed potatoes, etc. A tablespoon adds 4 grams of fiber. Did you know that you can make an added-sugar free jam by using fresh fruit and chia seeds? There is still plenty of sugar in the fruit – so be careful. But there is no additional sugar needed to make a jam, when using chia seeds. That is a significant reduction in sugar. Just add a tablespoon of chia seeds to a cupful of fruit, puree in a blender and cook until thick. When it cools, it will gel very nicely.

- Psyllium husk whole flakes: almost 100% fiber, have no real flavor and can be sprinkled onto almost anything. The flakes will absorb a lot of water if it is available. On a salad, that is not a problem. When you are making lasagna (see Appendix 5 for a kale lasagna) you can sprinkle a bit of psyllium husk whole flakes as you create the layers. It has the added benefit of absorbing water as it cooks, so if you ever made lasagna that was watery – with this technique it will not be watery! Anything that you normally add bread crumbs to can benefit from psyllium husk whole flakes or chia seeds, as these will absorb water just like the bread crumbs. For example: meatloaf, meatballs, and crab cakes.

- Sunfiber ® disperses readily in almost any liquid or moist food with no impact on flavor or texture. Stealth fiber!

To summarize how to get over 50 grams of fiber into your diet:

Every day:

- 100 grams of a green leafy vegetable with your dinner: 3 grams of fiber

- One chocolate chip cookie (50 grams) Special High Fiber, Low Sugar recipe in Appendix 3: 10 grams of fiber, with 210 calories, 6 grams of protein, 14 grams of fat, 25 grams of carbs, 5 grams of sugar and 5,700 ORAC units. These are available from The Biome Bakery ™ at www.biomebaking. com.

- 100 grams of Biome Bakery ™ All-In Biome Balance ™ Bagel: 16 grams of fiber and 6 grams of protein, 6 grams of fat, with only 200 calories, 36 grams of carbs, and less than 0.5 grams of sugar. These are also available from The Biome Bakery ™ at www.biomebaking.com.

- Psyllium husk whole flake or psyllium husk powder shake: 10 grams of fiber

- Two tablespoons (10 grams) of Sunfiber ® added to a glass of water or any moist food

- Whole wheat bread (3 slices a day): 6.8 grams of fiber

Then pick a few of these every day:

- A large salad like the Special Salad in Appendix 1: 19 grams of fiber

- Oat bran cereal with cocoa powder, chia seeds and cinnamon powder: 12.4 grams of fiber

- 50 grams of pistachio nuts: 10 grams of fiber

- A serving of a high fiber cereal: 16 grams of fiber

- The veggie pate in Appendix 8: 7.6 grams of fiber

I eat one of the bagels every day, either with lunch or dinner, with butter, cream cheese, mayonnaise or if I want to eliminate the fat, dip it in balsamic vinegar. This alone gives me 16 grams of fiber, so in combination with the psyllium shake in the morning, a few tablespoons of Sunfiber ®, veggies, and a high fiber cookie for dessert after dinner, I'm at over 40 grams of fiber. By adding oat bran cereal, the Special Salad or pistachio nuts, I can easily break the 50-gram barrier. By adding a few grams of cocoa, ginger or cinnamon here and there as we prepare meals will add up too. Sometimes I cheat and just have a second cookie! Or double up on the psyllium shake. Get creative and design your own recipes with fiber. We can do this! Every day. Just think how happy your intestinal microbiome will be.

Conclusions About Diet

A few critical points to keep in mind as we select what to eat:

- Some foods are better than others, but there are no bad foods, only bad diets. If we manage what we eat and compensate for the occasional indiscretion, we can eat almost anything. Quantity is more important than what we eat. Calories matter.

- Always include low caloric content foods in your diet. Soup and vegetables are great ways to fill up the belly, while delivering beneficial fiber and antioxidants.

- Fruits and grains, including whole wheat bread, are good to have in the diet for fiber, complex carbs, antioxidants and for sheer enjoyment.

- Meats, fish and cheese are good for protein.

- Nuts are great for delivering protein, low melting point oils, antioxidants, and fiber, but are high in calories. A handful is fantastic.

- Select foods that have at least two to three times as much fiber as sugar.

- Spices and seasonings such as cocoa, cinnamon, ginger, turmeric and cloves are great for delivering fiber and antioxidants.

- Pistachio nuts and unsweetened chocolate are great for snacking, when you absolutely cannot make it to the next meal, or to replace a meal.

- Cocoa powder, cinnamon powder, chia seeds, nuts, wheat bran, wheat germ and psyllium husk whole flakes can be sprinkled onto almost any recipe with beneficial results in texture, flavor, ORAC and fiber content.

- The idea is to incorporate many different kinds of fiber from different foods into our diet every day. The different sources of fiber will feed the many different types of bacteria in our microbiome, enhancing not only number but also diversity.

- The magic number for fiber is 50 grams daily. That is probably five times your current intake. Eating more broccolis won't do it! Start off slow and increase your intake until you are consistently, every day above 50 grams. Design your own recipes using high-fiber ingredients like polydextrose,

Sunfiber ®, psyllium, chia seeds, cocoa, nuts and oat bran. They work! Make these ingredients part of your diet. We are not dieting. We are building a diet that is sustainable and enjoyable for the rest of our lives. Your intestines will be singing, not to mention pooping very happily!

The real beauty of achieving a lifestyle change where we are sustainably and easily consuming a diet high in fiber and antioxidants every day is that what we eat and when become less and less important. Quantity still matters. Chronic overeating and high sugar consumption are unhealthy and must be avoided. But you will find your weight, blood glucose and blood pressure automatically start going in the right direction. And if we want to overeat once in a while, or eat a donut, we can do it without causing harm. When our body is in balance and in control, it is able to safely manage the occasional deviation in diet without harm. This is where we want to be. It requires a few changes:

- High-fiber diet containing 50 grams per day from a variety of sources including vegetables, resistant starch in bread, polydextrose (in the cookies), nuts (especially pistachio nuts), oat bran, spices (cocoa, cinnamon, turmeric), and psyllium husk.

- High antioxidant diet containing a target of 25,000 ORAC units per day from a variety of sources. This is not so hard to do when you consider that our Special Salad alone delivers over 14,000 units! Turmeric and cinnamon have about 1,400 units per gram, so about 5,000 units per teaspoon. Cocoa and dark chocolate deliver about 500 units per gram. Don't get too hung up on ORAC numbers. There is building evidence that the number is not as meaningful as once thought. Meaning, the ORAC value doesn't always correlate to the antioxidant value in the body, but it is still useful as a guide. Our bodies are very good chemists and change many ingredients into more functional forms. We just need to provide the building blocks in our diet.

- Balance – eat a variety of foods, the broader the better. And when you do overeat or eat something with sugar in it, compensate by adjusting your diet over the next few days to get your overall diet for that time into alignment with your goals. Watch the scale – it doesn't lie!

- Exercise, activity, moving, skipping for joy!

- And enjoy life – attitude, life force.

Timing

Timing when we eat allows the blood glucose system to cycle between glucose and fat metabolism. This is a healthy thing to do in order to increase insulin sensitivity and keep the amount of stored fat in the liver and muscles below the point of causing insulin resistance. We will talk in depth about how to do this in Chapter 8. Basically, there are two modes of metabolism: glucose metabolism and fat metabolism. Our bodies are in one mode or the other. Either we are using glucose to power our bodies, or we are using fat. Interestingly, our bodies will not use fat when there is glucose around. What we eat and when, determines which mode we are in.

Eating by the clock is one of the worst things we can do. Of course, we all do it because it is convenient and often socially responsible to eat when everyone else is eating. When we must eat by the clock, try to eat low-carbohydrate foods like meat, and bulky foods like salads and veggies. Not carb free, but low to moderate carbs. It is best to eat only when we are hungry and not according to the clock. This allows the mechanisms in our body that control satiety and food intake to work. Hunger is the body telling us that we have depleted blood glucose. The absence of hunger tells us the opposite – blood glucose levels are adequate and there is no need to eat. We don't always need to or want to respond to hunger by eating. We want our bodies to occasionally go into fat metabolism, even if only for a few hours. After a few hours in fat metabolism we will eventually start to feel hungry again. We probably haven't depleted our store of fat (unlikely) but we have accomplished our goal and can celebrate (a little) by eating. And yes – food does taste better when we are hungry!

Breakfast – the Most Important Meal (Not)

I often hear people state that breakfast is the most important meal. Nutritionists and even doctors will say this. It is a myth. An extended overnight and morning fast is the way to get our body into glycogen and fat metabolism, allowing blood glucose and insulin levels to drop to baseline. The worst thing we can do in the morning is have a big glass of juice or a pile of pancakes with syrup! If you absolutely must eat, avoid sugar.

There are several important benefits to an extended overnight fast. Our blood glucose level will naturally drop as the glucose from the last meal we ate is absorbed and depleted. Soon after the blood glucose level drops, blood insulin level will also drop. This will occur while we are sleeping, so we won't feel hungry. If we wake up in the middle of the night, we need to avoid eating anything. Drink some water and then go back to sleep. The low blood insulin level switches the body from glucose metabolism to fat metabolism. This is the way our body was designed to work. Our body will break down some of the fat that we have stored. Yea! This is a good thing.

The second benefit of an extended overnight fast is that it allows us to reset the glucose control system. Blood glucose and insulin levels fall to baseline. And, very importantly, insulin sensitivity improves.[41] The control mechanism works better and the beta cells that produce insulin in the pancreas get to take a beneficial rest.[42]

The third benefit to an extended overnight fast is that it will reduce our intake of calories. As we get older, our metabolism slows and for lots of reasons we simply are not as active as we used to be. Watch a 5-year-old run around and you will appreciate this. The simple fact of the matter is that we need to reduce our intake of calories or gain weight. It's often not easy or comfortable. Nobody likes starvation diets. Most of us love to eat and even live to eat. Eating is social and cultural and difficult to control. Eliminating one meal a day may give us the ability to eat more freely at lunch and dinner. We can still enjoy eating, maybe even have dessert while being able to achieve and maintain a good body weight.

Some people feel lightheaded or irritable if they don't eat breakfast. This is likely due to insulin resistance – the beginning stage of diabetes. The lightheaded feeling is due to abnormally low levels of blood glucose. This is not a normal or healthy situation. We got this way from eating carbs as soon as we wake up – just like the nutritionist told us to do. The mechanism to switch from glucose metabolism to fat metabolism doesn't work efficiently, so instead of burning fat and maintaining a healthy blood glucose level, the body continues to metabolize glucose, resulting in an abnormal drop in blood glucose levels that cause us to feel lightheaded. We need food. Wrong! Actually, what we need to do is slowly retrain our bodies to efficiently switch into glycogen metabolism. Instead of eating carbs when we first wake up in the morning, eat a low or no-carb food like a cup of coffee (no sugar), pecans, peanuts, or almonds. This will help us feel less hungry and lightheaded. Slowly extending the time when we eat breakfast, will eventually enable us to make it all the way to lunch without eating carbs.

CHAPTER 6

Maintaining a Healthy Weight

Another big challenge to extending our healthy, vibrant lives is our body weight. Being overweight is unhealthy for many reasons, being both the cause of disease and the result of it. Gaining weight is terribly easy and most of us fall victim to it. It happens so slowly that we don't notice until it is there. Getting off those extra pounds is not easy, as reducing weight means reducing body fat. We never want to reduce muscle mass and we cannot reduce or change our bones, so it all comes down to fat.

There are over 90 different diets currently circulating and being presented as the best way to control weight and health. This is worse than the Tower of Babel. The cacophony of conflicting advice being thrown at people today is mind numbing and overwhelming. Most of these diets will help in the short term and may improve eating habits and health, but not one has been shown to be effective over the long term. It's interesting to note a study that compared weight loss and blood chemistry on several different diet regimes ranging from Atkins (high fat, very low carb, meat-based) to Dean Ornish (very low fat, high carb, plant-based), and found no significant difference! The conclusion was that almost any diet regime that limits the intake of food can result in successful weight reduction and an improvement in health metrics. The study was unable to quantify the long-term effects of the diets, but we have to conjecture that eating a high-fat, low-fiber, meat-based diet, as is done in Atkins, could have long-term negative health consequences.[43]

Dr. Ornish, in a beautifully written review, compares his program with the diet developed by Dr. Atkins, and makes the logical assertion that if calories matter in weight loss, then reducing fat intake must be an important consideration, since fat has more than twice the caloric content of protein or carbs.[44] In addition, the preponderance of evidence showing not only the benefits of fiber, but also the negative consequences of a low fiber diet, predict that long term, an Atkins regime will be damaging to health. Fiber reduces the caloric content of food and increases satiety, helping us to eat less. And fiber feeds our intestinal microbiome. All good things. The study also notes that in selecting a diet, weight management is only one criterion, albeit a big one.

Eating too many calories, even for a relatively short period of time, can cause insulin resistance, the beginning of diabetes. What we eat and when are important, but even more important is how much we eat. The body has mechanisms for managing over-nutrition. The liver and muscles are designed to store surplus calories as glycogen initially and when the store of glycogen reaches capacity, to store the excess as fat. Having glycogen and fat storage is a good thing if the body is to survive not only periods of overnutrition, but also periods of undernutrition. When food is scarce, we can tap into the stored calories to maintain body functions. The brain and muscles especially need a constant supply of energy in order to function. The brain has little or no storage capacity, so it relies on a constant supply of glucose in the blood that comes from the liver and kidneys when food is unavailable. The muscles have their own storage capacity for short-term and long-term use in the form of glycogen and fat. When these are exhausted, the muscles use fat from other parts of the body or even scavenge protein from the muscles themselves. This is how it is supposed to work. But if we never experience undernutrition, then the fat is never utilized and only accumulates, leading first to weight gain, then insulin resistance, eventually to obesity and finally diabetes. Even skinny people can be diabetic because excess fat storage doesn't mean that they are fat. Actually, the visible belly fat is the least harmful of all. The invisible fat stored in the liver and muscles is the most damaging. Skinny people may not have a lot of visible body fat, but their liver and muscles may be storing too much fat. They are skinny/fat. To avoid storing excess liver and muscle fat, we don't need to starve, but we need periods of undernutrition (fasting) to allow the system to cycle like a battery, in order to maintain our weight and blood glucose control system in healthy condition. If the system never cycles, eventually it loses the ability.

The main problem with the popular diets is that in order to be simple enough for people to follow, they focus on one aspect of nutrition. For example: low fat, low carb, high protein, no meat, no white foods, no gluten, caveman, pineapples, etc., etc. I suppose if we ate only pineapples, we might lose weight, but is that going to produces healthy results long term or be sustainable? Or eating no carbs as the Atkins diet proposes? Is that healthy long term or sustainable? There is an element of truth in all of these diets;

otherwise, they would not work for anyone. But clearly nutrition is more complex than just one factor. And to be effective, a diet should not be something we do for a few months, but rather a change in our eating habits that is sustainable for the rest of our lives, so that the benefits are long term, not just to drop a few pounds and then go back to our old ways and regain the weight. This cyclic gain/loss/regain is the unhealthiest practice of all. We want a diet that we can benefit from and live with for the rest of our lives. We will not be successful unless we also consider the social and lifestyle factors, as eating is a social act and we may become outcasts by restricting our diet to foods that no one else in our social group is consuming. Our restrictive diet sets us apart and denies us and them the benefits of belonging to a family or a social group. Eating is about nutrition of course, but it is much more, and if we don't take these other factors into consideration, we will fail long term.

The basic factors to consider in selecting what we eat are:

- Quantity (calories and volume)

- Composition (moisture, carbs, protein, fat, fiber, minerals and vitamins)

- Timing (time since the last meal)

- Balance (different foods that complement each other)

- Variety (eat lots of different foods)

Sorry. This is not as simple as just avoiding white foods! Good nutrition is more complex than that. On the other hand, we can identify some basic guidelines for selecting what to eat and when to eat so that we can be successful in achieving a healthy diet that fits our lifestyle and social group.

We also need to keep in mind that there is much we do not know about human nutrition and diet. When the science is lacking, it is difficult to separate fact from myth, the proven from the emotional, truth from belief. The field is mired in emotion and beliefs with not enough science to dispel the misinformation.

One of the most difficult things in life can be trying to put all of these things together.
-Humpty Dumpty

We make approximately 220 decisions each day about the food we eat. In a lifetime, we will eat approximately 80,000 meals. These decisions matter, and in the long run impact our health, physical capabilities and lifespan. The World Counts estimates that over one billion people on the planet are hungry and that 17 million people die each year from starvation. At the same time, they estimate that over 800 million people on the planet are obese. It is ironic that starvation and obesity coexist to almost the same extent globally. Food is a major contributor to disease, and as people in other parts of the world adopt a western diet, there is a concurrent rise in the Metabolic Syndrome, where these diseases were virtually unknown before. The point is that the food we eat has a significant impact on our health and on how we feel. The decisions we make about food selection and diet are not trivial and we make a lot of them every day. Making these decisions consistent with our lifestyle can enable us to make these numerous diet decisions in a rational, consistent and expeditious manner that can save us from spending time and energy to consider each one separately. The problem is that we will not realize the impact of the decisions we make today until the consequences have accumulated for several decades. We don't want to wake up one day thirty years from now to the realization that we are overweight and unhealthy. How did that happen? How can we prevent it from happening?

Diet and Disease

The impact of diet on disease is a controversial subject with many unknowns. We are certain that too little of some nutrients in our diet will cause disease. Insufficient intake of Vitamin C results in scurvy, for example. Too little protein will cause muscle loss. There are minimum levels of consumption for each nutrient, below which we risk the onset of disease, and there are maximum levels of consumption for some nutrients, above which there is a risk of toxicity. Clearly, we want to always be above the minimum intake in order to avoid the risk of disease, and below the level that causes toxicity. What is not so clear from the science is the level at which each nutrient is optimal for health, which may be many times higher than the level required to avoid disease. The optimal level is difficult to determine, as it varies depending on many factors including the individual, lifestyle, activity level, overall diet, etc. Therefore, there is no consensus in the scientific community about optimal intake levels to guide us.

Using Vitamin C as an example, it is well accepted that to avoid scurvy, daily intake should be at least 10 mg. of Vitamin C. The US RDA (Recommended Daily Allowance) is set at 75 and 90 mg. per day for adult women and men respectively, to allow for a reasonable excess over the minimum required to prevent disease. There is evidence of benefit from consumption of up to about a gram per day, which is over one hundred times the level required to avoid scurvy. The point is that the optimal level of consumption for many nutrients is higher than what is required to prevent disease. In theory, if we are consuming a variety of foods, we will get at least the minimum amount of nutrients we need to avoid disease, but perhaps not attain optimality. This is where our awareness and intent come into play. If we want to achieve optimal levels of nutrients, we must intentionally modify our diet to include foods that contain those nutrients at high levels.

Atkins vs. Ornish

The Atkins and Dean Ornish diets are exact opposites, with South Beach and others somewhere in between. All these diets are attempts to provide a simple way to eat in order to reduce weight and improve health. They get some parts of the puzzle right and some wrong, but fail to achieve a holistic healthy, sustainable diet.

Atkins was right that we need to eliminate carbs in order to allow the body to switch into fat metabolism so that we can reduce stored fat and lose weight. There are benefits to doing this. But Atkins went too far. Eliminating carbs from the diet for days, weeks or more is unhealthy. In order to eliminate carbs from the diet, we must eat more protein and fat. Long-term consumption of a high-fat, high-protein diet can lead to ketosis, kidney damage and other serious health impacts. Elimination or drastic reduction in carbs will also greatly reduce dietary fiber intake that is critical to establishing and maintaining a healthy and diverse intestinal microbiome. The bacteria in our guts that produce so many health benefits will literally starve on a low-carb diet. And there are too many foods we like, such as bread, fruit and veggies, that are excluded under Atkins. The absence of these foods makes it difficult to stick to the diet long term.

On the other hand, Dean Ornish is also right that we can benefit from a high-carb diet rich in dietary fiber and antioxidants. On the Ornish diet, the intestinal microbiome will flourish. High-carb foods from grains and vegetables contain fewer calories and more bulk, making it easier to reduce total caloric intake and thereby achieve weight loss. The problem with the Ornish diet is that it eliminates many of the foods we like or are culturally important, making it difficult to follow and adhere to long term. The best results achieved by Ornish were with people who attended his camps and strictly adhered to his diet regimen, largely because of calorie restriction.

How about we take the advice of both Atkins and Ornish? For fourteen to sixteen hours each day, much of which passes while we are sleeping, we follow Atkins, allowing our bodies to switch into fat metabolism with all the benefits of that regimen. Then for the other eight to ten hours, we follow Ornish and feed our microbiome with plenty of dietary fiber and complex carbs. This way, we get the best of both disciplines in a twenty-four-hour period.

Healthy Weight

Maintaining a healthy weight is important for a lot of reasons. Every excess pound of fat that we carry around puts stress on our legs, joints, heart, and respiratory system, in addition to retaining higher levels of toxins and causing inflammation. Being overweight is not good for longevity and not good for our health. Obesity slows us down, wears us out and will convince us that we cannot do today what we used to do. It reinforces the attitude of aging and death. We are all different, so it's not possible to define ideal weight without some study.

Body Mass Index (BMI) is almost useless, as it doesn't adequately adjust for body size and muscle mass. According to BMI, Tom Brady is obese – no. he's not. A better indicator is body fat content. This is not so easy to measure, but some trainers and clinics have the ability either through a scanner or a dip tank. We need some fat on our bodies to store calories and to regulate hormones. Women need a bit more than men for good health. Male world-class athletes achieve body fat levels near five percent with women closer to ten percent. If you are not a world-class athlete, fifteen to twenty percent is a reasonable goal. Any more than that is extra weight to carry around. We don't want to be there.

What was your weight when you were a young adult? Assuming that you weren't already overweight, chances are this is when you were at your ideal body weight and most healthy. How many pounds above this weight are you now? Most people have tacked on forty or fifty pounds since that time, probably all fat. Our bones are the same bones we had then. They have not grown bigger or stronger. Our joints are the same. Our heart and lungs are the same. Our muscles may have gotten stronger, but more likely are the same or weaker. Our body is the same body as it was back then, except now there is all this extra fat to carry around and support, putting extra stress on organs, muscles and joints. It's no wonder that we cannot do what we used to do. Calculate how much extra fat you are now carrying around and then go find a stack of books or a sack of potatoes or something that weighs that much and go walk around with it for a few minutes. The extra weight will instantly be noticeable and cause us to tire more quickly. This is what we are putting up with every day, except that the fat accumulated slowly so that we never noticed it. When we can take it off, we will notice it!

My personal experience with weight control started in 2006 when I first started to see Dr. Jeffrey Life. He was at Cenegenics at the time, pioneering the concepts of longevity and health enhancement for older people. I weighed 225 lbs., but at a lanky 6 feet 4 inches, I wasn't obviously overweight. In the 12 years since then, I have reduced my body weight by 30 lbs., but a scan reveals that I added 15 lbs. of muscle with the loss of 45 lbs. of fat, for a net loss of 30 lbs. That is a significant change in body composition. I'm still not skinny, with about 25% body mass as fat. But I'm stronger, leaner and in many ways more physically capable today at 65 than I was at 53 years of age.

Nutrition is complicated and there are many factors to consider in a healthy diet. But there are a few facts that can put it into context. If you are above your ideal body weight, you are eating too much. Sorry – it doesn't get any straighter than that. You will have to eat less, if you want to lose some pounds or maintain an ideal weight. Buy a scale and weigh what you eat in order to calibrate intake. You are probably eating more than we think. Too much 'healthy' food is not healthy.

It takes a little over 4,000 calories to make a pound of fat. If we overeat by 100 calories a day, in about two months, we can gain a pound of fat. This is really easy to do, because 100 calories are only a couple of chocolate chip cookies. Doesn't seem fair, does it? Exercise is very important for good health, but we will not lose much weight by exercising. The only way to control our weight is to control what we eat. Carbohydrates are a required nutrient – if we don't eat carbs, we will die. However, if we eat too many carbs, we will get fat. The trick is to balance our carb intake with our physical activity level. If we are running marathons, we had better be eating big bowls of pasta every day, or we will literally starve to death. If we are a couch potato or computer jockey, and exercise for us is opening the microwave oven, then we had better reduce our carb intake. Reduce – not eliminate! We need carbs to live. How much? It depends on how active we are. Carbs are the fuel that our bodies run on. A healthy diet for a reasonably active person could include 300 grams of carbs per day. That sounds like a lot, but it's only 1200 calories of the 2000 or so that we need in a day. The remaining calories are fat and protein. Our brain consumes about half of these carb calories, our muscles the rest. Any excess that is not consumed is converted by our liver into glycogen, where it is stored for rapid conversion to glucose when we need it. At some point, it is converted to fat for long-term storage. That is the problem. Most of the fat we store, stays there forever and we keep adding more until we wake up some day with an extra forty or fifty pounds of blubber that restricts our movements, wears out our joints, makes our lives miserable, makes us unhealthy, stores toxins, and causes heart disease, inflammation, hormonal imbalance, hypertension, diabetes, cancer, and so on. All bad, no good. We don't want to be there, and we don't have to be.

It is worth emphasizing that the goal is not to be skinny! Too little body fat can also be harmful. Fortunately, most of us are at little risk of that ever happening! But consider the target of twenty percent body fat. Our 150-pound person, therefore, has a target body fat content of thirty pounds. That is not a trivial amount. If you ever saw a thirty-pound bucket of fat, you would be disgusted. The fact is that most of that thirty pounds of fat in the body is distributed around as thin layers that insulate, protect and lubricate our muscles and organs. It allows muscles to move freely and protects organs from shock and damage. Fat absorbs hormones and moderates hormone levels. Fat is also a protective storage site for stem cells, which are important for repair and recovery. Fat has a negative side too. In addition to the weight it adds to our bodies, it absorbs and stores fat-soluble toxins and causes inflammation. Fat is an important part of our bodies and we would literally die without it. We don't want to eliminate fat but control it. Fat is a good thing, but remember, too much of a good thing is often not a good thing.

Weigh yourself twice a week and watch out for changes. Don't obsess over it, but when you see a change, try to figure out what caused it. Set some guardrails for yourself. I aim to stay within +/- 5 pounds of my target weight (note that I didn't say ideal!), which is 200 lbs. When I overeat during the holidays, I can hit the top guardrail in a few days. Then for the next few days, I cut back a bit until I'm back in the range. Keep cutting down on carbs until you start to see the numbers moving slowly in the direction that you want. When you get to your target weight, learn what and how much you can eat in order to maintain it. We need to enjoy ourselves sometimes, so when we go to a fancy restaurant, we should eat as moderately as possible, but we will likely overeat. Then we should compensate by eating less over the next few days to bring our overall diet for that period of time into alignment with our goal. There are no bad foods, only bad diets. This means that we can eat almost any food, as long as we balance the overall quantity of what we eat over a period of a few days.

One of the worst habits imposed on us as children was the need to 'clean your plate'. Please don't impose this burden on your children or on yourself. Cleaning our plate will almost surely result in obesity at some time in our life. We need to stop eating when we have had enough. Enough does not mean full or sated. Eating until we are full on Thanksgiving is a tradition and certainly fun. But we don't want to eat like this every day. We need to learn how much we can eat in order to maintain our healthy body weight.

When people tell me that they are eating Paleo, like cavemen did, I like to remind them that in order for it to work, they really do have to eat like a caveman. Cavemen and women did not eat three or more meals a day. They feasted when the hunt was successful and fasted or ate subsistence items like nuts and dried fruits until the next good hunt, which could be several days away. Feasting and fasting may be the best combination for us as well. We can feast when we want to enjoy a really good meal, and then fast for a day or two to allow our body to digest, process, metabolize and clear out the waste, before another round of feasting begins. Fasting doesn't mean starving. It means reducing caloric intake for some period of time below the maintenance level, enabling the body to use stored glycogen and fat. The amount of feasting and fasting must be balanced to maintain a healthy body weight. When we feast daily, but fail to fast, the result is obesity and disease.

Fasting has been practiced, often for religious or cultural reasons, for thousands of years. Only recently, we seem to have forgotten how to fast. To underscore this point, one of the most informative books on extended fasting was written by Upton Sinclair in 1911 – yes, the Jungle guy[45]. It is called *The Fasting Cure*. Sinclair was not a doctor, but he had personal health issues that he found he could improve by fasting. He popularized fasting as a cure and collected testimonials from people who followed his advice. Many found relief, as he did, from several different diseases thought incurable by doctors at the time. Interestingly, he found no negative effects of extended fasting.

A modern book on the subject by Jason Fung MD finds the same[46]. We don't understand how a diet that is deficient in a required nutrient, such as Vitamin C for example, can cause disease, scurvy in this case, where a complete fast is well tolerated and causes no such disease. The only good answer is that the human body is exquisitely designed for extended fasting. Fasting can be a powerful tool for rebalancing, detoxifying, and resting our overworked biological control mechanisms, allowing the body to heal. In addition, fasting can get off unhealthy excess fat not just on our bellies, but also in our muscles and liver where it causes insulin resistance and diabetes.

When was the last time you saw an overweight squirrel, bird or any animal in the wild? Domesticated animals are another story. We feed our dogs and cats like we feed ourselves – constantly and too much, with a similar result. Our pets become obese and then suffer from the same diseases as we do – diabetes, hypertension, arthritis, heart disease, cancer, etc. Animals in the wild naturally restrict their diet, stay active and healthy.

Listen to Your Body Talk

We need to listen to our body talk. It talks to us with feelings, pleasure and pain. Thirst, hunger, satiety, exhaustion and many other signals give us a clue as to how our bodies are performing and what steps we should be taking to keep our body healthy. However, some of the signals can be misleading and need to be managed in balance.

Physical intelligence resides in our body. Our cells and organs have intelligence. In fact, it is possible that there may be more intelligence in our body than in our brain. As an example, Dr. Michael Gershon wrote a book on his discoveries about the neural processing capabilities that surround our intestines[47]. He estimates that there are over two million neurons wrapped around the intestines, controlling digestion and waste elimination for the body. That is roughly ten times the number of neurons in the brain of a fruit fly, and they can fly and do all sorts of annoying things. This is the second largest concentration of neurons in the body, second only to the brain. Did you know that your intestines were so smart? The liver is able to control blood glucose levels depending on what we eat and how active we are. It does this with limited input from the brain.[48] The brain is our main source of intelligence; however, we should not overlook the fact that there is intelligence in all parts of our body.

> When wealth is lost, nothing is lost;
> when health is lost, something is lost;
> when character is lost, all is lost.
> -Dr. Billy Graham

The first step in using our physical intelligence to help us live healthier, longer lives is to be aware of the presence of this intelligence. We are not used to thinking that our livers or feet are smart! But the fact of the matter is that these organs perform complex functions with little or no input from our brains. This means that they have an innate intelligence that enables them to operate and perform complex tasks. Our task is to realize this and learn to pay attention to it. Now that we know that our feet have intelligence, perhaps we can notice when they feel good or complain. Their complaints are not idle. The complaints that come in the form of pain or discomfort contain information that could be very useful to us. Learn to listen and then respond with a change in behavior or shoes!

> If we don't change direction, we will end up where we are headed.
> - Yogi Berra

Obesity

The underlying causes of obesity include:

- Lack of understanding about nutrition and essential nutrients

135

- Lack of availability of fresh vegetables (frozen is a good substitute, canned not so much)

- High cost of fresh vegetables

- Lack of skill in preparing fresh vegetables in a palatable manner that people want to eat, especially kids

- Overnutrition, especially carbs (high-carb foods are generally less expensive than high-protein-or-fat-containing foods, therefore people on low incomes often overeat carbs and paradoxically, become obese)

As we consider the nutritional properties of food ingredients, it is useful to measure or rate ingredients on the basis of the following criteria:

- Nutritional content (protein, fat, fiber, carbs, sugar, essential nutrient content, antioxidants)

- Availability (seasonality, knowledge and the existence of 'food deserts')

- Cost of the ingredient (per Kcal, per protein, per fat, per fiber, per antioxidant, per other essential nutrients)

- Convenience (preparation methods, waste)

- Knowledge (training, upbringing, cultural awareness and acceptance, recipes)

- Flavor (can be adjusted to local taste in the recipe)

- Texture (can reduce acceptance to novel ingredients, especially among children)

- Fun and enjoyable (includes foods served on holidays, parties and special occasions as well as snacks, desserts and treats)

If we consider what kinds of education or intervention needs to take place to improve this situation, we can include:

- Nutrition education

- Awareness of novel ingredients

- Recipes

- Preparation methods

The causal factors of obesity center around a lack of awareness and can therefore be improved via education. There could be utility in learning how to develop recipes that combine ingredients to achieve an improved nutritional profile while minimizing the impact on blood glucose. This is a challenge that is not typically presented in cook books, even books purporting to offer 'healthy' recipes.

To be successful, a diet needs to provide a good nutritional profile, be affordable, available, convenient, good tasting, fit our lifestyle and be fun. Only then can a diet be enjoyable, sustainable and successful!

CHAPTER 7

Maintaining Strength

Extending our healthy lives will require maintaining or enhancing several of our vital strengths: physical strength, immune strength to fight pathogens, mental strength, aerobic strength and circulatory strength. A commonly expected and accepted consequence of aging is a loss of strength. A leading cause of death, in otherwise healthy people, is loss of immune strength. When our immune system weakens, we can develop pneumonia and die from a common cold. Losses in mental, aerobic, circulatory and physical strength cause us to reduce activity, which results in a further loss of strength, which causes a further reduction in activity, and so on in a declining spiral. We want to minimally maintain our strengths, but with some effort, we can actually learn how to enhance them over time. Don't settle for less! We must stay strong.

> It's a great life, if you don't weaken.
> - John Buchanan

Healthy Immune System

If we are going to be successful in extending our healthy life, we must maintain a healthy immune system. We suffer when our immune system is overactive or underactive. When we are younger, the greater danger is that the immune system is overactive, resulting in issues such as allergic reactions, autoimmune diseases and inflammation. As we age, the immune system function slowly declines, making us more susceptible to pneumonia, infections, the flu and food poisoning; events that a healthy immune system can usually handle. One way to slow or stop aging is to keep our immune system functioning.

The world is an 'eat or be eaten' place! There is a constant battle raging inside of and on the surface of our bodies between the bacteria that want to eat us and the immune system that protects us. When the body dies, decomposition begins within minutes after the immune system stops functioning. Immune system function and failure originates in the intestines. Our skin is the outer, visible barrier, while our intestines are the interior, invisible barrier, protecting us from the outside world. The intestines isolate and protect us from toxins and bacteria in the food we eat. They act as a screen, keeping undigested food materials out of the body while allowing necessary nutrients to enter. If we want to maintain a healthy immune system, we must maintain a healthy gut. We have talked a lot about the importance of a diet containing sufficient dietary fiber to feed and nourish a thriving and balanced microbiome in our intestines. A healthy microbiome is also important to maintaining a healthy immune function and is a significant factor in immune system decline and eventual failure.

Inflammation is the most common and easily resolved issue resulting from an overactive immune system. Inflammation is basically retention of water in specific tissues as a response to damage. When there is real damage to a tissue, such as a bruise, insect bite, cut, infection, etc., the inflammatory response is beneficial to prevent further damage and aids in recovery. When there is no damage and the inflammation is persistent over weeks or months, the response is harmful. The effected body parts appear bloated, puffy, slightly red in color, tender to the touch and maybe even warm. Inflammation can affect any part or all parts of our body, including internal organs that we cannot see. Persistent inflammation is harmful and is often the result of a diet that is out of balance between foods that cause inflammation and antioxidants that fight it. Eating less of the foods that contribute to inflammation and more anti-inflammatory foods and antioxidants will help.

We breathe a toxic material called oxygen! Most of the oxygen we breathe is converted into harmless carbon dioxide and water via respiration. However, about 5% of the oxygen we breathe goes a different way and produces unbalanced molecules called free radicals. Free radicals are charged molecules that react with other molecules in the body in a very short time, causing damage. The damage accumulates and manifests over time as aging, disease and cancer. Life manages oxygen and free radicals by producing antioxidants. There are many different free radical molecules and also many different antioxidants.

Inflammation also can be seen in the mouth. Gingivitis is a

gum disease that has been linked as a causal factor of many other diseases including heart disease and Alzheimer's.[49] Gingivitis causes inflammation of the gums due to the presence of bacteria in the plaque that builds up in between the teeth and gums. The immune system detects the foreign bacteria and attacks them by sending white blood cells to produce free radical molecules that act like bullets to shoot at the foreign bacteria. Unfortunately, the shot is like a shotgun blast, hitting the target plus whatever is in the vicinity, including healthy cells in the gums. The result is damage to the gum cells and inflammation. The inflammation opens up the skin covering the gums, allowing the invading bacteria to enter the bloodstream, where they travel throughout the body, finding a safe place to hide in some organ. There, the bacteria produce inflammation-stimulating molecules that travel through the bloodstream eventually causing heart disease and Alzheimer's. The way to stop this complicated story from happening is first to prevent plaque from forming by brushing and flossing. Then have adequate antioxidants in the mouth to squelch the inflammation. Killing the bacteria, which is what most mouthwashes do, is actually harmful, as it also kills good bacteria. Like in the intestines, when we have a healthy quantity and balance of bacteria in the mouth, the pathogenic bacteria have a more difficult time getting established.

It is also beneficial to take an antioxidant supplement every day. Curcumin and grapeseed extract are excellent antioxidants, and there are foods that we can make part of our daily diet to assure an adequate supply. I personally take a liposomal curcumin supplement every morning and have seen the benefits. I also take Fuller Life C60, a Carbon 60 product in a convenient edible strip that you place on your tongue to dissolve. I developed this unique product and have a patent on the process to manufacture it. C60 is the most powerful and smallest of all antioxidants, allowing it to diffuse throughout the body into cells and mitochondria, where it neutralizes free radicals by absorbing the extra electrons and protons. I have more energy, sleep better, heal faster, and feel great. And my ankles are never swollen anymore. See the recommendations in the section on supplements in Chapter 3.

Another nutrient that is important to our immune function is magnesium. There is evidence that most of us are consuming a suboptimal amount of magnesium. Getting an optimal intake of magnesium from food is difficult and hard to assess. Read Dr. Carolyn Dean's book called *The Magnesium Miracle*[50] She links dietary magnesium deficiency to immune system failure, hypertension, diabetes, obesity, anxiety, depression, headaches and insomnia, among other common ailments afflicting many of us today. My conclusion is that magnesium is one more piece of the puzzle. One more small change we can make in our lifestyle for the rest of our lives. The cost is low. The risk is nothing, while the potential benefits are large.

Autoimmune diseases are a destructive consequence of an overactive immune system. Initially the immune system is improperly sensitized, which results in an active attack on healthy tissues in the body. These diseases are part of the Metabolic Syndrome that starts in the intestines with a leaky gut.

Allergic reactions are caused by an extreme sensitization of the immune system to a specific food protein. When exposed to this protein, the immune system identifies it as foreign and immediately launches a full-scale response that includes the production of histamines, swelling of body parts, rashes, hives, diarrhea, and vomiting. The most severe immune reaction is anaphylaxis, where the airway to the lungs swells and closes, resulting in asphyxiation and death within minutes. There are 138 specific proteins in foods that have been documented as causing an allergic response in a sensitive person somewhere. Please note that protein means a polypeptide, not the individual amino acids that are the building blocks of the protein. This is an important distinction, because we cannot be allergic to an amino acid or even a di-peptide, which is composed of two amino acids. It takes at least four amino acids in a polypeptide in order for the immune system to respond. Polypeptides get into our bloodstream via a leaky gut and should not be there.

The incidence of severe allergies has been increasing worldwide for the past fifty years, but not uniformly. Peanut allergies in the US are common and rising rapidly, while in Asia this is not happening.

Peanuts are consumed in both areas, but in Asia they are mostly prepared by boiling, whereas in the US boiled peanuts are rare and most peanuts are prepared by roasting. Does roasting change the peanut protein to make it more allergenic? Another interesting fact is that kids who grow up on farms in closer contact with animals have fewer allergies than city kids. Does exposure to more 'dirt' in the environment help to develop a healthy immune system? It is not clear.

Allergies to foods can develop later in life. Shrimp, for some reason, is a common food allergy that people develop in their fifties and later, even though they have safely enjoyed eating shrimp for their entire prior life. If we want to extend our healthy lives, we need to be aware of food allergies. Usually, sensitization starts slowly and then advances to more extreme reactions, until a full-blown allergic response occurs. The early signals are mouth or tongue swelling, numbness or tingling, vomiting and swelling of a body part that came into direct contact with the allergenic material. If you suspect that you have experienced an allergic response, you can avoid exposure to that food again, which could be overreacting, as maybe it was a false alarm. Certainly, you should approach the suspect food cautiously next time. Take a small bite and wait a few minutes to see what happens before you eat more. If the reaction reoccurs, especially if it is more severe the second time, then you should stop eating that food and see an allergist to confirm. You don't want to risk having a severe or anaphylactic reaction. If one or a partner has a severe allergy, you both need to carry an Epi-Pen, which is a portable syringe with epinephrine in it. It contains enough epinephrine to slow the advancing severe allergic reaction in order to allow time to get to a hospital emergency room.

Celiac disease is an extreme sensitivity to gluten protein. It is now known to be caused by a sensitization of the immune system that occurs during a viral infection[51]. If a child is introduced to gluten protein while the virus is active in their system, they will develop celiac disease and be sensitive, often for the rest of their lives. The only solution is strict avoidance of all foods that contain gluten protein. Gluten protein is found in wheat, rye, and barley grains.

Immune Summary

Some steps that we can take to maintain and build the immune system include:

- Positive attitude

- Strenuous exercise and lots of activity in between

- Develop a healthy microbiome. A diet that includes lots of fiber to feed the microbiome. Beta glucan enhances insulin sensitivity and modulates the immune system, enhancing immune function when it is low and decreasing it when it is too high.

- Optimal levels of vitamins, minerals and antioxidants, especially magnesium

- Sufficient sleep

Maintaining the Ability to Heal

As we age, the healing process slows down and eventually stops, resulting in death. The root cause of this slowing is a limit on the number of times that cells can divide. Cell division occurs during growth, when we are young, and all during our lives as part of the healing process. When a cell dies, or is injured, a nearby cell divides to take its place. Leonard Hayflick, in 1962, discovered that a normal human cell can divide a maximum of about seventy-five times, after which it cannot divide further. This was an important observation, and the first evidence that there was a built-in mechanism that causes aging. From an evolutionary standpoint, it was thought that aging was an intentional process designed to limit the life of an organism. When an organism became "old" and no longer able to contribute to the group, it was beneficial for the rest of the group that this organism died. Later, it was discovered that the programmed aging was due to a structure in genes called a telomere, a section of DNA that resides on the ends of each gene, like a cap. The telomeres assist in the multiplication and separation of the genes that occurs during cell division. Every time a cell divides, the telomeres shorten. Initially, each telomere contains about 25,000 DNA base pairs, but after seventy-five divisions, the telomeres are shortened to around 5,000 DNA base pairs, and the division process comes to a halt. Healing, which requires that new cells be formed, slows or stops and death soon follows, when bodily functions can no longer be maintained.

Not all cells age. The reproductive cells in our bodies, bacteria and many animals do not age and are capable of dividing without limit. An enzyme called telomerase repairs the telomeres after each cell division, to maintain the original length. There is no shortening of the telomeres and no limit to the number of times the cell can divide. Our cells had telomerase to perform this function when we were young and numerous cell divisions were required for growth and development. After adolescence, the amount of telomerase drops rapidly, and the programmed aging clock starts ticking.

Telomerase is naturally occurring in some plants and is available as an extract for oral or topical application. No negative side effects have been reported in people taking these extracts in order to restore telomere length. In theory, this can restore the ability of the cells to divide freely and reverse the apparent age of a cell. There is a test that measures telomere length and estimates the 'age' of the cells in the body. Some people claim to have reversed the age of their telomeres by this treatment. This technology is available now, but is new, expensive and as yet, not fully proven.

There are several other ways in which we can improve and maintain our ability to heal. These include:

- Antioxidants: reduce or prevent inflammation, oxidative stress and damage

- Eat less: too much food puts a stress on the body. Managing the impact of over-nutrition, and the resulting buildup of fat and eventual obesity are all negative

- Exercise: Any activity is beneficial by keeping muscles strong, blood flowing and burning excess calories

- Attitude: A strong will to live (life force) reduces stress, and gives us the reason to take the necessary steps in diet and exercise

- Stem cell therapy: puts actively dividing cells (stem cells), harvested from our own body, into places in the body where repair and active cell division are needed. This therapy is not yet approved by FDA, but extensive research is showing benefit.

Maintaining Healthy Blood Pressure

Hypertension is another condition that coincides with 'old age'. Arteries may harden, the reduced flexibility of the arterial walls results in it more resembling a metal pipe than a living conduit that works with the heart to convey blood to the body. Partial blockages due to buildup of arterial plaque or calcium will also restrict flow. These changes in the circulatory system will contribute to a rise in the blood pressure. But are these the real cause of hypertension? Dr. Thomas Cowan writes at length about the real causes of hypertension and hardening of the arteries in his book titled *Human Heart, Cosmic Heart*[3]. We already talked about his book and how blood flows due to electrical charge inside the capillaries. His claim that this is the root cause of hypertension and heart disease is a real eye opener. According to Dr. Cowan, the conventional wisdom is wrong and the treatments applied today are only treating symptoms, not root causes. The result is that hypertension and heart disease continue to rage as significant risks to longevity. We don't want to go there. We need to learn from Dr. Cowan how to prevent the disease and, if we already have the symptoms, how to address the root causes in order to reverse the condition. If we want to extend our healthy life, we must maintain a healthy blood pressure.

There is no evidence that high sodium or salt intake causes hypertension. If we don't have hypertension, eating salt will not cause it. If you already have hypertension, reducing salt intake will reduce blood pressure, so reduce salt intake. On the other hand, there is evidence that reducing salt intake, in otherwise healthy people, could increase heart disease. The best advice is to avoid hypertension and use salt moderately.

The root causes of hypertension, as best we know today, include:

- Stress (number 1): Distress not eustress. Good stress (eustress) is energizing, healthy and not a cause of hypertension. Bad stress (distress) is severely damaging and debilitating on many levels. Sometimes the difference between the two is due to attitude. If you accept life's challenges as opportunities to be welcomed, these could create eustress. If you bear life's challenges as burdens, unfairly placed on your shoulders, alone in the world, with no way out, these same challenges will create distress. Worry is also a cause of distress. Some people naturally worry about everything, even those things that they cannot change or control. Attitude means a lot. Having a Plan B ready in case Plan A bombs can reduce stress.

Another option is to talk about our problems with a friend. Getting what seem to be insurmountable issues out into the open air can detoxify them or at least get them off our chest. Burying our problems and worries inside allows them to build and fester with predictably bad consequences. We are not an island or an Atlas carrying the burden of the world on our shoulders. Stress can be measured by testing blood for cortisol. Cortisol is a hormone that our body produces during periods of stress to enhance alertness and certain body functions, like increasing blood pressure and blood glucose level to enhance the ability to fight or take flight. When cortisol levels remain high due to persistent stress, there are many negative side effects, including hypertension and poor blood glucose control.

- Lack of sufficient sleep.

- Lack of exposure to the sunlight and earth energy: Try to get sun on as much of your body as possible for ten minutes every few days. If this is not possible, radiant energy from a wood stove, fireplace, hot shower, sauna or hot tub can substitute. Walking barefoot in the grass restores our electrical charge and feels great. Absorb earth energy into your body by doing Chi Gong. Take an earth energy pill (Oh – sorry, I haven't developed that yet!)

- Diet lacking in adequate antioxidants, vitamins, minerals, protein, essential fats, complex carbs, or dietary fiber. And predictably containing too much sugar.

- Imbalanced or underdeveloped microbiome: This is caused by diet and the factors we already talked about in leaky gut syndrome. The short chain fatty acids produced by the bacteria in our intestines are absorbed into the bloodstream where they clean up the high melting point fatty materials.

- Insufficient consumption of good fats and oils: We thought incorrectly for many years that saturated fats or cholesterol caused heart disease. We now know that a diet rich in oils from fish and nuts, as well as olive oil, safflower oil, sunflower oil, canola oil and even soybean oil will protect the arteries from the high melting point fats like coconut oil, palm oil, lard, butter and cocoa butter. Synthetic trans fats had even higher melting points, but these have been removed from our diets and are no longer a concern.

- Alcohol in excess.

- Lack of exercise. Exercise is necessary, especially the kind that pushes the cardiovascular system to the limits.

- Insufficient hydration: We need to drink enough water to keep our bodies hydrated. This is actually a controversial topic because some think that excess consumption of water will dilute or wash out body minerals. I'm not sure who is right! It's safe to say that we don't want to be dehydrated. And probably wise not to over-hydrate with too much water consumption. Balance!

There is evidence that a diet high in fiber and antioxidants will reduce blood pressure significantly.[52]. Proceed slowly as you increase fiber; monitor your blood pressure along with your blood glucose in order to observe how your body reacts. Like blood glucose, blood pressure needs to be controlled in a relatively tight range. Lower is generally better, to a point.

Avoiding hypertension will require many steps, many of the same steps that we need to take to avoid other ailments such as diabetes. The body is a holism and these ailments have a common set of root causes.

Exercise

Exercise and physical activity are critical to a healthy and properly functioning body.[53] The older we get, the more important exercise becomes. Without exercise, we lose muscle quantity and tone. We need strong and flexible muscles in order to move, hold our skeletons in place, digest our food, keep our blood circulating and to breathe.

Dr. Otto Siegel, Genius and Longevity Coach, discusses the importance of exercising properly and not causing injury.[15] In our personal coaching sessions, he pointed out that the goals of exercise should be progressive:

- First, to prevent injury (avoid what hurts and what you don't like)

- Second, to preserve your existing capabilities (maintenance, no loss with age)

- Third, to recover capabilities (get back to where you used to be, but lost due to inactivity)

- Finally, to develop capabilities (expand capabilities beyond where you are now or were in the past)

Lack of physical activity results also in obesity, hypertension, constipation, poor circulation, diabetes, and an overall malaise (bad attitude!). Let's start with a definition of exercise: Exercise is repeating a motion in order to challenge a muscle or set of muscles.

Let's differentiate between exercises that challenge muscles and those that challenge the cardiovascular system. Of course, our lungs and heart are powered by muscles, so an exercise that challenges those, is challenging muscles. If our cardiovascular system has good capacity, an exercise that challenges our legs may not challenge our heart and lungs. We need to pay attention to both. Any activity is good. Any exercise is good. Learn exercises that challenge various muscles and find ones that you can do enough of to challenge your heart and lungs. Start slow and increase intensity and repetitions as your strength and capacity improve.

The Canadian Air Force exercise routine is especially instructional on how to exercise. It starts out ridiculously easy, or so we think at first. For example, for pushups, it starts out with a few pushups done from the knees, which almost anyone can do, and requires that we perform just a few of these each day, then increase by one rep and continue daily. When we can repeat the exercise several days in a row, we add another rep, and so on for twelve cycles, at which point the intensity of the exercise is increased. After a few months, we are doing a respectable number of full body pushups, which of course was the goal, and it continues to advance in difficulty. The important thing about this program is that progress is manageable and therefore we don't hurt ourselves. If we do too much, or advance too rapidly, our body isn't ready, resulting in a pulled muscle or aggravated joint. The exercise must stop for a few weeks or longer until it heals. This is a good example of the tortoise and the hare – the tortoise will win this race!

Most people don't know how to exercise, thinking that for it to work it must cause pain. Then they avoid exercising because they don't like pain. Who does?! Pain could be an ache that indicates that a muscle has been pushed beyond its limit, resulting in increased endurance and strength once it has recovered. That could be a good thing. Or pain could be from a pulled muscle, or a damaged joint. While we are waiting for that pulled muscle to recover, we avoid any exercise that challenges that muscle. Meanwhile, that muscle and others nearby atrophy from lack of use. The other problem with pain is that it may (and maybe should) prevent us from doing more exercise. That is not a good outcome. A better approach would be to find exercises that we enjoy doing and that don't hurt. We will find our strength and endurance improving, which is the idea. And as our strength increases, we will actually want to do more. Let's go there.

Any activity where the muscles are in action can be exercise. Walking is exercise. Stretching is exercise. Talking – is not exercise! We can build exercise into our daily routine and everyday activities. For example, when we take a shower, we can stretch and tighten muscles as we move to wash ourselves. It is amazing how much of a workout we can get just by pushing and stretching our muscles as we move. It's a great time to do it because the warm water will help loosen up tense muscles, reducing the risk of pulling a muscle. Stretching is a great form of exercise that we can do often during the day. I love to stretch in bed. Every time I wake up during the night, and in the morning, I stretch my legs and back. Watch your dog or cat. Every time they get up, they stretch. Watch and learn!

Before we embark on any new exercise routine, it would be smart for us to get a physical checkup to make sure we are capable. The best way to do this today is to get a complete body scan. The price has come down to a few thousand dollars. The benefit is that it allows the doctor to assess our entire circulatory system to identify any blockages or developing blockages that could lead to a heart attack or stroke. Keep in mind that blockage of the arteries comes from at least two sources – fat and calcium. We can have low cholesterol and run several miles a day and still have a life-threatening arterial blockage caused by calcium deposition. The scan will also identify aneurisms, which are silent time bombs. There are many advantages to learning that we have a partial blockage of arteries. If the blockage is severe enough, a stint can be installed now to open the artery. If the blockage is minimal enough that no treatment is needed now, we can make lifestyle changes in order to reverse the blockage or prevent further advancement. On the other hand, if we get a clean scan, we have validation that whatever we have been doing is working – keep it up. We can relax mentally and get to work physically, knowing that our body can take the stress.

When we first start to exercise vigorously, it will hurt a little (good hurt), but after a few weeks the body will actually crave the work. The benefits to exercise are numerous and additive:

- Exercise builds muscle

- Muscle burns calories

- Muscles remove glucose from the blood, reducing blood glucose level

- Burning calories allows us to eat reasonably while maintaining a healthy weight

- Muscles look good!

- Muscles feel good

- Muscles build our confidence and improve our attitude

- Muscles help pump blood in the extremities

- Muscles hold bones in alignment and improve posture

- Muscles help move food and waste in the intestines

- Exercise improves insulin sensitivity

- Muscles improve our balance

- Muscles absorb shock from bumps and falls so we don't get hurt

- Muscles allow us to do what we want to do

- Muscles make us feel strong, be strong and feel younger

- Exercise builds endurance and improves circulation

- Endurance allows us to do what we want to do

- Exercise tires us so that we can sleep well.

Two great books to read on exercise and diet are by Dr. Al Sears, *PACE: The 12-Minute Fitness Revolution*[54] and Dr. Jeffrey S. Life, *The Life Plan: How Any Man Can Achieve Lasting Health, Great Sex, and a Stronger, Leaner Body*[55]. In his book, Dr. Sears exposes the fallacy of cardio training. He shows how to use interval training techniques to challenge our cardiovascular system and muscles to induce real growth and improvement in capacity. It is strenuous, so it's important that we are physically able to handle it. If you are good to go, read the book and get to work. Interval training requires that we perform several repetitions of an exercise, getting ourselves to exhaustion as quickly as possible. We can do different exercises, but intensely enough to get to exhaustion within five minutes for each one. As our capacity increases, we will need to increase the intensity in order to get to exhaustion in five minutes or less.

The first time I did this, I rode my exercise bike and got to exhaustion in a minute. Apparently, I wasn't in as good a condition as I thought! The good news is that when you challenge your body like this, it responds. I added fifteen seconds every few days and within four weeks I was up to five minutes of bicycle time. And I could feel the strength returning to my body. Personally, I don't like riding the exercise bike. To me it is painful and dragging myself to do it is a real chore. I have since found other exercises using small weights and a Bowflex® that I actually enjoy. The result is the same. I can push myself to exhaustion in a few minutes doing a strenuous exercise that I actually enjoy. What a concept! Experiment and find a set of exercises that you like to do and then use them to push your body to the limits. Go slowly and incrementally increase the intensity as you feel your body getting stronger and more capable. It is an exhilarating feeling. Make it fun and it becomes a sustainable activity we want to do every day for the rest of our vibrant, healthy lives.

One of the main reasons why we don't exercise is that we are not motivated. We can find a hundred reasons not to exercise now. There is always something else on our to-do list that must be done now. It is an example of the urgent pushing out the important. If we don't schedule the time to exercise, we probably will find ourselves tucking into bed, realizing that our good intention to exercise didn't happen, again. Sometimes, when I don't feel like jumping into a strenuous exercise routine, I trick myself to get started. "I'll just do thirty seconds on the exercise bike." When that is done, I can almost always convince myself to go another thirty seconds, and so on until I find myself at the goal. Easing into it slowly works. Having a routine also works, as we get used to doing it, and even crave it. And that is the bottom line – we must do it!

Roger Clements had a long, successful career as one of the top pitchers in baseball history. He attributes his success to many factors, and one is his unique exercise routine. He worked himself to exhaustion every day, discovering that it was important not only to his physical health, but also to his mental and emotional health. Exercise produces endorphins, which give us a calm, good feeling all over. This feeling is good not only for muscles, but also for our brains, and it reduces stress. Find a plan that works for you and then get good at it.

Another beneficial side effect of exercise, especially the high intensity kind, is the impact it has on blood glucose. When you start measuring your blood glucose often, you may notice that even a little bit of activity drops the level. That is the good news. A brisk walk, a few jumping jacks, jumping on a small exercise trampoline (my personal fav), even walking around while reading or watching TV is better than sitting. Look at how we have designed our work and our relaxation times – usually sitting or lying in a recliner. We couldn't have invented a more destructive lifestyle if we tried. We were not designed to sit around. We were built for movement. In fact, we were designed to run. An enlightening book on that subject is *Born to Run: A Hidden Tribe, Superathletes, and the Greatest Race the World Has Never Seen* by Christopher McDougall[56]. In the book, he analyzes the design of the human body and concludes that we were intended to be long distance runners. In fact, our species was successful because we were designed to run, enabling us to run prey to death. There is no animal on the planet that is capable of running the way we do, for as long as we can. In fact, there is recent evidence that Neanderthals, our most recent ancestor, had a rigid rib cage that limited them to breathing by expanding their diaphragm. We are capable of expanding our diaphragm as well as rib cage, to take in more air with each breath, enabling us to run faster and longer. A running cheetah can only take one breath per step, as their spine and rib cage flex on each step they take. We have no such limitation and can take multiple breaths per step. We are running machines, sitting around idle most of the time. When was the last time you ran anywhere? We need to move and keep moving.

Living with Pain

Pain often is an unavoidable part of life. My father used to say, with his characteristic feigned lack of empathy, 'Enjoy the pain; when it stops you're dead!' Pain and pleasure are inseparable. Without pain, we would not know pleasure, and vice versa, but too much pain can cause the body to go into shock and even lose consciousness. Continuous pain is debilitating and exhausting, wearing down our energy and temper, but we cannot and don't want to completely avoid pain. We need to learn how to manage pain, accepting it when we must, while adjusting our behavior when possible. The first step is to differentiate between 'good' pain and 'bad' pain.

Good pain is usually muscle pain. If we haven't used a muscle in a while, the first few times we stress it, the muscle will give us some aching pain, stiffness or spasms. This is a good pain, because it doesn't indicate damage. The muscle isn't damaged; it is exhausted, sore and needs to recover. After it recovers from the stress in a few days, it will be stronger and better able to handle the stress. If we experience muscle cramps after increasing the intensity of an activity, first make sure to hydrate sufficiently and if that doesn't work, take a magnesium supplement to ease the cramps. Antioxidants also help. We want to continue stressing this muscle in order to expand its endurance and strength, accepting the good pain as an indication that we did it right. This is growth.

Bad pain feels different. It can occur anywhere in the body and is an indication of damage. Bad pain is usually more than an ache. We may describe it as shooting, burning, or stabbing. We need to listen to bad pain, identify the cause and take action to remove the cause. Then we need to do what we can to help the body heal. This may mean avoiding whatever activity caused the damage. Bad pain requires our response. The body knows when something is wrong or when damage has occurred, and it indicates where the damage has occurred by pain. We need to listen, act and modify our behavior in the future. This is how we learn.

When my knee was hurting, I tried to relieve it of some weight and movement, which caused additional strain on my other knee and hips, both of which started to complain as well! When the intestines are in suboptimal condition, eating can cause bloating and pain. Meanwhile, virtually every part of our body also suffers, and since we cannot see our intestines to assess their condition, we go unaware of the underlying cause. That is why it is so important to listen to the wisdom of your body. The organs and parts send a signal when something is wrong. The hard part is recognizing and understanding the message. Pain is the most obvious signal and the easiest to recognize, but it is not the only one. Being tired or "not being able to do what I used to do" are also signals. How often do we hear people say that? "Well, you know at my age it's normal not to be able to do what I used to do". "At my age, it's normal to be in pain". Do we have to accept this as truth? Why are we putting up with it? Why aren't we listening to our body and supporting it so that we can do what we used to do or even more?

We want to avoid taking pain-relieving drugs when experiencing muscle pain. Pain has a purpose and muting the signal may allow us to continue the action that caused the pain and inflict further injury. Pain-relieving drugs have negative side effects that are worse than the pain and will not be evident until years later. Some pain-relieving drugs are addictive, even after only a few uses. I prefer to avoid pain-relieving drugs unless I absolutely need them, and then only use them intermittently. Never take these drugs continuously or prophylactically. If I really am in pain and need a good night's sleep, then occasionally taking an over-the-counter pain medicine may be a smart move.

Avoiding activity may actually be the worst thing we can do when we are in pain. The body loses muscle tone and endurance in a matter of weeks. Many injuries, especially to joints, are the result of poor muscle tone. Avoiding activity will make it worse. We need to find an exercise that doesn't hurt the damaged joint in order to strengthen the muscles around the sore joint. This will help with recovery and prevent loss of muscle tone while we recover. We want to prevent spreading the injury to other parts of the body, as we avoid use of the hurting part.

If we are to successfully extend our healthy, vibrant lives, we need to learn how to manage pain. This means learning how to do the things we want to do without injuring ourselves. Perhaps we need to wear knee braces when we do strenuous activities involving the knees, for example. Maybe we need to learn what activities injure us and then avoid those activities or find an alternative approach that permits us to play and not get hurt. Over and over, I have learned the hard way that I have to experiment and find another way. When we get hurt, we need to learn how to heal ourselves. There are many kinds of therapy that can be useful including chiropractic, myofascial, acupuncture, massage, etc. Hot tub soaks and sauna treatments are also great for sore, stiff muscles. Experiment and find out which work best for you. Try everything; don't give up. We will need to be good at this!

CHAPTER 8

Maintaining Healthy Blood Glucose

Maintaining a healthy blood glucose level will likely be one of the biggest challenges that you will face in extending your healthy life. Failure to control blood glucose is called diabetes, but a multitude of health issues start long before the clinical disease state is reached. It is one of the most serious threats to a long and vibrant life, because it is pervasive, insidious, slow-developing, progressive, debilitating and ultimately deadly. Most of us are already exhibiting symptoms of inadequate blood glucose control, and too many of us will end up with diabetes. We must figure out how to prevent this from occurring. Doing so will require that we make some changes, and the sooner we start, the better. There are many interrelated factors that make solving the diabetes dilemma difficult. It will take some pages to unravel the details. Suffice to say for now that the solution involves diet and activity, but it is not so simple.

This is a personal story, because this is a battle that I also fight. I found, while researching for this book, that I was on the path to becoming diabetic and was already showing signs of being prediabetic. Denial was my first reaction. I checked my medical records for the past ten years and found that my fasting blood glucose level had been steady over that time at 118. This is not considered to be diabetic, and my doctor had never pointed it out as an issue, but based on what I was learning, this is not where I wanted to be. I began reading everything I could find, as well as testing my blood glucose often. What I learned from both shocked me. There are hundreds of studies that focus on one tiny part of the diabetes puzzle, identifying the root causes that gradually lead to the disease: excess eating, excess sugar, lack of fiber, and inactivity. But no one was putting together the pieces of the puzzle to create a comprehensive picture that would allow us to take steps to prevent the progression of the disease. I had a mission and a personal interest. I don't want to become diabetic. I want to extend my healthy life for as long as possible, and to do that I would have to learn how to retrain my body to properly manage blood glucose. I am happy to say that it is possible, and I am doing it. Now, I hope that I can help you to do the same.

One thing certain about diabetes is that the disease is rapidly increasing. In 2015, there were 392 million people diagnosed globally compared to only 30 million in 1985.[57] The CDC estimates that in the US about six million, or twenty five percent of those who meet the clinical definition for having diabetes, have not been diagnosed. The WHO estimates that the extent of underdiagnosis could be as high as fifty percent in some countries. Diabetes is the seventh highest cause of death in the US, reducing life expectancy by ten years. Diabetes is out of control, poorly diagnosed, poorly understood and likely to get worse because we are not taking the necessary steps to avoid it.

It is useful to understand that the body's ability to control blood glucose deteriorates slowly over time. It is a progressive disorder, meaning that the body progresses slowly from a healthy state to a disease state over a period of several decades. It happens so slowly, that we and our doctors often miss the warning signs and fail to take action soon enough. We are all on the path to diabetes, the only question is where and how fast we are moving towards it. Unless we take action now, we will become diabetic.

There is uncertainty about what causes diabetes – poor diet, obesity, age, genetics, lack of exercise, gender, lack of sleep, excess liver fat, intestinal microbiome imbalance and many other factors all contribute. The clinical definition is complicated and restrictive, resulting in failure to diagnose people early enough to enable them to take preventative steps. Instead, treatment is often delayed until the disease state is reached and drugs or injections of insulin are the only options. Diabetes and obesity are often observed together, with diabetes exacerbating obesity and obesity contributing to diabetes in a vicious cycle, but even skinny people can develop diabetes.

Additional complexity comes from the fact that there are several ways by which the blood glucose control system becomes compromised, which include: failure to produce sufficient insulin, insulin resistance in the liver, brain or muscles, overproduction of glucose by the liver, and failure of the liver and muscles to remove excess sugar from the blood. This complexity makes it difficult to detect, diagnose and to prevent.

There is a long chain of events that starts with diet and activity and ends with diabetes. But diabetes is not the end of the chain or the story. Inadequate blood glucose control is the first step in another long chain of health impacts that includes depression, physical capability and stamina, brain function, sleep disorders, obesity and finally other disease states such as heart disease, hypertension, stroke, kidney disease, cancer, and autoimmune diseases. Ultimately, if not controlled, high blood glucose levels can result in loss of limbs, eye damage and death.

Diet is a critical factor in developing and preventing diabetes. Chronic overeating, high sugar, and low fiber are the dietary factors that lead to diabetes. The foods we eat and even how we combine them into meals makes a difference in blood glucose control. We decide to have the salad and then drench it with a high calorie dressing loaded with sugar and fat. We drink sugar-laden juices thinking that they are healthy. We rationalize that we can have that chocolate cake for dessert because we did ten minutes on the exercise bike this morning, when in reality the cake contains 500 calories and we burned 100! When it comes to eating, we do just about everything possible wrong. We have done this to ourselves. The problem is us, not the food we eat. We do not know how to avoid diabetes and unless we teach ourselves, most of us will eventually become diabetic. We have a lot to learn.

> People need to know that walking around the block doesn't burn off a hot fudge sundae.
> -Penny Kris-Etherton (Penn State University)

Our bodies, age, genetics, behaviors, diet, activity levels, etc. are different, making it important that we learn about ourselves in order to discover what works best for us. We will need to gather data, make observations and even experiment a bit to find what works best. A blood glucose test kit costs $25 and is easy to use. We will need to have one and use it to learn how our body responds to fasting, eating certain foods, exercise, etc. to enable us to learn what to do and what to avoid in order to improve our ability to manage blood glucose. A blood pressure meter is also cheap and easy to use – we need to have one and use it often, as the changes we will make to improve glucose control will also lower blood pressure. It has taken several decades for us to train our bodies to manage blood glucose the way we do today. If that is not working so well, then some retraining will be required in order to improve, and this will take time and numerous changes in our diet and lifestyle. It took us decades to get where we are. It will take a year or more to regain control.

Lastly, don't allow age or any other factor be a limit on what you can do. This is another fallacy perpetuated by our medical system today. If we are sixty years old and our fasting blood glucose level is 115, like mine, our doctor is likely to advise us that we are 'normal' for our age and there is no need to do anything. The normal fasting glucose level for a twenty-five-year-old is under 95, so why should we be satisfied with 115? Can we do something about it instead of enduring another decade of denial, while blood glucose control continues to deteriorate to the point that we will be prediabetic or actually diabetic? The answer is that we can do something now and we should not wait.

What Is Diabetes?

The control of blood glucose and the factors that eventually lead to diabetes are complex and interrelated. I will try, in this section, to explain these factors in as simple a manner as possible, but please understand that in order to make it simple, I must leave out a lot of the details. The details can be found in other chapters in this book or in the reference articles that I cite. If you want the chemistry and the details, please go to these articles, keeping in mind that the science is not yet completely agreed on. Even among the experts and scientists, there is considerable disagreement.

There are two routes to diabetes: a lack of sufficient insulin production and insulin resistance.

- Insulin is produced in the beta cells located in the pancreas. After years of high sugar intake, the cells wear out and fail to produce sufficient insulin, allowing glucose to build up in the blood uncontrolled. A catastrophic failure of the beta cells to produce insulin causes Type 1 diabetes. In Type 2 diabetes, the beta cells are able to make insulin, but the amount produced is out of proportion to the amount of glucose present in the blood, allowing glucose to build up in the blood uncontrolled.

- Insulin resistance happens when the insulin receptor sites throughout the body become blocked or do not bind insulin efficiently. The result again is that glucose builds up in the blood uncontrolled.

There are many organs involved in the production and metabolism of glucose. When any of these become resistant to insulin due to prolonged exposure to high insulin levels over many years, the system becomes less efficient and fails to control glucose properly. Excess glucose accumulates in the blood because it is not being removed efficiently by the liver, muscles and brain, and the liver and kidneys continue to produce glucose even when there is sufficient or excess glucose in the blood. It is common that both issues exist: organs have become insulin resistant and insulin production has fallen to suboptimal levels, both due to excessive levels of sugar and insulin over many years.

Now, let's consider blood glucose level and define what is normal and what is diabetic or prediabetic.

Healthy Blood Glucose:

Healthy blood glucose levels range from 80 to 126 mg/dl. Below 80 is hypoglycemic, meaning too low and anything higher than 126 is hyperglycemic, meaning too high.

Morning Fasting Levels:

Blood glucose level should be lowest after an extended fast, as we experience when we do not eat overnight. Healthy fasting levels range from 80 to 100. The fasting level is a measure of how well your liver and kidneys are controlling blood glucose. If the fasting level is above 100, the liver or kidneys are not functioning properly. Test your blood several mornings in a row to allow you to learn about your body's fasting level. A big meal or dessert the night before could be the culprit. We will talk about the liver and steps to take to keep your liver healthy in a little bit.

Levels After Eating (Postprandial):

It is normal after eating a meal, especially one that contains sugar, for blood glucose levels to rise, peak and then decline again. If the peak level rises above 140, the meal contained more sugar than the system could manage, and therefore you should reduce sugar consumption in the future. If it goes over 140 after consuming a meal that contains a moderate amount of sugar and carbs, then insulin control may be the cause, meaning either that not enough insulin is being produced or the system has become insulin resistant. The only way to differentiate these possible causes is to test blood insulin levels after eating. This must be done by a doctor.

There is considerable controversy about where to draw the lines between normal, prediabetic and diabetic blood glucose levels. My interpretation and preference is to draw the lines lower so that we take action sooner. My suggestions are to define prediabetic and diabetic as:

- Fasting blood glucose between 100 and 125 is prediabetic; 126 or above is diabetic

- Postprandial blood glucose above 140 is prediabetic; above 200 is diabetic

The only test that we can do easily at home is for blood glucose. After eating a meal, test your blood glucose every fifteen minutes until the level returns to baseline. Watch how the level rises, peaks and then drops. Make note of the peak level and how long it took to drop. If it drops back to near fasting levels within 2 or 3 hours, the system is working. Peak levels above 140 are a sign that something is wrong, and the best response may be to change your diet to consume less sugar. If the level doesn't drop to below 100 within three hours after eating, again something is wrong. Try reducing sugar in your diet and see if the same pattern persists.

The Glucose and Fat Metabolism Model

When we eat a meal that contains carbs or sugar, the level of glucose in our blood rises, causing a proportional rise in insulin. Carbs must be digested and broken down into glucose before they can be absorbed. Glucose passes through the intestinal wall, directly into the bloodstream. The rate at which the glucose enters the bloodstream depends on how complex the carbohydrate is – basically how long it takes for the digestive system to break it down. Simple starches start to break down into glucose in the mouth as the food is chewed. Complex carbohydrates take more time to break down and may not be converted for hours or days, when the food reaches the intestines where there are bacteria capable of digesting it.

While blood glucose and insulin levels are both high, our bodies metabolize the glucose and we feel satisfied. After some time, our stomachs are emptied, and the rapidly digestible sugars have been absorbed. The level of glucose in the blood drops. The insulin level in the blood drops as well, but not right away – there is a lag of some time, maybe thirty minutes, depending on many factors. When blood glucose level is low and insulin is still high, during this lag phase, we feel hungry. There are two possible routes we can take:

A. Our body is telling us that the glucose is gone, and we need to replenish it – we feel hungry and we eat a snack or meal that contains carbohydrates. Our blood glucose level rises, the hunger dissipates, and our bodies continue to metabolize glucose.

B. Alternatively, when we feel hungry, we can avoid eating or eat something that is low in carbs, like a glass of water, or some nuts. If we wait for the lag phase to end, our blood insulin level will drop and when at a sufficiently low level, our bodies will go into fat metabolism. The liver converts stored glycogen and fat into glucose and the hunger goes away, even though we haven't eaten any carbs or sugar.

Scenario B is what we want to happen at least once a day. If we stay in scenario A, our bodies will not metabolize glycogen or fat. This is what happens when we eat carbohydrates several times a day. Some people even wake up in the middle of the night to have a midnight snack to quell the hunger they feel. This is the worst thing we can do. If we don't allow our bodies to go into fat metabolism, then we never metabolize fat. We're putting money in the bank and never taking it out. With money, this may be a good, if miserly, behavior. With fat, it is a disaster that results in obesity and disease.

This model predicts that in order to avoid insulin resistance, excess stored fat and obesity, we should:

A. Never eat carbs late at night or during the night. If you must put something into your stomach late at night or during the night, choose something that has no carbs, like water or nuts.

B. Fast in the morning for as long as you can or eat a low-carb breakfast like eggs, or nuts with coffee or tea (without sugar). By doing this, we can extend the overnight fast for another four hours. The goal is to spend twelve to fourteen hours in glycogen metabolism.

C. Eat three or fewer times a day with little or no carb-containing foods in between meals.

We will find that to reverse the conditions of insulin resistance, excess stored fat and obesity, we will need to take more drastic steps.

Healthy Blood Glucose Levels

If you are already diabetic, you will need to follow your doctor's advice and take the pills or injections that they prescribe. Failure to do so could kill you. Unfortunately, we don't know how to reverse diabetes once the disease state is reached. There are some anecdotal reports of success using herbs. Let's hope they are real. However, if you currently have healthy blood glucose levels and your body is able to adequately, even if not perfectly, control blood glucose, then you can benefit from reading this section. The steps we will discuss could prevent you from becoming diabetic in the future. It is critical that you learn how to do so.

I say 'learn' because you will need to test yourself to learn how your body is reacting to the foods you eat and to the activities you perform. Everybody is different, so what works for me may not work for you. A fasting blood glucose test once a year during your annual checkup is only measuring one aspect of glucose management – how well your body manages glucose when you are fasting. Where did that glucose come from if you haven't eaten any sugar or carbs in twelve hours? It comes mostly from your liver, where stored glycogen is converted into glucose to keep your brain and organs functioning, even though you haven't eaten anything. A good fasting blood glucose level for a healthy twenty-five-year-old is about 95. When you are fifty years old, your fasting blood glucose level might be 110. This means that your body is not managing blood glucose as efficiently as it did when you were in your twenties. This happens to people, when they don't do anything to maintain their ability to manage blood glucose.

The other test that is useful, but more difficult to perform, is the A1C test. This test estimates the average blood glucose level during the past two or three months, by measuring the degree of glycation of hemoglobin in the blood. Sugar in the blood reacts with the hemoglobin via a reaction called glycation and 'sticks' to the red blood cells for months. The higher the blood glucose, the higher the level of glycated hemoglobin. Good values are reported as below 5.7%, prediabetic is from 5.8 to 6.4% and above is diabetic. If I dip you in two pools of water, one at 70 degrees F and the other at 130 degrees F, on average you are at a comfortable hot tub temperature of 100 degrees F, but you are dead. Averages don't mean much, when blood glucose is spiking too high, and the A1C will not catch it.

We are learning that many organs of the body are involved in glucose management, including the brain, pancreas, liver, kidneys, muscles, intestines and probably more. There are glucose and insulin sensors located throughout the body that stimulate the production of insulin, glucagon and incretins. Incretins are proteins produced in response to glucose in the intestine that stimulate insulin to rise even before it is absorbed into the bloodstream. There are receptor sites on the surface of cells throughout the body that insulin specifically binds to in order to enable the passage of glucose across the cell membrane, into the cell where it can be metabolized. When these sensors and receptor sites become insensitive to insulin, the ability to manage and metabolize glucose is diminished. This is how most of us get on the path to diabetes.

Insulin and glucagon are the two hormones that control blood glucose level. Insulin is the primary control, with glucagon level depending on insulin. In essence, insulin down-regulates blood glucose, preventing it from getting too high and glucagon up-regulates blood glucose, preventing it from getting too low. Insulin performs several functions in the control of blood glucose:

- Insulin promotes the absorption of glucose by muscles, the brain and the liver, removing excess glucose from the bloodstream. Decades of high sugar and insulin levels cause these organs to become resistant to insulin, meaning they fail to respond to the elevated insulin. Excess glucose is not efficiently removed from the blood, allowing blood glucose levels to rise out of control.

- Insulin shuts down the production of glucagon when blood glucose is adequate. When blood glucose drops, insulin drops, and glucagon production commences. Glucagon stimulates the liver and kidneys to produce glucose, keeping the level of blood glucose constant. When the alpha cells in the pancreas that produce glucagon become resistant to insulin after decades of high sugar and insulin levels, the alpha cells continue to produce glucagon in spite of the rising insulin level that occurs normally after a meal containing carbs.[58] The result is that the liver and kidneys continue to produce glucose, even though the level in the blood is adequate, resulting in high blood glucose levels.[59]

Sugar increases glucose in the blood, which stimulates insulin production, which results in the glucose level dropping – when the system is working properly. Protein, on the other hand, directly stimulates the production of insulin, which results in the glucose level dropping. This is how high protein, low sugar meals and diets reduce blood glucose.

We train the system by the amount of sugar we put into it. An excessive amount of sugar overloads the control mechanism and eventually damages the system's ability to properly control blood glucose. The system becomes insulin resistant, meaning it takes more insulin to control the same glucose level. This resistance increases gradually with continued excessive sugar intake, until at some point the body cannot make enough insulin to control the glucose, with the result that blood glucose level rises uncontrolled. This is the diabetes disease state. This happens progressively, creeping up slowly and insidiously. If we know that our fasting blood glucose level is climbing, can we do something about it to prevent the onset of the disease state? That is the key question. If we want to extend our healthy lives, it is imperative that we maintain good blood glucose control. Diabetes is a debilitating disease with many negative side effects. We don't want to go there.

In order to learn how our blood glucose control system is working, we need to test our blood glucose level at several critical times:

- First thing in the morning when we wake up

- Fifteen minutes after we eat, repeated until the level drops back to baseline

- After exercising

- Whenever we feel hungry

- Especially if we feel lightheaded or dizzy.

- We want to know what is happening to our blood glucose level and how well our body is managing it at different times of the day and after different activities. Armed with this information, we can start to figure out how to retrain our system to improve control. Here is what we want to learn:

» How well is the liver controlling blood glucose while we fast?

» How much does blood glucose level rise after a meal?

» Are there activities that drop blood glucose level?

» How low does blood glucose level go and when during the day?

» How high does blood glucose level go and when during the day?

» How long does it take for blood glucose level to return to baseline after spiking due to a meal?

We retrain our blood glucose control system by achieving low baseline levels of blood glucose and insulin. We do this by fasting. Avoid eating anything after dinner or between meals. Water is OK anytime. By morning, we have gone ten to twelve hours without eating. Blood glucose and insulin levels should be at baseline. Try to wait as long as you can before eating breakfast. You can drink coffee or tea without sugar. Or even a diet soda. Anything without carbs or sugar. If you feel lightheaded or dizzy, test your blood glucose. If it is below 80, eat some pecans or walnuts and retest in fifteen minutes. If it is still below 80, break the fast and eat some carbs. You don't want to pass out. The goal is to get your blood glucose level down to the low to mid 90s, by exercising or working while we extend the fast as long as we can. With some practice and time, you should be able to wait until lunch to eat carbs. And then for lunch eat a low-carb meal such as a salad. For dinner, eat a moderate amount of carbs, in balance with your activity level. Remember – you need carbs to live, so don't eliminate them. What you want to see in your testing is that your fasting blood glucose level is in the 85 to 100 range. After eating a meal, it may jump up twenty to thirty points, and then after a few hours drop back down again. The less it jumps up after eating, the better. The faster it recovers back to baseline again after eating, the better. Ideally, your blood glucose level stays level all the time at or near your fasting baseline level, in spite of eating and activity. The more it spikes up after eating and the further away it gets from the ideal 85 to 100 range, the closer you are to becoming diabetic.

The Role of the Liver in Glucose Control

If your blood glucose level remains high or even goes up after a fast, it is an indication that your liver or kidneys are overproducing glucose. After using up all the glucose from the last meal we ate, blood glucose levels should drop, then after a short lag, insulin levels should also drop, signaling the liver to begin converting glycogen into glucose so that the blood glucose level does not drop too far. The brain must not be starved of glucose or we will get lightheaded and if the drop is extreme, even lose consciousness. The liver is supposed to maintain a steady level of glucose in the blood. If the levels after a fast are too high (over 100), then the liver is not functioning properly. In extreme cases, it could be an indication of liver disease such as cancer, cirrhosis or Hepatitis.

More likely, it is an indication of excessive amounts of fat stored in the liver, called non-alcoholic fatty liver disease (NAFLD). The excess fat stored in the liver interferes with the function of the liver. There is little known about NAFLD, how to identify it, how to prevent it, or how to reverse it. It is thought to be due to prolonged overconsumption of food in general, and fructose specifically. The liver is supposed to remove excess glucose from the blood and store it as glycogen initially and then as fat, when the glycogen store is saturated. It also removes fructose from the blood, but as already discussed, it converts some of it to glucose and some to fat, without any apparent control. The problem occurs when the amount of fat in the liver becomes excessive. It can happen quickly, in a matter of weeks, or over a period of years. There is evidence that it can be prevented by maintaining a moderate food and carbohydrate intake. Drs. Mann and Chisholm[60] recommend forty to sixty percent of calories come from carbs. In a 2000-calorie-per-day diet, this translates to 200 to 300 grams of carbohydrates per day. If a person is overweight, they suggest reducing daily caloric intake by 500 calories below maintenance, which means to about 1500 calories per day, depending on activity level, in order to lose weight. They do not advise carb intakes below 130 grams per day, even on a restricted calorie diet.

The only food that has been clinically proven to reduce the excess fat in the liver and reverse NAFLD is beta glucan. Beta glucan is a soluble fiber found in oats and especially oat bran. It is also found in the cell wall of yeast and is available as a dietary supplement. George Inglett[61] with USDA developed Oatrim®, a concentrated beta glucan derived from oat bran and performed research on oat fiber to prove its efficacy in reducing stored fat in the liver and blood cholesterol levels.

Oat bran is a good food for breakfast. See Appendix 4 for the recipe. Eggs are also reported to be good.

Insulin Resistance

Insulin resistance is not well understood. The term is used to describe a prediabetic state, where insulin receptor sites located in the muscles, liver and pancreas can be blocked by the presence of excessive amounts of accumulated fat. These organs are supposed to store fat, and convert fat to glucose when needed, but when the amount is more than they can handle efficiently, the system fails. Insulin cannot bind to the cells to stimulate glucose uptake and metabolism, with the result that glucose builds up in the blood uncontrolled. High insulin levels are undetected by the pancreas and it continues to call for glucose production by the liver and kidneys. The liver and kidneys continue to convert fat into glucose, even though there is sufficient glucose in the blood and glucose levels rise uncontrolled.

There are several ways in which the glucose control system can become resistant to insulin:

- The muscles become insulin resistant when excessive amounts of fat build up inside the muscle tissue. Some level of fat is normal and good, but not too much.

- The brain becomes insulin resistant. We don't know how

this happens, but there is evidence that an insulin sensor in the brain triggers the central nervous system to control glucose production by the liver and kidneys. When this fails, the liver and kidneys overproduce glucose.

- The alpha cells in the pancreas become insulin resistant and fail to respond to high insulin levels. The result is the continued production of glucagon that stimulates the liver and kidneys to produce glucose in spite of adequate blood glucose.

- The liver becomes insulin resistant due to excessive amounts of fat stored in the liver with the result that it continues to produce glucose in spite of adequate blood glucose.

The excess accumulated fat in the liver and muscles happens in several ways:

- Eating too much over many years. Excess calories are converted into fat. The fat accumulates and is never removed.

- Too much fructose in the diet. The liver converts some fraction of all fructose consumed into fat.

- Lack of exercise. Every muscle stores fat that it alone will use. Any muscle that is not exercised sufficiently to use up stored fat will accumulate fat to excess levels and become resistant.

Insulin resistance develops slowly over many years as the capacity of the system to respond to persistently elevated insulin levels deteriorates.

The Pieces of the Diabetes Puzzle

Our goal is to put together the pieces of the diabetes puzzle. First, we must figure out if we have an issue. We want to know where on the path to diabetes we are now so we can take steps to prevent or reverse it.

The first step is to identify if we have an issue with blood glucose control.

1. Start by testing your fasting blood glucose level first thing in the morning, before you have eaten anything or exercised. Do this for at least five mornings. If the level is consistently above 100, you should go further to find out why. If the level is above 140, you should see a doctor. You want to do this test yourself, as the test performed at a clinic or doctor's office is delayed. The activity you perform in the morning before getting your blood drawn at the clinic is enough to drop the blood glucose level, giving a false low reading.

2. Test your blood glucose level before and after eating a meal. It's not necessary to eat anything special. Eat as you normally would and see what happens. Test your blood before starting to eat and then every fifteen minutes for three hours. The intent is to see how much your blood glucose level goes up after eating and then how long it takes to come down again.

3. Try some different activities. Test your blood glucose before and after exercising. Try different types of exercise to see what happens. I bought a 36-inch exercise trampoline and use it several times during the day, especially in the morning. Just two minutes of jumping around can reduce my blood glucose level by fifteen points or more. This is fun and involves the biggest muscles in the body – the legs. The idea is to use your muscles to burn glucose and get it out of your blood. I find that strenuous exercise like stationary bike or lifting weights is even more effective at lowering blood glucose level and have seen my level drop from 130 to 92. I was happy with that! On the other hand, I notice that after I have successfully lowered my blood glucose by some activity, all I have to do is sit at my desk for half an hour and it rises back up again.

4. Test your blood glucose when you don't feel right. If you are lightheaded, dizzy, tired or even very hungry, test your blood

to see if the glucose level is the culprit. If blood glucose drops below 80 mg/dl, you are likely to feel lightheaded, dizzy or tired. Test it again in fifteen minutes. If it is still below 80, eat something.

5.   Experiment with different foods, in different combinations. Make it a game and have some fun.

What to Do

If your glucose is always between 80 and 100, no matter when you test it, you are good and can focus on maintenance. If your fasting glucose is 126 or above, your glucose after eating a meal is over 140, or any single reading is above 200, see a doctor now. If your glucose is below these numbers, but above 100 after fasting, then you are prediabetic and need to take steps now.

1.   Exercise of any kind is beneficial to reducing blood glucose. The more, the better. The more strenuous and intense, the greater the drop. The idea is to use the muscles to metabolize glucose and remove it from the blood. The drop is temporary of course, but any drop is beneficial. Repeated exercise can build muscle mass and strength, which increases the amount of glucose that your body can burn, even when not active. The benefit is cumulative and builds over time. Exercise is also known to improve insulin sensitivity, reversing insulin resistance for three to four days, which is why regular exercise is so important to managing blood glucose and reversing insulin resistance. Find exercises that you enjoy and do them often during the day. After dinner, take a walk.

2.   Unless you are already thin, losing weight is also known to improve blood glucose management.[62] Obesity is both a cause of diabetes and a result of it. It is a vicious cycle that must be broken in order to get better. Obesity reduces the effectiveness of exercise, and certainly makes it more difficult to exercise. Excess stored fat changes your body chemistry, hormone levels and liver enzymes. Men need a minimum of five percent body fat to be healthy. Women need about

ten percent body fat for proper hormone control. Most of us are nowhere near these levels, so not a worry. We should all aim for fifteen to twenty percent body fat as a reasonable and achievable goal.

3. Change your diet.[63] Start by eliminating as much sugar from your diet as you can. We do not need to eat any sugar. There is often sugar hiding in the foods you eat. Do you take sugar with your coffee or tea? If so, reduce the amount slowly until you no longer need it. Stop drinking sugar-containing beverages like soda and juices. There is no evidence that sugar substitutes are harmful or interfere with blood glucose management, so use them in moderation if you need sweetness. Yogurt, except the unsweetened varieties, often contains a lot of sugar, especially ones with fruit. If you eat cereal, eliminate the types with added sugar and don't add it yourself. Sugar is everywhere, so you will need to be diligent.

4. There is a lot of evidence that changing your diet drastically to a low or very low carbohydrate diet is beneficial to improving blood glucose management. The normal recommended level of carbs in a diet is about sixty to seventy percent of caloric intake, which for a 2000-calorie-per-day diet is 300 grams. One study suggests that we should go back to pre-industrial levels of carbs, which they estimate to be 43% or 215 grams per day. A low-carb diet contains about 130 grams per day, which is the minimum recommended by ADA. A very low-carb diet contains 50 – 75 grams of carbs per day. Unless you are extremely diligent, achieving that level of carb intake every day will be difficult. It is more reasonable to aim for the 130 to 215 grams of carbs per day. However, to see any benefit may take over three months. This is why most people fail to see the benefit – they don't persist long enough or drop carb intake low enough. It's not easy and unless you are obese, probably unnecessary.

5. Chronic overeating causes oxidative stress, which causes insulin resistance, which causes NAFLD, which causes diabetes. This long chain of events obscures the cause/effect relationship between overeating and diabetes. Remarkably, a study by Knudsen showed that overfeeding combined with inactivity increased insulin resistance in healthy young men in only fourteen days.[64] The body has a mechanism for handling excess calories in the diet, initially storing the glucose that is not needed at that time as glycogen in the liver and muscles, but there is a limit. When the limit is reached, the next step is to convert the excess glucose into subcutaneous adipose tissue or belly fat. This is the biggest store of fat in the body. But again, there is a limit to the rate at which excess calories can be processed and deposited. When this rate limit is exceeded, meaning we are taking in more calories than the storage mechanism can process, the additional calories get stored as ectopic fat in the liver. The result of too much fat stored in the liver is NAFLD, insulin resistance and diabetes.[65] Chronic and persistent overeating is one of the biggest risks to our health long term. We must eat less. If we eat less, what we eat becomes far less important. If any of the 90 or so popular diets did any good at all, it was in helping people eat less calories.

6. Fasting is an excellent practice to recalibrate the blood glucose control system and improve insulin sensitivity. The goal is to avoid solid food for some period of time so that there is no sugar, carbs, fats or protein entering the bloodstream. We need to continue to drink liquids even when fasting so as not to dehydrate. Make morning fasting a part of your daily regimen as a great way to reduce overall daily caloric intake to help control weight. Do a twenty-two-hour fast once a week to push your control system into fat metabolism. See the section on glucose management for a full discussion of the benefits of fasting on fat metabolism. Fasting will be found to be highly beneficial in prevention and perhaps reversal of insulin resistance and diabetes.

7. Now, I'm going to tell you the opposite about diet! Eliminating sugar or changing to a low or very low carb diet is difficult to achieve consistently for a sufficient time to have an impact. For lasting impact, you will have to make these changes for the rest of your life. Most of us are not willing or able to make that kind of commitment. And there is even good reason not to make these drastic changes. By eliminating fruit and sugar-containing vegetables from our diets, we reduce our quality of life and also eliminate beneficial nutrients and vitamins. Remember the chapter on life force? Living without bananas, strawberries, oranges, chocolate chip cookies and donuts will not be fun and will weaken your life force. This could be detrimental to your health. In light of this realization, here are two points to consider: First, unless you are willing to go extreme in eliminating sugar and going low carb long term, what you eat is not going to matter very much. The fact is that how you process what you eat is more important than what you eat, and this depends on the health of your microbiome, your activity level, whether you are insulin resistant or not and whether you are producing sufficient insulin or not. Secondly, there are other ways to manage blood glucose that are not so demanding. And finally, by eliminating whole groups of foods from our diets, we may unwittingly cause the next wave of diseases and not know it for thirty years.

I suggest that you eat the foods you like, reducing sugar consumption as much as possible, while still enjoying fruits and snacks in moderation. Then, focus on the other steps that you can take to manage blood glucose such as exercise, eating less, losing weight, periodic fasting, increasing fiber intake, increasing antioxidants, adding some new items to your diet, etc. You are more likely to stick to a moderate approach and therefore more likely to be successful.

8. Add some new things to your diet. There is evidence that the following foods can be beneficial:
   a. Dietary fiber – There are a lot of benefits from increasing dietary fiber intake. Fiber produces short chain fatty

acids, increases the viscosity of food in the digestive system, allows more time for bacteria to ferment sugar, slows absorption of sugar into the blood stream[66], reduces the permeability of the intestinal wall (leaky gut), improves blood glucose control, reduces blood pressure, enhances satiety, improves weight control and more. Americans consume about 11 grams of fiber per day. The USDA Guidelines for Americans now says we need over 30 grams per day. I've seen recommendations for between 50 and 100 grams a day. Fiber and exercise are the two most important elements in blood glucose control and health overall.

b. Oat bran – Oat bran contains beta glucan, a beneficial dietary fiber that has been clinically shown to reduce the amount of fat stored in the liver and improve insulin sensitivity. Beta glucan can also be derived from yeast cell walls and is available in convenient 500 mg capsules. This is a game changer. Take it every day. Almost all of us have an excess amount of fat stored in our liver, which is the cause of fatty liver disease and liver dysfunction in blood glucose control. You will also see and feel the benefits in your digestive system.

c. Vitamin D3 – has been shown to be important in glycemic control and prevention of diabetes.[67] We should be getting Vitamin D from exposure to the sun, but most people don't get enough. You need to take a supplement of 6,000 IU twice a day. Have your blood tested to assure that you are near the top of the 30-100 ng/ml recommended range.

d. Vinegar – Take an ounce of vinegar a day. Put it on a salad, dip bread into it, mix it into a beverage (yuk) or if you're really tough, sip it! Make it part of your meals. Cider vinegar, especially the unfiltered kind, is supposed to be the best, but Balsamic is great too.

e. Fenugreek seed – Take a teaspoon a day (three – four grams) of powdered fenugreek. It is a good source of fiber too. I add it to my oat bran cereal.

f. Cinnamon – Add a little to something that you eat. I add it to my oat bran cereal every morning.

g. Antioxidants[68] – have many benefits in our diet including: slowing aging, reducing inflammation, neutralizing free radicals, eliminating AGEs (Advanced Glycation End products) from the body, preventing cancer and improving blood glucose control. All antioxidants are good, and you want to include several in your daily diet. Curcumin (also called turmeric spice) is one of the best. The spice itself is good, but the prepared versions are far more active. The best is the liposomal form, which is highly absorbable by the body. Cocoa powder and ground cinnamon are also powerful antioxidants that are easy to incorporate into your daily diet, but be careful not to overdo it. Two tablespoons of cocoa powder a day is good. A teaspoon of ground cinnamon a day is good too. Grapeseed extract and lutein are available as capsules. There are other good antioxidant foods that you may like, but are a little rough, such as ginger and cloves. Coffee, tea, and red wine are also good. Carbon 60 is the smallest and most powerful antioxidant of all. Take the solubilized form made by Fuller Life C60 for maximum activity and benefit. The idea is to incorporate a little of each into your daily diet in order to get enough antioxidants. If you have inflammation of your ankles, arms or face, you likely need more antioxidants. If you like to analyze your diet, look up the ORAC value of the foods you eat. It stands for Oxidation Radical Absorbance Capacity and is a measure of the amount of free radicals that a material can neutralize, which is what antioxidants do.

h. Milk Thistle Oil and Powder – reported to detoxify the liver.

9. There are also some things to avoid in order to improve your blood glucose management. There is no evidence that

sleep improves blood glucose control, but a lack of adequate sleep will likely make it worse. Likewise, stress is harmful. Alcohol in excess is also a stress on the liver to avoid.

When we put all the pieces together, it creates a complex and not so surprising picture. Exercise, fasting, good diet, eating less calories, losing weight if indicated, increased dietary fiber, antioxidants, keeping hydrated, getting adequate sleep and avoidance of stress. Those are all good things to do in any case. Why wait until we develop indications of being prediabetic? Start now.

Summarizing the Diabetes Scenario

1. **The path to diabetes**

    - Blood glucose is one of the most tightly controlled materials in the body, with very good reason. Too much glucose or too little have severe health consequences, so tight control is critical. Only about 4 grams of glucose are circulating in our blood at any one time. This is less than a teaspoonful.

    - Just about everything has an impact on blood glucose control, and blood glucose control has an impact on just about every system in the body. The body truly is a holism. When blood glucose control is out of balance, everything is out of balance and the consequences are manifest and extensive throughout the body. Adequate blood glucose control is critical to our vibrant, extended health.

    - High intake of sugars stresses the ability of the system to control glucose in the blood.

    - Failure to adequately control blood glucose results in high levels of glucose in the blood, further stressing the system.

    - Control progressively declines until the disease state is reached.

2. **The main factors in causing diabetes**

    - There is considerable scientific evidence that diabetes is caused by the confluence of three main factors over many years:

» Poor condition of the intestine, especially a compromised mucosal layer and a depleted, imbalanced bacterial population
» Chronic overeating, and high sugar consumption
» Lack of physical activity, especially challenging cardiovascular exercise.

3.　Diet and Diabetes

- Blood glucose control starts with the food we eat. When the systems are functioning properly, we can literally eat anything and process it efficiently and safely. But the stress we put on the system by chronic overeating and high sugar intake eventually degrade the ability of the system to adequately control blood glucose and we start on the path to diabetes
- Limit the amount of sugar
- Increase consumption of complex carbohydrates and fiber
- Balance the amount of protein and fat in a meal
- Select a combination of foods in a meal to minimize blood glucose spikes
- Select a combination of meals to create a diet that controls calories and nutrients
- Be aware of the long-term accumulated impact of what we eat
- Fast fourteen hours, three to five days a week (eat two meals a day)
- Fast twenty-two hours, once a week (eat one meal a day).

4.　Exercise intensely to exhaustion 3 times a week

5.　Add **Good Stuff** to Your Life

» Antioxidants (Carbon 60, curcumin, cocoa, cinnamon, whole grains)
» Vitamin D3 (6000 IU twice a day)
» Vinegar (20 ml once or twice a day)

» Eat fermented foods such as yogurt, kefir, kombucha, and sauerkraut

I hope this scenario begins to point towards a solution to diabetes. We may not be able to reverse the disease state, but at a minimum we can take steps long before progressing there to avoid diabetes.

CHAPTER 9

Managing the Aging Process

We have considered many factors that contribute to aging and what we can do to slow, stop or even reverse these factors. The perspective we want to develop is that there is an opportunity to balance and optimize each one. Too little of one or too much of another is imbalance, resulting in a failure to optimize the benefits. Too much of something is often as harmful as too little. The optimal amount of each depends on many things, including the uniqueness of our own bodies, our activities, our attitude, our environment and many other criteria. Optimizing one factor is powerful. Optimizing many factors is life-changing. It is wrong to oversimplify, or prescribe based on the average, as most diet and self-help books do. It is risky to extrapolate from incomplete data and correlations to recommended practices and avoidance diets, as some experts do. We must learn about the factors, assess, and then based on our unique situation, do what is optimal for us.

To summarize the main points that we have discussed so far, here are some factors to consider in our quest for a longer, healthier, vibrant life:

Diet and Nutrition:

- Body weight management – what is the scale indicating? How much body fat do we have?
- Balancing carb intake with activity level
- Fasting for twelve to fourteen hours at least three days a week (this means eating two meals)
- Fasting twenty-two hours once a week (this means one meal that day)
- An extended 4-day fast twice a year
- Getting an optimal level of vitamins and minerals (not minimal to prevent disease, but sufficient to optimize health)
- Getting 50 grams a day of fiber every day
- Getting at least ½ gram a day of Beta Glucan every day
- Getting sufficient antioxidants to prevent inflammation

Exercise:

- Exercising to exhaustion to develop strength and endurance
- Exercising too little or too much (less than three days a week is too little and more than five days a week is likely too much unless you are a serious athlete)
- Allowing the body to recover in between sessions
- Constantly pushing to achieve higher levels – incrementally, slowly like the Canadian Air Force regimen
- Seeing the benefits, especially endurance and strength
- Exercising properly, good technique, good equipment, etc.
- When was the last time you ran?
- Physically capable of doing what we want to do
- Improving, staying the same or gradually losing strength and endurance
- If we stay on the path we are on now, where will we be physically in ten years, twenty years, or even fifty years?

Attitude:

- Attitude, mostly positive
- How often do we get into bad moods?
- When we get into a bad mood, how long do we stay there?
- How do we get out of a bad mood?
- How is our walking posture? Do we look at the ground most of the time or all around?
- When was the last time we skipped just for joy?
- Do we use essential oils to stimulate our parasympathetic nervous system?
- Do we feel stressed? What is our cortisol level?
- Do we get 'upset' when things go wrong? Does it help us or anyone else, when we get 'upset'? How is that working for us? It is a choice.
- Do we enjoy our life? Do we love our life? Do we love ourselves? If not, why not?

- Do we want to live another fifty years as we are now? What changes do we need to make?

Breathing:

- Practice deep, full lung breathing at least twice a day for a minute or more
- After deep breathing, do we feel more relaxed?

Hydration:

- We need water to live even more than food. Only air is more urgent. How much is enough? How much is optimal? I leave this to you to research - Homework!

Reflection, thinking

- Reflection is good as long as we don't get stuck in the past. The past was what it was, and we should enjoy it and reflect on it occasionally. After all, there are some great experiences there that we want to enjoy. Thinking is actually a skill that we can practice getting better at. We can benefit from some five-year-old questioning and wondering about it all. I enjoy asking Siri questions when one pops into my head. What is the normal body temperature of a vulture? And does its high body temperature allow it to eat dead stuff and not get sick? Hmm…
- The best question in the past used to be 'why?' This often led us to learning. Today, I suggest, the best question is 'why not?' The opportunities today are endless and overwhelming. We truly live in an age where the streets are paved with gold. The gold of opportunity, possibility – but only if we are open to it.

Reading

- What are we reading? It will impact our attitude and mood. I suggest a well-rounded range of topics to keep us thinking and on our toes.

- Go back and read or re-read some of the classics. Maybe my life experience has changed my perspective, allowing me to appreciate them more the second time. Some of my favorites include: *Frankenstein* by Mary Beth Shelly (the original – it is an elegant and intellectual story); *Moby Dick* by Herman Melville; *War and Peace* by Tolstoy; *anything* by Dostoevsky, Hemingway, Steinbeck.

- Are we reading what I call 'crazy' books that can expand our mind? I've referenced a few already, like *Lab Girl* by Hope Jahren[21], and *Living without Death* by James Strole and Bernadeane[1]. Here are a few more that are bound to bring about a mood change!: *Life* by Keith Richards[69]; *Honey from a Weed* by Patience Gray[70]; *Just Getting Started: Fifty years of living FOREVER, Insights on agelessness and immortality*[71] by James Strole and Bernadeane, with Joe Bardin; *Infinite Jest* by David Foster Wallace[72]; or *Shamanic Reiki: Expanded Ways of Working with Universal Life Force* by Llyn Roberts and Robert Levy[73].

Working

- Work is such an important part of our lives and our identity. Whether we are just starting out or retired, we need good work to do. The biggest mistake we make is looking for the perfect job or my favorite – "work that we enjoy". Good luck with that! Work is, after all, a four-letter word! There are no perfect jobs and even the best jobs and bosses have their bad moments. Flip it around! If we want to succeed, we need to enjoy the work we are doing instead of looking for work that we enjoy. We will be a lot happier and more likely to be successful instead of miserable. It is a choice! Once again, attitude is critical.

- The happiest people have work to do and do it well. Ever wonder why successful rich people keep working? It's not about the money. It's about the satisfaction from working hard and being successful. Success against a respectable challenge is a reward far more powerful and satisfying than money.

Dreaming

- Dreaming by its nature is forward looking and optimistic. If we want to extend our healthy lives, we need to keep dreaming, learning, planning and, of course, doing.

Sleep and Relaxation

- We all have different requirements for sleep. The key is to know your body and give it the sleep that it needs, when you can. And when we cannot, compensate by taking naps or resting when we can. The biggest mistake is to wait until the weekend, or until vacation to catch up. The best advice is to take care of ourselves every day.

- Relaxation doesn't have to mean sitting in a chair watching TV. It also doesn't have to mean lying in a beach chair all day. Sleep and relaxation are like required nutrients; our bodies don't have any ability to store excess today for use in the future. We must have the minimum daily requirement today or accept the consequences. And the optimal level is unique to our body and lifestyle.

Stem Cells

- Stem cells – Not yet approved by FDA, this new technology is being practiced with reportedly excellent results for many diseases and ailments. The concept is simple: harvest your own stem cells from belly fat (we all have plenty of that), grow them to increase the number, inject them into the body where repair is needed and finally, store them for future use. The cells that are harvested and stored now are going to be younger and more active than the cells in our body will be in ten years when we may need them for some issue, so it is prudent to act now, even if we don't need the treatment now.

Other Stuff

- There is an awful lot of other stuff out there to consider regarding life extension and health that is beyond the scope of this book, or perhaps any book. Technology is advancing rapidly, and even more impactful discoveries will be made soon. We will need to observe, experiment and learn how to use what is available in order to extend our healthy, vibrant life.

Those who dream with their eyes open are dangerous people, as they work in the daylight to make their dreams come true.
-Alexander Pope

Attitude

I started this book talking about the importance of attitude, and now I am going to end the book on that subject. Attitude is extremely important in extending our healthy lives. A vision of what we hope to achieve is the basis of our attitude. If I can visualize living for another fifty years or even one hundred years, and keep that vision in mind every day, it will change my attitude about today and how I behave. Knowing that I have a future, changes how I act today. That is worth repeating – I have a future! And because I have a future, I will take on bigger and more adventurous projects, perhaps even ones that will take many years to accomplish. Good! I will think about taking extreme care of myself today and every day so that I will be healthy and vibrant into that future. Good! I will look differently at how I spend my time today, perhaps more focused on achieving some goal, but also including some time to enjoy life. Good! It will likely change the way I plan my life. What is meaningful activity? What is wasting time? Am I learning? Am I reading and expanding my horizons? The answers to these questions will change dramatically if I have a future vision in mind to guide me. All good!

The great French Marshall, Louis-Hubert-Gonzalve Lyautey walked thru his garden one morning with his gardener. He stopped at a certain point and asked the gardener to plant a tree there the next morning. The gardener said, "But the tree will not mature for one hundred years". The Marshall replied, "In that case you had better plant it this afternoon."

-John F. Kennedy

The point is that there is no time to lose. Let's use our time wisely and not waste it on frivolous or useless activities. Let's take time to build, develop, contribute, support and nurture our life force in order to enjoy and love life more fully. The world is a beautiful place, if we take time to discover and see the beauty. While I was writing this, outside my window were two cardinals sitting on a branch next to each other. It was springtime, so the birds were courting and building nests. The male cardinal flew down into the grass and picked up something, returned to his mate and transferred whatever gift he had found from his beak into hers. Life is so beautiful. Let's take time to notice and appreciate it.

Whatever you can do or dream you can, begin it.
Boldness has genius, power and magic in it!

-Goethe

The Final Word

I've tried to hit the most impactful topics, but a lot depends on us. We are all different and what is impactful for you may be different. Extending our healthy lives will take learning and experimenting. Make it a goal to change or learn one little thing every week. It could be a new exercise, a new ingredient we use in our diet, a new Yoga pose, a new friend, or catching up with an old one. We are pushing the envelope as we move into the unexplored and uncharted territory of healthy life extension. We are, in many ways, the modern version of explorers, embarking on an unpredictable journey of adventure and discovery. Our lives are literally at stake. The world could be flat, and we might fall off the edge, like some experts have warned us. Or maybe they are wrong, and the world is round, and we will find a new world of opportunity on the other side of the seemingly endless ocean of obstacles. Who knows what possibilities we will find on the other side of the horizon? A journey of one thousand miles begins with a single step. Let's take that first step, then go on to discover the many steps we can take to live a healthy, vibrant life, for as long as we dare!

Appendix 1:

Recipe – Special Salad Meal
1/11/15 Len Heflich

Who says that you cannot eat a salad for dinner?

Well, here is a salad that will fill you up and satisfy you as well as provide some great nutrition, flavor and texture. You will enjoy eating this as a meal.

Special Salad Meal	
Ingredients:	
30 grams (1 cup)	Arugula or other salad
110 grams (1/2 fruit)	Avocado
3 grams (1/2 teaspoon)	Cinnamon Ground
3 grams (1/2 teaspoon)	Ginger ground
10 grams (2 tablespoons)	Pine Nuts
25 grams (3 tablespoons)	Almonds (diced)
25 grams (3 tablespoons)	Sunflower seeds
30 grams (2 tablespoons)	Walnut Oil
100 grams (1/2 cup)	Papaya (cubed)
25 grams (2 tablespoons)	Pomegranate seeds
40 grams (3 tablespoons)	Balsamic vinegar
401 grams TOTAL	

Preparation:

- Place the arugula or salad greens in a large bowl.

- Add the avocado, cinnamon powder, ground ginger, chia seeds, pine nuts, sunflower seeds, sliced almonds, Papaya, Pomegranate seeds and then drizzle the walnut oil and balsamic vinegar over the top. If you cannot get papaya, you may substitute mango (available frozen), watermelon, bananas, cantaloupe or blueberries. You can be creative based on availability and season.

- Check that the sunflower seeds, pine nuts and almonds are not rancid. Rancidity is easy to detect – just open the bottle or bag and take a quick sniff. If it smells like paint, it is rancid. Store the nuts and sunflower seeds in the freezer to make sure.

- I like to cut across the salad to reduce the size of the arugula and to mix in all the ingredients.
- It's fast, it will fill you up, it doesn't heat up the kitchen and it is very nutritious.
- Ready!

Nutritional Profile – Special Salad:

	Weight (grams)	Calories	Protein (grams)	Total Fat (grams)	Saturated Fat (grams)	Omega-3 (grams)	Cholesterol (mg)	Total Carbs (grams)	Sugar (grams)	Fiber (grams)	Sodium (mg)	ORAC (umol TE)
Totals	401	924	15.2	78.6	7.7	3.3	0	51.3	19.0	19.3	38.2	14,513

Summary: this recipe is high in protein, good fats, omega-3 fats, fiber and antioxidants (ORAC). It is low in cholesterol and sodium. At 401 grams total weight, it will fill you up and it tastes great. Can you believe it – this recipe contains almost 20 grams of fiber? It's a great start towards reaching the goal of 50 grams of fiber per day. Your microbiome will love you!

January 11, 2015 L. Heflich

Appendix 2:

A few comments are appropriate and necessary about this list. First, it is taken directly from the USDA Database, so not every food is represented, only the most common. For example, foods and ingredients like psyllium husk and polydextrose are not on the list, and are useful in your diet, as these are 90% fiber, higher than any other food. Second, many of the foods that are highest in fiber are spices. These are good to use and incorporate into a diet for flavor, fiber and antioxidants, but since we cannot tolerate high amounts of these, individually, they cannot be significant contributors of fiber. However, a little of several spices, used in different meals, adds up.

DIETARY FIBER CONTENT OF POPULAR FOODS AND INGREDIENTS

USDA NUTRITION DATABASE

		WATER PER 100 GM	KCAL PER 100 GM	PROTEIN PER 100 GM	FAT PER 100 GM	CARBOHYDRATE PER 100 GM	DIETARY FIBER PER 100 GM
1	CINNAMON, GROUND	10.58	247	3.99	1.24	80.59	53.1
2	CARAWAY SEED	9.87	333	19.77	14.59	49.9	38
3	CHIA SEEDS, DRIED	6.3	490	15.6	30.8	40.54	37.7
4	PAPRIKA POWDER	11.24	282	14.14	12.89	53.99	34.9
5	CHILI POWDER	10.75	282	13.46	14.28	49.7	34.8
6	CLOVES, GROUND	9.87	274	5.97	13	65.53	33.9
7	FENUGREEK SEED	8.84	323	23	6.41	58.35	24.6
8	DILL SEED	7.7	305	15.98	14.54	55.17	21.1
9	TURMERIC, GROUND	11.36	354	7.83	9.88	64.93	21.1
10	POPPY SEED	5.95	525	17.99	41.56	28.13	19.5
11	PISTACHIO NUTS, DRY ROASTED, W/SALT	4.5	446	18.55	19.4	53.75	18.4
12	BUCKWHEAT FLOUR, WHOLE-GROAT	9	342	12.29	1.33	75.87	18.3
13	CAROB FLOUR	11.53	364	19.3	6.04	60.65	17.4
14	ARROWROOT FLOUR	9.44	354	12.48	2.3	73.48	17.3
15	PEANUT BUTTER, SMOOTH STYLE, W/ SALT	7.8	327	52.2	0.55	34.7	15.8
16	BARLEY, HULLED	10.09	352	9.91	1.16	77.72	15.6
17	OAT BRAN, RAW	6.5	246	17.3	7	66.2	15.4
18	MILLET, COOKED	6.55	246	17.3	7.03	66.22	15.4
19	ONION POWDER	5.39	341	10.41	1.04	79.12	15.2
20	GINGER, GROUND	9.94	335	8.98	4.24	71.62	14.1
21	SESAME SEEDS, WHOLE, DRIED	3.3	565	16.96	48	25.74	14
22	PALM HEARTS, RAW	3.1	344	10.9	2.1	82.4	14
23	WHEAT BRAN, CRUDE	11.12	360	23.15	9.72	51.8	13.2

24	SORGHUM FLOUR	12.42	332	9.61	1.95	74.48	13.1
25	BEANS, NAVY, MATURE SEEDS, CANNED	10.06	343	20.96	1.13	64.19	12.7
26	WHOLE WHEAT FLOUR, HARD WHITE, WHOLE GRAIN	10.42	340	10.69	1.99	75.36	12.7
27	MUSTARD SEED, GROUND	5.27	508	26.08	36.24	28.09	12.2
28	TRITICALE FLOUR, WHOLE GRAIN	12.76	329	15.4	1.92	68.03	12.2
29	RYE FLOUR, DARK	10.97	349	10.88	1.52	75.43	11.8
30	CHESTNUTS, EUROPEAN, RAW, PEELED	9.45	374	6.39	4.45	77.31	11.7
31	SUNFLOWER SEEDS, DRIED	1.2	582	19.33	49.8	24.07	11.1
32	NUTS, HAZELNUTS OR FILBERTS	5.79	629	13.7	61.15	17	11
33	BEANS, FAVA, IN POD, RAW	73.32	93	5.6	2.12	17.31	11
34	TOFU, SALTED & FERMENTED (FUYU)	8.43	347	24.33	1.31	61.91	11
35	RICE FLOUR, BROWN, WHOLE GRAIN	10	357	7.46	2.08	79.26	11
36	NUTS, PINE NUTS, DRIED	5.9	629	11.57	60.98	19.3	10.7
37	WHEAT GERM, CRUDE	10.74	340	13.21	2.5	71.97	10.7
38	KAMUT, COOKED	11.02	338	14.57	2.43	70.19	10.7
39	ORANGE PEEL, RAW	72.5	97	1.5	0.2	25	10.6
40	ALMONDS, DRY ROASTED, W/ SALT	2.8	607	21.23	55.17	17.68	10.5
41	BEANS, NAVY, MATURE SEEDS, RAW	63.81	140	8.23	0.62	26.05	10.5
42	BEANS, CRANBERRY (ROMAN), MATURE SEEDS, RAW	64.65	136	9.34	0.46	24.46	10
43	BARLEY, PEARLED, COOKED	9.75	343	13.25	3.4	71.5	10
44	GRAPE LEAVES, RAW	76.1	69	4.27	1.97	11.71	9.9
45	TEMPEH	5.16	436	34.54	20.65	35.19	9.6
46	PEANUTS, ALL TYPES, DRY-ROASTED, W/SALT	6.39	570	26.15	49.6	15.82	9.5
47	PECANS	1.12	710	9.5	74.27	13.55	9.4
48	COCONUT MEAT, RAW	47	354	3.3	33.5	15.2	9
49	MACADAMIA NUTS, DRY ROASTED, W/SALT	1.75	594	17.3	51.45	25.35	9
50	BEANS, PINTO, MATURE SEEDS, RAW	62.95	143	9.01	0.65	26.22	9

51	CORN, HOMINY, CANNED, WHITE	8.67	378	11.02	4.22	72.85	8.5
52	CORN, WHITE	10.83	364	8.75	5.09	73.89	8.4
53	DATES, DEGLET NOOR	20.53	282	2.45	0.39	75.03	8
54	SPELT, COOKED	8.82	367	13.3	2.38	73.13	8
55	MILLET, PUFFED	3.4	380	10	3	78	8
56	APRICOTS, DRIED, SULFURED	30.89	241	3.39	0.51	62.64	7.3
57	BULGUR, COOKED	10.37	365	9.42	4.74	74.26	7.3
58	CORN BRAN, CRUDE	10.91	361	6.93	3.86	76.85	7.3
59	PLUMS, DRIED (PRUNES), UN-COOKED	30.92	240	2.18	0.38	63.88	7.1
60	BARLEY FLOUR OR MEAL	8.21	361	10.28	1.84	78.3	7.1
61	ELDERBERRIES, RAW	79.8	73	0.66	0.5	18.4	7
62	WHOLE WHEAT BREAD, COMMERCIAL	38.6	247	12.8	3.2	41.4	6.8
63	AVOCADOS, RAW, CALIFORNIA	72.33	167	1.96	15.41	8.64	6.8
64	FLAX SEED	2.03	574	29.84	49.05	14.71	6.5
65	KUMQUATS, RAW	80.85	71	1.88	0.86	15.9	6.5
66	RASPBERRIES, RAW	85.75	52	1.2	0.65	11.94	6.5
67	TOMATOES, SUN-DRIED	53.83	213	5.06	14.08	23.33	5.8
68	CRANBERRIES, DRIED, SWEETEND	16	308	0.07	1.37	82.36	5.7
69	ARTICHOKES (GLOBE OR FRENCH), RAW	84.94	47	3.27	0.15	10.51	5.4
70	BLACKBERRIES, RAW	88.15	43	1.39	0.49	9.61	5.3
71	LETTUCE, GREEN LEAF, RAW	79.1	74	2.6	0.1	17.23	4.9
72	CURRANTS, RED & WHITE, RAW	83.95	56	1.4	0.2	13.8	4.3
73	GOOSEBERRIES, RAW	87.87	44	0.88	0.58	10.18	4.3
74	TOMATO JUICE, CANNED, W/SALT	73.5	82	4.32	0.47	18.91	4.1
75	POMEGRANATE, RAW SEEDS	77.93	83	1.67	1.17	18.7	4
76	COLLARDS, RAW	90.18	33	2.71	0.72	5.65	4
77	CHICORY, WITLOOF, RAW	92	23	1.7	0.3	4.7	4
78	RAISINS, GOLDEN SEEDLESS	14.97	302	3.39	0.46	79.52	4
79	MUSTARD, PREPARED, YELLOW	82.65	67	4.37	4.01	5.33	3.3
80	BROCCOLI, RAW	89.25	35	2.38	0.41	7.18	3.3

81	SWEET POTATO, RAW, UNPREP	75.78	90	2.01	0.15	20.71	3.3
82	OLIVES, RIPE, CANNED (SMALL-EXTRA LRG)	79.99	115	0.84	10.68	6.26	3.2
83	PEARS, RAW	83.96	57	0.36	0.14	15.23	3.1
84	CARROTS, RAW	90.17	35	0.76	0.18	8.22	3
85	ARUGULA, RAW	90.35	35	0.64	0.13	8.24	2.9
86	FIGS, RAW	79.11	74	0.75	0.3	19.18	2.9
87	DANDELION GREENS, RAW	89.8	33	2	0.6	6.4	2.9
88	BEET GREENS, RAW	89.13	27	2.57	0.2	5.46	2.9
89	PUMPKIN, BOILED, DRAINED	89.97	34	1.1	0.28	8.09	2.9
90	WATERCRESS, RAW	96.1	13	0.4	0.2	3	2.9
91	COLLARDS, BOILED, DRAINED, WO/SALT	91.8	26	2.1	0.4	4.9	2.8
92	BROCCOLI RAAB, RAW	91.41	33	3.83	0.52	3.12	2.8
93	CABBAGE, SAVOY, RAW	92	24	1.8	0.09	5.41	2.8
94	RICE, WHITE, SHORT-GRAIN	10.46	370	6.81	0.55	81.68	2.8
95	WHEAT FLOUR, WHITE, ALL-PUR-POSE, ENRICHED, BLEACHED	11.9	364	10.3	1	76.3	2.7
96	CORN, SWEET, YELLOW, RAW	76	86	3.2	1.2	19	2.7
97	BANANAS, RAW	74.91	89	1.09	0.33	22.84	2.6
98	CABBAGE, RED, RAW	90.84	29	1.51	0.09	6.94	2.6
99	BRUSSELS SPROUTS, RAW	88.9	36	2.55	0.5	7.1	2.6
100	OAT BRAN, COOKED	84	40	3.21	0.86	11.44	2.6
101	EGGPLANT, RAW	89.67	35	0.83	0.23	8.73	2.5
102	SPINACH, RAW	91.21	23	2.97	0.26	3.75	2.4
103	ORANGES, RAW, ALL COMM VAR	86.75	47	0.94	0.12	11.75	2.4
104	APPLES, RAW, WITH SKIN	85.56	52	0.26	0.17	13.81	2.4
105	CAULIFLOWER, RAW	93	23	1.84	0.45	4.11	2.3
106	WHITE BREAD, COMMERCIAL	36.7	267	8.2	3.5	50	2.2
107	CHARD, SWISS, RAW	92.65	20	1.88	0.08	4.13	2.1
108	LETTUCE, BUTTERHEAD (INCL BOSTON & BIBB TYPES), RAW	94.61	17	1.23	0.3	3.29	2.1
109	ASPARAGUS, RAW	93.22	20	2.2	0.12	3.88	2.1
110	KALE, RAW	91.2	28	1.9	0.4	5.63	2

111	BEETS, RAW	87.06	44	1.68	0.18	9.96	2
112	STRAWBERRIES, RAW	90.95	32	0.67	0.3	7.68	2
113	APRICOTS, RAW	86.35	48	1.4	0.39	11.12	2
114	PAPAYAS, RAW	88.06	43	0.47	0.26	10.82	1.7
115	MANGOS, RAW	83.46	60	0.82	0.38	14.98	1.6
116	PEACHES, RAW	88.87	39	0.91	0.25	9.54	1.5
117	ONIONS, RAW	87.86	44	1.36	0.19	10.15	1.4
118	TOMATOES, RED, RIPE, RAW, YEAR- ROUND AVERAGE	94.34	18	0.95	0.11	4.01	1.2
119	KALE, SCOTCH, RAW	91.2	28	1.9	0.41	5.63	1.2
120	CELERIAC, RAW	92.3	27	0.96	0.19	5.9	1.2
121	GOURD, WHITE-FLOWERED (CALABASH), RAW	95.32	15	0.6	0.02	3.69	1.2
122	LETTUCE, COS OR ROMAINE, RAW	95.64	14	0.9	0.14	2.97	1.2
123	TOMATOES, GREEN, RAW	94.52	18	0.88	0.2	3.89	1.2
124	PEPPERS, SWT, GREEN, RAW	91.87	28	0.92	0.2	6.7	1.2
125	RADICCHIO, RAW	92.73	21	2.71	0.4	3.11	1.1

Appendix 3:

This cookie makes it possible and healthy to snack. For me, being able to have an espresso and a cookie after dinner is part of making a diet sustainable.

The ingredients in this cookie contain only traces of sugar, except for the chocolate chips. Even an eighty-five percent cocoa chocolate contains about fifteen percent sugar. I only know one place to buy them online and they are expensive! Semi-sweet chips contain sixty percent cocoa and almost forty percent sugar. These cookies when made with the eighty five percent cocoa chips contain about 4 grams of sugar per one-ounce cookie. And since the formula has about 10 grams of fat per cookie, the rate of absorption of glucose into the bloodstream will be moderate, so you shouldn't see a big glucose spike after eating one of these. If you used the more popular semi-sweet chocolate chips, which are sixty percent cocoa, the sugar would go up to 6.5 grams per cookie. Not so bad. Quantity matters, when it comes to calories and blood glucose, so one cookie is good, two is pushing it and more is a problem!

If you want to reduce the sugar further, reduce or take out the chocolate chips. A good option is to replace the chocolate chips with sunflower seeds or diced pecans. These add great texture, flavor, more fiber and good fat.

HI FIBER, LO SUGAR CHOCOLATE CHIP COOKIES, LALAYD 2020

THE BIOME BAKERY™ DECEMBER 5, 2019

INGREDIENT	PERCENT	GRAMS	ENGLISH	FIBER PER 100 GRAMS	FIBER PER 28 GRAM COOKIE
WHOLE WHEAT FLOUR	28.0	174	1 ½ CUPS	3.6	1.1
WHOLE EGGS	8.8	55	1 LARGE EGG		
BUTTER, SALTED	18.4	114	1 STICK		
BAKING SODA	0.6	4	2/3 TEASPOON		
MONKFRUIT JUICE CONC.	2.0	12	1 TABLESPOON		
DEXTROSE	2.0	12	1 TABLESPOON		
GLYCERINE	2.0	12	1 TABLESPOON		
COCOA POWDER SPECIAL DARK	4.5	28	4 TABLESPOONS	1.5	0.4
SUNFIBER™	9.0	56	1 CUP	7.7	2.3
PSYLLIUM GEL (1:10 IN WATER)	5.3	33	2 TABLESPOONS		
CHOCOLATE CHIPS SEMI SWEET	19.4	120	¾ CUP	3.1	0.9
TOTAL	100.0	620		16.3	4.9

PROCEDURE:

- BLEND FLOUR WITH COCOA POWDER AND BAKING SODA
- CREAM SOFTENED BUTTER (ROOM TEMP, NOT MELTED) WITH DEXTROSE AND SUNFIBER™
- ADD PSYLLIUM GEL, MONKFRUIT JUICE CONC. AND EGG AND MIX WELL – WILL BE ROUGH
- ADD FLOUR/COCOA/BAKING SODA AND MIX/KNEAD UNTIL SMOOTH
- FLATTEN WITH ROLLING PIN TO ¼ INCH, CUT 2.25 INCH ROUNDS WITH A CUP (30 GRAMS EACH)
- OR CUT INTO ANY SHAPE YOU LIKE!
- PLACE PIECES ONTO PARCHMENT PAPER ON A STEEL BAKING PAN
- BAKE 12 MINUTES AT 375 DEG F.
- MAKES 20 COOKIES (1 OUNCE EACH)

Nutritional Profile – Hi Fiber, Low Sugar Chocolate Chip Cookie

	Weight (grams)	Calories	Protein (grams)	Total Fat (grams)	Saturated Fat (grams)	Omega-3 (grams)	Cholesterol (mg)	Total Carbs (grams)	Sugar (grams)	Fiber (grams)	Sodium (mg)	ORAC (umol TE)
TOTALS 1 COOKIE	28	120	2	7	4	0	23	14	3	4	85	2535
TOTALS 2 COOKIES	56	230	4	15	9	0	46	29	6	9	170	5070

Optional: Remove the Chocolate Chips

Nutritional Profile – Hi Fiber, Low Sugar Chocolate Cookie

	Weight (grams)	Calories	Protein (grams)	Total Fat (grams)	Saturated Fat (grams)	Omega-3 (grams)	Cholesterol (mg)	Total Carbs (grams)	Sugar (grams)	Fiber (grams)	Sodium (mg)	ORAC (umol TE)
TOTALS 1 COOKIE	28	103	2	6	4	0	29	14	1	5	105	980
TOTALS 2 COOKIES	56	206	4	13	8	0	57	28	2	10	210	1960

Optional: Replace the Chocolate Chips with Sunflower Seeds

Nutritional Profile – Hi Fiber, Low Sugar Chocolate Sunflower Cookie

	Weight (grams)	Calories	Protein (grams)	Total Fat (grams)	Saturated Fat (grams)	Omega-3 (grams)	Cholesterol (mg)	Total Carbs (grams)	Sugar (grams)	Fiber (grams)	Sodium (mg)	ORAC (umol TE)
TOTALS 1 COOKIE	28	117	3	8	3	0	23	13	1	5	85	790
TOTALS 2 COOKIES	56	234	5	16	7	0	46	25	2	9	170	1580

Optional Substitutions:

1. You can leave out the chocolate chips and make a chocolate cookie. It is also quite good and satisfying. Look at what happens to the nutritional values! Sugar drops from 3 grams to 1 gram per cookie, while fiber increases from 4 to 5 grams per cookie. Two cookies now deliver 10 grams of fiber. Not a bad snack.

2. Replace the chocolate chips with sunflower seeds or diced pecans to drop the sugar and increase the fiber. This will also increase the fat and calories, but not so bad.

3. You can use several different flours instead of whole wheat flour. For example, you can use Whole Grain Rye flour instead. Or oat flour, teff flour, flax seed meal, even corn starch if you prefer. If the batter comes out too sticky, add two tablespoons of the flour you used and remix. Add more if necessary, until the batter is silky and easy to roll out. If the batter is too dry and stiff, add a tablespoon of water and remix. Repeat until the batter is silky smooth.

Appendix 4:

Oat Bran Cereal

April 25, 2017
L. Heflich

This is a good breakfast recipe, but it can be eaten anytime to get more fiber and antioxidants into your diet. It will raise your blood glucose due to the high-carb content, but you can moderate this by adding some fat. Butter works great and tastes good, but I also use flax oil or coconut oil.

Ingredients:	
340 grams (3 tablespoons)	Oat bran cereal
13 grams (1 tablespoon)	Chia seeds
7.4 grams (1 tablespoon)	Cocoa powder
6 grams (1 teaspoon)	Cinnamon powder
1 gram (1/3 teaspoon)	Ginger powder
0.25 grams (1 pinch)	Clove powder
45 ml (3 tablespoons)	Milk or half-and-half (optional - it really helps the texture)
15 grams (1 tablespoon)	Butter
225 ml (1 cup)	Water

Procedure:

- Sift cocoa powder, cinnamon powder, ginger powder, clove powder to remove lumps.
- Mix all dry ingredients together in a cereal bowl.
- You can use preheated hot water or cold water and microwave
- Add half the water, stir with a spoon until smooth.
- Add remaining water and stir until smooth.
- If you used cold water, microwave on high for 2 minutes, stir and microwave for another minute.
- Add oil or butter, and optional half-and-half and stir.

- Let it sit a few minutes and eat.

Nutritional Profile – Oat Bran Cereal

	Weight (grams)	Calories	Protein (grams)	Total Fat (grams)	Saturated Fat (grams)	Omega-3 (grams)	Cholesterol (mg)	Total Carbs (grams)	Sugar (grams)	Fiber (grams)	Sodium (mg)	ORAC (umol TE)
Totals	300	305	11	20	9	1.9	32	39	1	13	135	13,890

If you want to eliminate the cholesterol, use coconut oil instead of butter. The added fat helps to moderate the absorption of glucose into the bloodstream, reducing the impact of the carbs in this meal on blood glucose.

Appendix 5:

Kale and Eggplant Lasagna

April 25, 2017
L. Heflich

This is an easy and delicious way to get more fiber and antioxidants into your diet. I usually make a large baking dish of this recipe, and then after it cools, I cut it up into meal-sized pieces, refrigerate a couple to eat in the next few days and freeze the rest. It's a simple matter to reheat them in the microwave or oven when I need them.

Ingredients:

8 grams (2 cloves)	Garlic
300 grams (1 large)	White onion, diced
45 grams (4 tablespoons)	Olive oil
250 grams (1 medium)	Eggplant, cubed ½ inch
45 grams (3 tablespoons)	Sundried tomatoes in oil, drained
15 grams (2 tablespoons)	Turmeric powder
3 grams (1 teaspoon)	Ginger powder
800 gms (3 cups)	Tomato sauce
200 gms (1 bag! or 5 cups)	Baby kale (can be frozen)
60 grams (6 tablespoons)	Chia seeds
60 grams (6 tablespoons)	Parmesan cheese, grated
200 gms (7 ounces)	Cheese, sliced (mozzarella, Swiss, etc. all work well)
50 grams (5 tablespoons)	Wheat germ

Eggplant Filling:

- Sauté in a covered pot with olive oil, minced garlic, diced onion and cubed eggplant until tender.
- Add sundried tomatoes, turmeric and ginger and cook for another 10 minutes.

- Mash together to form a uniform paste (put it into a food processor to make a really smooth paste).

Layering the Ingredients:

- Spread half of the tomato sauce on the bottom of a large 10 X 15 inch glass baking dish.
- Sprinkle half of the chia seeds evenly on top of the tomato sauce.
- Place a layer of half of the kale leaves, breaking up the leaves into pieces no bigger than 2 inches, removing any thick stems (this is especially easy if the kale is frozen).
- Evenly spread the eggplant filling over the kale, smoothing it with a spoon.
- Spread the remaining tomato sauce on top of the eggplant filling layer.
- Sprinkle the remaining chia seeds evenly on top of the tomato sauce.
- Add another layer of the remaining kale leaves in the same manner as before.
- Place a layer of sliced cheese on top of the kale.
- Sprinkle evenly the grated parmesan cheese on top.
- Last, sprinkle the wheat germ evenly on top to keep the cheese on top from burning in the oven.

Bake:

Preheat oven to 350 Deg F

Bake for 1 hour

Serve:

Cut it up into squares, about 5 by 5 inches and place in bowls or covered containers. Serve immediately or refrigerate what you will eat within 48 hours, and freeze the rest.

Nutritional Profile – Kale Lasagna

	Weight (grams)	Calories	Protein (grams)	Total Fat (grams)	Saturated Fat (grams)	Omega-3 (grams)	Cholesterol (mg)	Total Carbs (grams)	Sugar (grams)	Fiber (grams)	Sodium (mg)	ORAC (umol TE)
Totals	339	384	17.5	23	17.5	1.8	35	31	4	10	225	7515

Appendix 6:

Morning Kickstart

I call this recipe my Kickstart because I take this in the morning on days when I am extending my fast until lunch. When I am fasting until lunch, the Kickstart helps me avoid eating. The Kickstart is high in fiber but is very low in sugar, which is what I want to avoid during my morning fast.

It contains fiber to feed the bacteria in the intestines, charcoal to absorb toxins in food to protect the good bacteria, and antioxidants to reduce inflammation. The oils will give you your daily requirement for linoleic and linolenic fatty acids, needed for a healthy gut. The L-Glutamine and psyllium feed and aid in developing the layer of bacteria in the intestinal wall. The charcoal powder absorbs toxins in the food to prevent damage to the good bacteria. Cinnamon and cocoa powder are high in dietary fiber and are also powerful antioxidants. Note that while beta glucan is one of the best dietary fibers for feeding beneficial bacteria, you shouldn't take more than a quarter gram per serving. That is too small to measure without an expensive analytical scale, but for 10 servings that's 2.5 grams or a teaspoon full.

You can make it by the serving, but I like to blend the dry ingredients in advance, enough to make 10 servings and mix it really well in a small container. Be careful to keep the lid tightly closed as it is dusty. It stores unrefrigerated and will keep for months. This way, when it's time to make the shake, I just spoon out what I need and don't have to measure all the ingredients each time.

Morning Kickstart Shake!		
For One Serving	**For 10 Servings**	**Ingredient**
1 tablespoon	10 tablespoons	Psyllium husk fiber, whole flake
1/2 teaspoon	5 tablespoons	Cocoa powder
1 tablespoon	10 tablespoons	L-Glutamine (optional)
1/3 teaspoon	3 tablespoons	Charcoal powder (optional)
1/3 teaspoon	3 tablespoons	Cinnamon powder (optional)
1/10 teaspoon	1 teaspoon	Beta glucan fiber (optional)

When you are ready to make the shake, take a glass of water (12 ounces), add two tablespoons of sour cream or unsweetened yogurt to improve the flavor and consistency. Stir in the dry ingredients. If you made the 10-serving mix, then you would need to add up what you put into it and divide by ten to get a single serving amount. You can use a blender or just mix it with a spoon. Then, while blending or stirring it, I dribble in a tablespoon of grape seed oil and a teaspoon of flax seed oil. Drink this every morning and your intestines will send you a message – hopefully a happy one!

When I need to lose a few pounds, or compensate for a few meals where I let myself go, I will fast until lunch time and then take the Kickstart for my lunch. This way, I can go until dinner time without taking in any substantial calories and no carbs. It's a great way to get back on track after a little binge, as the fiber and antioxidants are high, and the sugar and calories are very low.

Appendix 7:

101 changes that we can make to improve our health and longevity:

I bet you can think of 100 more!

1. Stretch in the shower
2. Vigorous drying after shower
3. Stretch while sitting at a meeting
4. Eat a banana a day
5. Take Vitamin D
6. Curcumin
7. Take C-60 solubilized form (FULLER LIFE C60)
8. Magnesium threonate (most absorbable form of Mg)
9. Fiber to 50 g daily
10. Daily multivitamin
11. Time Release Vitamin C
12. Melatonin before bed
13. Take a nicotinamide (NAD) booster for more energy (Nuchido™ is the best!)
14. Fish oil
15. Collagen
16. Beta glucan
17. Linolenic and linoleic acids
18. Lions mane mushroom powder tea
19. Coffee (good antioxidant)
20. Learn a new Tai Chi move
21. Learn a new Yoga pose
22. Learn a new Chi Gong position
23. Do sit-ups
24. Do pushups

25. Hot tub or sauna daily
26. Reduce sugar in diet
27. Test your blood glucose often and know your body
28. Sun exposure 3X per week for 5 minutes (without sunscreen)
29. Skip for joy!
30. Go to level II skipping (sideways)
31. Run
32. Climb stairs
33. Listen to music
34. Meditate
35. Jump rope (even without a rope!)
36. Jump on a little exercise trampoline
37. Go to the gym and start out real slow
38. Get a massage once a month
39. Myofascial therapy at least monthly
40. Find a chiropractor you like and go monthly
41. Call an old friend
42. Hug a friend (please note that you cannot give a hug without getting one!)
43. Tell someone that you love them
44. Count your blessings
45. Say thank you
46. Envision 50 years from now
47. Create something
48. Plant a tree or bush
49. Plant a garden
50. Exercise to exhaustion 3X each week
51. Plan a trip to anywhere
52. Make a one-year to-do list
53. Review your long-term to-do list and make a list for today and get it done!

54. Reward yourself when you complete something
55. Take a Coursera on anything
56. Work on a hobby
57. Learn a word in a foreign language
58. Learn an instrument
59. Teach
60. Do something a little daring
61. ASK: "What is there that I cannot do, but if I could, would it change everything?"
62. Organize something (socks!)
63. Instead of asking 'why', ask 'why not'!
64. Give someone a gift
65. Commit a senseless act of giving
66. Overtip for great service
67. Write about an experience
68. Travel someplace new
69. Try a new recipe
70. Go to a new restaurant
71. Go home a different way
72. Get lost on purpose and use your GPS to find your way home
73. Laugh
74. Have a party
75. Take a vigorous walk
76. If something hurts, ask why, then do something about it
77. Fast 14 hours, 5 X per week
78. Fast 22 hours, once a week
79. Fast 4 days, once or twice a year
80. Test your hormone levels, fix
81. Read a new book
82. Reread a classic
83. Play a game (nonviolent)

84. Open the Bible and read a random page
85. Read a new magazine
86. Watch the sun rise
87. Exercise your creativity
88. Oat bran cereal
89. Add cocoa to something
90. Add cinnamon to something
91. Eat an orange peel
92. Take Zinc Carnosine
93. Take L-Glutamic acid
94. Sing
95. Tell a joke
96. Read this book!
97. Give this book to a friend and tell them you want them to be here with you in 50 years
98. Take a trip (even a short one)
99. Write a poem
100. Make a small beneficial change at least once a week and make it part of your lifestyle
101. Smile and think a positive thought!

Appendix 8:

Recipe – Vegetarian Pate (Faux Chicken Liver à la Julia Childs)

This is a very tasty pate that can be eaten directly, on crackers, with whole wheat toast or as a dip. It's easy to make and has a great nutritional profile. At 5.3% fiber, it is about the same as plain beans, but tastes a lot better! The ginger gives it a pleasant, bright, slightly hot flavor. It tastes similar to the classic chicken liver pate (à la Julia Childs) it is meant to replace! But contains no animal products.

Ingredients:	
Chia seeds	10 grams (1 tbsp)
Water (warm)	55 grams (2 oz.)
Ginger Powder	5 grams (1/2 tbsp)
Pecans	25 grams (1/4 cup)
Sundried tomatoes	25 grams (1/8 cup)
Feta Cheese	40 grams (1/4 cup)
Black beans (canned)	40 grams (1/4 cup)
TOTAL 200 grams (1 cup)	

Note: this makes a 200-gram total batch.

My little food processor took a double or 400-gram batch to mix well.

Preparation:

- Soak the chia seeds in the warm water for at least 2 hours or overnight to form a nice gel.
- Add all the ingredients to a food processor and puree until creamy smooth.
- Done!
- Serve with crackers or lightly toasted whole wheat bread.

Nutritional Profile:

	Weight (grams)	Calories	Protein (grams)	Total Fat (grams)	Saturated Fat (grams)	Omega-3 (grams)	Cholesterol (mg)	Total Carbs (grams)	Sugar (grams)	Fiber (grams)	Sodium (mg)	ORAC (umol TE)
Veggie Pate (see recipe)	100	220	7	17	1.1	1	0	12	0.6	5.3	1.5	4,600
Crackers (6 Triscuits or slice of whole wheat bread toasted)	30	100	3	1	0	0	0	15	1.5	2.3	140	350
Red wine (1 cup)	246	205	0	0	0	0	0	7	2	0	10	11,126
Total	376	525	10	18	1.1	1	0	34	2.3	7.6	152	16,076

Summary: this recipe is high in protein, good fats, omega-3 fats, fiber and ORAC. It is low in saturated fat, cholesterol, and sugar. Note: you don't have to consume 200 grams of the pate at one time. It makes a great dip appetizer. 100 grams per serving is plenty.

Dec. 17, 2014 L. Heflich

References:

1 Jim Strole and Bernadeane, Living Without Death: The Experience of Physical Immortality, (Scottsdale, AZ: People Unlimited Inc., 1999)

2 Dr. Abdul Wahab Pathath, "Theories of Aging", The International Journal of Indian Psychology, Vol. 4(3), April-June, 2017, pages 15-22

3 Ernest Becker, The Denial of Death, (New York: The Free Press, 1973)

4 Mary Ann Bakerji, Milay Luis Lam, and Rochelle Chaiken, "Insulin Resistance and the Metabolic Syndrome", Chapter 37, in Leonid Poretsky, Principles of Diabetes Mellitus, Third Edition, (Cham, Switzerland: Springer International Publishing AG, 2017)

5 Collins, Jim and Porras, Jerry I, Built to Last: Successful Habits of Visionary Companies, (New York: HarperCollins Publishers, October 26, 1994)

6 Eckhart Tolle, The Power of Now: A Guide to Spiritual Enlightenment, (Novato, California: New World Library, 1997)

7 Dr. Stuart Brown, Play: How It Shapes the Brain, Opens the Imagination, and Invigorates the Soul, (New York: The Penguin Group, 2010)

8 Leonard W. Heflich, Balanced Leadership: A Pragmatic Guide for Leading, (Bloomington, Indiana: iUniverse Publishers, June, 2018)

9 Rachel Brazil, "Nocebo: the placebo effect's evil twin", The Pharmaceutical Journal, March 15, 2018, pages 1-11

10 Launa Colloca, "Nocebo effects can make you feel pain", Science, Vol 358, Issue 6359, October 6, 2017, Page 44

11 Bob Monroe Associates, Hemi-Sync by Monroe Products, Lovingston, VA 22949, www.hemi-sync.com

12 Dr. Thomas Cowan, Human Heart, Cosmic Heart, (White River Junction, Vermont: Chelsea Green Publishing, 2016)

13 "How Elements are Formed", The Science Learning Hub, www.sciencelearn.org.nz

14 Carlo Rovelli, The Order of Time, (New York: Riverhead Books, 2017)

15 Otto Siegel, Ph.D., personal communication, www.geniuscoaching.com

16 Tim Ferriss, Tools of Titans: The Tactics, Routines, and Habits of Billionaires, Icons, and World-Class Performers, (Boston: Houghton Mifflin Harcourt, December 6, 2016)

17 Valerie Ann Worwood, The Complete Book of Essential Oils and Aromatherapy, (Novato, California: New World Library, 2016)

18 Robert M. Pirsig, Zen and the Art of Motorcycle Maintenance: An Inquiry into Values, (New York: William Morrow and Company, 1974)

19 Astrid Kolderup and Birger Svihus, "Fructose Metabolism and Relation to Atherosclerosis, Type 2 Diabetes, and Obesity", Journal of Nutrition and Metabolism, Vol 2015, Article ID 823081, June 7, 2015

20 Peter J. Havel, DVM, PhD, "Dietary Fructose: Implications for Dysregulation of Energy Homeostasis and Lipid/Carbohydrate Metabolism", Nutrition Reviews, Vol. 63(5), May 2005, pages 133-157

21 Hope Jahren, Lab Girl, (New York: Alfred A. Knopf, 2016)

22 Scott M. Grundy, "Overnutrition, ectopic lipid and the metabolic syndrome", J of Investig Medicine, Vol. 64, 2016, pages 1082-1086

23 D. El Khoury, C. Cuda, B.L. Luhjovyy, and G.H. Anderson, "Beta Glucan: Health Benefits in Obesity and Metabolic Syndrome, A Review", Journal of Nutrition and Metabolism, Vo. 2012, Article ID 851362, 2012, pages 1-28

24 JM Keenan, JJ Pins, C Frazel, A Moran, and L Turnquist, "Oat ingestion reduces systolic and diastolic blood pressure in patients with mild or borderline hypertension: a pilot trial", The Journal of Family Practice, Vol 51(4), April 1, 2002, page 369

25 D. Gentilcore, R. Chaikomin, KL Jones, A. Russo, C. Feinle-Bisset, JM Wishart, CK Rayner, and M. Horowitz, "Effects of fat on gastric emptying of and the glycemic, insulin, and incretin responses to a carbohydrate meal in type 2 diabetes", The Journal of Clinical Endocrinology and Metabolism, Vol. 91, 2006, pages 2062-7

26 Felipe De Vadder, Petia Kovatcheva-Datchary, Daisy Goncalves, Jennifer Vinera, Carine Zitoun, Adeline Duchampt, Frederik Bäckhed and Gilles Mithieux, "Microbiota-Generated Metabolites Promote Metabolic Benefits via Gut-Brain Neural Circuits", Cell, Vol 156, January 16, 2014, pages 84-96

27 Paul Stamets, Growing Gourmet and Medicinal Mushrooms, Ten Speed

Press, Berkeley, 2000

28 Manu S. Goyal, Siddarth Venkatesh, Jeffrey Milbrandt, Jeffrey I. Gordon, and Marcus E. Raichle, "Feeding the brain and nurturing the mind: Linking nutrition and the gut microbiota to brain development", PNAS, Vol 112(46), Oct. 6, 2015, pages 14105-14112

29 Megan W. Bourassa, Ishraq Alim, Scott J. Bultman and Rajiv R. Rutan, "Butyrate, neuroepigenetics and the gut microbiome: Can a high fiber diet improve brain health?", Neuroscience Letters, Vol. 625, 2016, pages 56-63

30 T.S. Dharmarajan, "Psyllium versus Guar Gum: Facts and Comparisons", Practical Gastroenterology, February 2005, pages 72-76

31 RRWJ van der Hulst MD, MF von Meyenfeldt MD, NEP Deutz MD, PB Soeters MD, RJM Brummer MD, BK von Kreel PhD, and JW Arends MD, "Glutamine and the Preservation of Gut Integrity", The Lancet 341: Issue 8857, pages 1363-1365, May 1993

32 Toshikazu Yoshikawa, Tomoyuki Yoneda, Yashiro Nishimura, "Inflammatory Bowel Disease Preventive and Curative Agent Containing Zinc L-carnosine Salt as Active Ingredient", United States Patent 5,238,931, August 24, 1993

33 A. Mahmood, AJ Fitzgerald, T Marchbank, et. al, "Zinc Carnosine, a Health Food Supplement that Stabilizes Small Bowel Integrity and Stimulates Gut Repair Processes", Gut 2007: 56: 168-175

34 Steven R. Gundry, MD, The Plant Paradox: The Hidden Dangers in "Healthy" Foods That Cause Disease and Weight Gain, (New York: HarperCollins Publishers, 2017)

35 Mahesh S. Desai, Anna M. Seekatz, Nicole M. Koropatkin, Nobuhiko Kamada, Christina A. Hickey, Mathis Wolter, Nicholas A. Pudlo, Sho Kitamoto, Nicholas Terrapon, Arnaud Muller, Vincent B. Young, Bernard Henrissat, Paul Wilmes, Thaddeus S. Stappenbeck, Gabriel Nuñez, and Eric C. Martens, "A Dietary Fiber-Deprived Gut Microbiota Degrades the Colonic Mucous Barrier and Enhances Pathogen Susceptibility", Cell: 167, 2016, pages 1339-1353

36 Dr. Natasha Campbell McBride MD, MMedSci(neurology), MMedSci(nutrition), Gut and Psychology Syndrome: Natural Treatment for Autism, Dyspraxia, A.D.D., Dyslexia, Depression, Schizophrenia, (Cambridge, UK: Medinform Publishing, January 2017)

37 Mohamed Al-Saleh Ali, Barbera Corkey, Jude Deeney, Keith Tornheim and Ethan Bauer, "Effect of artificial sweeteners on insulin secretion, ROS, and oxygen consumption in pancreatic beta cells", FASEB Journal, Vol. 25, April 2011

38 Bianca Martins Gregório, Diogo Benchimol De Souza, Fernanda Amorim de Morais Nascimento, Leonardo Matta, and Caroline Fernandes-Santos, "The Potential Role of Antioxidants in Metabolic Syndrome", Current Pharmaceutical Design, Vol. 22(7), February 2016, pages 859-869

39 Sam Kean, Caesar's Last Breath: Decoding the Secrets of the Air Around Us, (New York: Little, Brown and Company, July 2017)

40 AS Naidu, Redox Life, Bio-Rep Media, 2013

41 N Halberg, M Henriksen, N Söderhamm, B Stallknecht, T Ploug, P Schjerling and F Dela, "Effect of intermittent fasting and refeeding on insulin action in healthy men", Journal of Applied Physiology, Vol. 99(6), December, 2005, pages 2128-2136

42 LK Heilbronn, SR Smith, CK Martin, SD Anton and E. Ravussin, "Alternate-day fasting in nonobese subjects: effects on body weight, body composition, and energy metabolism", American Journal of Clinical Nutrition, Vol. 81(1), January, 2005, pages 69-71

43 Michael L. Dansinger, Joi Augustin Gleason, John L. Griffith, Harry P. Selker, and Ernst J. Shaefer, "Comparison of the Atkins, Ornish, Weight Watchers, and Zone Diets for Weight Loss and Heart Disease Risk Reduction", Journal of the American Medical Association, Vol. 293, No. 1, January 5, 2005, Pages 43-53

44 Dean Ornish, MD, "Was Dr. Atkins Right?", Journal of the American Dietetic Association, Vol 104(4), April 2004, 2004, pages 537-542

45 Upton Sinclair, The Fasting Cure, The University Press, Cambridge, 1911

46 Jason Fung MD, The Complete Guide to Fasting: Heal Your Body Through Intermittent, Alternate-Day and Extended Fasting, Victory Belt Publishing, Las Vegas, 2016

47 Dr. Michael Gershon, The Second Brain: A Groundbreaking New Understanding of Nervous Disorders of the Stomach and Intestine, (New York: HarperCollins Publishers Inc., November 17, 1999)

48 Mazen Alsahli, Muhammad Z. Shrayyef and John E. Gerich, "Normal Glucose Homeostasis", Chapter 2, in Leonid Poretsky, Principles of Diabetes Mellitus, Third Edition, (Cham, Switzerland: Springer International Publishing AG, 2017)

49 Debora MacKenzie, The Hidden Cause of Disease, New Scientist, August 10, 2019, Pages 42-46

50 Carolyn Dean, M.D., N.D., The Magnesium Miracle: Discover the Missing Links to Total Health, Ballantine Books, New York, 2017

51 Romain Bouziathttp,Reinhard Hinterleitner, Judy J. Brown, Jennifer E. Stencel-Baerenwald, Mine Ikizler, Toufic Mayassi, Marlies Meisel, Sangman M. Kim, Valentina Discepolo, Andrea J. Pruijssers, Jordan D. Ernest, Jason A. Iskarpatyoti, Léa M. M. Costes, Ian Lawrence, Brad A. Palanski, Mukund Varma, Matthew A. Zurenski, Solomiia Khomandiak, Nicole McAllister, Pavithra Aravamudhan, Karl W. Boehme, Fengling Hu, Janneke N. Samsom, Hans-Christian Reinecker, Sonia S. Kupfer, Stefano Guandalini, Carol E. Semrad, Valérie Abadie, Chaitan Khosla, Luis B. Barreiro, Ramnik J. Xavier, Aylwin Ng, Terence S. Dermody, Bana Jabri; "Reovirus infection triggers inflammatory responses to dietary antigens and development of celiac disease"; Science, Volume 356, Issue 6333, April 7, 2017, pg. 44-50

52 S.P. Whelton A.D. Hyre, B. Pedersen, Y. Yi, P.K Whelton, J. He, "Effects of dietary fiber intake on blood pressure: a meta-analysis of randomized, controlled clinical trials", Journal of Hypertension, 23(3): pages 475-481, 2005

53 Paddy C. Dempsey, Neville Owen, Thomas E. Yates, Bronwyn A. Kingwell, and David W. Dunstan, "Sitting Less and Moving More: Improved Glycaemic Control for Type 2 Diabetes Prevention and Management", Current Diabetes Reports, Vol. 16, October 3, 2016, page 114

54 Al Sears, M.D., P.A.C.E.: The 12-Minute Fitness Revolution, (Royal Palm Beach, FL: Wellness Research and Consulting, 2010)

55 Jeffrey F. Life, M.D., Ph.D., The Life Plan: How Any Man Can Achieve Lasting Health, Great Sex, and a Stronger, Leaner Body, (New York: Atria Books, 2011)

56 Christopher McDougall, Born to Run: A Hidden Tribe, Superathletes, and the Greatest Race the World Has Never Seen, (New York: Alfred A. Knopf, 2009)

57 GBD 2015 Disease and Injury Incidence and Prevalence, Collaborators,

As I La

A REHOBOTH BEACH MEMOIR

As I Lay Frying
A REHOBOTH BEACH MEMOIR

By Fay Jacobs

A&M Books
2004

As I Lay Frying
A Rehoboth Beach Memoir
By Fay Jacobs

Copyright © 2004 by Fay Jacobs

Printed in the United States of America
First Edition

Cover Design by Murray Archibald
Printed by Dover Litho Printing Company
Dover, Delaware 19901

ISBN 0-9646648-6-0

To BJQ, you made it all possible
and Anyda & Muriel, an inspiration

Spring 2004

ACKNOWLEDGMENTS

Many people helped me get this project off the computer and onto the page. Thanks to Anyda and Muriel for having faith in me, coaxing me, then pushing me, and finally making the book a reality. Thanks, too, to Steve Elkins and Murray Archibald, without whom I wouldn't have written the first word in 1995, and without whom I wouldn't have corrected the last punctuation errors not too many weeks ago. They are my heroes for what they give to the community of Rehoboth Beach and for the enormous help and inspiration they have given me. My deep appreciation goes to my-son-the-actor Eric Peterson for his insight, perspective, cleverness, and willingness to spend entire weekends sifting through piles of my rantings. Many thanks to proofreader and reality checker Kathy Weir, the staff at Dover Litho, and my father, who taught me that even the worst event is not so awful if you can eventually tell a good story about it. And, special thanks to my *Letters* readers for being there.

A heartfelt thanks to you all.

Foreword
AS I LAY FRYING: A REHOBOTH BEACH MEMOIR

In the summer of 1996, I was adopted by a lesbian couple. That shouldn't be an unusual story; gays and lesbians are raising children all over the country these days. But my story was a little different because...well...I was 25 years old at the time.

At the time, I was making a living, pursuing an acting career on the side...and coming out of the closet. When I was ready to tell my friends Fay and Bonnie that I thought I might be a homosexual, they didn't miss a beat.

"What are you doing next weekend?" Fay asked.

"I don't have any plans," I responded.

"Yes, you do," Bonnie said. "You are coming to Rehoboth with us."

If you've ever been to Rehoboth Beach, Delaware you know why Fay and Bonnie brought me here. They love it. In 1995, they brought their 27-foot boat to Rehoboth for an eight-week stint. And in a very real sense, they never left.

Even before they eventually sold their boat, bought a condominium, and sold their Maryland residence to become year-round Rehoboth Beach residents, this place quickly became their home.

"Everyone's so nice," they kept saying. Which was why it was so surprising when a homophobic miscreant began shouting obscenities at them at a hamburger joint just outside town one day. Fay immediately fired off a letter to *Letters from CAMP Rehoboth*, a magazine for Rehoboth's large and diverse gay and lesbian community. The CAMP acronym stands for Create A More Positive Rehoboth, and that's just what the newsletter and its founding organization CAMP Rehoboth succeeds in doing.

The letter was printed, and after a subsequent conversation with *Letters* editor Steve Elkins, Fay began work on an essay about boating to Rehoboth. Steve and his readers liked the article, and Fay's been writing for *Letters* ever since.

What began so inauspiciously on that summer day in 1995 has become nothing short of a Rehoboth tradition. For years, Fay's been sharing her personal stories with the residents of Rehoboth Beach—she's been nearly run over by a cargo ship, hunted down by the AARP, and known to shuttle stray animals across state lines. She lived through a frightening (and serious) family medical crisis in 2000 and eloped to Canada in 2003... and of course, she and her partner "adopted" a 25-year old gay son (look for me in "What I Did on my Summer Vacation").

I'm so pleased that Fay asked me to prepare a forword for this, her first collection of columns. I can't pass up this opportunity to thank Fay and Bonnie for everything they've ever done for me—while my family of origin has turned out to be wonderfully supportive of me, I still owe Fay and Bonnie an emotional debt that I'll never be able to repay.

At the same time, on behalf of all of Fay's readers, I feel that I must extend my sincere and heartfelt gratitude to the idiot homophobe at that long-forgotten hamburger place, who inadvertently prompted her to put pen to paper, thus beginning a career that the faithful readers of *Letters from CAMP Rehoboth* (myself included) are richer for having experienced.

Finally, enjoy the book. I know that in its pages, Fay's long-time readers will find themselves reliving the events and literary adventures of their old friends, and those who are discovering them for the first time will grow to love my lesbian moms almost as much as I do.

Onward.

Eric C. Peterson
March 17, 2004

1995

Cruising to Rehoboth 1

1996

Just the Fax, Ma'am 4
Weekend Warriors 7
The Renters are Coming! The Renters are Coming! 10
A Separatist Beach Bum 13
Ham and Cheese at 30 Knots 16
Is it Hot in Here or Is It Me? 19
And You Must Be Bonnie 22
Dumbstruck 25
What I Did on My Summer Vacation 28
Truth Justice and the DeGeneres Way 31
Lady of Spain I Abhor You 35
Ram-a-Lam-a-Ding-Dong 39

1997

Three Dog Nights—Oy to the World 43
My Life as Ballast 48
Lord Help the Mister 52
Not Responsible for Soiled Clothing 55
Got a Pair of Dykes? 59
Don't Fog on my Parade 62
A Family Town for All Families 69
Fickle Finger of Fate 72

1998

Writer's Schlock 75
There's Life in the Old Boy Yet 79
I See London, I See France 82

As Old as Vinyl and Twice as Scratchy 86
It Was the Best of Boats, It Was the Worst of Boats 89
Happy Trails to Howdy Doody Time 93
The Well of Schmuckiness 96
Much Ado About Not So Much 99
Counting Blessings Instead of Sheep 102
Max 106

1999

No Grout About It 107
It's Geek to Me 110
Stop the Beltway, I Want to Get Off 114
You're Gonna Make It After All 118
Change is Good; Transition Sucks 121
Be It Ever So Humble, There's No Place Like Homeless 124
I (almost) Cannot Tell a Lie 127
A Weakness for the Preakness 130
Postcard From the Very Edge 134
Changes to Normal 138
Fay Jacobs, This is Your Life 141

2000

Auld Lang Insane 144
Just When You Thought It Was Safe to Go Back 147
Life, Liberty and the Pursuit of Free Weekend Minutes 150
It's Enough to Make You Sick 154
She's Not Just My Friend, She's My Partner 158
Days of Whine and Morphine 162
Reality Bites 165
The Return of Leadfoot 169
Slower Mower Delaware 172
Pork Snouts in Sussex 175
Too Close to Call 179

2001

Be In The Moment 182
But We ARE in Kansas, Toto 186
Coming Out of the Walk-in Closet 190
Not a Dog Story 194
Rules to Move By 198
There'll Be Bluebirds Over 202
Answering the Call 206

2002

Underground Railroad 210
The Anniversary Waltz 214
Bullie for You 218
Adventures in Livestock, Film at 11 222
Closets Are For Shoes 225
Show and Tell 228
We'll Leave the Light on For Ya 232
Running Hot & Cold 235
Oh, The Follies of It All 238
If Fay Ruled the World 241
No Fleas on Me 244

2003

If It Bleeds, It Leads 247
Crime and Punishment 250
E-Male 253
Smile, You're on Digital Camera 257
Too Much Information 261
Hitting the Speed Limit 264
Get Me To the Insurance Office On Time 267
We Did, We Did 270

August 1995

"I wish we could buy a place in Rehoboth," I whined last winter, knowing full well that every cent of our disposable income was tied up in that hole in the water into which we'd been throwing money—our 27-foot cruiser "Bay Pride." That's Bay, with a "B" and a wink, for folks who see us cruising the Chesapeake Bay and waving our rainbow flag.

"Why don't we just *move* our place to Rehoboth?" the captain adventurously suggested.

And so it began.

On Friday June 30 our four-woman crew left Annapolis and headed up the Bay, past Annapolis and Baltimore to the C&D Canal. By Saturday we'd crossed through the canal alongside huge tankers, ventured out into Delaware Bay and took refuge from a tremendous thunderstorm in the Cohannsey River on the Jersey shore.

Best we can figure, the Cohannsey is noted only for swarms of green head flies. Until we could anchor and retreat below deck, our crew looked like Bogart and Hepburn in the pestilence scene from *African Queen*.

As we waited out the thunder and lightning, we relaxed in our air-conditioned quarters, cooking shrimp in the microwave and chatting by cellular phone with friends in Rehoboth. Ah, camping.

On Sunday we headed to Cape May, where, to the amazement of an assortment of deep-sea fishermen, our all-gal gang executed perfect docking techniques. Leaving on Monday morning July 3, macho captains all around patronizingly patted their wives heads, saying, "See honey, you *can* learn to drive the boat."

Fortunately, we were out of their earshot as we crossed the wide-open bay towards Cape Henlopen and admitted being humbled and yes, a little frightened by the incredible expanse of

1

BIG water. When the Jersey shore disappeared into the mist behind us and we couldn't yet see Lower Slower Delaware, heebie-jeebies set in.

"Maybe we've strayed into the ocean." "Maybe we're heading for Portugal." "Is that a Russian periscope or a sea gull?"

Before too long we spied a black and white speck ahead, which, as we gained on it, turned out to be the Cape May-Lewes Ferry. Our captain's compass heading had been perfect. We, ahem, knew that.

At the entrance to the canal in Lewes, DE, we phoned our Rehoboth buddies. "We're here!" I said into the phone to alert the folks who promised to watch us arrive under the Rehoboth Avenue Bridge. "We're here, we're queer, get used to it," echoed all hands on deck.

As we cruised toward the bridge I got my binoculars out. "I think there are three people. No, four. Wait a minute, I think there are more." At least 10 Rehoboth campers waved at us, blowing noisemakers, waving streamers and taking pictures. We felt like passengers on the QE II.

Unfortunately, a few minutes later it seemed like we were *on* the QE II—the entrance to Rehoboth Bay got very, very shallow. Only skillful maneuvering by the captain kept us from being skewered by the submerged rocks along the entrance.

By the time we got to the Rehoboth Bay Marina in Dewey, our welcoming committee had arrived, too. Bay Pride, with its rainbow flag flapping in the breeze, its all-woman crew, and its jubilant welcoming committee, caused quite a stir.

Since our arrival July 4th we've spent as much time as possible living on our floating condo, enjoying everything about Rehoboth and returning to Maryland "for just a few days" each week.

This past Sunday evening, just as the captain and I zipped up the canvas preparing to "lock-up the house," a set of grandparents arrived on the pier to watch their nuclear family members on rental jet boats.

Gramps, watching us batten the hatches said, "You girls do

all the work and your husbands get to drive the boat!"

"There are no husbands on this boat. Women do the work and women get to drive," I said.

Granny gave us a "thumbs up." We love it here.▼

February 1996

"Supreme Court okays editor's suggestion."

Sounds like a landmark freedom of the press case, right? It was closer to home. Last summer, *Letters* editor Steve Elkins wrote a little editor's note after my story about arriving in Rehoboth by boat. He knew we'd spent weekends last summer on Rehoboth Bay, and suggested that we continue to weekend here after boating season, too. Well, the spirit was certainly willing, but the devil was in the details.

Last August, when it was time to think about putting the boat into drydock, we started looking for a condo. After all, we'd had a taste of Rehoboth life, and it was tough to think of weekends anywhere else. Between boating on the bay, soaking up rays at the women's beach at Gordon's Pond, and getting involved, for the very first time, in an out and proud gay community, the idea of leaving town for a long, cold winter was unthinkable.

When the going gets tough, the tough go shopping for real estate.

First stop, a squatter-inhabited bargain basement. Management assured us the place would fumigate just fine. We'd been inside five minutes, stepping over crushed beer cans, pizza boxes, and laundry, when one of the piles of clothes sat up, groaned like Frankenstein and fell back down. We fled.

Next we saw a perfectly fabulous apartment on the perfect block. Only it was a third floor walk-up; a two-bedroom Stairmaster. We imagined dragging up there with luggage. We envisioned planting sod on the balcony for the dog. We worried about the stamina of pizza deliverers. We came to our senses.

Schlepping around town, we saw a handyperson's special affectionately referred to thereafter as the Amityville Horror House. Next up, a place with a basement so wet ducks swam in it. Then came palaces way beyond our means.

"I have one more to show you," said the agent. It was *the*

one. Three doors from the boardwalk on a quiet block, this old house converted to four contemporary condos was perfect. We could be three-season weekenders in town, and in the summer, move aboard our boat while renters paid our annual condo mortgage. "Write the contract," we squealed.

At first, things seemed normal. When we learned the condo was owned by a bank we figured someone else's loss was our gain. And we didn't flinch when told the contract could only become ratified after Oct. 5, 1995 at the expiration of some kind of litigation. That's what settlement attorneys are for. Don't worry; be happy. You live and learn.

We learned that the builder, having lost the property at a Sheriff's sale, fought the simple foreclosure all the way to the United States Supreme Court. Talk about making a federal case out of something.

So Fay and Bonnie had to wait until the first Monday in October, thank you, to hear whether Ruth Bader Ginsburg and the Supremes would let us buy our beach place. Eventually, they did.

But then the mortgage company got wind of the story and wanted to know the whole gory litigation history. The mortgage man needed to talk to the bank who needed to talk to the lawyers, who needed to talk to the investors, who had to check the documents, so they could call the courthouse so that ultimately we could live in the house that jerk built. Silly me, I thought Slower Lower Delaware was just a clever t-shirt logo.

If I made one phone call a day to hustle up the facts, I made ten. As the clock ticked on my loan commitment and Nov. 28 settlement date, we played telephone tag. Finally, after I harassed three quarters of the lawyers in Sussex County, somebody hollered "uncle" and my fax machine started to grind out a 23-page opus detailing the condo's pathetic legal history.

Hold the victory lap. Was there a lawyer left in town who'd never represented or been sued by the foreclosee? Hardly. One newbie attorney surfaced and I called his office two weeks before settlement to give the firm a heads up on the legal mess.

His administrative assistant told me not to worry; they were working on settlements for the next day and they'd work on the Nov. 28 settlement on or about Nov. 27. I tried to warn them.

On Nov. 18, the day I was leaving for a Thanksgiving trip to Palm Springs, I got a call from a genuinely surprised assistant to the settlement attorney. "This is a difficult case to research," she said. "Did you know it was a foreclosure?" "AUUU-UGGGGGG!!!!!...."

I was still feeding *War and Peace* into the fax machine for the title insurance company when it came time to leave for the airport. I spent the better part of my vacation wrestling information about condo documents, parking easements, and insurance out of any number of lawyers and funneling it to unsuspecting title company flunkies.

Jet-lagged and harried, we made it to settlement on Nov. 28, with the last legal hurdle having been leapt mere minutes before. As we signed the deed and promised to love, honor and obey the mortgage company until the year 2025, we realized that for once, nobody even batted an eye over our non-traditional union. We knew we liked Rehoboth. They may be slower in lower Delaware, but they made us feel very welcome.

Two weeks later, we drove to town in a blinding snowstorm only to discover the outlets closed, the gas stations closed, the 7/11 closed. But Cloud 9 Restaurant was open. Gay people are nothing if not spunky.

So now that the weather is finally breaking, our victory before the high court of the land seems most worthwhile. If the Supreme Court would only do as well on upcoming discrimination and sodomy cases, we'd really be home free. ▼

April 1996

Morning coffee in hand, I sit in my sunny front room and watch Rehoboth wake up. Early-birds come by for a look at the ocean; I wave as a man I recognize zips past on roller blades; dozens of people and their dogs head towards the water for a last board-walk stroll before the April doggie ban.

I feel like I've always been here.

In fact, I can't even remember the day my lover and I stopped reciting "the speech."

Do you know the one I mean? Driving home after visiting friends at their new beach houses we'd tell each other "their place is great, but we'd hate driving all that way every weekend. Besides, we wouldn't use it enough to get our money's worth. And we'd be bored going to the same places all the time. And getting home so late on Sunday, Yech! It's not for us. Besides, with summer rentals we'd only have it off-season. No way we're driving to the beach in the snow."

So now I have a beach house with a mortgage that won't be paid off until 2025.

We worried about not using the place enough? We're ubiquitous. Rehoboth can't get rid of us. I blame the few missed weekends on the Maryland lottery. They haven't picked my numbers yet and I had work obligations.

The not-driving-in-the-snow thing was a lie. Not only didn't the wicked weather keep us from our appointed round trip, but we're the only idiots we know who drove to the beach in a blizzard so we could be stranded here, not home.

The next tradition to collapse was the get-home-early thing. At first it was 4:30 at the latest to make it home for *60 Minutes*. Then we started staying for our cherished ambush journalism. And once it got to be 8 o'clock, well, we started getting sleepy, and...it got harder and harder to go home.

Now our alarm goes off at 5 a.m. Monday so we can hot-foot

it home (except through those rural speed traps!) see sunrise over the chicken coops by Elmer's Market and be at work by 9.

It's the same on the other end. Last fall we'd arrive Friday nights for a late dinner, having taken time to change clothes and pack after work. By January we were leaving clothes at the condo, jamming toiletries into a backpack on Thursday night and taking off a little early on Friday—getting out of our corporate drag in the car. By the first sign pointing to "Shore Points" we were dyked-out and waving at all the other rainbow-stickered cars heading East.

Last Friday I called in sick with mad cow disease and we packed and left on Thursday night.

Even with our gradually expanding weekends we couldn't live up to my arrogant statement about being bored with the "same old places." We're regulars at the restaurants which stayed open this winter, having gotten to know the wonderful folks at our favorite places. If we miss Sunday brunch on Wilmington Avenue they file missing persons reports. We've been accused of living in a condo without knobs on the stove. I don't know, I haven't looked.

And we don't just dine here. The three of us (me, Bonnie and Max the Schnauzer) all have haircuts in Rehoboth now, although not at the same place. Hey, I'm sure our respective stylists would swap scissors for clippers and vice versa in a pinch.

And Max loves strolling Baltimore Avenue, sampling from water dishes provided by the merchants as if he were wine tasting. He drags us right to the courtyard bookstore on our way into town each Friday so he can catch up on news and chat with his friends. And he's discovered that most of the shops serve dog biscuits to shoppers of a canine orientation.

In fact, all of Rehoboth is a shopper's paradise. From paper towels on up we're tax-free-shopping groupies. By now, the only groceries we shop for at home are the perishables. And last week I smuggled a fish packed in ice over the Bay Bridge.

This jaded, native New Yorker just can't get enough of Rehoboth's small-town feeling with its special sensibility. As more of our friends settle here—some full-time—and we make new friends from Delaware and Philly, it's getting tougher to spend weekdays away.

But we really got panicky last Sunday when I heard myself saying "I love the beach, but I don't think I could live here full time. I'd miss the theatre, the city, the pace. It's nice to have both but I really don't think I could...I mean what could we do to earn a living? Maybe when we retire, but I don't know...."

Bonnie slapped her hand over my mouth and kept driving West. For now. ▼

May 1996

I was late. For me. Only an hour and a half early for my flight. My spouse, used to my neurosis that the plane might, just this time, leave early, ignored my muttering as we walked briskly to the gate. Reluctantly I put my purse on the conveyor belt and watched it disappear. I'd rather have my breasts x-rayed than my purse. What if there's scissors or matte knife in my bag? I haven't been down to the bottom of the thing since 1986. Are tweezers a weapon? Nervous and hassled, do I look like a terrorist?

It had been a bad week. We had to pack up the beach condo for our first-ever renters.

"What promise?" I said to Bonnie as she caught me stuffing a set of dishes and a cherished cork screw into the lockable owner's closet.

Oh right. That brave mumbling last fall about buying inexpensive furniture and not putting anything that means anything to us in the condo. Now I was clutching weird bathroom kitsch, running in circles and shouting "the renters are coming!" I'd already replaced the $39 bedspreads with $24 bedspreads and was obsessing over *their* fate.

Bonnie, shoulder to the bulging closet door, was just slamming the vault when Chicken Little appeared with matching green coffee mugs.

"Get a grip," she hollered, "they were a dollar each!"

So we locked up the condo and didn't look back. If we had, we'd have noticed the rainbow flag still hanging in the window. I hope the first family that moves in doesn't mind.

Back in Maryland we packed for my conference in Chicago; Bonnie was going along for fun. After years of devoted *Oprah* watching, a friend had secured her a scarce ticket for a taping.

So here we were, waiting (...and waiting...says Bonnie) for take-off.

Once aboard we shared an aisle with a passenger suffering from, at a guess, Ebola Fever. And the flight was not smooth. It wasn't as bad as our turbulent Palm Springs flight when they showed the film *Apollo 13*. The plane was bouncing and free-falling as Tom Hanks is shouting "Houston we have a problem" with video of debris being blown out the side of a fuselage. What were they thinking?

Anyway, we arrived in Chicago more or less intact. My conference (to cure baby boomer technophobics like me of fear of merging onto the information highway) was a success. We had great networking sessions, where I networked myself into a group familiar with Chicago's gay nightlife. That gaydar thing is really the only technology I seem to understand.

As for Bonnie, after years of waiting for a heartwarming, healing, touchy-feely subject for her at-long-last *Oprah* tickets, she got a show about Mad Cow Disease—a disgusting hour about the filthy things in your dinner.

We're in Chicago, sirloin butcher to the world, with the best steakhouses known to humankind, and an expense account waiting to be abused, and Bonnie turned vegetarian at 11:30 that morning. This mad cow wound up with spaghetti and tomato sauce for dinner.

On our flight home we finished obsessing about tainted meat and began obsessing about renters tainting the condo. We conjured up smokers, drinkers, barfers, Crayola fiends and air-conditioning abusers.

They arrive to storm the beach next week. I'm scared. At our settlement walk-through we found a VCR with a cassette slot stuffed with pretzels.

Fears aside, we're going to close the door and not look back. In fact, we'll be back on the boat for summer weekends beginning Memorial Day. And Bonnie won't let me go near the condo 'til the last renter is gone in the fall.

"Imagine the fun you'll have, using your terrorist tweezers to extract pretzels from the appliances," she said.

In the meantime, I hope the renters find the twelve sets of

11

coasters I left strewn about. And if you know where I can get $12 bedspreads, let me know.

    • *Author's note: As it turned out, Oprah was slapped with a lawsuit by Texas Cattlemen over the "Mad Cow" show and it became a hot topic...with Bonnie coming to love the fact that "Mad Cow" was the one Oprah show she caught!*▼

May 1996

We were seated at the worst table in the restaurant. Valley-girls, juggling trays of fried food that looked like heart attacks on a plate wiggled by, adjusting their tiny skirts, not bothering to say "Excuse me" for slamming my chair with the kitchen door.

It was Happy Hour at a popular Annapolis restaurant. The place teemed with prom night couples, Naval Academy Midshipmen and their dates, politicians, and yacht clubbers. And the two lesbians at the table by the kitchen. I gulped my beer, fought the raucous din, and hollered to my spouse, "Get the check! We'll eat dinner at the beach!"

I couldn't believe what I was thinking. Help! I'm becoming a separatist!

Well, not a guitar-strumming-get-naked-in-the-woods-separatist. Not that those lesbians aren't heroic for embracing the land and its rustic life. But for me, a Noo Yawka who, until 1982, didn't know vegetables grew in dirt, going back to nature is oxymoronic.

In fact, on my first night in the first house my lover and I shared, I threw open the window, gasped at a frightening moan I heard and started dialing 911. A drunk was being rolled in the gutter. Never mind that the fledgling subdivision didn't have a street much less a gutter.

When Bonnie told me I was hearing a cow I got confused. Who'd want to rob a cow in the gutter? They have no wallets (they are wallets, but that's another story).

No, my spouse, who, by this time was talking real sloooow so I would get it, explained that what I was hearing was a local cow, making a normal cow noise. I was sure she was nuts. Finally, still in our pajamas, we had to drive around the corner so I could see that some old MacDonald had a farm abutting our property. A shock to say the least.

The next day I almost drove over a chicken crossing the road

(Stop that. I have no idea why he was crossing). I cheerily reported seeing this darn chicken with floppy-looking red stuff on its head. It seems I was hopeless.

But I digress. My original point was that I was in Annapolis, a town I've loved and enjoyed for many years. But now, I wanted to rush back to the nurturing atmosphere of Rehoboth and be a separatist beach bum.

I wanted to hunker down in Rehoboth with gay men and lesbians, and all of the gay and lesbian-friendly shops, restaurants and beaches. Plus all of our straight but not narrow friends. Is this so much to ask?

I'm sure my condition is a result of Rehoboth emersion therapy. Being in town almost every weekend for a year does something remarkable to your expectations. Comfort becomes the norm.

Waving shopkeepers and conversations with folks on the street—even one's you've just met—are a delight. In most cases, the rapport is so instantaneous you feel you've known these strangers for years.

Dining out is really cool. You can toast to your anniversary and gaze into your mate's eyes without giving the waiter an aneurysm. And the only other place you hear restaurant staff call everyone "sweetie" or "hon" is Baltimore—but there, instead of attractive, sincere people, you get octogenarian waitresses with bad teeth and beehive hair. It ain't the same.

I still can't believe how my spouse and I sauntered into our Rehoboth furniture store to buy a headboard and didn't wince saying "for our bedroom, for our king size bed...we'll use our credit card."

Back in civilization (and I use that term loosely), we used to shop in shifts for sheets, consulting in the parking lot. Anything to avoid embarrassing gaffs or evil-eye salespeople.

Once we were at a non-Rehoboth furniture place with friends. One woman loudly exclaimed "I love You!" and her partner dove behind a sofa. Turns out the message was "I love Yew," as in the choice of wood for the bedroom set. We got the attention of everyone in the store.

14

Before coming to Rehoboth, I'd only experienced gay-friendly cities on vacations. By the time I got used to shedding my "outsiders" protective armor, it was time to go home. But now, feeling—for once—like a first class citizen, it's mighty tough to go back to those old defensive and destructive ways.

And, after being ruined, in a fabulous way, by my new hometown, I guess I wasn't in fighting trim for Annapolis. I stared at odd-looking middle-aged men in Sansabelt pants and worried that the profusion of polyester violated the fire code. I tried to eat, drink, be merry and avoid saying, doing or touching something I shouldn't. Unhappy Hour.

I felt like an outsider again. Before experiencing the freedom of Rehoboth Beach, I hardly noticed that sense of "otherness." It was part of life; I dealt with it. But Rehoboth showed me it doesn't have to be that way.   As we hurried toward Route 50, a car behind us honked. We're used to that—our rainbow sticker always gets friendly honks and waves. But this driver came around on our right, cut us off and angrily gave us the finger. "Uncle!!!" I cried. "Get me back to the beach!"

Arriving in town, we bee-lined to a lovely center table at the window of one of our favorite places. We ate wonderful food and watched Wilmington Avenue come alive for the night. Several folks waved as they passed by; our favorite waitress welcomed us back; the music was strictly Streisand and Sondheim.

Spying a straight couple outside on a bench, kissing and pawing each other, I shook my head. "Blatant heterosexuals. Get a room! Why do they have to keep flaunting it like that?"

There's really is no place like home, Auntie Em.▼

June 1996

We're baaack, but we're different.

The captain and I pulled our floating mini-condo into our slip on Rehoboth Bay on a drizzly, yucky Memorial Day weekend. The first thing we did was blow-dry the dog and take hot showers.

The miserable weather had its up side. Drizzle usually flattens the water. This was good, since a friend with a history of motion sickness was aboard. She chose our trip from Annapolis to Rehoboth to face down her demons in a personal Outward Bound experience. We were flattered, I think, as we armed ourselves with every pharmaceutical, herbal, homeopathic, and velcro seasickness cure marketed.

So the Captain, First Mate, First Dog and Mal De Mer poster girl set out on a gloomy morning. Our fledgling crew member steered the boat to keep her mind off her gag reflex.

With Captain Bonnie at the throttle and navigational charts, the dog and I had nothing to do. So Max monitored the seagulls and I pondered.

I continue to revel in being part of Rehoboth's mainstream. And while I've been pretty "out" for years in a relaxed, non-confrontational way, I never realized just how "out" I wasn't.

My mate and I never celebrated an anniversary in suburbia like we did at the Back Porch Restaurant this year. No shrinking in horror at a loud, proud "Best Wishes on your 14th Anniversary" from the waiter; no stares from gay or gay friendlies in the room; no embarrassment at "good for you!" toasts from perfect strangers at the next table.

I've got the freedom of unedited conversations with shopkeepers and new acquaintances. I can join straight neighbors in casual chatter about everyday details of married life no different from their own. I don't have to wonder if people think "why does she always have to bring up homosexuality?" when we're really just describing our lives. Amazing.

I glanced starboard and saw sea gulls. Not swimming. Walking. I could see their bony little knees. As I turned to relay the bad news, the boat lurched and landed on a sandbar.

"What's the depth finder say?" muttered the captain.

Now if you ask me, a depth finder is a useless instrument, proudly revealing how shallow the water is around the thing you've already hit. We were in 1 ft. 8 inches of water. That's putting the drama in Dramamine.

"I thought it felt unusually calm here," said our crew member, who, despite our best efforts, had obviously been monitoring every pitch and roll for the last four hours. Fortunately, we were quickly re-floated and back in the channel.

Returning to my ponderments, I realized that my beach personality was creeping into weekday life.

Recently, my spouse and I were immersed in a production of the show *Side By Side By Sondheim* in Annapolis. The mostly straight company included longtime friends as well as folks we'd just met. While we've always been quietly open with theatre friends, we shut the closet to others until we gauge their comfort level. It's exhausting being unflaunting lesbians. This time, unconsciously, we arrived with matter-of-fact "we're here, we're queer, get used to it" attitudes.

In the show, I expressed my identity by staging an appropriate ballad with the singers wearing red ribbons. On opening night it looked great, except for the clueless soprano with her ribbon pinned upside down.

After the opening, the company did the bonding thing. Among everyone's getting-to-know-you details were casual questions asking how long Bonnie and I've been together and unsolicited support for sending us to Hawaii to get hitched should the court okay gay marriage there.

I was interrupted. "Is it lunchtime?" asked the captain and pilot-in-training. That everyone wanted lunch was a good sign.

I volunteered to make sandwiches while we kept going, since it would be cruel to ask a person who was, incredulously, not yet hanging over the rail, to eat lunch meat and pickles in a boat bobbing at anchor like a rubber ducky.

I absently juggled ham, cheese, plates and condiments while continuing my attitude adjustment review. Last week at an Eddie Bauer in a mall near home, a salesperson and I connected gaydar blips. As she totaled my spree at the register, I said, "Well, it's no more than my other half is probably spending for a leaf blower downstairs."

"Well, then he can't be mad," said another clerk.

"She won't say a word," I said. "I know what leaf blowers cost."

The salesdyke fought back a grin as I took my receipt, smiled sweetly at the open-mouthed clerk, and left.

Reality intruded again, as the waves picked up, sending tomatoes rolling, cups catapulting and an open mustard jar into the air. The mustard itself flew faster than the jar (that Isaac Newton thing, I guess) and a huge glob became a heat-seeking missile, Grey Pouponing what would have been my lap if I'd been sitting down. I shouted a bad word.

The real captain (as opposed to the intern), thinking I'd been hurt, instantly throttled back. The boat stopped but I kept going, landing butt first in Max's water bowl. Now I had a lap, with ripe tomatoes and a huge vidalia onion coming at it, in a simultaneous application of Newton's and Murphy's laws. I became a hoagie.

Miraculously, lunch got made, everyone ate, nobody turned green, and we reached Lewes on schedule. Loyal but wind-whipped friends waved at us from the Rehoboth Avenue Bridge as we made our second annual arrival in the canal, and cheered the success of the former barf queen's aversion therapy cruise.

Heading to our marina, I remembered wondering last year if the Bay Pride and its rainbow flag would be welcome. Upon arrival, we had been a curiosity. This time, several marina neighbors, strangers when we pulled in last year, waved, hollered "what took you so long!" and offered helping hands for docking and dispensing beverages.

I'm so glad to be back. And if anyone asks "Have you any Grey Poupon?" I can say. "Yep, all over my pants." ▼

June 1996

We're turning into our parents. Well, not entirely.

I don't think our parents had the fun in middle age that baby boomer gays and lesbians have. But in other ways we're becoming them whether we like it or not.

Last week I heard myself making the same noise my father used to make getting out of a chair.

And lately, no matter who we're with, sooner or later somebody says "hormones" or "health care" and we start discussing fat grams, forgetfulness and other topics I can't recall at the moment.

I do remember the 1950s (short term goes first) and my parents and their friends discussing the new tranquilizer Miltown. Now we speculate about Prozac. Same-same.

We have a dermatologist friend about to give up his practice. These days, the phrase I hear most is, "He's retiring, so I went to get something taken off." Then we compare the moles we've got left and look for ticking time bombs.

Remember Fire Island or P-Town, when you'd baste yourself like a turkey and lay frying on the beach like an omelette? Now we slather with so much Coppertone #25 epoxy that sand sticks to us like Shake-n-Bake. If every 40-something lesbian I know shook off before leaving the beach we could cancel our beach reclamation project.

And it's a good thing my spouse and I were home and not in the grocery last Wednesday when she leapt up and started ripping off her clothes. In seconds she was down to birthday suit and deck shoes.

Gape-jawed, I asked, "Hot flash?"

"Power surge," she said.

They're happening all over. Ever watch a waiter try to adjust the air conditioning at a 50th birthday bash? The men and premenopausal women turn into popsicles while the rest sauté in their seats, fanning themselves with menus. And I'm petrified that my significant other might do Gypsy Rose Lee during the salad course.

When the waiter comes back from adjusting the thermostat for the third time, and finally starts taking our order, the game begins.

The first guy or gal to fumble for reading glasses gets to order first, then passes the drug-store specs to each succeeding party-goer. At least one person, too vain to admit to needing glasses, stretches his arms so far to be able to read that the menu hits the candle and bursts into flames.

The crowd starts to sing Happy Birthday but quickly realizes it's just another menu going up.

And speaking of smoke, it's been ten weeks since one of our buddies traded smoking for nicotine gum. "But just try and get that stuff," she says. "When I went to the store they were out. I said 'what do you mean you don't HAVE any? We're all hooked on this shit and NOW you don't HAVE any???' Then they tried to sell me cigarettes!" She was one angry woman.

So I whined to her about my doctor-prescribed diet pills. I'm losing tons of weight, but the HMO refuses to pay for the medication despite all their "wellness" crap. Losing the equivalent of half of model Kate Moss doesn't count?

So I swallow 90 bucks worth of pills a month. It's better than downing an equal amount of beach fries. Pills don't need salt and vinegar, and the seagulls won't use you for target practice while trying to steal them.

And so it goes. On our last boat trip we forgot the blender but everybody aboard remembered dental floss. And after chic Southwestern food one night we all shared somebody's package of Beano like we used to share a nickel bag of grass.

I have this theory. One day on the news you'll hear about Thelma and Louise robbing a Nicorette Gum truck. Then a local woman, a writer in fact, goes berserk after six months of eating nothing but vegetables, fat-free cream cheese (what is that stuff?), decaf cappuccino with skim milk, and the occasional hard pretzel. Armed with a stale baguette in her pocket, she holds up the local candy stand, making off with a pillowcase of taffy—then continues to the Gourmet shop where she demolishes the fat free honey mustard bottles, and takes the entire stock of Boursin cheese and caviar hostage. The crime spree ends at the custard stand in a hail of chocolate jimmies.

No longer will disgruntled postal workers get all the press. A militia of nicotine chomping, sunscreen wearing, fat-gram counting, people of a certain age will hole up on a Montana ranch and dare the FBI to turn off the electric. What the heck, they can't stay awake much past 9 p.m. these days anyway.

These radicals will demand that the government fly in the best plastic surgeons, the most delicious low-fat cuisine, a tub of Retin-A and personal trainers who look like Jody Foster or Brad Pitt. Soon, their energy will return, extra chins will disappear and they'll set fire to their stockpile of Zantac, Ibuprofen and Metamucil.

After a three-month siege they'll emerge looking and feeling like they did when The Village People were popular the first time. And then....

Excuse me. My mate is talking to me. "Honey, I'm trying to finish up my column. What? They want to meet us at Blue Moon for a drink? Now? Sounds great."

I gotta go. The sky is full of stars and we're heading to Baltimore Avenue for Absolut Vodka and some laughs. Maybe we'll see sunrise on the beach. After all, the night is young. When my parents were this age they would never have gone out after *Gunsmoke* and the 11 o'clock news. Armed with antacids, I'm on a roll. ▼

June 1996

Syndicated columnist Deb Price's book is called *Say Hi to Joyce*. No columnist is an island if they have a spouse.

I loved Deb's book about starting a syndicated column about gay issues. But I had no idea that just as Deb's column publicly outed her lover Joyce, so would my writing catch my significant other like a deer in the headlights.

When Steve first asked me to write a column I figured I was in it alone. Just me and my laptop.

Wrong. It seems I never do anything alone. I'm not complaining, mind you, but my credibility would be history if I misled people into thinking I actually know how to start the engine on my boat. Mix drinks, yes, back it into the slip, no. Although I did help back it into the dock once. (That was expensive.)

So the not-so-Lone Ranger had to find a way to acknowledge Tonto. Phyllis Diller chose to call her husband Fang. If I went that route I'd soon be doing a lot of important things alone.

And what about friends who naively socialize with us only to read about their embarrassing moments ("You're not going to write about this are you???") two weeks later?

One wonderful man who shall remain nameless makes me swear he's "off the record" before I step in the door.

So I've taken to using friends' addresses instead of names ("...the Hickman Street boys visited Mr. Maryland Avenue, who told Ms. Newcastle Street that...) The subjects stay anonymous but it's obvious I'll not only be passed over for a Pulitzer, but Steve will weep trying to edit the mess.

But Tonto had me stumped. Advocate writer Janis Ian conquers the problem by using the term of endearment Mr. Lesbian. My thesaurus produced only the well-worn "significant other-lover-spouse-mate-and/or better half."

One day, after typing "significant hardware fanatic" for my lover and the poetic "household dog" for my Schnauzer, I

22

became literarily unglued and started naming names.

My lover Bonnie's name was all over the page like a rash. "I now know how Mr. Bombeck felt," she muttered.

Dog mentions came in second, although Max might have been flattered being called Fang.

I fared the best. My name tops the article and that's it. If people read a byline at all, they completely forget the writer's name by paragraph two. I'd have to refer to myself in the third person to keep up with Bonnie's press. "Fay Jacobs thought that referring to oneself in third person sounded pompous and silly."

So everybody now knows all about Bonnie.

Last week as I filled out a raffle ticket the seller said "Oh, you're Fay Jacobs who writes for *Letters*." Before I could say "thanks for reading my column," he turned his back on me and said to my companion "You must be Bonnie. Do you really do all those nutty things?" She shot me a venomous look and muttered "I'm afraid so."

On a recent stroll past a store with backyard fountains, the proprietor overheard Bonnie describing her plan to decorate the dock behind our boat. "Say, aren't you those girls who wrote about driving the boat down Delaware Bay to Rehoboth?" he asked.

That's funny, I don't remember Bonnie writing about it.

Recently, a local waitress teased Bonnie about hitting a sandbar in the Lewes Canal. City Hall sent Bonnie a completed parking sticker application since they know where she lives, what she drives, and where she generally parks. Unfortunately, the Route 1 police know exactly when she'll fly by on Monday mornings. I've revealed so much minutiae about my mate that Trivial Pursuit is coming out with a Bonnie edition.

It's all been in good fun, of course—such good fun that Bonnie was starting to enjoy seeing her name in print. Then tragedy struck.

A regretfully misguided burst of creativity made me write a column about aging baby boomers, hot flashes, and squinting at restaurant menus. No longer relying on euphemisms like "significant hot flasher," there was nothing to do but relate how Bonnie was handling estrogen warp.

"Are you nuts, Jacobs?" I thought to myself (That's me, Fay Jacobs, the name on the byline, as you have probably forgotten by now). "You can't print that story about Bonnie having a hot flash and ripping all her clothes off. She'll kill you."

So I asked her permission to use the story. Flushed from recent quasi-celebrity, (or a hot flash, now that I think of it), she suffered temporary insanity and said "sure, why not."

WHY NOT????? Because since my last article came out, our friends, along with perfect strangers, have been telling Bonnie "power surge" jokes, winking at her when she squints at a menu and offering her Pepcid AC with pizza. Nobody says a word to me. They can't remember the name of the idiot who wrote the article.

My spouse is NOT amused.

At least the dog is still talking to me. Although there's a great story about Max getting spooked and backing right off the dock into the water. Clad in his tiny life jacket, he dog paddled until Bonnie....▼

July 1996

According to a local wise-ass, Rehoboth recently suffered its second major event of the year. The first, according to said wise-butt, was the Delmarva blackout. So the second was Hurricane Bertha, right? Wrong...although that minor incident happened the same weekend.

Mr. Smarty Pants deemed this columnist being struck totally silent by laryngitis as the season's second defining event.

It started Friday, July 12 with the good news that Hurricane Bertha had been downgraded to a tropical storm packing mere 40 mph wind gusts. Heck, I could do that telling a good story. That is, before Thursday night when sinusitis turned me into a Canadian Honker.

By Friday I had no voice at all. That seemed to tickle a certain bookstore manager, who turned gleeful town crier to spread the news.

Then, a noted artist asked if I was contagious and if so, would I please spend time with the editor of this publication (now we'll see just how committed said editor is to freedom of the press). And these folks were not alone. Our young actor friend, with us for the weekend, kept imitating that scene in *The Miracle Worker* where Anne Bancroft teaches Patty Duke to sign the word for "water." Only he was teaching me the sign for vodka.

One sarcastic fellow said "Gee, if I'd known, I would have come prepared." With what, a long-winded story like I usually tell so turnabout could be fair play?

My spouse, thrust into the unaccustomed role of communicator general, interpreted my gestures (to suit her opinions, I might add), and kept up our social obligations. Once she learned how to turn the boat phone on, folks getting her calls were sure something tragic had happened. Actually, it had. To my horror, Bonnie started plagiarizing my versions of family stories, while I stood by, smiling weakly, like the village idiot.

Soon Her Royal Chattiness cheerily broadcast what fun she was having as our domestic partnership's public information officer. In the face of her unbearable gloating I resorted to rudimentary sign language, featuring only one digit.

The vicious but good-natured (I think) kidding lasted all day, as folks asked me questions, then saw me shake my head and clutch my throat.

Then the bad news: by late afternoon, Old Bertha was a hurricane again, packing 100 mph winds and heading directly for us. Now up to this point, our marina, nestled between ocean and bay on a narrow strip called Dewey, seemed to cry "location, location, location." Unless, of course, there was a hurricane coming our way. We needed to seek safe harbor.

Casting off, we drove to a protected canal where friends, off in sunny Florida, had left us their house key. Since radio forecasts put the storm's arrival at noon the next day, we tied up to the pier and joined friends for dinner and a movie—where, to my relief, it's fashionable not to talk.

Repeated lulls in dinner table conversation prompted me to mouth "this is when I would be talking" over and over until somebody finally noticed me.

Back at the boat, our marine radio re-confirmed Bertha's Saturday mid-day arrival, so we decided to sleep aboard. At dawn we'd retreat to the house to await the storm. No sense having to wash guest room and sofa bed sheets if we didn't have to. So the three of us—the boat captain, our buddy the actor, and I—went to sleep on the boat.

Now I'd like to know where our local weatherpersons learned meteorology.

At 4 a.m. we awoke to a vicious howling and the guttural moaning of ropes on pilings ("or is that you trying to talk, hon?" asked the captain.) The rain, falling in sheets, blew sideways, and the boat rocked like that Boardwalk arcade ride where people pay money to be shaken like a Vodka Gimlet.

And I couldn't even yell "Mayday!"

"We've got to abandon ship," said the captain quite calmly.

Now this scared me. Unlike me, the captain is not a hysteric.

The actor was still sleeping (now that's focus) so the captain shook him and said, "Abandon Ship!" He said, "Five more minutes." Finally he opened one eye, saw an ashen-faced street mime gesturing wildly over his head and realized we were having a monsoon.

The three of us grabbed shorts, shoes and shirts, and headed topside. The six-inch trip from the boat to the dock was tricky since both places were moving. "Careful, careful, remember Natalie Wood," I rasped, quite unheard, adding, "This is where I would be screaming!" as we ran (or were blown) into the house.

Sleepy, drenched, and pissed at the forecasters, we turned on the TV to find a big, disgusting "4:39 a.m." at the bottom of the screen and a map of our favorite shore points. Remember the blob that landed on Sigourney Weaver's face in Alien? It was on radar, sucking up the Delaware shore.

From the kitchen window we saw wind and rain bend trees, blow shrubs sideways, and threaten to launch lawn furniture to Kansas. But by 9 a.m. it was all over except my not shouting. No damage, no problem.

By noon, "I survived Hurricane Bertha" T-shirts were already in stores and I began a new day as the target of merciless razzing. Bonnie was in rare form, blabbing about the joys of talking for two.

And then it happened. At a Saturday night gathering, during an especially virulent—but clever—round of harassment, several of my friends suddenly realized the pen might just be mightier than the cord. "She may not be able to talk, but she's going to write about this," said one frightened harasser.

They backed off so fast the resulting suction practically pulled the pen from my hand. We all laughed.

Heck, the ribbing was fun. Sort of. But now that my voice is almost back—I sound like Talullah Bankhead—I want everyone to rest assured that although Bertha's gusts are just a memory, I'm back up to hurricane strength. Start looking for safe harbor. ▼

August 1996

Even now, as an adult (chronologically, anyway), I get weak in the knees around Labor Day. Though I know in my heart it won't be me going to junior high on that awful Tuesday morning, I still panic at back-to-school ads.

And as much as I hated seventh grade (feeling different, not knowing why,) I hated writing that stupid first assignment "What I did on my summer vacation" even more. Why would I want to write about my best friend discovering dumb boy-girl parties and ignoring me the entire month of August? Or my parents desperately buying me "pretty" school clothes and making me take ballet. That was humiliating.

So when I sat down to write a column this August I was struck momentarily queasy—but then I had this delicious fantasy. What if I could stand up in front of my old homeroom class and tell them what I did on my vacation this summer.

Cool. I know just what I'd say.

First, my spouse (that would be the woman I've lived with for 14 years) and I spent weekends in delightful Rehoboth Beach, part of a tremendously supportive community.

In fact, we're among the many people helping to host Sundance this year. It's the biggest party of the year, where thousands of folks get together to dance, dine, and support the Sussex County AIDS Committee and CAMP Rehoboth. Lots of our friends—make that our big, friendly, everyone-welcome clique—will be there, no Pink Lady satin jackets or varsity sweaters required. Do I sound bitter? Sorry.

And this is just *one* of the many fantastic boy-boy, girl-girl, boy-girl parties this town throws each season. Bet you never thought I'd be having the time of my life partying!

And I have to tell you about my very functional family, too. It sure makes liars out of the grown-ups who told us "you can pick your friends but not your relatives." Gay people can select both.

We have the luxury of having friends who *are* our families. And we're forever celebrating somebody's 15th, or 20th anniversary. These may not be legal marriages—yet—but many of us seem to have a knack for this commitment gig.

Oh wait! I almost forgot my biggest news. Remember how you thought me hopeless for not having a single Barbie? Or called me queer for going to football games instead of practicing for motherhood by babysitting?

Well, it turned out okay anyway. My spouse and I are thrilled with our new son. No, I did not just have a baby at my age. But my mate and I informally adopted our-son-the-actor (imagine me, a Jewish Mother after all) as he turned twenty-something. We got an intelligent, thoughtful son without going through diapers, tonsils, carpools, orthodontics or tuition. And he likes our generation's Broadway musicals.

We met our young actor two years ago, but he just recently asked to meet some of our friends, saying he thought—but wasn't sure—he might be gay.

So we loaned him books, talked a bit, and arranged for him to visit us in Rehoboth. At the bookstore, the manager took lots of time finding him just the right books to introduce him to our community. Then friends escorted the wide-eyed novice to Poodle Beach, where the scenery was great and rude kids didn't kick sand in people's faces. There were a few children around, but they were the well-behaved offspring of gay couples.

Anyway, I was telling you about our son's coming out. By Saturday night at dinner he started to look very comfortable, but we were still wary. Though we hoped for the best, we knew he might still turn out to be straight. I mean either you are or you aren't. It's not like there's a choice.

Whatever happened though, we promised to be non-judgmental...not that we wouldn't be a little wistful about the many wonderful parts of the gay culture he'd never get to experience.

But by Sunday brunch, over mimosas and Steven Sondheim music, it became clear we had a gay son and our actor had two mommies.

And for the rest of the summer, the three of us have been entertaining straight and gay friends visiting Rehoboth, using the TVs mute button to bleep out the Republican Convention and enjoying the unseasonably delightful weather.

And that's how I spent my summer vacation. (I hope I get an A+.)▼

September 1996

Until I heard about *Ellen* I was perfectly content spending my summer without TV or newspapers. Being the village idiot was quite relaxing, actually.

I'm no longer a newspaper, magazine and TV news junkie. Bonnie's jaw dropped last week when she heard I cancelled the weekend *Washington Post*. I was sick of paying for a bag of newsprint that went from the driveway to the recycling bin without ever passing my eyeballs.

Get this. The only newspaper headline I read all last week was "Anna Nicole Smith's Boobs Explode." And I only saw the tabloid by accident (as if anybody would read that stuff on purpose) in the checkout line at the grocery.

Instead of poring over *Newsweek*, I've been sitting on the pier, dog in lap, with the both of us staring at chorus lines of Herons and Cormorants drying their wings.

But it was the Ellen DeGeneres thing that finally got to me. My urge to break my self-imposed media blackout became overpowering the day somebody at the beach asked what I thought of the big news about *Ellen*. "What news?" I whimpered.

"What news? What news?" she gushed, implying I'd been under a rock when the emergency broadcast network announced nuclear war. "The stuff in the *Post* yesterday. About Ellen's character coming out on her TV show."

Whoa. This was bigger than an A-bomb.

How could I find out more? A band of renters were laying siege to my condo, holding my television hostage.

As Bonnie and I headed back to our media-free boat I sought a plan. "*Entertainment Tonight* will have it and I'll be saved," I muttered.

"Yeah. Where are you going to watch it?" Bonnie said, "our investment television is occupied." Investment TV? It occurred to me that Bonnie had a more practical view of our condo than I had. But I had to get the scoop on *Ellen*.

I fed the dog, changed out of my beach attire and then, quite casually said, "I'm going to K-Mart. Want to go?"

"To buy a television?" she said. "No thanks." We've been together so long my brain waves must come in through her dental work. Too bad she couldn't tune in *Entertainment Tonight* on her wisdom teeth.

After promising to look for hardware too, we went to K-Mart and bought assorted screws, bits, and miracle waxers plus a 13" television.

Back at the boat, we got nothing but static. So we opened the forward hatch and telescoped the rabbit ear antenna up on deck, turning the vessel into *My Favorite Martian*.

"Did it ever occur to you that one hundred percent of people in Rehoboth have cable for a reason?" Bonnie said. Not until that moment.

We found three channels with images resembling the reception you get on HBO when you don't subscribe to it. And none of the squiggles was *Entertainment Tonight*.

We did manage to watch five blurry minutes of Jersey Shore news, ("Leading off tonight, romance comes to a farmer's prized bovine...") until we required No-Doze. Failure. Then I thought about the Internet.

To this point, I've viewed this new technology with a suspicion reserved for electric nose hair clippers and vegematics. I use my office account mainly for stuffy research and the occasional "Dear Senator Helms" diatribe.

The internet for news? Forget it. I'm a print journalist. The Internet will never work. You can't take it into the bathroom with you. But suddenly it made sense. I could sign on and search for truth, justice and the DeGeneres way.

I clicked a menu on my laptop and searched. Sure enough, I found a dozen Hollywood gossip sites. How long has this been going on?

It seems that no less than *TV Guide* had floated a trial balloon from the producers that maybe, just maybe, the character of

Ellen Morgan would come out of the closet as a lesbian by the end of the season.

There it was, in black and white. Blue and green, actually. What's more, I was invited to post my opinion on a message board set up just to discuss Ellen's future. "Will she or won't she?"

For the next few hours I scanned Ellengrams on several different *Ellen* boards. And you know what? There are some incredibly glib and articulate people posting messages day and night.

Folks who wrote "by allowing millions of viewers who already know Ellen as a friend to see her come out will be a huge step forward for us all," and "Ellen: You go girl...I'm a 65 year old heterosexual woman and I think you are terrific. There are gay people in life, why not on TV?" Or the short note "like Ellen's coming out would be news. Anybody notice that poster of k.d. lang over her bed in her apartment?"

Sure, there were morons. Like the woman who wrote "I'm a church-going mom of three and we watch Ellen all the time. Showing her in her true homosexuality light will make me turn the TV off and stop watching." I want to know what a homosexuality light is and where I can order one.

To the imbecile who wrote, "Homos aren't normal. How do you procreate? Homos are ruining society," an internet watcher answered. "It's heterosexuals who are producing homosexual offspring. Should we blame them?"

Next, we saw a message noting "I'm sick and tired of a lifestyle I don't agree with being shoved down my face. Our kids will turn gay if there's a gay character. This is terrible."

Before I could type a reply, another message appeared. "Hey, we all didn't turn black when Bill Cosby was the first black TV star in *I Spy.*"

"You tell him!" I typed. Then I thought about saying something witty but rude to the person having the gay lifestyle shoved down his face, but figured the humor would elude him.

The next message said "Letting Ellen out of the closet is uncalled for. Do what's wright. Go to an uncensored cable channel. Teach our children some morales."

I say teach this person some grammar and spelling. Then some jerk added "I'll never watch again if Ellen is to become lesbianism. Don't tell me sexually orientation is born. They choose to be that way and its unnatural."

Lovely sentence construction. The next message said "why do homophobes spell so badly? Are they born that way or is it a choice?"

I laughed until I cried.

And so it went. Lots of messages, 90 percent positive.

Some terrific dialogue is taking place; stuff that really may be educating and changing people's attitudes. Meanwhile I have a message for the bad speller who wrote the fulminating epistle about the wicked gay lifestyle threatening all of society. Get a load of my wild gay lifestyle, bud: sitting at my laptop late at night, typing and laughing.

As for Ellen, "You go, girl!" ▼

I missed the Jazz Festival last weekend.

Now before you conclude that I don't support Rehoboth's very successful jazz weekend bringing big tourist bucks to our shops and restaurants, I have to be perfectly honest and come out of the closet. Yeah, yeah, I've been out with the gay thing, but this is much tougher.

My ex-husband was an accordion player.

And, along with his wedding and bar mitzvah gigs (if you've never heard *Jeremiah was a Bullfrog*, played on an accordion, you can't really know the kind of hell I'm talking about), his hobby was playing jazz accordion. Apparently that's not as oxymoronic as it sounds. He was good enough on the squeeze box to play a gig at the White House, but frankly all that notoriety didn't make me like his sound of music any better.

To this day I go into anaphylactic shock if I hear *Lady of Spain*.

My sordid past includes too many nights in smoky afterhours clubs listening to my very own Lawrence Welk pitch the melody to the bass player, who tossed it to the drummer, after which it disappeared altogether and I couldn't go home until it came back.

Thankfully, my days in the musician's wife business ended almost 20 years ago (the accordion was minor among the irreconcilable differences), but I was left with permanent jazz damage. I admit it. I'm jazzphobic.

Here's how bad it is. Several years ago, Gary Larson drew a cartoon with the top half showing St. Peter saying "Welcome to Heaven, here's your harp," and the bottom quoting Satan's "Welcome to Hell, here's your accordion." Within days, newspaper clippings of the cartoon started jamming my mailbox like letters to Kris Kringle in *Miracle on 34th Street*. Most just said, "Thinking of You."

When I had my hysterectomy a friend sent a card that read "it you have to lose an organ…" Inside was a picture of an accordion.

As for Jazz Festival, I might have enjoyed some of the acts, since I do like blues and Dixieland, but I wouldn't dare wander blindly into a concert. If some earnest bass player was "taking it" I'd have to be air-lifted to the emergency room. I'd probably serve my time and be back on the street before the extemporaneous solo ended. I've seen people celebrate consecutive birthdays during a single drum solo.

Instead of hiding in my condo all weekend, Bonnie kept me in Maryland for the jazz duration.

We missed our gay news, so we went into a card shop/newsstand to pick up *The Advocate*. They had every magazine ever published. Along with *Newsweek, Brides, Kiplingers* and *Field and Stream* they had a tremendous selection of filth. Appalled as I was, it was like that horrible turnpike accident. You don't want to look; can't take your eyes off it.

The rags were on display racks at about pre-teen height: *Hustler, Busty, Big Butt, Small Tops* (that one took me by surprise), *Leg Show*, ("Fabulous Foot Fetish edition") and *Pulsating Pink Pix*.

Disgusted, I retreated to the more mundane racks to pick up *The Advocate* and *Out*. You guessed it. There were no gay magazines in the store.

Bonnie marched to the counter, asked if they had *The Advocate* and got an attitudinal "No" with the sanctimonious clerk pointing to a *Bible* display.

"You have…" I glanced back to the displays, *"World Class Ass Club*, you have *Nasty*, and you won't stock a gay news magazine?" I hollered from the doorway. "This is your idea of religion? *Rump Runners*?!!!"

We headed back to the house without any gay newspaper. I should have known that staying home for a weekend would come to no good.

Back home, we opened the front door and got hit with the smell of smoke.

"My God! Something's on fire!" Bonnie screamed, running around, sniffing and feeling the walls.

"Grab the photo albums!" I yelled, racing back out to toss Max into the car.

I passed Bonnie struggling down the stairs with a leaning tower of scrapbooks as I ran to grab the two kitchen phones— separate area codes—punched 911 on both, and, sandwiching my head, held the receivers to my ears.

"Fire and Rescue" said one, then the other.

"House fire!" I barked, summoning battalions from two counties.

The smell worsened. Hearts pounding, we sniffed and searched like pigs seeking truffles. Then came the sirens. "Let's get out," I hollered, fearful of smoke inhalation, but noting it was getting smellier not smokier.

Just as the fire truck and ambulance pulled up, with jurisdiction two in hot pursuit, I saw a trail of smoke from the dishwasher.

Clawing the door open I found a smoldering lump of plastic, formerly a slotted spoon, hanging over the heating element like spew from Mt. St. Helens. Wrenching it free, I ran out the front door waving my steaming, smelly trophy.

Now this pretty much stopped the squad of fully outfitted fire fighters running toward the house.

"Sorry, sorry, never mind, it's okay," I hollered, waving my blackened Olympic Torch to the honking, flashing, throng— which included all our neighbors leaning out their front doors wondering what those crazy lesbians had done this time.

With great fanfare, the lead firefighter picked up his walkie-talkie and barked, "Attention!! Fried Tupperware. Fried Tupperware. All units back in service."

"Fried Tupperware" echoed a half dozen two-way radios, "Fried Tupperware. Over and Out."

"I'm so sorry," I said to the Fire Investigator.

"Don't be," he said. "Happens all the time. Glad it wasn't a fire. But lady, next time, just call one county and let us decide if we need a second alarm."

"Thanks," I said. "At least we know our escape plan works."

So we liberated Max and the photo albums from the car, opened every window in the house to dissipate the stink, and eventually got through the rest of the weekend.

I missed the beach. Maybe next year the Jazz Fest ads could carry tiny disclaimers saying "Warning: this concert contains material which may be offensive to women formerly married to tuxedoed accordion players who insisted on playing inappropriate selections, like *Age of Aquarius* and *I Can't Get No Satisfaction* on the squeeze box. Oy, I'm having a flashback....▼

November 1996

I used to think it was age. That 40-plus thing where you get downstairs to the kitchen and forget why. Or you find yourself digging through your desk for something but it's anybody's guess if you'll know when you find it.

"I'm going nuts," I thought this morning, when I lost my credit card between the gas pump and the car. I had it in my hand after pumping, but by the time I got into the car it was gone. Like Houdini.

There's nothing as pathetic on a rainy morning as a woman in corporate drag, crawling under her car looking for Mr. Visa.

He did not turn up.

But in taking the compulsory actions to cover the disappearance, I realized just what's wrong with us. Our brains are full.

I have a friend who knows all the lyrics to every show tune ever written. Once, when she was launching into the mercifully obscure *Jubilation T. Cornpone* from *L'il Abner,* I asked, "How do you remember all this crap?"

"It's where algebra should be," she said.

At that moment I discovered the concept of the finite brain. Kneeling in a gasoline puddle frantically pawing for my elusive Visa card, I recognized my problem as brain-RAM failure.

My skull is so full it couldn't process what happened to the little grey card in my hand. And what happened next proved why our brains are so overloaded.

Soaking wet and defeated, I headed for the office where, as the first one in, I had to disarm the burglar alarm with code 20901 (not the real number) so I could get in to call Credit Card Central. After dialing the area code and number on the office phone system, I had to key in my department number 007 (not the real number) and personal code 911 (not the real number) so my office can track who's calling numbers where somebody named Bambi answers.

Once I got through to Visa I had to give them my social security number 000-00-001 (not the real number. I just feel that old), and my mother's maiden name, Kelsey (True. How that happened to the little Jewish family at Ellis Island is another story.) and convince the operator I couldn't read her my credit card number because I lost it, and she'd better hurry and cancel it because as we were speaking some terrorist organization was probably charging para-military uniforms from L.L. Bean.

Next I called the bank to find out how much cash I had since I was now cut off from plastic.

"Welcome to your automatic reply line. Press 1 for savings accounts (what's that?) 2 for bill payment (familiar territory) and 3 for account balances...."

Then I had to punch in my lengthy account number, pin number (my dog's birthday), zip code, and maiden name thing again.

By the time I got the depressing balance, my voice mail button was blinking and I had to punch in my mailbox code 666 (not the real number, but what the hell) to retrieve my message.

It was my daily spousal call (look how low I've sunk to shore up my once-sharp memory) to make sure I pick up the dry-cleaning.

Next I powered up the computer and typed my convoluted virus-avoiding cryptogram password (I'm not even going to make one up here. With my luck I'd accidentally give those terrorists with my credit card access to the Federal Reserve) and typed in about a million http//dotcoms. I was looking up information about my recent cholesterol test results.

I typed my good cholesterol numbers and my bad cholesterol numbers and my e-mail address MVNoozy@aol.com (I think I'm telling the truth here) so some skinny doctor could analyze my fractions and tell me never to eat another Twinkie.

Then I checked my e-mail, wracking my bulging brain to recall which deliciously campy screen name went with which Tom, Dick or Larry. When I finished typing computer gibberish, I had an epic voice-mail message with instructions for contacting a colleague by beeper.

Oh, for a few stolen moments with an old-fashioned ink-smeared *Washington Post*—perhaps in the bathroom, where computers fear to tread. So far.

The phone rang. "I just opened the cellular phone bill and it's $856!" shrieked Bonnie. "What have you been doing, conferring with the Psychic Network on your way home?"

"No! If I had I would have known when to intercept the bill!!!"

So I called the phone company ("Your call is very important to us so stay on the line until hell freezes over") to learn that some computer geek had electronically cloned my cell phone number and was, by now, shouting orders to the credit-card wielding terrorists in Paraguay.

They assigned me another password, admonishing me, for safety sake, just to memorize it, not write it down. I told them not to worry. If I wrote it I'd only forget where I put it. Maybe I should just tattoo my compendium of codes and passwords on my person.

The final straw came later, when having a pizza delivered seemed the only sensible way to end the day. Now I don't know about you, but I find that businesses using clever wordplay for their phone numbers make me nuts. My brain is teeming with anagrams for pizza (227-FAST) and plumbers (1-800-HOT-WATER) but I never find the matching key pad digits fast enough to stave off the telephone company distress signal. Craving pepperoni and urgently hunting for the alphabet on the phone, I slowly tap F-A-S-T, get through, and order the damned pizza.

"Phone number?" the dispatcher asks.

I pull it up from my grey matter.

"Address?"

I spout my street and house numbers.

"Name?"

Um...um...it takes forever for me to spit it out!

It's any wonder I can remember it at all. After all, I hardly use it anymore. Whole days go by when my bank, HMO, personal computer, and e-mail haven't a clue Fay Jacobs exists. She's a pin number, account number, screen name, social security number, or zip code.

Now I'm sitting here madly calculating dog years to figure out when those puppies were born so I can come up with my ATM pin number. I feel like a 386 in a world of pentiums.

I'm absoutely sure humans were designed for a simpler time. If God meant us to store this many codes and passwords he'd have given us upgradable memory.

Luckily, I don't have room on my hard drive to worry about it. ▼

April 1997

Years ago, my father told me that the little infuriating things in life —and even some of the really big bad things—aren't half so bad if you wind up with a good story to tell.

It's been his best advice to me—especially since the rest from that era tended toward "It wouldn't kill you to wear a dress to your sister's wedding" and "You'll never find a husband if you buy a house with another girl."

We've come a long way since then. For the record, wearing a dress to the wedding didn't kill me, but the shoes almost did. And buying the house with Bonnie pretty much covered that finding-a-husband thing. And go figure—Dad even sent us an anniversary card this year.

But the advice about turning lemons into stories about lemonade really stuck. I try to find something worth smiling about in just about every stupid, annoying or awful thing that befalls me. It's gotten me through some tough stuff.

But I thought I'd met my Waterloo last fall when Bonnie and I found out our dog Max was sick. There was nothing to smile about—not his three surgeries to remove the cancerous cells, not the uncertain prognosis, and surely not the staggering vet bills.

But now that it's spring and woman's best friend is doing better than expected, I realize that despite our fragile feelings on the subject there are some tales to wag.

First, there was the ritzy New York Animal Medical Center our vet referred us to after she removed a cancerous tumor from Max's leg.

Virtually indistinguishable from a people hospital, the Center had signs directing visitors to Admitting, Cardiac Care, Dialysis, Surgery, and of course, the Cashier.

"Dr. McKnight to Oncology" crackled the loud speaker as scrub-coated aides and concerned "parents" accompanied spaniels, retrievers and Siamese felines from place to place.

I don't know what this says about the state of our own hospitals, but one thing I didn't see was a hallway full of moaning, abandoned patients.

In Admitting, Bonnie, Max and I sat amid other patients and their companions. Nearby, a woman clutched a squiggling tube sock to her chest. This worried me, as I refused to see ANY movie at Midway until *Anaconda* departed, lest I see even a poster.

So I was greatly relieved when a bald rodent popped out of the sock. Somebody get the Rogaine. The woman's beloved ferret was being treated for hair loss.

To our right sat an Armani-clad cover girl type with a white poodle shaved into topiary; on our left was an unshaven, rumpled bag man clutching a cat carrier. He got the same VIP service as everyone else.

When our turn came, Max went to Oncology, where his new specialist ordered tests to see if Max's aggressive form of cancer would respond to radiation. He would stay for six weeks of treatment at a cost roughly equivalent to our spending the same six weeks in Barbados—but there would be a 95 percent chance of remission.

Unfortunately, tests revealed a cancerous lymph node and poor Max underwent the knife again—eliminating the radiation option and sending us home to a course of Schnauzer chemotherapy.

Not funny. Especially not the sobering visit to the hospital cashier, or the added insult of having to drive back to the beach on Thanksgiving Eve, the worst travel day of the year. We had 10 hours to creep and weep our way down the Jersey Turnpike with a groggy post-op dog.

But from there things got so weird we had to laugh.

First it was the pills. Doggie chemo is taken orally. Not, however, willingly.

For the first week, we spent ten minutes, three times a day prying Max's jaws open, depositing five dollars worth of pills, and having him spit them back at us until—worn to a frazzle by

Bonnie's refusal to give up—he'd gulp.

By week two he pretended to swallow and ran, making us race to find whatever chair, sofa or shoe he used for a spittoon.

So we started embedding the fistful of pills in people food like smoked salmon cream cheese, frozen custard, and hummus. Max's palette was getting so sophisticated he should have been doing the restaurant reviews for this publication.

Along with the chemo, Max took Tagamet. Great. With my gallbladder gone, I no longer subsist on Tums but I'm paying $9 a week for antacids anyway.

Another medication had Max constantly gulping water. Every night from November to March, Bonnie or I had to drag our butts out of bed in the middle of the night so Max could visit a fire hydrant and impersonate it. We had one, two and sometimes three dog nights.

Would he use newspaper? No way. We'd say "Please, Max, here's an old issue of *Letters from CAMP*. I swear, Steve won't mind...." But no. Lucky for her, June Allyson missed Max modeling Depends.

Totally sleep deprived, we barely survived the holidays, our workweeks, and the inevitable exhaustion-caused snippiness.

Meanwhile, between pees, Max slept like the Gerber Baby since his regimen also included drowse-inducing Benadryl.

After spending our nights jumping up and down to let him out, we got some measure of revenge every morning by not letting sleeping dog lie. "Wake up! Max, rise and shine," we'd holler, shaking him awake. One morning I could swear he said "Ten more minutes...."

Meanwhile, as his thirst subsided, ravenous hunger took over.

Once a picky eater, Max started swallowing everything but his bowl. And who could deny a poor ailing creature?

Before, when Rehoboth shopkeepers gave him treats, he'd just push them around. "He doesn't like to eat out," I'd sheepishly explain. Now, Max shoves his furry face through the door at our pet shop, rushes for the dog cookies and runs up a tab.

On one beach commute, our formerly polite pooch waited until Bonnie was busy paying the Bay Bridge toll, lunged up like Jaws and—just when you thought it was safe to go through the toll booth—separated Bonnie from her Big Mac.

Naturally, Max started porking up and bursting out of his tiny Canine Klein T-shirts. Short of sending him to Jenny Craig, we tried lo-cal Rawhide chews. Now he's addicted to them and needs Rawhidette gum.

Lest you think the dog is suffering, let me tell you he's having the time of his life. He goes everywhere with us, like a pampered European pet—including being invited into certain Rehoboth coffee bars which should, in the name of propriety, remain nameless. He can, however, tell you where to find terrific Biscotti.

And he's far more socially plugged in than we are. Max and I crossed Rehoboth Avenue last week to hear somebody call, "Hi ya Max!" What am I, chopped liver?

We were shopping one day when somebody we barely knew ran up to us and asked if Max could wait—her mother was just finishing up at the cash register and would be right out to see him. I feel like his personal assistant—"Have your people bark at my people and we'll do lunch."

The dog turned 13 last month ("Max will be barking the Torah at 11:30 with luncheon to follow") and celebrated his Bark Mitzvah. Okay, okay, I realize we may be in denial, but Bonnie and I have been sublimating our fear of losing him and making every day count.

But now that the chemo treatment is over, it's a little harder. When he was swallowing 14-k gold pills, we felt we were being pro-active. Now we just wait to see what happens.

We're hoping for the best, but know that things can go downhill fast. But in the meantime, we feel like we've done everything possible for Max—even if we've been overly permissive parents. In fact, I think we've turned him into a spoiled SCHNAP (Schnauzer American Prince).

Last week during my Ellen-Comes-Out party he begged

hummus and pita, accepted an offer of Boursin cheese and crackers, snagged several slurps of Merlot and, in a brazen move, made off with a slice of pizza while my back was turned.

If he lives, we're gonna kill him.▼

May 1997

MY LIFE AS BALLAST

The realtor caught us by surprise. "There's a gay square dance group in town May 1. You want a rental?"

It was waaay too soon. The thought of stuffing a whole winter's debris into our owner's closet and schlepping onto the boat seemed idiotic, especially with morning frost still on the boardwalk and the boat on land in a big baggie. Besides, no way we'd give up our favorite spring mornings in town.

"They're willing to pay a lot."

"Show me the money!" we hollered and started packing. And I confess, I was less nuts this time. Last year I stripped the place of so much stuff it looked like an abandoned crack house. But now that I know the tax advantage of buying stuff for a rental, I'm encouraging our tenants to break or steal things so I can buy them again this fall.

With the condo secured, we arranged to do launch and drive the boat back to the marina in Dewey. Our actor son joined us and naturally, we'd picked a cold, rainy day.

With clothes, bedding and bare necessities (TV, blender, CD player), we set out from our winter storage site up river back to Rehoboth Bay.

At best it's a dicey trip, since one narrow channel is the only route our boat with its 3-foot draft can travel. Go an inch off course, and the propeller hits bottom, getting chewed up like a spoon down a garbage disposal.

So we set out—and couldn't find the channel markers. They were missing. The Delaware Coast Guard must have taken them to the dry cleaners and forgotten to pick them up.

We blundered forward in the rain and fog, with Bonnie watching the depth finder plummet to 2 feet, 5 inches. And some of that was mud.

"Go stand out front," Bonnie said to me, "maybe it will help raise the prop in the back."

Great. I can call my autobiography *My Life as Ballast*.

"You look like Barbara Stanwyk, heading for a Titanic lifeboat," said the actor. "Are we stuck?"

"Not yet," said Captain Bonnie throttling forward into the goo and then jolting to a stop.

"Now we're stuck," I said, from the bow pulpit at the boat's nose where I'd landed from the short stop. Below me, the water was ankle deep.

The leading man joined me on my perch and we both leaned over and stared.

"Ohmigod, those are clams," he said.

Then Max trotted out to join us and Bonnie hollered, "That's it, everybody back in the cockpit."

Easy for her to say. The three of us clung to the teeny platform like survivors from Wallenda's seven-man pyramid. Finally the captain had to crawl onto the deck herself, and with outstretched hands, guide the three wimps back into the boat.

"We could be stuck here all day. Call the marina and ask somebody to come get us," I said, thinking it a valid solution.

To Bonnie it ranked with "stop at the gas station and ask for directions" or "call Microsoft Tech support"—not to be tried in the first two hours of any crisis.

"Maybe somebody will come by and tow us home," Sir Laurence Olivier wished outloud.

"There aren't any other morons out here," I said, glancing at the depth finder. Two feet, three inches. "Maybe we should just get out and walk back."

By this time Bonnie had the boat in reverse, trying to dislodge us from the muck.

"We won't be missed until Steve wonders why I didn't turn in a column this week."

"And I've got an audition on Thursday...to be or not to be...."

"Forget that," it looks like the dog is thinking, "to pee or not to pee, that is the question."

Bonnie finally had enough. "Will you two cut it out. You aren't helping."

We didn't know we were supposed to.

"Just what she needs," mumbled Marlon Brando, "two sissies in the front seat giving her moral support."

With that, Bonnie gunned the engine and we shot backwards, sending everything in the boat flying. But we were afloat.

After that, I don't think the captain found the channel, as much as dug a new one.

Back at our marina, gusty winds and tsunami waves rocked the boat while the cabin had sheets, towels, and small appliances flung everywhere. I couldn't tell if I was home or in a Goodwill Collection box.

Out on the pier I found a note from the phone installer. "Your phone service is working. I installed the line as far as the Rate of Demarcation Point near the marina. If you have any questions call 227- whatever."

I had a question. If my phone service was on and I was paying for it, where the heck was my phone jack? Bonnie and I went out onto the blustery pier to look for it, but found none behind our boat or anywhere between the slip and the parking lot. As we lay on our bellies searching for under-dock wiring we wondered if Natalie Wood had been looking for her phone jack when she went down.

Wind howling around me, I called the phone company from a nearby pay phone.

"What problem are you reporting?"

"I can't find my phone."

That stopped the conversation.

I explained that I'd expected to find a phone jack installed on my dock.

"What? I can't hear you. You'll have to speak up."

"You can't hear me because I'm outside at a pay phone, we're having a cyclone and I can't find my f-ing telephone. We both started to laugh and she assured me that an installer would return the next day and fix me up.

Back in the boat, Bonnie, Max and I huddled for warmth and surfed off to sleep, dreaming of lucky square dancers do-si-doing back to a warm condo which wasn't pitching and rolling.

By morning we dragged ourselves out of berth, threw on crumpled clothes and drove to town for breakfast...driving by the condo to gaze wistfully at it on our way.

At our favorite coffee shop, our favorite waitperson took one look at us and said, "Whoa. Rough night?"

"First night on the boat," Bonnie grunted, "We have renters."

With that, a gaggle of women in fringed shirts and cowboy boots came in. One couple asked another, "How's the place you're staying?"

"Great," said a rested-looking woman, "it's a beach block condo and it's real homey. Not stripped down like lots of rentals."

Bonnie poked me in the ribs and winked.

So we slunk off to await the phone man and clean our floating house. With the weather improving, we phoned in our pizza order and waited for the dock party to begin. Pity the poor renters with their parking tickets, and kids screaming for T-shirts and beach fries, while we watch a gorgeous sunset and imagine all the tax deductions we'll buy for the condo come fall.

Home sweet boat. ▼

May 1997

By the time Thursdays roll around I've pretty much had it up to
my eyeballs with people assuming everybody is heterosexual.
That's why I love beach weekends—with all the diversity in this
community, gay people get a breather from the insulting
assumptions we hear most everywhere else.

And when Rehoboth burst to life on Memorial Day weekend,
I counted dozens of reasons why my comfort level is so high.
Between an awesome women's dance at the convention center
(even if Bonnie and I were the oldest women on the dance floor),
and Baltimore Avenue teeming with gay people, we were everywhere.

Insulting assumptions were mercifully hard to come by.

Unlike last week when Bonnie and I were at our local mall
and a salesman eyed the two of us, looked at my credit card and
asked, "What are you, sisters, or something?"

Now this happens to most lesbian couples I know, even if
they're as different as Jack and Mrs. Sprat. The only exception
(and I'm not even including race here) is when only one lesbian
has grey hair. Then they ask the embarrassing, "mother and
daughter?"

But mostly it's the sister thing. When one lesbian offers a
credit card to pay for purchases for the pair, salespeople make
the only assumption they're conditioned to make: it's not a husband and wife or parent and child, so these women with financial ties must be, uh, um, sisters!

When the clerk asked if we were sisters or something I wanted to ask if he was a moron or something, but I settled for telling
him we were merely "or something."

Gay people need an ad campaign to let the world know that
alternative spousal relationships exist. We could plaster busses
and billboards with photos of great looking lesbian couples saying "We're no sister act." Or posters of three embracing cou-

ples—two men, two women and a mix 'n match, with copy reading "Just friends? Think again."

And the first place I'd post them would be hotels.

Recently we checked into the Fairmont in Chicago, where a clerk asked us "Can you make do with one bed or do you want two?"

Boldly, without hesitation, I said "One will be fine."

The clerk looked at us and said "Are you sure? Because I can get you a room with two."

"I'm sure," I said with conviction, "We'll take the room with one."

"Well, let's check a minute," she continued, tapping on her keyboard.

"Really, it's not..." I protested.

"Oh! Here we go! I *do* have a room with two beds," she said triumphantly, handing me a key.

Invisible lesbians. I don't think she would have listened if it had been my picture instead of Ellen DeGeneres on *Time* magazine with the "Yup, I'm Gay!" headline.

Then there was the gallstone incident.

I arrived at the emergency room with what felt like a Subaru Outback lodged in my gut. I'm doubled over in a triage room chair and they shove a financial responsibility form under my nose asking me to check, among other things, single, married or divorced. I was in no mood to debate. I qualified to check all three, so I did. Hours later, after being told I needed surgery, they got me again.

"Mrs. Jacobs, er...Miss, er, Jacobs...er..." (I guess they read the financial form.) "We're taking you to X-Ray. Is there any chance you're pregnant?"

"No, not a chance."

"Are you sure?"

"Absolutely."

"There's not the slightest chance you could be pregnant?"

"No. I don't sleep with men and my biological clock stopped ticking before the lesbian baby boom."

Now this got her attention, but she couldn't seem to process the information.

"So you're sure?"

"That I'm a lesbian? You bet." Morphine is really good stuff. I never did find out what she checked on the form.

In my pre-op haze I recalled other such indignities. Like the ignorant transmission man who assumed I was scamming him when I brought the car in under Bonnie's warranty; the insensitive people who ask Bonnie "are you still with Fay?" when they'd never dream of asking married friends the same question; and the legions of Americans who assume that straight couples are the only ones working hard, paying taxes, and living in the suburbs with station wagons and dogs.

Finally, a nurse came to take me to the O.R. and asked who'd be in the lounge awaiting word of my condition. I gave her Bonnie's name. "Friend or relative?" the nurse asked. Another trick question!

"Um, relative."

"Sister? "

"No. Um..."

I finally lost it and whimpered "Spouse...." To her credit, the nurse, with a hint of apology said, "Oh. I guess we need some time to get used to these situations so we can do better."

Well, the rest of the world should take a lesson from Rehoboth. Capping the weekend, Bonnie and I were half a foursome celebrating a birthday at a Wilmington Avenue restaurant. Behind us, two straight couples in their late 60s or early 70s celebrated a birthday too, and we exchanged toasts.

When they asked where we were from, I pointed to the boys and said "These guys have a home here, and we're from Maryland, but spend weekends here on our boat."

And lo and behold, the quartet had not a moment's hesitation processing our non-traditional coupling. And that's how it should be. No if, and, or assumption about it. ▼

June 1997

Partway through our rainy, windy, miserable spring, I heard an explanation for it on the weather channel—something about a jet stream screw-up causing El Niño winds. I was explaining it to my friend the accountant who said "then El Niño must be Spanish for f-ing cold."

He had a point.

And while we were reduced to wearing ski jackets in June and passing the dog around for warmth, El Niño really got on my nerves when my best friend from high school visited the beach with her family.

Too cold for beach or boat, and too inappropriate to suggest spending the day downing Bloody Marys, we did the beach fries, funnel cake, T-shirt thing, then bowed to the 10-year-old's request to visit the boardwalk amusements.

First we played Whack-a-Mole, where you take a heavy mallet and bash small plastic forest creatures popping up through holes in a table. I was terrible at it—always a day late and a mole short. Bonnie, Best Friend, and the kids gave those moles migraines from hell, scoring 180 to my 40. By our sixth round I hiked my score to 60 by hovering over only one hole and whacking the daylights out of its lone inhabitant.

I was pondering Whack-a-Mole as an allegory for coming out of the closet at a Southern Baptist Convention when the youngest player asked "What do you get for winning Whack-a-Mole?"

"Carpal Tunnel Syndrome," I said.

"Aunt Fay, want to go on the bumper cars?" a young-un asked.

"No, you go." I said, wondering why anybody would pay to get whiplash when you have such a good chance of getting it for free on Route One.

Suddenly, fog rolled in from the ocean, plunging the board-

walk into a dense haze. Best Friend and I lost sight of the kids—
including Bonnie.

By the time we saw them again they were in some sort of
line, which I inadvertently joined when I walked up to ask what
they were waiting for.

"Great, you're going with us!" Bonnie said with a finality
cinched by the 40 people now behind us in line.

It seemed I was going on some sort of circular contraption
painted like a wagon train, with little two-person cages harm-
lessly rocking back and forth. It didn't look bad.

I didn't see the sign until I was next in line to board. "Not recommended for pregnant women, people with high blood pressure, heart problems, bad backs or with any other medical problems...." It included everything but toenail fungus.

I'd have cut and run but there were too many eight-year-
olds behind me. I stepped into the gently swinging cage, sat
down and pulled the security bar across my lap. That should
have been my first clue—it was encased in about a foot of foam
rubber.

Sharing my cage was Best Friend's son, the recent college
grad, who asked, "You're going to be okay with this, right Aunt
Fay?" Clue two.

With a sickening grinding of gears our cage shot forward,
and promptly turned completely upside down, hanging me by
my thighs and emptying my pockets of a whole winter's stash of
parking meter quarters.

"Oh my god!!!" somebody, who turned out to be me,
screamed as I closed my eyes and saw myself hanging over
Rehoboth like a sloth.

As we righted ourselves, sixteen dollars in quarters came
back and hit me in the face. Best Friend watched in horror. If her
face looked that bad and she was on the ground, what did my....

"AHHHHHHH!! Houston, we have a problem!!!!" We flipped
again, and this time I was sure I was falling out, that stupid bar
no match for a well-fed woman who was, at that moment, regret-
ting the funnel cake.

With visions of a Barbara Walters expose on amusement park accidents flashing before me, I clung to the bar, blood rushing to my brain, and centrifugal force flinging my breasts back where they hadn't been since puberty.

"Here we go again!" hollered my cage-mate, either to warn me or drown out my moaning.

Again and again the cage whirled in circles, turning us upside down until I was finally heard screaming "I'm almost 50 years old! What in the El Niño am I doing here !!!!"

Then, mercifully, it stopped. I was helped from the cage by my solicitous escort, who politely noted my sea-green complexion and went to get me a Coke.

"Well, what did you think?" asked Bonnie, whose face was still its natural color and who seemed to be getting a perverse thrill in knowing I wanted to kill her.

"I think I'm going to barf," I said, to the laughter of my companions. It was obvious that my entire entourage thought I was a whack-a-mole-challenged, bumper car-fearing, easily nauseated, amusement-phobic ninny.

I staggered toward the old-fashioned Shooting Gallery arcade, where you could fire a rifle at targets on an outhouse door, a moonshine jug and the back of a piano player's head. I especially liked that one. I used to be married to a keyboard guy.

Bonnie, Best Friend and the kids looked at this antiquated amusement with no lights, no virtual reality, no joy stick and no computer graphics, turning up their noses.

Fine. I borrowed two quarters, plunked them into the slot and started to fire. Bam. Down went a duck. Bam. Open came the outhouse door. Bam. A whole bunch of geese bought it. Bam, Bam, Bam. To my great glee the pianist was history. 25 shots, 25 hits.

More quarters were offered.

I didn't know if I was Annie Oakley or an Earp brother. 50 shots, 50 hits and the piano player got it twice just for spite. Did I see some respect blooming on the faces of my entourage?

"Wow" said the pre-teen; "Impressive," said the young man;

"Doesn't this worry you, Bonnie?" asked the Best Friend.

"No," said Bonnie, "but I suggest we let her have her way for the rest of the day."

It was on the way out of the amusement area, between the Tea Cup ride and the hamster cage thing, that I spied the professionally printed sign that pretty much sums up my experience. It said NOT RESPONSIBLE FOR SOILED CLOTHING.

If not them, then who? El Niño? And what exactly are they trying to say, really? It's there on the wall by the Haunted House. If you get down that way check it out and let me know what you think. And look for my quarters embedded in the boardwalk.

But a word of warning: funnel cake or hamster cage. Never both. ▼

June 1997

"Why the hell don't you write fiction," Bonnie said, "then maybe these stupid things wouldn't happen to us all the time." She had a point.

We were stranded in the middle of Rehoboth Bay with a boat full of actors and a big metal crab pot stuck to our propeller. The actors were a trio of musical comedy folks set to perform that night in Lewes.

We'd planned a leisurely afternoon cruise. At 3:30 p.m. we were ten minutes from completing the ride, leaving plenty of time for the actors to get back to Lewes and rest up for the evening—when the submerged crab pot, no warning float attached, attacked our propeller. Cruuunch, thud, short stop, beer everywhere.

"There's good news and bad news," I said. "The bad news is we're dead in the water; the good news is we have a dozen free crabs."

"Right," said the captain, "repairs alone will make those free crabs worth about a hundred bucks each."

Bonnie and I stared at the twisted metal mess behind the boat while the actors retreated to the bow to argue over who'd be a better Ginger from *Gilligan's Island*.

"Let me take a look at the situation," said a passenger we'll call Kayak Man. He offered to get into the water to survey the damage. "How deep is it here?" he asked.

"Shallow. I doubt if it's over four feet," I said. "We're always running aground."

He climbed down the swim ladder and completely disappeared. He was pissed, but we'd finally found the channel. Bobbing for air, Kayak Man noticed that our new crabs were still very much alive. "I'm not touching those things, they're snapping at me!" crab phobic Kayak Man said, scrambling back aboard.

"This will be great material for another story," somebody said to me, prompting my grabbing my little notebook to take down details.

"Put the damn book away and start flapping your arms in the distress signal for a tow," Bonnie hollered. The actors joined me and I couldn't tell if we were calling for help or doing *Hello Dolly*.

I grabbed the cell phone and called for a rescue party. We waited, trying not to think of the clock ticking toward show time. "Have you ever been stuck before?" asked a performer.

"Once or twice," I allowed.

I told of a particularly memorable incident on the Chesapeake Bay where our boat, stocked with a quartet of lesbians, suffered a dead ignition switch. We needed a hot wire, and loathe as I am to admit this, not one of us had that skill.

A good Samaritan came along, climbed aboard, and flopped onto his back beneath the boat's dashboard to play with the wires. Bonnie handed him requested tools.

"Screwdriver." She handed it over.

"Wrench." She handed it over.

"Pair of dykes."

Excuse me????? We looked urgently at each other, knowing we had two pair aboard, but not knowing which couple to sacrifice. The four of us clamped our mouths shut and clutched our sides to keep from exploding into hysterics.

"Dykes. You know, needle nosed pliers, have you got any?" asked the mechanic, mercifully unaware of his double entendre and ensuing commotion.

"Oh, right!!!" Bonnie said, handing him the proper instrument. Fortunately the engine turning over covered our roaring laughter.

The next day we conducted an informal tool survey—needle nosed pliers really are called dykes.

Back to the present, our stranded crew was amused. "Hey, we've got a pair and a spare here" said one of our crew, pointing at me and Bonnie, then herself.

"Are they really called that?" asked an incredulous actor.

"I've never heard of such a thing."

"I hadn't either," I said.

"Somebody was putting you on," said Kayak Man.

With that, we saw our marina rescue boat heading toward us. Pulling alongside, the mechanic boarded our craft, looked down at the crab pot stuck to the prop and the first thing out of his mouth was "Do you have a pair of dykes?"

"I...rest...my...case," I managed to spit before stuffing my hat in my mouth to keep from howling. Now there were seven people clutching their sides, screaming with laughter. The mechanic had no idea what he'd said.

Since the only pair of you-know-whats we had aboard were human, we had to be towed back to the marina for repairs. The actors fled as soon as we hit terra firma.

Bonnie was about to do the butch thing and jump in the water to yank the damned crab pot off the back of her boat when the rescue team directed us to stand on the bow to help lift the prop out of the water. "Woman's work," Bonnie muttered. "Now we can call your damn book "*Our* life as ballast."

Then, Kayak Man, who was the remaining man on the crew, was asked to stand behind the boat and do the honors with—what else—a pair of dykes.

In a burst of machismo, Kayak Man slipped into the water, grabbed the aforementioned rudely-named tool, followed instructions for cutting part of the mangled metal away, and freed the propeller. Triumphantly, he waved his pair of dykes in the air. Our hero.

So the actors made it on stage in time, the boat seemed no worse for wear, and we all proved what we'd surely suspected: you never know when a pair of dykes will come in real handy. ▼

July 1997

People thought I was kidding when I vowed to recreate one of history's most famous journey's—not Lewis & Clark, not Amelia Earhart, but Barbra Streisand's *Funny Girl* tugboat trip in New York Harbor. I intended to take our boat to the Statue of Liberty, climb out on the bow and sing *Don't Rain on My Parade*.

Then Bonnie and I planned to keep a promise made a decade ago in Fire Island. We saw two women having cocktails on their boat in Cherry Grove and said, "Someday that will be us."

"You're taking that little boat in the ocean? To New York?" folks said, laughing.

And when they heard that our friends Bob and Larry—men who'd never spent one night on a small boat, much less ten— were joining us, they were sure we were making it up.

But we were prepared. Each couple was permitted a reasonable amount of clothing, toiletries, food, and drink. The guys did great limiting themselves on clothes and toiletries, but I'd never seen that much yogurt in my life.

Robert's eager anticipation seemed based on the thrill of seeing New York harbor as well as the challenge of keeping the boat really, really clean for the next ten days.

Larry was worried about keeping busy enough, so I gave him the task of ship's accountant—calculating the amount of boat gas and associated expenses needed for our travels. Then I made him swear to keep the total to himself. The golden rule of boating is NEVER, under any circumstances, divide the amount you spend in a season by the number of days you use the boat. Former boaters are in rubber rooms from coast to coast from doing that equation.

Our ship's log tells the tale.

Day 1 (July 3) – Rough start. Worst Delaware Bay crossing ever. Wind made five foot waves, drenching us and our new red shirts, dying our white shorts pink. Robert crawled across the deck to get Larry a life jacket. I requested one too but he didn't hear me for strains of *There Has to be a Morning After* in his ears. When the worst was over, we almost injured ourselves rushing for the vodka.

Made it to Cape May for crustaceans to go, and toodled up the Intercoastal Waterway behind Jersey towns of Wildwood and Stone Harbor. Collected ourselves and cooked a lovely lobster dinner at a marina in Avalon. It's 70 degrees and windy. No A/C needed tonight—just open up those hatches and breathe!

Day 2 - Yeah. And inhale a lung full of gnats. Robert woke us up coughing and slamming the hatches.

Too rough for ocean route today so we continued on the Intercoastal through the great black fly fields of New Jersey. No wonder the houses have no decks. As we were swatting, shooing and snapping the flies to death with towels, it crossed my mind that the backwaters of New Jersey may have given birth to the *Macarena*.

Arrived at Barnegat Bay marina 5 pm. and fired up the blender while Robert and Bonnie hosed sea spray off the deck. We're exhausted and ready for sleep. In the distance we hear fireworks, but we're too tired to care.

Day 3 – Gorgeous. Cruised calmly up the Jersey shore past long white beaches, Ferris wheels and roller coasters of Ocean City N.J. Small planes trailing ad banners buzzed overhead as we raced north. At Asbury Park, we saw something in the distance.

"Is it a tanker with smokestacks?"

"I don't think so," said the captain, squinting into the haze. "It looks like buildings."

One more look and I got goose bumps—the twin towers of Manhattan's World Trade Center rose on the horizon. But it was just a tease, as the towers disappeared when we veered west around Sandy Hook, N.J.

At a marina, we relaxed, read and napped, waking at one point to hear some seafarers behind our boat asking each other what kind of yacht club flies a rainbow flag. An exclusive one, I thought.

After yet another fuel fill-up, we capped the day watching fireworks on the beach.

Day 4 - We did it! At 11 a.m. with a clear sky and barely rippling water, we cruised under the Verazanno Bridge and right up to the towering Statue of Liberty. As her inscription says, "Give me your tired, your poor...." Well, here we were. Awesome.

At first, feeling very insignificant amid the tour boats and tankers, I was more like Yentl arriving with the immigrant tide than Babs defiantly singing on the front of the tug boat.

"You're not really going out front are you?" asked Robert as the boat bounced and pitched from the wakes of passing tankers.

"I came all this way and I'm gonna do it," I said, a poor, tired, huddled mass, inching my way to the nose of the boat and humming "No-body, no no-body, is gon-na rain on my...."

We all took turns hanging onto the bow pulpit for photo ops and Captain Bonnie stayed calm even when the Staten Island Ferry threatened to crawl up our stern.

Then we cruised around the tip of Manhattan, under the Brooklyn Bridge and up the East River for spectacular views of the City skyline.

A thousand Kodak moments later, we docked at the 23rd street marina—in the shadow of the Empire State Building, lit up red, white and blue for the holiday. After venturing to Times Square for dinner and returning to our boatel, those patriotic lights were the last thing we saw before falling asleep.

Day 5 - We wanted to wake up in the city that doesn't sleep and here we are. But we didn't know that Sinatra's next lyrics about "king of the hill and top of the heap" referred to our dirty laundry. It threatened to sink the boat. We're debating sending it home FedEx.

It rained this morning and it turns out that London Fog is not foul weather gear. Yogurt is holding out. We're all still friends. And to think there were skeptics. Tomorrow, a short run to Fire

Island. Hey, if we can make it there, we'll make it anywhere.

Day 6 - Okay, so it was a little hazy on our way down the East River, but not what I'd call bad weather—until we rounded Coney Island and carefully ventured into the ocean. Suddenly, a thick fog completely socked us in, making it difficult to see the front of our own boat much less Coney Island. We would have stuck to our plan to hug the shore, only now we couldn't find it.

Then we heard the chilling moan of a foghorn. Omygod! The Titanic?

The guys studied the nautical charts and navigation instruments. "We're okay, I know where we are," said Larry.

We didn't have the heart to tell him that our knowing where we were wasn't the problem. Please let whoever blew that foghorn know where we were.

So we sounded our own deafening blast every 30 seconds, stayed as still as possible and wished we had radar instead of matching shirts.

And just when it got so creepy I thought I'd scream, an enormous tug boat trailing a thick tow line appeared. It was hauling a barge the size of Pittsburgh and was just a hair-raising 75 yards to our side.

My eyeballs changed sockets and I practically peed myself. Bonnie was struck dumb. "Anybody else mess their pants?" I cheerily asked. "That was close. Just a little farther and we would have been in that tow line...."

"But we weren't," said Robert, happily. You gotta love that attitude.

As the fog lifted we saw other small boats but still no shoreline. "We're here, we're queer, but where are we?" somebody muttered.

Before I could suggest otherwise, Bonnie hollered to a passing fisherman "Which way to Fire Island?" I thought she should ask for directions to the Rockaway Channel and leave it at that.

The unsavory-looking boater pointed sort of East and we took off before he could see the guys' pink shorts.

Still fogged in, we inched along the shore, with dozens of

jetties coming into focus in the nick of time for us to avoid crashing onto the rocks.

Somehow we found the channel and puttered past the Fire Island Lighthouse toward our destination. Our three-hour hop had become a tense six-hour ordeal by the time we reached Cherry Grove—but the welcome made it worthwhile. We docked at tea time with the speakers at Cherry's bar blaring *I Will Survive*.

It didn't take long for us to tie up and mix cocktails to the sounds of *I Like the Night Life* and *YMCA*.

If there were two women at the bar watching our happy hour on deck and saying "someday that will be us," I had two words for them: "Get radar."

So we took a water taxi to the Pines for a luscious dinner, shopped at the local Gay Mart and headed back to the boat. The piano bar was going full blast and the Ice Palace promised dancing 'til 4 a.m. We were all asleep by 10:30.

Day 7 - Took a lovely walk through the Grove with its grid of boardwalks, unfurled rainbow flags and houses named Think Pink, Peckerwood, and YMCA annex. Perfect beach day and entertainment—swimwear is optional in Cherry Grove, although not for us, thank you very much.

Late in the day folks warned us that a big storm was brewing and the marina was a notoriously unprotected harbor.

We battened the hatches, put all our fenders out, tied the boat as tightly as possible and got the hell off—some of us more successfully than others.

With no finger piers alongside the boat and just a deteriorating foothold board along the seawall, every debarking was a crapshoot. We all share the humiliation of the one of us who took a header into the water as an entire Fire Island happy hour crowd watched and hummed *It's Raining Men*.

Then, from a restaurant overlooking the slip we ordered an exquisite meal, watched the boat blow back and forth, and repeated, "What the heck, we're insured."

At the next table, a woman and her husband eyed the predominantly gay crowd, including some large and lovely drag queens. The man leaned over to the four of us (seated across from, not next to, our respective partners) and said "pretty strange crowd, if you know what I mean...." wink, wink, wink, followed by a Beavis and Butthead laugh.

"Yeah, and we fit right in," Larry said proudly.

The man swallowed his shrimp, tail and all.

The sky turned black, but then the wind backed off, a few raindrops fell and it seemed we'd dodged the bullet.

Later, we sang show tunes at the piano bar, caught the Ice Palace drag show, and returned to the boat under clearing skies and calmer water. Now we're gently rocking in the slip with hopes for good weather tomorrow.

Day 8 - The storm was not over. At 1:30 a.m. the boat started to pitch and roll, waking everybody up so we could hang onto our bunks. "My God, we had sex three times and we didn't have to move" said Larry.

At 4 a.m. most of us were up watching for flying cows or trying to hold onto the evening's expensive dinner. By dawn we couldn't wait to get the hell out of what was arguably the worst marina (albeit the best music) in the world.

"Don't you guys try to shave or it will look like *M*A*S*H* in here," I warned, casting off our lines.

Miraculously, as we neared the Jones Beach inlet to the ocean, sun and blue sky reappeared, turning the water absolutely flat. We set our heading for Asbury Park, N.J. and the four of us settled into doing what we did best: Bonnie cheerfully at the helm, Larry navigating, Robert obsessing over dirty footprints on the deck and me writing it all down.

A few delightful hours later, we pulled into a marina with wonderful facilities, showers and a pool. I'll take clean bathrooms over Donna Summer and the Village People any day. Tomorrow: Atlantic City.

Day 9 - The good news is that it was another perfect boating day for our cruise to Harrah's Marina. The bad news is we used all our luck on the weather. Bonnie and I escaped from the casino with just enough cash to get us home. Atlantic City may be gaudy and ostentatious with its Trump's Taj Mahal and 100' yachts but it's Jersey all the same. It did our hearts good to see folks on the half a million dollar yacht next to us beating their monogrammed towels at the black flies.

Day 10 - Another gorgeous day. This time, Delaware Bay was a lake. As our happy crew, dirty laundry, and leftover yogurt returned to port, we bid a fond farewell to Fay, Bonnie, Robert & Larry's Excellent Adventure.

It was thrilling and exhausting—and if we learned anything, it's this: a boat's radar arch is not merely a design feature, London Fog is not really foul weather gear, and invest in fly swatters. But nobody, but nobody, rained on our parade. ▼

July 1997

Fantastic! I looked at the enormous crowd of women at our state park beach, settled into my chair and took out my decorative book.

I don't know about you, but in all my years at the women's beach at North Shores or the mostly men's sandy outpost at Poodle Beach, I've never actually finished a page of text—too much to look at. Although holding a book still gives me the reassuring sense I have the option to read if I ever want to.

One of the options I don't exercise is actually getting into the water. I swore off three summers ago, when my spouse lured me into the surf ("Don't worry, it's calm") from my comfortable chair amid a dozen friends staked out at water's edge.

I gingerly followed Aquawoman toward the breakers, turned to look at the waving crowd behind me, heard "Lookout!" and was instantly wiped out by a wave.

Being swept bass ackwards out to sea, then dribbled on the ocean floor like a basketball was bad; washing up on shore flat on my back with the entire lesbian caucus leaning over me like a shot from an old Busby Berkley movie was worse. Their sincere concern for my safety soon gave way to amusement that my bathing suit had left its moorings. First I thought I was dead, then I hoped I was dead.

So, rather than disturb my domestic tranquility, it's the ocean and I who are no longer speaking. Fortunately, I love lots of things about the beach exclusive of swimming. Like being surrounded by a whole bunch of terrific women, their friends and families.

Women of all ages, body sizes, bathing suits, haircuts and attitudes cram the beach. Oooh-wheee! Look at all the lesbian couples, lesbians with kids, lesbians with men and lesbians with dogs—we are fam-i-ly!

There were even lesbian luminaries. I was seated near

Human Rights Campaign Executive Director Elizabeth Birch and her friends. A lot of the time I spent not reading was spent wondering whether to go over and tell her how much I appreciate her efforts on our behalf—and to say I admire her for enduring a job where it's impossible to please everybody. I opted for letting her enjoy the beach without thinking about the office.

But as if we didn't know from her job success, no fool she— Ms. Executive Director walked waaaaay down the beach before boogey boarding—no washing ashore in front of the whole membership for her.

That night at a cookout, we heard tales about the gay merchants and homeowners who've been contributing to Rehoboth's evolution for a half-century or more. How I'd love to talk to some of those old-timers who had the foresight and spunk to start a community here.

I was thinking about those pioneers and how I might find out more about them last Sunday, when Bonnie and I spent the entire day relaxing at the marina.

As the temperature climbed past 95 degrees, I inflated my tiny three-ring (age 3 and up) swimming pool, and sat down cross-legged in it to cool off and read.

A story in the local press described some homeowner's questions for the candidates for City Commissioner. Buried among issues like traffic, parking and zoning was the phrase "keep Rehoboth a family town" and the ubiquitous cry for "family values."

Ouch. Those gay entrepreneurs, shopkeepers and homeowners who took a chance on Rehoboth years ago—developing and maintaining their properties, encouraging a vital resort economy and sharing their aesthetic sensibility, have certainly played a large part in the evolution of the great "family town" folks find worth keeping. I wonder if the family values crowd knows that our families have value, too.

Just then, two good-looking young men walked up the pier toward us. Certain they were headed past us, Bonnie shifted her chair to let them through. But they stopped two feet from us, looked down at me in my baby pool and asked, "Are you Fay Jacobs?"

I wished I wasn't. I considered telling them Fay was at the beach and I was the boat sitter; I rejected the notion of flipping onto my hands and knees doggy-style and struggling to my feet. I finally chose to admit it was me, and sit there, pretending I didn't feel like the star of *Free Willy*.

"We were just reading your boat story in *Letters* and we saw the rainbow flag on the boat and thought this must be you. We have a boat in this marina and...."

I'm looking up at these guys, trying to concentrate on what they're saying, pretty sure they've noticed I'm sitting in three inches of water, with my hips lodged in a K-Mart inflatable pool.

Bonnie, who smelled revenge, whispered, "Good, you can write about this so you'll be the laughing stock in the story for once," sweetly offered the guys a drink, then disappeared to make mudslides.

It turned out that these Philly guys work hard in the city all week and spend weekends at the beach just like we do. We compared notes on the cost of boating and martinis. And, I have to tell you, these men were classy. They pretended not to notice when, after another half-hour of sitting like a pruny pretzel, I finally pulled the plug on my playpen and ungracefully hauled my soggy ass back up into a chair.

We talked about keeping Rehoboth a "family" town. We talked about our gay families and friends. And we agreed that we should all demand that the Commissioners keep Rehoboth a family town for all kinds of families.

Last week I found myself trolling Maryland Avenue peering into my own apartment windows to gauge what havoc the family value renters wrought. Where's that Mars Pathfinder when you need it. "You're stalking your own condominium," Bonnie told me. "Get a grip."

Yeah, I reluctantly admit, Rehoboth should be for all families. But keep the pretzels out of the VCR.... ▼

October 1997

FICKLE FINGER OF FATE

Our adopted-son-the-actor has a theory. He thinks that the muse of essay writing has been smiting me with bizarre life circumstances so I'll have inspiration for my column.

I've pooh-poohed the idea for a while now, but as I sat in the Hand Clinic at Baltimore's Union Memorial Hospital, with the middle finger of my left hand poised decorously on the x-ray plate, I began to think he was onto something.

"Make a fist except for that finger," the technician requested. Um, okay.

The resultant brightly illuminated x-ray of me flipping the bird to the consulting physicians had the whole room screaming with laughter.

So why the x-rated x-ray? I'd been cultivating a bump inside my fingertip for some months, but it suddenly grew painful. Personally, I think the actor is right. These things don't happen to people who don't have to come up with an idea for a column on a regular basis.

Suffice to say I was in the operating room the next day, awake, but numb (somewhat my natural state) and listening to the surgeon proclaim, "Whoa! This is no princess and the pea." Apparently, the finger tumor (that's the first time I've ever typed those two words together) was a whopper, although fortunately it turned out to be a benign tumor of the digit (the correct terminology).

Unfortunately, the doctor was a sadist and proceeded, despite my plea for a double-digit bandage, to wrap my middle finger alone in a humongous swaddle of gauze and send me home. Now it's bad enough that my spouse took one look and burst out laughing, but complete strangers in the hospital elevator also had a cathartic hoot at my expense. I had a giant dildo attached to my hand (don't go there).

So we drove home, being careful not to accidentally raise

my hand above window level lest I incite road rage from passing motorists.

The next day I drove to work, hand propped on the steering wheel, with this digit thing making a perpetual left turn signal. It was not a good day, what with my staff, several clients and the entire board of directors having their funny bones tickled at my expense. By 5 p.m., all I wanted to do was go home and try to get a glass of Absolut to my lips without dunking my club finger. Alas, utensils would be a challenge, so dinner would be, as they say, finger food.

I walked in the front door to find a note: "At the vet. Max sniffed something up his nose."

Now this raised more questions than it answered. I've seen the dog sniff. In addition to typical canine hydrant sniffing, I've seen him aspirate things like drywall dust, kitty litter (that was a nice moment) or an entire vodka gimlet. It makes him sneeze. So????? What did he do, hoover up a Yorkie?

I was still trying to imagine exactly what would constitute a sniffing emergency when the front door opened.

"We're back," said Bonnie, canine DustBuster in tow. "The vet said she was glad Max was still around to do these dumb things."

To hear Bonnie tell it, Max had gone out for an innocent backyard pee and when making his site selection, took an extra energetic sniff at the lawn.

"He came back in the house with his snout all scrunched up, unable to stop sniffing and sneezing. It went on for 15 minutes before I called the vet."

And?????

"Well, they said it could be serious so I rushed him over there."

According to Bonnie, just as they were pulling into the parking lot, Max let out a thundering sneeze, giving himself a very bloody nose.

With the bloodied dog in her arms, Bonnie raced into the office, whereupon the receptionist gasped, "Hit by a car?"

"No!" Bonnie hollered. "Something up his nose!"

That stopped everybody in their tracks.

As it turned out, Max had to have a 9-inch blade of crab grass extracted from his left sinus. You just don't see Grassectomies every day on *E.R.* Which brings me back to my original theory: my whole family has to lay low for a while and let some ridiculous things happen to other people for a change.

So here I am, trying to type with this gauze-covered zucchini on my hand, determined that until this last column of the season is written I'm not doing anything or going anywhere an adventure could possibly happen.

"But aren't we going to the Punkin' Chunkin' Festival?" Bonnie asked.

"Are you kidding? I could be hit by catapulted pulp."

"Are you going with me across the Bay to take the boat to dry dock?" she ventured.

"Not on your life. There's a crab pot with my name on it just waiting to sabotage us. Or I'll get Physteria. Pay somebody else to be ballast."

Bonnie looked exasperated. Only her sense of propriety prevented her from—as the x-ray technician put it—making a fist except for that finger.

"Well you can't just sit here in the condo until deadline."

Yes I can. And wish all *Letters* readers a happy Thanksgiving, a terrific holiday season, great outlet shopping, a delightful January and many wonderful adventures until we get together again in February.

"Okay Max, you can go out, but follow the Bill Clinton presidential role model: don't inhale." ▼

February 1998

WRITER'S SCHLOCK

When I first sat down to write this column I had plenty of time. It was the holiday season and coming up with copy in time for Valentines Day seemed like a piece of cake.

I knew I was in trouble when all I had to do was type the word cake and I was out seeking dessert like a truffle sniffing hog. Then I figured it was stupid to go back to the keyboard on an El Niño-inspired 67 degree day. So Max and I took a December 26 boardwalk stroll. If this is global warming, I'm all for it.

That night we went to a cocktail party, which validated my theory of the genetic discrepancy between most gay men and women. If Bonnie and I bring a party appetizer we buy a pound of something yummy and plop it on a paper plate.

We show up with our mound of crabmeat slathered in cocktail sauce or caviar ladled over a sturdy block of cream cheese and it's piteous compared to the guys' exquisite contributions— delicate china carrying dainty sculptured works of art posing as canapés.

So we went to this party with a typically sturdy offering and stood in awe of our brothers' contributions. One of the guys tried to teach us to recognize the perfect consistency for lemon curd —in case hell froze and we had to make curd for, say, insulation. Terms like mousse and meringue failed to connect with us until somebody said "Stir until it resembles spackle." That we understood.

"Fay's going to write this one up," said a cheerful passerby.

"Not likely," I said. "I have writer's block."

A week passed. No column.

When the going gets tough, the tough go shopping. Not so Bonnie, who hates shopping. She will, however, go getting. When she needs a specific item, she goes and gets it. But no browsing. I dragged her to Route 1 anyway. Not only did I come home without a story, but she violated one of our basic relationship rules and bought more than I did.

New Years Eve arrived. Surely a column idea would surface. Small elegant dinner party; wonderful friends; lots of laughs; some bubbly at midnight; went home. We've got to do something about this wild gay lifestyle.

When I couldn't find anything to rant and rave about by January 10, I panicked.

So while Bonnie watched Bob Vila wallpaper Saskatchewan, I locked myself and my laptop in our condo's tiny bedroom, popped the TV on and hoped for a revelation to get me typing. Holed up in the bedroom, I found no small irony in news footage of the Unibomber's cabin being trucked to court to prove that any person willingly holed up in a 10x12 room writing manifestos was most surely certifiably nuts.

Another week, no progress. For our next cocktail party offering, I tried to be as inspired as the guys. I made hard-boiled egg penguins, based on a scene in the Rosie O'Donnell movie, *Another Stakeout*.

She made eggs with black olive heads, arms and feet, perched on a white bread glacier, surrounded by blue Jello water. The last time I assembled so many parts, it was a model airplane. "Stick whole olive A atop egg B for penguin's head; align egg torso to fuselage C...." If I'd had glue I would have sniffed it.

I toothpicked quartered olives to the egg for arms and put half olives under the egg for feet, anchoring them with shin splints. At least I didn't need decals and paint.

Finally, with the pathetic penguins rolling around the counter, I said screw blue Jello, draped a blue plastic grocery bag over a plate for water, and sturdied my penguins on a crustless white bread iceberg.

Ugh. In the end, I brought my usual mound of shrimp salad to the party.

Surely I'd get some literary juice at this soiree. While no one said "Oh, you're the lunatic who makes a spectacle of yourself in print," I suspected they recognized me. After all, what's the chance that every person in the room was in the witness protection program, unable to divulge name, career or interesting tales? Would nobody say anything printable?

I've got it! I'll write about a recent family gathering, so truly weird readers would find a simple re-telling hilarious. Saved! I finished the story and read it to my spouse. "It's hilarious, every word is true, it's a great column, and if you use it I will have to kill you."

This was a first. This long-suffering woman has seen every stupid thing we've ever done show up in print and never once used a line item veto. That includes the infamous Hot Flash article, which, if you missed it, I don't dare repeat lest I get the hot flash cold shoulder all over again.

But, of course, she was right. Making fun of ourselves is one thing but making fun of people we care about is a topic of another color. That I almost blew it gives you a glimpse into my wretched state. I pushed delete and the column went bye-bye.

By January 17, I would have done anything for an idea—evidenced by my driving 30 miles to the Midway Slots. Have you been there? It's like the Space Shuttle ejected a payload of slot machines onto a cornfield. Rural roads, a lonely gas station, alfalfa fields, chicken coops, !!!CASINO!!! Can you say oxymoron?

Can you say moron? I lost $20 in twenty minutes. One lady fed a hundred dollar bill into the video slot machine, poked the PLAY button a bunch of times, shrugged and walked away empty-handed. She wasn't alone.

The place sported hundreds of people, some in 70s leisure suits, playing one-armed nautilus machines—all to the migraine-inducing clatter of buzzers, bells, blinking lights, and blinking people. As for scenery, I especially liked the man with a towering pompadour who tripped on a roll of nickels, fell down and broke his hair. I went home broke. Without a topic.

With a column due in mere hours, I lunged for the laptop and typed at warp speed, trying to make readable drivel out of the past few weeks. My kingdom for a topic. What the heck can I write about? Why isn't there anything interesting going on? I did my best, finished up and prepared to turn in my column.

"Are you watching the news?" Bonnie rushed in to ask. "Some White House intern is claiming she and Bill Clinton....

Now you tell me.▼

March 1998

W.C. Fields warned us never to work with kids or animals. He was afraid we'd learn something.

You might recall that our Schnauzer Max was diagnosed with cancer in November '96. After two surgeries, a course of chemo, and paying off the vet's mortgage, he was pretty much his old self again—and spoiled beyond reason.

Now, as Max approaches his 14th birthday, our family is dealing with geriatric dog issues we never thought we'd have a chance to experience. And I remind myself how lucky we are to have this extra time with Max, even if he's driving us nuts.

First off, we've got the world's only two-seater station wagon. After a shortstop sent Max sliding off the back seat, Bonnie took a thick slab of foam rubber and lodged it from the back of the front seat to the front of the backseat—so Max can travel like Cleopatra on a barge. Not even Bonnie's penchant for short stops can send him flying. Of course, if we have to take an extra passenger, I get stuffed in back with the spare tire.

As if his travel accommodations aren't special enough, we also cut a hole in the dog barge and flush-mounted a water bowl so Max can drink and drive.

So we got the traveling down, but the staying home was problematic. Max, who used to bark to go out with such regularity you could use him to set Greenwich mean time, now makes us guess when he needs relief. Since he's hard of hearing, we figure he thinks nobody can hear, so why bark? If we don't guess YES by a certain time, pass the rug shampoo.

So now we just toss him out the door every four hours, overnight included. It brings new meaning to the term wee hours. But now things have gotten even more complicated as Max's vision has deteriorated.

I know. We've been asking ourselves if it was, euphemistically, "time." But both the vet and Max say, "No." After all, the dog still eats like a goat, wags his tail once he notices we're there, snuggles up to "watch" TV and can sniff beach fries at 50 yards. Last week at the pet shop he shoplifted two biscuits and a jerky chew.

But we do have our hands full keeping Max from hurting himself. Since he navigates by caroming off the walls like Schnauzer hockey, we went to K-Mart to pick out a playpen for him to occupy when we go out.

We got lots of advice from local moms who saw us shopping for Fisher Price and suspected the gayby boom was about to strike again. We didn't have the heart to tell them our little one wears a flea collar.

Most recently, I've been sleeping in gym shorts and a t-shirt so I can accompany the dog into the moonlight for his 3 a.m. pee break—a move made necessary one night when he couldn't find the back door and forced me to scoot around the yard barefoot and indecently dressed to fetch him. Now that was a full moon.

And while we're all trying to adapt with a sense of humor, the truth is, he's just not the same dog. We really miss his mischief, bounding energy and effusive unconditional love. But just when we were assessing his quality of life (forget about ours), he surprised us.

Friends visited the beach with their adorable 4-year-old.

At first Katy shied away from Max, with her Dad telling us an encounter with a big dog had left her wary. Seeing how calm Max had become, Katy's Mom said, "This will be great. We've been wanting to get a pet and Max will help Katy get over her fear."

Mom and Dad explained to Katy that Max was very old and couldn't see, so she should be careful not to move fast and scare him. Well, that's all it took. Katy instantly signed on as practical nurse.

With admirable gentleness, this kind 4-year-old miracle worker guided Max around the condo, fed him as many treats as we'd allow and made sure he could find his wa-wa—her Anne Bancroft to his Patty Duke. On Saturday night Katy clutched Max like Tickle Me Elmo until she fell asleep.

In a charming corollary to her canine care giving, Katy inquisitively whispered to Dad, "Did Aunt Bonnie and Aunt Fay's husbands die?" When Dad told her we didn't have husbands, she answered with concern "But who takes care of them?"

Say what you will about the message society is still sending our kids, this 4-year-old was bright enough to sense we had an alternative household.

"They take care of each other," said Dad, which seemed to make perfect sense to Katy as she quickly returned to her full-time job as Max's personal assistant.

On Sunday, by the time Katy packed up, kissed Max and waved goodbye, her parents were betting she'd ask for a dog by the time they hit Route 1.

Well, the kid and the dog showed us that Max is still very much here. Not only did the weekend erase Katy's fears, and cultivate a next generation Schnauzer lover, but it proved to us that our old man can still make a difference.

I'm going to the powder room to put the toilet seat up so Max can have his 5 p.m. cocktail. Cheers. ▼

June 1998

I SEE LONDON, I SEE FRANCE,
WE LOST BONNIE'S UNDERPANTS

Bonjour! Bonjour!

Okay, we didn't see London, but we did see France, and we did lose Bonnie's underpants.

We're reluctantly back and would return in a heartbeat. But if we never get the chance it's okay, since this vacation was, simply, the trip of a lifetime. Our quartet toured the Riviera, Provence, Chateau Country, and Paris with lots of great food, wine and tourist madness.

We drank Chateauneuf du Pape at the actual Pape's chateau, sipped Cote du Rhone in that very countryside, had Salade Nicoise in Nice, and ham and cheese with Dijon mustard in, where else, Dijon. We walked where Cezanne got his inspiration, explored where Toulous Lautrec met his models and sat on the Pont Neuf spanning the Seine in little nooks history says are reserved for lovers.

And we kept our promise and took our *Letters* photo in front of the Eiffel Tower. By the time we got there, late in the trip, the back issues and the four of us all looked pretty tattered. But we had a ball.

This was despite the fact that most of my obsessive tourist preparations turned out to be for naught. The dual current hairdryer never worked anywhere. For 16 days I looked like the Bride of Frankenstein. The plane was so packed we'd have blown out a window or a flight attendant if we'd inflated our cervical pillows, so we arrived with jet lag *and* whiplash. And on day two, one of our troop drowned our emergency compass in the bathtub, leaving us geographically befuddled.

But those security wallets staved off the swarms of pickpockets—mostly doe-eyed youngsters under parental guidance, working every major tourist site. They would have had to commit third degree sex crimes to get to our credit cards.

And speaking of underwear, our throw-as-you-go plan (discarding our underwear after its daily use), really worked. We had all sorts of packing room for souvenirs. Although on our first day at each hotel, the chamber maids thought we idiot Americans didn't know trash cans from hampers.

Actually, Bonnie took throw as you go a little too seriously, packing her very worst underwear. Apparently, sagging elastic got the best of her during a chateau tour and she confided that for comfort reasons she'd ditched her drawers in the Louis Sixteenth toilette. Archeologists may conclude Catherine De Medici wore Jockey for Women.

Since one short column is no match for this simply astonishing and eye-popping journey, I'll just share some random thoughts.

The Principality of Monaco, high on a rock jutting into the azure Mediterranean, with it's yachts, Grand Prix track and Monte Carlo Casino was something I thought I'd only see in a James Bond movie. It looks even better in person. And it certainly explains what Grace Kelly saw in Prince Ranier.

And I wasn't prepared for the glorious mountaintop towns, walled cities, narrow winding streets and ninth century cathedrals. And of course, I took so many photos I have carpal tunnel finger.

Although, where photo ops are concerned, every single French historical site is under renovation. Want a picture of the Paris Opera? It's got scaffolding on it. Notre Dame? Scaffolding. Versailles? Scaffolding. The only structure not covered by scaffolding was the Eiffel Tower, which of course IS scaffolding.

O'er the ramparts we walked, in medieval walled cities with churches and homes built up to 1500 years ago. With tile roofs, stucco walls, stone streets, windowsill flower boxes and charm to spare, I managed, for sixteen whole days, to deny the existence of vinyl siding.

Think we have grand homes in this country? The chateaus those Louies built for their wives, mistresses, horses, boyfriends, you name it, beat anything Claus Von Bulow ever built for Sunny.

By comparison, American mansions are outhouses.

And the only thing I can say about Versailles and its gilt-covered, gaudy, wretched excess, is that one look explains the entire French Revolution. The masses took a gander and said "That's it, cancel the royal Visa card and cut off their heads."

French highways are manic. The speed limit is 130 kilometers, or about 80 mph. You can drive that fast in the right lane and have itty-bitty Renaults whip past you on the left. Leadfoot Bonnie drove our little rental car.

Bonnie: "It's incredible, I'm going 115 miles an hour and nothing's out of alignment, nothing's shaking."

Front seat passenger: "Except me."

The four of us got along splendidly, with everyone viewing the trip from their own particular perspective. Larry the Accountant translated what everything cost and made sure we knew that the 130 speed limit meant "kilometers, not miles per hour, Bonnie!!!"

Fastidious Robert, who, on our last trip did such a great job keeping our boat spotless, made sure we got a tour of French car washes, and was overheard at Versailles' Hall of Mirrors wondering what it cost to clean the place.

As for Bonnie, her fascination with home improvement had her studying flying buttresses and vaulted ceilings in case the French government ever contracted her to renovate Notre Dame.

And I just shopped 'til I dropped a whole lotta French francs.

As for the food glorious food, after one week Larry calculated that if he kept eating at a similar pace, he'd soon be his own principality. After two weeks, we were sweating butter. On our way home, we expected to pass through airport security x-rays and proceed directly to Angioplasty.

Our only food faux pas was a seafood appetizer Bonnie ordered. It arrived looking like a plate of French fries, but a closer look found the fries looking back in the form of little fried whole fish. My girl toughed it out but subsequently insisted on complete disclosure before ordering.

What you've heard is correct. French food is fabulous. We

avoided 3-star places in favor of small bistros and some new, innovative Parisian restaurants. France has a nifty tradition of every restaurant offering a three-course plus tip fixed-price meal. We stuck to these Le Menu meals and ate like royalty.

And that rumor about the French not being friendly is pop-pycock. All over the country, folks couldn't have been more helpful to the four Americans sputtering broken French.

Toward trip's end we left the guys in Versailles for an extra night while Bonnie and I headed to Paris. At the hotel, it appeared we were being told, in rapid French, that something was wrong with the reservation. But then a cute male clerk came up and translated. "Zare is some troooble with zee reservaaceeone. Zee bed, it is a doooble. Non zee twin."

"Ah!" I said. "Zee doooble is, um, good, er, bonne, er, tres bonne."

The clerk eyed the two women in front of him, smiled with recognition and said, "Oui??? Yes, this eeez good?"

Then he looked back at the reservation book and asked "Zee other room, pour tomorrow, Les Monsiours, zee same?"

"Oui," I said. The clerk smiled, helped us with our luggage and for the rest of our stay made sure the four of us had everything we wanted.

I have stories galore but space prevents it. I haven't yet told you about the beautiful mostly naked girls (and boys) in Paris' famous Lido show, or the scenic drive to St. Tropez, or being trapped on the Paris Metro with, of all awful flashbacks, a strolling accordion player. Mal de Mer. At least he was playing *La Vie En Rose*, not the *Beer Barrel Polka*.

Bon Soir, Mes amies!▼

June 1998
AS OLD AS VINYL AND TWICE AS SCRATCHY

They found me. It was inevitable, but it was still a jolt.

Every day for the past several weeks I'd skulk into the house, sweat trickling down my back, terrified of seeing the mail. And every day I'd say, "Whew. Just bills."

But with every day it wasn't there, I knew I was closer to the day when it would be. And that, sports fans, was yesterday.

I got my application to join AARP.

For readers too young to understand the stake through my heart, the AARP (American Association of Retired Persons) is an omnipotent organization for persons over the BIG 5-0. Irritatingly, you don't even have to be retired. You can still have years of office politics, bad coffee and homophobic bosses to go. But the second anyone ever born gets within spitting range of fifty, AARP's database lights up like your birthday cake. Forget the CIA, FBI, or the Royal Mounties. AARP should be on the trail of Jon Benet Ramsey's killer and the abortion clinic bomber.

This is a group that recruits.

Their tactics include brainwashing recent applicants so they cough up names of equally decrepit friends. "Are you now or have you ever been about to turn 50? Can you provide names of your comrades?" Somebody ratted on Al Gore this week and he, too, got his letter bomb.

So I stood staring at the envelope, hearing the theme from *Hawaii 5-0* in my ears, wondering how I got this old. I mean unless I make 100 I'm not even middle aged anymore.

About a decade ago, when I was already feeling old, but I now know *that* I was really quite young, I visited St. Augustine Florida's Fountain of Youth.

I was sitting on the stone wall in front of a painting of Ponce De Leon with Bonnie. A friend, camera in hand, stepped back to get the scene in focus. As he was about to snap our photo with the words "Fountain of Youth" above our heads, a juvenile delinquent in a pick-up truck roared by, leaned out the window and yelled, "You still look just as old!"

We laughed so hard the photo is blurry.

Well, I'm here to tell you that staring at my AARP invitation, I not only still feel as old, but apparently it's now official.

I began to realize my fate a few months ago when some zit-faced talking head on MTV called Bob Dylan the Grandfather of Rock 'n Roll. Mr. Lay Lady Lay a grandfather? The times they are a changin'.

Then I was watching a TV sitcom, blithely laughing out loud at the episode where a mother was apoplectic about having a birthday that ended in a zero. Very well dressed and exceptionally youthful-looking, she was, nevertheless the leading man's mother for heaven's sake, so I didn't understand why the scriptwriters had her so upset about turning 60. But I thought the show was hilarious.

That is, until Bonnie told me I'd made a tragic assumption and the entire show was actually based on the angst of somebody's TV mother turning 50. Since we don't have natural gas and I couldn't put my head in the oven, I spent the rest of the night with my head in a glass of Absolut.

Then I got *People* magazine's "50 Most Beautiful People" issue. The fact I didn't recognize a single person was a big clue that my blip is slipping off the radar screen of contemporary culture. I mean how did these people get famous without my knowing about it?

And the government isn't helping me stay youthful and fit either. This morning, I was huffing and puffing on the treadmill when I heard about the feds' new Body Mass Report. By adjusting the national weight barometer, even as I was pounding the treadmill, and without gaining an ounce or eating a Twinkie, I was declared fatter than yesterday. There is no justice.

But the mirror incident topped all. Sometime back in my forties I began to notice occasional random little hairs on my chin. Hey, I realize nobody ever talks about these things, but girls, it happens. Have tweezers, will travel.

Then, several months ago the random follicle sprouts disappeared. Good news. It was only after my arms got too short for me to read anymore and I got bifocals that I discovered the harrowing truth—I'd been fuzzy all along, I just couldn't see it. My God! How long was I walking around like Billy Goat Gruff??? Now I have to wear my damn bifocals to the damn bathroom just to see in the damn mirror. I gotta tell you, I looked younger before I could see.

Woe is me. What's the next stop? Depends? Although, in honor of their upcoming customer base of Boomers they should rename the product Baby Bloomers.

And I just loved the recent news report that the music industry celebrated the 50th anniversary of the invention of the long-playing record. They're obsolete for pity's sake!!! What does that make me??? There I sat, still in my forties for a few days, staring at my AARP application.

Hmmmm. They offer travel benefits, credit cards, investment programs ("Buy Viagra and Polident"), health insurance...and spouses are eligible, too. Oh sure.

Just spoiling for a fight (I'm old. I can be cantankerous), I called AARP to ask if my same-sex spouse was eligible—and I was shocked and delighted to find out that apparently they are progressive old farts. Bonnie, being 14 months younger can now be an AARP spouse, causing her to go into her own pre-5-0 spasms, ha-ha.

So I wrote the $8 check, sent my application back and joined the largest lobbying association in America. And this morning, with my actual birthday only hours away, I'm moving from denial to acceptance.

Heck, Rita Mae Brown and Lily Tomlin are over 50. Gloria Steinem and Jane Fonda have been there a while. Meryl Streep has only a year to go. I could be in worse company.

And even old LPs are called classic rock.

Just as long as I don't start walking around in a plastic rain scarf, rolling knee high stockings down to my ankles, or covering Kleenex boxes with crocheted covers, I think I'll be all right. ▼

July 1998

Talk about change of life. Now I'm homeless.

Okay, I'm not sleeping in a cardboard box on Rehoboth Avenue, but metaphorically speaking, at least as far as weekends are concerned, I am temporarily without a home.

It started with the new puppy. Now when people hear this news, they clear their throats and whisper "does that mean that Max...er...."

No, the grand old dog is still hanging in there. In fact, we bought the puppy for Max—for company and to have somebody to boss around. It's worked out splendidly—for Max. It's Bonnie and I who've been housebroken.

The disintegration began as we headed for our first two-dog night aboard the boat. First, there was a three hour Bay Bridge tie up.

By the time we got to the marina, station wagon bulging with, among other things, puppy, puppy toys, and puppy food, (no puppy poop yet, hurry!) half of under-aged, liquored-up Dewey filled the parking lot. The crowd took turns barfing, urinating or hurling insults at these two women of a certain age trying to unpack the kennel club. It was disgusting.

With our duffels, leashes, dogs, collapsible puppy crate, Milkbones, chew toys, kibble, laptop computer and provisions, we had to run the gauntlet through the parking lot fraternity boys, recreating, I suspect, the Navy's Tailhook scandal.

Then, dragging our brood up the pier we looked like the Von Trapps fording every stream. Rough water made the boat a moving target. Transferring life-jacketed Schnauzers, our belongings, our bodies, and ourselves to the boat was hair-raising business.

And by the time we got the pups out of their personal flotation devices, stowed our stuff and collapsed for a breather, it was time to reverse the whole ugly process and take the boys back out for one last pee.

Then, the puppy, appropriately named Moxie, got his exercise by bouncing around the boat like a billiard ball. It begged the question, what were we thinking???

Is it any wonder that by morning, on our way for bagels, we wandered into a condo open house? And, following our typical cautious, deliberate modus operandi, we signed a sales contract in the time it takes most people to decide between an onion bagel and croissant. If all goes well, by mid-August we'll own a teeny, tiny downtown studio apartment with its very own Murphy Bed. It's got a bedroom and living room, just not at the same time. But we will be able to see who's coming and going on Baltimore Avenue. And it's double the size of the boat cabin. Cups and utensils don't have to be velcroed down, and we'd gladly pay the mortgage for the in-town parking spot alone.

Yeah, it meant putting the boat up for sale. But heck, we'd been threatening to unload our hole in the water into which we throw money for at least two years.

Of course, we secretly counted on the reputation of the used boat market to save us. People make it to the top of heart transplant lists faster than they sell used boats. You can stroll Rehoboth Avenue on a Saturday night in August and get a table for twelve for pizza faster than you can sell a used boat.

"Don't worry, Bon, we'll get the condo, keep advertising the boat, and be in the nursing home gumming Jello when the damn thing sells."

We had an offer in 24 hours.

Do you take Dramamine for seller's remorse?

When our vitals stabilized, we agreed it was for the best.

"I'll miss cruising with dolphins around Cape Henlopen and taking trips to Atlantic City," said Bonnie.

"Yeah, I'll miss crab pots stuck on our propeller, jellyfish sucked into the exhaust, and going to dinner in damp, wrinkled clothes," I offered. "On the other hand, it's bye-bye to fireworks on the Chesapeake, bounding out Indian River Inlet to the ocean and water gently lapping me to sleep."

"And waking up to black flies and jet ski exhaust," said my spouse, adding "don't forget marina bills, mechanic's bills, gas bills, and large unnumbered bills gone with the wind."

"But I will miss the folks at the pier," I said, wistfully.

"Yeah, and how about the drunken jailbait in the parking lot?" Bonnie said, sarcastically.

As Charlie Dickens might have said in his Tale of Two Biddies, it was the best of boats, it was the worst of boats.

So here I am, at 7 a.m. on the day we hand over the keys to Dave, Bay Pride's new owner. We don't close on the condo for three weeks yet. Friends have rallied with heartfelt offers to put us up, but most of them also remembered a visiting cousin, or long-anticipated trip to Botswana when they realized we come with a traveling circus of dogs and dog accoutrement.

A few hardy souls are willing to offer us shelter anyway and to them we say "you're brave."

So we've carted six years of boating debris to the car, folded our rainbow flag, and packed the blender. We left Dave the flyswatter, marine toilet paper and anti-mildew spray.

And as I sit in my cozy boat, gently rocking in the slip, pecking at my laptop computer and trying to finish this column before Dave shows up, I wonder if I can really part with this boater's life—the adventurous cruises, wonderful harbors, luscious sunsets, cocktails on board, frozen mudslides on the dock, the romance of it all....

"WOOOOOF!"

"Yip, Yip, Yip."

Oh no. The dogs are up.

"Bonnie, wake up. You get the life jackets, I'll find the leashes. Hurry! Here, grab the puppy. I'll take Max. Moxie wait! No!!! Bad puppy! I'll get the paper towels. Careful, don't let Max fall in the water...watch your step. Watch him. Hey, watch your keys, they're hanging out of your pocket. You're keys are...here, let me help you...."

Splasshhhhh!!!!

I think the old adage is going to be true. The two best days in a boater's life are the day you buy it and the day you sell it.

See you in town. ▼

August 1998

It's been a tough few weeks for Baby Boomer icons.

First we lost Roy Rogers, known to Gen Xers and thirty some-things for Double-R-Bar-Burgers, but to us boomers as the consummate TV cowboy.

I wonder how many of us FDAs (future dykes of America) used the Roy Rogers early warning signals. My mother should have known something was up when I threw a Halloween tantrum for being made to dress like fringe-skirted Dale instead of pistol-packin' Roy.

And when my sister's favorite toy was Betsy-Wetsy, the doll whose sole claim to fame was wetting her pants, I could never understand why my parents thought my fixation with Roy Rogers and Trigger wasn't sensible.

Eventually I moved on to annoying my family by mooning over Annette instead of Frankie Avalon, and relegated my Roy Rogers lunchbox to the junk heap.

Until we got word of Roy's demise, I hadn't thought about him in years. Except, that is, for noticing the occasional tabloid photo of Trigger and Bullet (Roy's German Shepherd) taxidermied for display at his Happy Trails Museum.

When almost everybody I know sheepishly admitted to wondering if Dale planned to have Roy stuffed, too, I realized that Roy and Dale had been much better publicity agents than I'd ever imagined. I know I'll be watching the *National Enquirer* for an update.

We'd hardly had time to sing *Happy Trails* to Roy when we heard that Buffalo Bob Smith, Howdy Doody's faux cowboy sidekick passed away at age 80. Since nobody but Bob ever accompanied Howdy on TV or to personal appearances, I had to conclude that on July 30 Howdy Doody breathed his freckle-faced last as well.

H. Doody, 51, entertainer. You didn't see that in the obits.

Now I hadn't spent quality time with Howdy in years, unless you count the occasional glimpse of him in grainy pre-video kinescopes on TV retrospectives. About a year ago I saw a poster for a nostalgic Howdy Doody personal appearance show right here at the Rehoboth Convention Center. Frankly, it struck me as unseemly for a woman of my age to want to go to the show, so I never even mentioned it to anyone.

But the truth is, Howdy meant a lot to me.

At age five I got to go to the TV studio where the *Howdy Doody* show was broadcast and sit in the Peanut Gallery. It was my very first live theatrical experience. Depending on how I feel about my own show business career at any given instant, that day either inspired me or screwed me up for life.

It was a seminal moment when I realized that the black and white Howdy I saw at home was actually a full color Howdy, who worked for a living. What's more, Clarabell was an actor getting paid to do a job, albeit squirting kids with seltzer. That day in the Peanut Gallery formed the essence of my thinking that acting and directing were actually viable career choices. Howdy should have warned me.

I was just getting over the shock of the Howdy thing when I heard about Lambchop. Man, that was pretty much all I could take. I loved Lambchop—the only good use I'd ever seen for a gym sock.

And what a trouper! Other 50s superstars like Perry Como or Kukla, Fran & Ollie were long gone from our screens, but Lambchop and Shari Lewis (both of them still looking like a million bucks I might add) were still going head to head with the likes of Barney, not to mention Beavis and Butthead.

Psychologists were all over the radio explaining to parents how to tell their children about the untimely death of Shari Lewis and I thought "who's gonna explain it to me??"

A sadistic friend gave me the book *On Women Turning 50* for my forty-tenth birthday. While my inclination was to pitch it at her head, I actually found some valuable wisdom in it—like the news that my 40s were the old age of youth but my 50s are the youth of old age. I don't know if that's good, but it's certainly catchy.

And now that most of the icons from my first childhood can only be seen in the Smithsonian, I guess it's time to start cultivating icons for my second childhood. But in the meantime, if I were Bozo, I'd start watching my cholesterol. ▼

August 1998

Once, when my father had one-too-many martinis, he laughed and said, "You and Bonnie are the only ones of my kids or step kids who have ever borrowed money and actually paid it back. You're schmucks!"

Now technically that can't be, since the Yiddish word schmuck refers to a body part neither Bonnie nor I own, but in the vernacular, I guess it's true.

And lately, we've radiated world class schmuckdom—including giving up our boat two weeks earlier than planned, so the new owners could bond with the vessel before their honeymoon. Would non-schmucks have been so accommodating if they had to scurry for lodging with friends for three summer beach weekends?

Meanwhile, back in Maryland, it was schmuckiness central, too.

Scrambling for cash for our impending condo settlement, I juggled bank funds, and broke and entered the piggy bank. As I sat in a puddle of coins, stuffing, at best, about two hundred dollars into those irritating paper sleeves, the phone rang.

"Hi! I'm calling for Whitman Walker Clinic. D.C. has cut our funding and we'll have to drop clients unless...."

"Put me down for $20," I said and went back to rolling nickels. What's wrong with this picture?

Meanwhile, Bonnie had to work all night Monday because she took the day off to donate platelets at Johns Hopkins ("They needed my blood type, I couldn't say no.") Would that be giving blood figuratively and literally?

On August 8 we drove to the beach just for the day. It was our very first Saturday-in-August arrival ever and my God! In the time it took to crawl down Route 1 from Red Mill to Rehoboth, the people in the mini-van next to us could have gestated a baby. I'll bet there are documented cases of families needing an extra crib at check-in.

Then, we drove home in the dead of night, fighting narcolepsy all the way, only to find a cat waiting on our doorstep. We don't have a cat.

Is there a sign on our roof saying "Schmucks live here, drop off your unwanted animals?"

"Enough," I said. "Don't let him in."

"Meooowww."

"No!" I said, mostly to myself.

So we put water out on the stoop and prayed the cat would be gone by morning. The following night he slept on the bed.

The next day, too few of the young, limber softball players on Bonnie's team showed up for a double header and she agreed to do home plate knee bends as catcher for both games. By Tuesday, Yogi Berra had to sleep on the sofa because she couldn't lift her legs high enough to do the stairs.

I was feeding her anti-inflammatories when the sellers of the soon-to-be-ours condo called. They couldn't possibly settle on August 14 because they wanted another beach weekend. Nonschmucks certainly would have threatened "no deal." I tried.

"But we're homeless, we have nowhere to..."

"Impossible," said the seller. "Monday the 17th or nothing." Another weekend in purgatory.

But the final straw was the grueling six-hour condo settlement. At the walk-through, when we went to check the stove, the sellers behaved as if we were asking them to put their heads in the oven to test it.

Later, at settlement, we wished they had. At one point they were so nasty we got up from the table and fled the room, leaving our unflappable settlement attorney to deal with these sellers from hell.

When the mortgage company faxed us the zillionth copy of the wrong loan papers, the evil sellers threatened to walk out entirely. At that point, Bonnie and I took the brilliant advice of the paralegal and fled across the street for a medicinal martini. Back at the Title company, the attorney convinced the irrational sellers to go away, leaving their signatures behind.

If all the mortgage papers were laid end to end the square footage would be ten times the size of the apartment we were trying to buy.

"I'm glad next week is my vacation," said the clerk.

"This *is* our vacation," said the schmucks.

By 7 p.m. we'd handed over our last dimes, got the keys, liberated the dogs from eight hours of maximum security at a friend's house, and staggered to town for dinner. As we explained our glassy-eyed condition to friends, two gentlemen at an adjacent table couldn't help overhearing our horror story.

"Where did you buy?"

We told them.

"That's where we are!" they said, asking us which apartment we bought.

"Hooray!!! The *%$*#&#* moved out!!!!"

Hooray, the schmucks moved in!

As we walked the half block home (I love it!), and settled into the condo for the night, we couldn't believe that those petty sellers had returned to the apartment before we took occupancy to turn off the air conditioning so we'd be sure to come home to a sweltering apartment.

"Can you believe that! Well if we're the schmucks and they're not, I'd rather be us," I said.

"Me too," Bonnie agreed.

So we toasted to the bride and groom's happiness aboard our former boat, set the alarm for 5 a.m., pushed the living room aside for the Murphy Bed and went to sleep. It was going to be a busy week. Somewhere between work, softball, and platelet donation we have to find a home for the cat.▼

September 1998

"Did you complete your column?" Bonnie asked.

"Well, taking a cue from President Clinton, it depends on your legal definition of the word complete," I obfuscated. "I've been working on it, on and off, for a long time but since I haven't printed it out yet, I'd say no, I did not do this thing."

And who can blame me? Just like everybody else I know, I've been busy reading the Starr Report about the President's sex life. Well, come to think of it, that's not legally true either. I had the newspaper read to me. Since I didn't do the actual reading, I wasn't the reader, I was just the readee, and therefore, I can legally state that although I now know the material intimately, I did not finish the whole report, so....

AUGGGHHHH!!!

On Friday afternoon, when the technological revolution as we know it reached it's zenith, and the Starr Report was posted on the Internet, all I could get from my internet provider was a busy signal. The blinding frustration I felt must have been something akin to that which the leader of the free world felt every time some pesky congressman rang up the oval office and caused Monica Interruptus.

I sat at my desk, hearing my computer modem's busy beep and thought that the Unibomber was right after all, and technology is evil.

On the other hand, if the world's collective race to read the smarmy details of one little tawdry office romance actually crashed the Internet, it could be just the thing to get teenagers back into reading newspapers.

Thanks to a busy beach weekend, I never actually had time to consider reading the Starr Report until the drive home on Sunday. And since I've been known to get car sick from simply reading the nutritional information on the back of a Snickers bar, drastic action was required.

"I'll drive home," I told Bonnie. "You can read the thing to me."

So she did. No offense to my spouse's oral interp skills, but both dogs were asleep and I was starting to nod off by the time we got to Milton.

And that was during the reading of the more salacious stuff. Let's face it. It cost Ken Starr 40 million of our dollars to produce something Sydney Sheldon could have knocked off in a weekend. I'm surprised Starr didn't have Fabio on the cover of this bodice ripper.

At one point, I started to sweat profusely and thought I was having some perverse nervous system event. I mean the stuff wasn't that steamy. Truth was that the newspaper section was so heavy, when Bonnie laid part of it down she accidentally activated the seat warmers.

By the time we got halfway home, Bonnie was getting a hoarse voice from reading, I was chugging caffeine to keep me on the road, and we were only up to the tenth time Monica accidentally loitered by the Oval Office. Just you or I try that and we'd be chained to the White House fence waiting for a SWAT Team to haul us off.

Forty million dollars and this was the best prosecutors could come up with? Unless it was a Cuban Cigar, I don't see anything impeachable here.

Don't get me wrong. I'm disgusted that Bill Clinton made such a foolish spectacle of himself. But this whole thing is a big case of TOO MUCH INFORMATION!!!!!!

We're having a national tizzy over a sophomoric office assignation that has turned the country into one big *Jerry Springer Show*. Elected officials all over the map are rushing up to the microphone to blurt out details of illicit affairs. Who asked them!

Has anybody stopped to think exactly how many people wouldn't be embarrassed to see the graphic details of their intimate romantic interludes (now matter how vanilla) in a special section of *The New York Times*?

If there's a sequel, who's it going to be, Newt? Madeleine Albright? Boris Yeltsin?

As for Ken Starr, give me a break. With those resources, and six years of investigating Clinton for everything from Whitewater to campaign financing, to come up with nothing more than Monica Lewinsky means he's either the most inept prosecutor since Hamilton Burger faced Perry Mason, or...and here's a novel thought...the Clinton Administration actually did nothing illegal.

The way Congress is behaving you'd think that Clinton and Monica conspired to sell arms to Iran. Oh, that's right, that wouldn't be impeachable either.

By the time we got home I had heard quite enough of the Starr Report and by 9 p.m. it was on the kitchen floor, under the puppy, where it belonged.

So now what? Are elected officials (a few of which we actually still respect) going to have nationally televised impeachment hearings about this stuff?

If I were a member of Congress I'd be embarrassed to suggest that our founding fathers meant the articles of impeachment to be used to judge this kind of behavior. If Ben Franklin warned Thomas Jefferson to stop fooling around with the servants, I have a feeling Jefferson would have told Franklin to go fly a kite.▼

October 1998
COUNTING BLESSINGS INSTEAD OF SHEEP

I dropped my spouse off at the Johns Hopkins Sleep Clinic last Thursday. She was told to arrive with a good book and her pajamas. To tell you the truth, I was envious. She'd be snuggling up with Patricia Cornwell while I was home doing laundry and dog sitting.

Sure, she was probably having little electrodes glued to her forehead as I was pulling into my driveway, but I was greeted by mounds of dirty laundry, the phone ringing with a computerized magazine solicitation, and a Schnauzer running through the backyard with a brassiere hanging out his mouth. Give me the electrodes. Please.

After chasing down the laundry thief, I secured the hamper perimeter and collapsed on the sofa. Bonnie wants to know why she's having trouble sleeping? Blue Cross should save big bucks and just ask me. She's not sleeping because life is nuts.

Our dog is old, the puppy's an underwear klepto, my mother-in-law used our Visa Card at Bingo World, we've got a Hoover upright that doesn't suck, and a White House intern that does. We should sleep? Maybe it's that we're trying to find affordable health insurance, they've recalled the Subaru, our lawn belongs in the Shock Trauma Burn Unit, the Redskins have the worst record since Lyndon Johnson was president, National-Boycott-the-Media-Day flopped since the press didn't publicize it, oh-so-Special Prosecutor Ken Starr took another document dump, and we don't know if the coming Y2K bug will kill our computers or just screw up our microwave popcorn.

Is it any wonder we wake up six times a night hoping we turned off the sprinkler, mailed the taxes, and gave the pills to the right dog? If we were sleeping soundly, I'd worry we'd lost touch with reality.

Actually, I have no idea how Bonnie will answer at the clinic when they ask why she's not sleeping, because the truth is, it's me who's not sleeping.

Now before I blab, please know I have a signed spousal release, giving me literary license for full disclosure without risking domestic tranquility. I'm discussing this on the chance readers might relate.

My spouse snores.

I'm doing 16 years to life with a nightly half hour of tossing and turning to what sounds like a squadron of Canada Honkers. Then I grab my pillow, one or more dogs and harumph off to the guest room. In hindsight, buying a cheap guestroom mattress, ("Heck, we don't want guests to be comfortable for more than a day or two anyway") was flawed logic.

At any rate, my only respite from back spasms is to fall asleep first. But even if I do manage to drop off, I'm generally awakened several times a night by the QE II Fog Horn. Or Harpo Marx, back from the dead and in bed with us.

Then, I wind up gently shaking Bonnie and whispering the most universally uttered marital phrase after "I Do."

"Honey, turn over, you're snoring." Failing to produce quiet, I resort to karate chops, after which Bonnie usually harumphs to the guest room.

This being the case, I fail to see how the sleep clinic, despite high-tech video, audio and body sensor surveillance, can get the complete picture without monitoring my defensive sleeping skills. Heck, they'd have to wire up the dogs, too. Can't you just see some HMO Administrator trying to preauthorize that.

(Also in the spirit of full disclosure, I promised Bonnie I'd reveal that once I do fall sleep I've been known to exert flapjack-like flips with such force that we had to sell the waterbed because I regularly launched our late cat into the hall. No, that's not what killed him! Ringling Brothers would have loved it. There, Bonnie, I hope you're happy.)

Well, at least the clinic will be able to determine whether my significant snorer has something called Sleep Apnea. That's where some people actually stop breathing during the night and wake themselves up gasping for air. It's either Apnea or a nightmare about being made to sit through the musical *Rent* again. If she's got Apnea, no wonder she feels lousy in the morning. My anxiety that she has it is just one more thing to keep *me* awake.

Anyway, I pictured Bonnie at the clinic, enjoying her *N.Y. Times* Best Seller, then dropping off into REM sleep, fluttering eyelids observed on TV by hovering interns. The dogs and I turned off the lights, locked the door and went to bed.

Why is it that the second I'm home alone, I hear Freddy Krueger shimmying up the A/C vents? I thought *Sixty Minutes* moved to midnight but it was just the bedside clock. It was so quiet I could do a traffic count on I-95, a road I had no idea was even in proximity. While the room was snoreless, it was a miserable, lonesome night.

Bonnie arrived home the next evening with news that "they wired me up like Frankenstein, put a red light on my finger (ET, phone home), stuck a tube up my nose and told me to have a good night's sleep."

"How could you?" I asked.

"I don't know," she said, "but I slept like a baby. Then they woke me up for cereal and a banana, told me to read a while, then asked me to take a nap, then woke me up and told me to watch *Rosie*, then told me it was naptime, then woke me up for lunch and *Oprah*, and...."

Was this a hospital or Canyon Ranch Spa?

In honor of October 11, Coming Out Day, Bonnie answered questions accordingly:

Doctor: "How long have you been having trouble sleeping?"

Bonnie: "Actually, it's my partner who's having trouble sleeping."

Doctor: "Oh, what's his problem?"

Bonnie: "Well, *she* says...."

It's going to take several weeks for data tabulation, diagnosis and suggested remedies. Meanwhile, we're trying a tip from the clinic brochure. Since people snore most on their backs, we're supposed to sew tennis balls onto her pajama backs to keep her from relaxing that way. While these lesbians don't sew, we do own a backpack. We'll fill it with tennis balls, tell Bonnie to strap it on (don't go there) and say, "G'night, Gracie." Romantic, no, but we're willing to give it a try.

As for the clinic report, we'll keep you posted. I feel a nap coming on....▼

October 1998

Max the Wonder Schnauzer died on Saturday, October 31, at age 14 and one half. A life-long resident of Laurel, MD, with a weekend place in Rehoboth Beach, DE, Max beat the medical odds by having two more enjoyable years of boating, Rehoboth Beach social life, and overturning trash cans following his 1996 cancer diagnosis. He leaves his devoted companions Fay and Bonnie, new puppy Moxie, and a host of friends, including Tucker R. of Critter Beach, Belle from Hell Galloway of Trumbull, CT, and Elmo Ramoy-McFall of Silver Lake in Rehoboth Beach. He was predeceased by his girlfriend Rita Mae Peters-LeLacheur of Rehoboth. Max was pleased to have survived long enough to mentor Moxie in all of his bad habits. In lieu of flowers, the family requests kibble contributions to local animal shelters.

February 1999

It's all Bob Vila's fault. Strange grunting sounds are coming from my shower stall, where Bonnie is trying to cut wall tile.

She's been working on this project for so many weekends, people seeing me alone around town are asking questions.

Well, everything's fine. It's just that wisely, my manual labor skills weren't requested, except to run for the occasional sandwich or caulk gun.

But we got lots of help. At one point there were so many assistants in the 32"x32" shower it looked like a Marx Brothers movie. How many gay people does it take to....

They sent me to Lowe's on the last day the old store was open. With its 60 percent off sale, it was day of the locusts in there. Every gay (and straight) person I know was in Lowe's. You think the Millennium 2000 gay rights march will be big? You didn't see the lesbians marching to the cash registers with power tools. The boys picked the place clean of designer faucets.

So now I'm sitting here with my laptop, hoping I'm out of grout splattering range. Is it just me, or do you also think spackle, grout and caulk are the same crap in different containers? They should simply call it groulkle. No matter what phase of the project we're on, there's a pail of the same white goo to step in. I'm convinced it's a hoax perpetrated on a nation of Vilaheads.

And speaking of hoaxes, let's face it, life's been weird. Did you hear about the National Security Agency banning this year's top toy seller, a furry robot called a Furby, in the workplace? Our nation's top spooks feared the fuzzies would record and divulge defense secrets. Apparently government intelligence (oxymoron alert) failed to notice that Furby entrails don't include tape recorders. No wonder we can't find Saddam Hussein.

But what really floored me was TV coverage of the president's Senate trial. On the trial's opening day, every single news program led off with 20 minutes on the retirement of dribbler Michael Jordan. It was a whole country telling Congress to take a quarter and call somebody who cares.

It's been weird locally too. Here in Sussex County we had the infamous trophy defacing—literally. A sore loser from the Punkin' Chunkin' festival went out of his gourd when festival judges failed to find the gourd he fired. So he sawed the face off the gargoyle atop the festival trophy. Jeeesh. If other people behaved that way, Barbra Streisand would have decapitated Oscar after losing for *Yentl*. (She didn't, did she???)

And for news of the weird even closer to home, here's a report for those of you who have been kind enough to inquire about Bonnie's diagnosis from the Johns Hopkins sleep clinic.

After I wrote about my spouse's snoring problem, we both took some heat. One person noted that I made good and sure Bonnie would never leave me. "Who'd go out with her after reading about the nighttime honking?"

Bonnie's comeback was "who'd go out with Fay and risk seeing every embarrassing thing they've ever done in print?" She had me there.

Well, it turns out that Bonnie does have sleep apnea and yes, it's being treated so we can both get some rest. Bonnie sleeps hooked up to a machine called a C-pap that blows air up her nose all night. No, I am not making this up.

Bonnie told me to tell you that she's sleeping like a baby, feeling rested, and the only downside is an inability to fall asleep at will during Ivory/Merchant films.

Of course, for me, it's like sleeping with somebody on life support. She's got this snorkel over her nose, hooked to a rubber tube from the air machine on the nightstand. Yes, a sense of humor comes in handy.

We visited friends in Connecticut and when our hostess spied the set-up she couldn't help howling, "My God, woman, you look like Lloyd Bridges in *Seahunt*." (If you don't remember Beau and Jeff's Dad's show on Saturday nights before *Gunsmoke*, you aren't AARP-eligible.)

Then we recalled when lots of people slept tethered by hoses to those big bonnet 1960s hairdryers. Heck, hostess and I got through our college social lives by having the roommate with the overnight guest put Keds on the wheels of the bed frame to reduce squeaking, while the roommate without the guest slept in the other bedroom with the hairdryer blowing on her head to muffle the er...noise.

This story got Bonnie's rapt attention, but hostess assured her that in those days, since I was still hanging in the closet with the bell bottoms and tie dye and had absolutely no interest in fraternity boys, hostess got most of the exercise while I wound up with a headful of split ends.

So on the whole, hearing the gentle whirr of the air machine is not unfamiliar to me. And it sure lets us get our rest.

Although we do have to report that one night when Bonnie heard the dog coughing that pre-barf thing dogs do, she instinctively leapt up, grabbed Moxie off the bead and headed for the bathroom. She forgot she was still leashed to the nightstand and got bungy-jumped back into the sack. The dog was so surprised he never did throw up.

So it's been pretty weird all over. With 65 degree weather in January, the Rehoboth off-season seems to have lasted about two days. In fact, I noticed hundreds of women milling about Baltimore Avenue and environs this weekend.

"I bet they're all here for the grand opening of the new Lowe's on Route One," Bonnie said, which sounded plausible until I realized it was just her way of telling me to fetch more spackle.

"I want the kind called Fast and Final." she said.

Yeah, like those two things could ever be true about one of our Bob Vila projects.

I'm going to turn in my column on the way. I hear that the new Lowe's is so big they hand out hiking maps at the door. If I'm not back by the next issue of *Letters*, hire a Sherpa guide and come rescue me. I'll be in the aisle with the groulkle. Or would that be spaulk?▼

March 1999

It was the day the Congressional report on the Y2K mess was released, with newspapers and TV all squawking about the coming computer crisis. Along with reports of the woeful unreadiness of government agencies came tales of survivalists digging shelters to hoard food and guns. They seem convinced that on January 1, 2000, when the whole country's power grid goes down (oh, if it were only that simple to stifle Jerry Springer...), with frozen ATM machines and people bartering toilet paper for Lean Cuisine, they expect Bill Clinton to revoke the Constitution, declare a dictatorship and end democracy as we know it.

Lock and Load! These rabid survivalists plan to lock shelter doors, load their AK47s and keep less prepared citizens away from their stockpile of Dinty Moore Beef Stew. One enterprising family ordered waterbeds for extra H2O storage. Yecccch!

All this sounds pretty alarmist to me, but then Congress recommends that "Americans should prepare for the year 2000 computer bug like they would a hurricane, by stocking up on canned food and bottled water in case vital services are cut off."

Now unless you've been under a non-digital rock, you know that many computers might not recognize the year 2000. To save expensive disk space, early programmers tracked dates with only the last two numbers of the year. If not fixed, many computers will read "00" as 1900, no doubt causing them to crash since computers weren't invented then. You gotta love one writer who called it a Geek Tragedy.

But so far, my all-time favorite Y2K comment comes from an e-mail memo now spamming the web. It's addressed to an unnamed company from an unnamed technical guru, noting "As you requested, staff has completed 18 months of work on Y2K Compliance. We have gone through every line of code in every program in every system, analyzed all databases, all files, including backups and historic archives, and modified all data to reflect the "Y-to-K" date change. All dates reflect the new standard: Januark, Februark, March, April, Mak, June, Julk, etc. as well as Sundak, Mondak, Tuesdak, Wednesdak, Thursdak, Fridak, Saturdak I trust that is satisfactory."

I'll say. So with Y2K scenarios in mind, Bonnie and I arrived at our Rehoboth condo the other night to find a total power outage. No lights, no heat, no welcoming frozen margarita. No frozen anything. In fact, sticky low fat faux ice cream was leaching out the freezer door.

In the blackness, I groped for the phone, hoped I dialed 411 and asked for the electric company's emergency number. When the operator started to spout numbers, I couldn't see to write it down. "Could you connect me? " I asked, having a flashback to days on Walton Mountain when operators did those things.

"You have reached the emergency number for Conectiv Electric. If you are reporting a gas leak, press 1, an electric outage, press 2...."

Who can see the numbers? I'm lucky I found the phone. I punched something, heard an odd digital burp and realized I'd punched redial. I had to start again with the operator.

"For a gas leak, press 1...."

I prayed for the kind of kinetic memory accountants get where their fingers memorize the calculator key pad. The only number I seem to know without looking is 227-FAST for pizza. Finally, I accidentally hit a key that got me to an actual person.

"May I help you?"

"Yes! I have no electric in my condo and it's freezing everywhere in here except my freezer. Can you send somebody to fix this?"

"How many units in the building are out? How many people have no electric?"

"Just two of us and a dog, but if that means you won't send somebody then there are a hundred of us here."

Fortunately, she laughed. And told me she'd send somebody out but that it might take a while. "Do you have plenty of blankets?"

This was starting to sound bad. Just because I'd been thinking about Y2K preparedness didn't mean I needed a drill.

"Do I have to stay here?"I asked, knowing that over on
Baltimore Avenue there were lights and comfortable bar stools.

"Oh yes, because if there's an appliance or circuit in your
apartment that caused the problem they want you to be there
when the electric goes back on."

They want me in here when it blows up? Not being a sur-
vivalist myself, it didn't make me happy.

After lurching around and groping for the walls like Audrey
Hepburn in *Wait Until Dark*, I managed to find a candle or two,
but no matches. So I left Bonnie and Moxie waiting for Godot
and went to the Blue Moon for a light. Hmmm. Nearly last call. I
wonder how long it's been since somebody asked for matches
because they actually needed a light, not a place to write a
phone number.

I hadn't been home long with the matches, with the condo
glowing like some retro counter-culture opium den, the three of
us huddling for warmth, when the Conectiv truck appeared.

A thousand apologies, they said. They'd meant to turn off a
neighbors electric, not ours. "Call the Claims Department and
tell them about the food you lost in the fridge."

Well, to be honest, there wasn't too much—half gallons of
Mudslides and Margarita mix, some fat-free cream cheese, and
a jar of Hellman's Real Mayo (just in case medical data reverses
itself and Mayo is prescribed to reduce cholesterol and stop hot
flashes). Oh yeah, there was that Heart Smart stuff we use instead
of butter, but that showed no signs of melting, like when you cook
with it.

And since our total culinary reputation lies in our making
reservations, I'm sure even the Conective Claims Department
would sniff fraud if we cited lost rump roasts and Tuna Surprise.

As these things go, our little Y2K preparedness drill put the
problem in perspective for me. Let folks in Montana dig their
bunkers; let New Years Eve revelers chance the air and cruise
lines. Let conspiracy theorists protect themselves from dictators,

banking paralysis and less reactionary neighbors trying to replace their canned Spam with fresh arugula, portobellos and moral pollution.

As for me, I intend to be here in Rehoboth with my friends, hunkered down with a stack of matches, a glow-in-the-dark Timex watch, and plenty of party food.

We'll lock (the door) and load (up the battery-powered blender) and welcome the Millennium. ▼

March 1999

Hi. What's new with us? Oh, nothing much. In the past three weeks I quit my job, sold the mini-condo, listed my Maryland house, took a great job in Rehoboth, bought a new house and we're moving to the beach!

On the single weekend when all of this was coming down, we dragged several of our buddies around looking at houses and then announced "Cocktails to celebrate our life change at the condo at 6 p.m.!"

When it was 6:20 and only our weekend guests were on hand, I worried aloud at the reason the others might be late. "They're probably huddling and planning an intervention," said a houseguest. Well, we probably are crazy, but there's no time for shrinks.

First, we had to complete an assignment from our realtor before putting the Maryland house on the market. Little stuff, like touch up paint, remove puppy gates, ditch dust bunnies, dispatch half the furniture, re-carpet the steps, take the buck naked Venus magnet off the fridge, pack up every stray possession we own and make the place look like an antiseptic model home.

"We can do that."

And by the way, said the realtor, "I want to have an open house next Sunday."

Oh good. God may have made the world in six days but he didn't have this much to do.

Gentlewomen, start your vacuums. Let the home improvement blitz begin. With gleeful abandon I went through the basement, storage room, closets and drawers, gathering up unwanted detritus from eleven years of residency.

I had bags for Goodwill, Bags for Sussex County AIDS Committee, bags for recycling, bags for the dump and, since I was staying up well into the nights doing this, big fat bags under my eyes.

Every morning on my way to work, I'd stop by the dump. There I was, in my Jones of New York corporate drag, hauling trash out of the Outback and chucking it into giant dumpsters. If it was after-hours for Mount Trashmore, I cased the neighborhood for deserted dumpsters, executing hit and run, drive-by dumpings.

By Wednesday, I'm loathe to admit, I stopped caring whether I was flinging my goodies into the right bins or not. Years of obsessive recycling came to a halt as this woman in a power suit tossed and ran, becoming an eco-terrorist, mixing green and brown glass, paper and cardboard, plastic and aluminum. One particularly ugly morning as I peeled into the dumpsite and got ready to shot-put old magazines and newspapers ("Clinton promises...") a rather, ahem, big-boned woman working at the site spied me. I figured she saw the rainbow on the back of the car and was coming over to help. No, she was coming over to laugh.

Meanwhile, back home, we worked like mules to fix stuff we'd happily ignored for over a decade. Bonnie, armed with screwdrivers, hammers, caulk and spackle (yet again), sanded, patched, painted and fixed the stove burner which hadn't worked since 1989, while I took care of ferrying massive piles of bric-a-brac to the garage.

Here's a yardstick: we had so much to do, that by late in the week I was reduced to actual manual labor. "Go paint the cellar steps," Bonnie told me, "You can't do too much damage to concrete."

Meanwhile, she was hauling a mound of dirt from the driveway to the backyard, hoping to shore up a sinkhole that appeared during the Iran-Contra scandal. A neighbor, coming to assist, spied me grappling with paint brush and bucket and called for reinforcements. "Bonnie needs help," he telegraphed to the cul de sac, "Fay's painting."

Actually, it was a combination painting and exterminating. Whatever crawly creatures lived on those steps suffered death by paint ball. Yo! Martha Stewart! Did you know that if you back into already-painted places, your butt does sponge painting?

After I painstakingly painted the top step, and slowly continued down the flight, Bonnie could stand it no longer. She poured the bucket of paint on the second step and proceeded to sweep the glop downward, completing my task in about a minute. To her, the Sistine Chapel would have been a half hour job.

On his way to Rehoboth Friday afternoon, our realtor stopped by to see what the place would look like when he returned for the Sunday open house. Boxes rose to the ceiling, the place was a wreck. He took one look and retreated to his Jaguar in horror.

With the clock ticking, we called two of our fussiest (in a good way) boyfriends to come do domestic science. Amid a flurry of Windex, we found the desk in the den with its drawers hanging open. Apparently, Quasimodo the carpet man, who single-handedly moved all the furniture to replace the carpet (with new stuff so cheap it shines like a bad suit), broke the desk drawers. Great. Prospective buyers will think the place has been ransacked.

We took a teeny martini break around 9 p.m. Friday night and, our luck, the garbage disposal choked to death on an olive pit. Fortunately, the plumber next door had a replacement disposal in his truck, disposing us of $60.

By midnight Friday we thanked the dust bunny twins and sent them home. Come Saturday morning, we touched up the last dog scratches by the front door, locked it and headed for the beach. The Open House verdict? "Great traffic, but no contract yet," said Mr. Realtor, "but congratulations, the place looks fabulous, I don't know how you did it!"

Frankly, neither did we. Not to mention spending the next two weeks living in an antiseptic bubble. For fear of crumbs, the only family member who ate in the kitchen was Moxie, while Bonnie and I sacrificed and went out every night. The stress of keeping the house pristine almost killed us.

But then we got the call, "Start packing. You've got a contract!"

Of course, as these things go, the contract fell apart, then the buyers found another lender, then we dickered about closing costs, then six calls later a deal was struck, then...somebody get the Dramamine.

Finally, we sold the place. I sure hope the people who bought it enjoy the bird who nests in our dryer vent every spring. She should be moving in, just as we're moving out.

At Passover Seder, the traditional end-of-ritual saying is "Next year, in Jerusalem." This year, we added "next year in Rehoboth." Actually, next week in Rehoboth. My very next column will be written as a full-time Rehoboth resident. If this is a mid-life crisis, I'm lovin' it. ▼

April 1999

After a hectic week of packing and shlepping, I arrived in Rehoboth more convinced than ever that I got out of DC just in time.

Between the government agonizing over ground troops— no, not for Kosovo, for the Tidal Basin to catch the bucky beaver chomping down the historic cherry trees, and *The Washington Post* carrying front page coverage of Fabio getting whacked in the schnozz by a low flying goose, it's been too weird to believe.

Did you catch the Fabio thing? The infamous romantic coverboy was dressed like Adonis and riding the lead car to inaugurate a new rollercoaster. Everything was ducky until the Fab must have closed his eyes in terror, because he never saw this humongous kamikaze goose heading for his face. The cover photo of Fabio's bloody beak was not Mr. I Can't Believe It's Not Butter's finest moment.

But if that wasn't disgusting enough, during my office farewell party, in the midst of wine and cheese, a pre-pubescent roller blader sidled up to the party room's plate glass window and, while executing a triple salchow, mooned the entire crowd. Now there was a sign that it was time to go.

We howled. The FBI could have dusted the big tush on the window for asshole prints.

As vivid a farewell as the moonie was, the sign outside the office was even better. My colleagues thoughtfully installed the letters "Farewell, Fay, thanks for the memories" on one side of the sign, but blushed when they were reminded that the back side said, "Get rid of bulk trash this Saturday." Yup. I was outta there.

I bid a fond farewell to my spouse, who is charged with handling the home fires for another few weeks until settlement. We'd have to make do with nightly phone calls. In the meantime, awaiting the move to our new home, I would camp at the condo.

So I arrived in Rehoboth on Sunday, April 11, no longer just a weekender, and a mere night's sleep away from my first new job in 17 years. As I tried to relax, channel surfing to keep myself company, it was no small irony that I stumbled upon the very first episode of the *Mary Tyler Moore Show*. I fell asleep watching Mary greet her new boss ("But Mr. Grant...."), new neighbors Rhoda and Phyllis, and totally new surroundings. I empathized.

Let me tell you, from the instant my alarm clock went off, things were gloriously different. In the hour I used to spend commuting, pouring coffee down my suit jacket, enduring public radio fundraising, and fighting road rage, I went to the gym, got a newspaper, and had coffee. Life was wonderful.

In fact, my new job seems to be wonderful, too. One of the things that attracted me to the position was the prospect of a one-person office. No more football pools, office politics, or staggered lunch hours. If I want to gossip around the water cooler I just grab the Britta jug and talk to myself.

Of course, being seriously hardware challenged (I know, it hardly seems fair, considering my lesbian credentials), the downside of office solohood is having nobody to call when machinery goes berserk.

Lest my new employers pale, let me assure them that I'm quite competent in the skills they sought at the interview. I'm just an office equipment klutz.

Like it took me three days to figure out that the printer wouldn't print because somebody had helped themselves to the printer cable. Once I leapt that hurdle, we had a paper jam. The machine is beeping and some cartoon geek on the computer screen is hollering commands. When I manage to liberate the shards of crinkled vellum, half a ream of paper shoots over the room. Suddenly I'm Lucille Ball at the chocolate factory, running around the desk and screaming for Ethel Mertz.

Meanwhile the phone rings. "Hello, Hello????" Nobody there. I'm thinking I got dissed by a heavy breather when I realize it isn't the phone, it's the fax. Another machine I flunked. Which is probably good. Otherwise, I might be tempted, as Murphy Brown once did, to fax my chest to the West Coast.

But the crowning glory of my first week came when I locked myself in the bathroom. While the office is in a cute little house, it's a very old little house. I went into the bathroom, closed the door, and the door handle fell off. Oh good. Trapped. Now here's a serious downside to the single-person office.

First I panicked, eyed the window and wondered if I'd be able to shimmy out without either killing myself or landing onto page one of the local press. I gave the window thing a good old college try and realized that this round peg would have lots of trouble getting through that square hole. By this time I was standing on the toilet, head and shoulders out the window, laughing like a hyena. I dethroned and took another look at the bathroom door. I figured out I could jiggle the lock open by sticking my pinky finger into where the door handle used to be. Sprung!

I've been flying solo almost three weeks now and I've started to leave little notes around the office. "Put letterhead in printer upside down, stupid." "Fax originals face down, moron." Luckily we don't have a shredder or my clothes would look like the costumes from *Les Miserables*.

Having negotiated this uneasy truce with my mechanical staff, I'm settling into my new job and new hometown. I miss the girlfriend, but her arrival is imminent. I've checked out the grocery, discovered mid-week dinner specials, walked the boardwalk after work, and generally enjoyed the heck out of myself. I think I'll take my rainbow embroidered baseball cap up to the boardwalk, stand on Rehoboth Avenue, toss the hat up into the air, and listen for Mary Tyler Moore's theme song.

I'm smiling. ▼

May 1999

Oh, the frustration of relocating my entire life.

Hell, just arranging phone service for our new house is life's work. What are there now, twenty thousand phone companies? And they all called me tonight during dinner. "Hi, this is a courtesy call from MCI...." If they were really courteous they wouldn't call at 6 o'clock.

Apart from connecting and disconnecting service, which now take a minimum of a month each on hold with a robot, my favorite phone company trick is slamming. Has it happened to you yet? While you sleep, no-name long distance companies steal your account. Then, when you make calls, your new company electronically selects the highest possible rate in the hemisphere. I'm paying a dollar seventy-five a minute. They should automatically dial 911 for you when the bill comes.

And just try to straighten it out. Short of having Amnesty International intervene, your only hope is spending the foreseeable future pressing 1 for Residential Service, 2 for Billing Questions, and 3 for the Spanish Inquisition. I was on the phone so long trying to get my phone company back that the operator, showing a refreshing sense of irony, ended our conversation with "Thanks for spending the day with Bell Atlantic."

Following that, the first call I got was from some cheesy long-distance company, interrupting yet another meal, to beg for business. Can't we pay them ten cents a minute to go away? Now I'm into the traditional kind of slamming—as in down the receiver.

As long as I was aggravated anyway, I called the cable company. First I was put on hold for the afternoon, forced to hear non-stop promos for Nicholas Cage movies. Then, the genius operator couldn't figure out how to order service at a new house where cable had never dared to go before. Duh. When she put me on hold, I came into a movie promo at the very words "It's *Dumb and Dumber*...." No comment.

Meanwhile, between calls to local utilities, Bonnie and I are holed up in our condo, belongings piled to the ceiling, waiting to get into the new house. The transition is even making the dog nuts. The poor little guy doesn't understand what happened to his backyard.

His frustration has manifested itself as a craving to chew wicker. Great. It's a beach rental. Wicker Central. A Moxie munching ground. Yesterday, for wicker du jour, he ate half a chair.

I'm easily amused these days. In my continuing transition to office maven, I called the people at Intellifax (Oxymoron Alert!!!) for help when the fax machine herniated itself. They told me, and I'm quoting here, "you're sticking it in the wrong hole."

But as frustrations go, by last week I finally had the mother of all irritants, an example by all future frustrations may be measured. It happened as we moved Bonnie's office stuff to Rehoboth. Try sitting in traffic, at a dead stop, on the Chesapeake Bay Bridge (always frustrating), only this time, as the minutes tick by, you are paying the moving van stuck behind you, $70 an hour. Tick, tick, tick....

So the upshot is that change may be great, but transition's a bitch.

I give credit to my friends Dan and Peter for that particular sentiment.

When we met them twelve weeks ago, Bonnie and I were in a Sarasota restaurant with my father, trying to explain why it was sensible for me to quit my long-time job, take a position for less than half the salary, sell the house, uproot Bonnie's business and move to the beach. Mission impossible.

As President of the Bank of Dad, he worried we'd evermore be dialing for dollars. No, we'd be fine, I said. We'd thought it all out, we had a financial plan. Then I told him that more than money, it really just came down to a sense of community. Our friends, the welcoming atmosphere, my opportunity to write for *Letters*, the diversity, the wonderful people we'd met....

He wasn't buying it. I talked and talked, but Dad looked wild-eyed, dwelling on that teensy "quit my job" part.

Just then, somebody tapped me on the shoulder. I turned to see a nice-looking stranger, about my age. "Are you Fay Jacobs, from *Letters from CAMP Rehoboth*?" he asked.

Now really, what's the chance of that happening a thousand miles from Rehoboth Avenue? A zillion to one?

I fessed up to it being me, as he introduced himself and his partner, glanced to my left and said "And you must be Bonnie. We have a place in North Shores and we enjoy reading *Letters*. We recognized you, Fay, from the picture. We just moved to Rehoboth full-time. Isn't it a wonderful place????"

My father was gape-jawed. Either he instantly understood our babbling about community, or, more plausibly, he wondered when the heck I'd had time to plant these guys in the restaurant.

Either way, after we chatted a while and the guys went back to their table, Dad cautiously endorsed our beach relocation plan and stopped stuttering "quit your job????" To this day, I'm sure he still thinks it was a set-up.

And now that we've completely uprooted ourselves, final push courtesy of our new Sarasota boyfriends, it's only fair that they got to counsel us last week over dinner. Yes, they said, change is good; it's just transition that's hell.

Well, if the end result is that a bad day negotiating for phone service at the beach is better than a good day anywhere else, we'll take the traffic-snarled moving vans, dialing for dummies and wicker chomping. Heck, I have to have something to rant and rave about.

Of course, while I'm typing, Bonnie's fending off a call from Sprint, Moxie's got his incisors around the coffee table leg, and we're so anxious to move in and get settled we're ready to gnaw the wicker ourselves. Change is good; change is good, change is good....▼

June 1999

I promise, these are absolutely, positively the last words I will EVER have to say about real estate. I know that reading about my move to the beach must be on your very last nerve by now, so I'll make it short: We didn't settle, we didn't move, we're nomads again. Rehoboth Hobos. (That's Hobo, with a b.)

Do I have the world's worst real estate karma, or what? Twenty-four hours before moving day we discovered that the builder forgot one teeny tiny detail for the new house—an occupancy permit. That's his job, for god's sake. It's like gay men forgetting hair gel. Or Rehoboth forgetting to install the parking meters. Or me forgetting to eat, god forbid. It doesn't happen.

But the moving van was on its way from Maryland, renters were heading to the condo and the settlement was off. I had two choices. I could walk into the ocean or laugh.

Ergo, here's the hyena from hell.

Nero fiddled while Rome burned and I just howled while my heroic real estate agent and crackerjack settlement team tried to locate a building inspector. What a hoot!

By 4 p.m. on moving day we got permission to unload the trucks, but we had to swear not to move into the house. Laughed, thought I'd die. Imagine the hilarity when I remembered I'd already arranged for the gas dryer delivery, cable installation, California Closet lady, and mail forwarding. Here's a hot one: If the phone number is transferred to the new house, but there's no one there to hear it, does it still ring?

With a mighty guffaw, Bonnie and I did the sensible thing and went to the bar at Blue Moon. "Ha-ha-ha, if we're too drunk to drive, we'll take a cab home!"

"Yeah, said my spouse, "What home?"

Beats me, ha-ha-ha.

Fortunately, friends leaving for vacation offered us refuge.

By the next morning, we raced to our 3-bedroom storage unit to meet the closet lady and spend a half hour surveying the walk-in closet, which is the longest I've been in the closet since 1978, ha-ha-ha....

And did you hear the one about the farmer's daughter who married the Jewish Princess and now they're both homeless because the builder forgot to get an occupancy permit, ha-ha-ha?

By Sunday night we cried with laughter as we packed bags at the house we'd just moved into to go back to the condo we'd just moved out of. Hot on the heels of the departing renters, we brought back much of the same crap we'd moved out forty eight hours before. What a gas!

I thought living out of a suitcase since April was bad, but it was just a chuckle compared to the rip snorter of having our belongings in a whole other house, four miles away. Twice on Sunday night we had to drive up and down the highway to retrieve necessities. Now that was a side-splitter. And speaking of splitting, let me tell you about the kind of headache you can get from all this. Hey, which house has the Tylenol??? A plague on both our houses ha-ha-ha....

Okay, a real estate agent, a mortgage man and a lawyer were all walking up Rehoboth Avenue trying to calm down a hysterical client, when...wait a minute, that's no joke, that's my life, ba-da-boom.

"It will all work out," Bonnie said, letting out an enormous guffaw. Or possibly a wail.

To paraphrase Henny Youngman, take my spouse, ple-assseee!!!

Or, as Groucho said, "This is the most ridiculous thing I've ever heard!"

"Dethpicable..." quoth Daffy Duck.

I know! We'll just click our Reeboks, whisper there's no place like home and find out we'd been in a tornado.

We've now been laughing for more than a week. So here are Fay J's top five reasons why we're still not in our house:

On Monday the builder said the plumbing inspection would be Tuesday;

On Tuesday the builder said the plumbing inspection would be Wednesday;

On Wednesday they discovered that they'd forgotten to fully insulate the ceiling;

On Thursday they delayed the final inspection until next week;

On Friday my realtor, shocked that I was still laughing, asked me what medication I was taking.

They're coming to take me away Ha-Ha Ho-Ho Hee-Hee to the funny farm where life is beautiful all the time and at least I will have an address for mail forwarding.

Ba-da-boom. ▼

May 1999

Bonnie made a liar out of me. To the police, no less.

Two weeks ago our intrepid editor invited me to join him for the Rehoboth Beach police sensitivity training session on hate crimes. I knew CAMP participated in the session every year and I was honored to be asked to join the team.

Realizing I'd have to prepare some comments in addition to being available for questions, I thought back to the hurtful occasion where Bonnie and I were threatened with a hate crime. It happened in Key West of all places.

It was a beautiful evening as four of us, dressed for a lovely dinner, walked towards the inviting lights of Duvall Street. As we dodged a huge puddle in the road (fearful of getting our prissy sandals wet), our quartet fanned out in opposite directions. Suddenly, from nowhere, a low-rider Chevy with dark tinted windows careened around the corner, almost mowing us down.

"Whoa," I said, motioning to the driver, mostly as a reflex, as he came within inches of my shoes.

"Hey!" hollered Bonnie, similarly.

The car screeched to a halt, a young man got out, screaming, "Dykes! Dykes! You f-ing Dykes were in my way, Goddammit. F-ing dykes," And then he let fly with a string of obscenities ttha would make a redneck blush.

Not only were we horrified for us, but a mother and her preteen daughter standing close by were appalled as the jerk continued to scream threats. I was scared for me, embarrassed for the scene, and sick to my stomach.

"Dykes! Dykes! I'll kill you, goddamn dykes!"

Bonnie ran to get the license plate number, I ran toward the nearest restaurant to call the police, and our brave friends turned on the creep, shrieked at him with a dose of his own medicine and watched his girlfriend haul him back into the car. When the vehicle finally squealed away, we stood, stunned, in the street.

"Are the police coming?" Bonnie asked.

"No, they said if nobody got hurt they don't bother."

But we were hurt. And it took a lot of tears, discussion, and venting our anger to calm us down. And none of us would ever think of Key West quite the same way again. It was a lesson I wanted to pass along to our local police force.

On the night of the sensitivity training, we joined the police chief and the summer police recruits to watch an excellent film about hate crimes. With its emphasis on racially motivated hate crimes, as well as synagogue defacing and gay bashing, I realized, eerily, I could speak to two thirds of the problem.

When Steve got up to speak, he introduced himself as a gay man, eloquently described the mission of CAMP Rehoboth, then introduced me by name, adding that I was a lesbian.

Oohph. That was the first time I'd been introduced to a roomful of people by my sexual orientation. And there was even a reporter from *The Washington Post* covering the meeting. Well, one of the things we try to explain about our lives is that the process of "coming out" is evolutionary. It's not just once; it's a thousand little "coming-outs" over a lifetime. For me, as open as I am about my life, this particular coming out was a milestone. I smiled at the fresh-faced young recruits to acknowledge the introduction, and turned my attention back to Steve.

His short presentation touched on the diversity of the gay community itself here in town and the expectations we have for professional conduct by the police, whether it be enforcing the laws or investigating criminal incidents. Steve made a special point of breaking down stereotypes; noting that not all gay men are effeminate and not all lesbians drive pick-up trucks. It was a light and humanizing presentation.

When it was my turn, I introduced myself as a non-pickup-truck-driving lesbian, evoking smiles from the normally reserved crowd. I went on to tell the Key West gay bashing story. "It ruined my entire vacation there," I said. "And it was the total indifference by the police which made it doubly hurtful. Here in Rehoboth, you have the opportunity to do better."

If racial, religious or anti-gay hate crimes, harassment or name calling occur here (and, let's face it, ignorant jerks happen) our police force has the chance to treat the incidents with the kind of sensitivity which could salvage people's feelings about their experience and our town. I told the crowd that they could really make a difference. And the eye contact and feedback I got from the presentation told me that we have a group of young men and women on the Rehoboth police force who understand the value of diversity in this community—and who will do their best to behave both professionally and sensitively.

For me, it was a wonderful evening, because I was doing just the kind of volunteer service I was never able to do in my hectic, suburban, commute-filled life back in Maryland.

Oh yeah, the liar part. Within days of identifying myself as a non-pickup-truck lesbian, Bonnie went out and bought a bright red Chevy S10. You should see this baby! Holy Sussex County! Why, we can plug in our radar detector and cigarette lighter at the same time! And here's good news—the doors stay open without the dome light shining, to keep from scaring off the deer during hunting season. I know I'll be using that feature a lot.

But if you see those police recruits, please tell them that it's Bonnie hauling concrete patio blocks and 2x4s from Lowe's. The only time I intend to get behind the wheel is for an annual power shop back at Nordstrom's. Yeee-Haw! ▼

June 1999

It's not enough that media hungry Rev. Jerry Falwell made a laughing stock of himself by proclaiming TV's purple Teletubby a gay poster boy, now he's messing with one of the powerhouses of popular music, the Lilith Fair.

Fallwell, or his editorial disciples, are warning parents to beware of the demonic legend behind the popular Lilith Fair concert series. Wheras his indictment of Tinky Winky made me go out and buy a plush Tinky for myself, this latest outcry sent me directly to the Internet for research.

I learned that according to ancient Jewish literature, Lilith was created by God as Adam's first wife, but left Eden after refusing to be submissive to Adam. Hmmmm.

According to Lilith tour publicists, the concert, featuring some of the nation's best women musicians, who played to over 800,000 music lovers last year, in 37 cities, "got its name from the character's original aspect, a woman seeking equality and independence."

But Falwell's conservative *National Liberty Journal* says there are many conflicting accounts of the Lilith character. Their favorite is the pagan legend, often associated with lesbianism, where Lilith dwelled with demons after leaving Eden and went mad after witnessing the execution of her children. That, in turn, caused a killing spree, where she seduced and murdered her own demonic male offspring. Oh good.

From reliable eye witnesses at last season's Lilith Fair in Columbia, MD, the most demonic thing the group did was leave the outdoor concert venue a lot cleaner than they found it.

By contrast, anybody ever sit in the infield at the Preakness? You want demonic? I've got demonic. It's a disgusting ritual at Pimlico Raceway in Baltimore, which I only attended once, which was more than enough. But the damn thing happens every year. Where was Falwell's warning in May about the demonic influence of the Preakness?

Bonnie and I were recruited (oh, no!) to take part in a crude (operative word) attempt at a heterosexual pride day, with a pagan band of Coors-worshipping idolaters. Our cabal set out in a van, armed with 18 cases of beer, three ice coolers, 40 fat-laden Italian subs, 100 yards of rope (what the heck for???), a dozen tomato stakes, two handcarts, a fold-up luggage carrier, a tent, and a port-a-potty. I prayed that the last two items would be used in tandem.

With backpacks, handcarts, tent and toilet, we set out for the races. Hundreds of other fiendish spectators, shlepping provisions and surging toward the track, jostled for position like the horses they'd come to bet on. People had extension ladders laden with beer cases, kegs in wheelbarrows, a ping-pong table piled with pilsner, and enough camping gear to make Falwellians suspect lesbianism was surely afoot.

Breaking through the crush, our wicked tribe charged the field, and staked out a 15x15 foot claim with the tomato stakes and rope. From our vantage point, through a maze of tents, canopies, coolers and bodies, you could almost make out the track fence. If the horses stopped, jumped up and waved, we might get a glimpse.

With a whoop, the ritual drinking began. A plastic cup of some awful red liquid came by and I sampled. Yum, vodka and red dye #2. I was told it was a Yucca Flat, named for the A-Bomb test site. This was 10:30 a.m., with post time for the first race at noon, and the Preakness at 5:30. All our coven did was drink, sopping up liquid with the occasional baloney/pepperloaf sub. A far cry, I'm sure from the tofu and pyramid of food groups revelers at Lilith Fair will be sampling.

Then some guys opposite our encampment, who had not thought ahead in the port-a-potty department, started making like garden hoses. Here's your tinky winky, Jerry. Where was the Falwell watch when you needed them? I'd never seen so much male equipment in my life. It was like a giant pee-a-thon. Ennui forced some disgusted women in our camp to start holding up paper plates with magic-markered numbers on them, rating the boys' endowments on a scale of Tinky-Winky to Ten.

Finally, our jury could only watch in horror as the infield turned into one enormous fist fight. With the drinking and pee-ing out of the way, all the revelers could come up with next was drunken brawls, as bored girlfriends and wives wished they'd stayed home watching QVC.

Finally, as a sure sign of higher power displeasure, the heavens opened with a Noah-inspired deluge of rain, turning the whole infield into a mucky mess, which then inspired mud-wrestling and trash bag luge racing. Yo! Falwell! Looky here. (And, now that I think of it, why doesn't Falwell have something to say about the position those guys have to take on that 2-man Olympic luge sled, anyway? Just wondering....)

We never did find out who won the Preakness. There were so many drunks on the yucca flat we had to step over mud-crust-ed bodies to get the hell out. Folks who'd had beer piled on lad-ders on the way in, used them as stretchers for the fallen on the way out. The four guys with the ping-pong table carried out a whole platoon of drunk and wounded. And the remaining infield was one big toxic landfill of beer cans and trash.

Holy Satanic Verses! Evil legend has it that this kind of infer-nal drinking and boys-will-be-boys reveling happens at race-tracks, ballfields and stadiums all over the globe. Why Lucifer himself tells tales of our very own Delaware Punkin' Chunkin' Fest, now endorsed by that conspiracy of male sensibility, the Promise Keepers (don't get me started). And Falwell is picking on Lilith Fair?

He's set his wily little eye on concerts where thousands of women, their men friends and not a few Tinky-Winky carrying children come to picnic on sensible food, drink additive-free beverages, listen to some of the best female musicians in the world, and clean up after themselves before they go? Besides, in every concert city, Lilith Fair donates thousands of dollars to the local battered women's shelters. It's demonic, I tell you.

The third and final tour Lilith begins July 8, and features

artists including founder Sarah McLachlan, Sheryl Crow, The Dixie Chicks and Queen Latifah. As McLachlan herself is quoted saying, "[Lilith] was a great example of strong women out there doing something they love, doing something really positive."

Of course, that's what Falwell and his kind find so demonic. Why doesn't he just admit it?▼

July 1999

It started with a postcard. A friend in L.A. sent me a postcard with her resume shot and agent's phone number on it. It's the kind of professional calling card those pursuing the "business" use for notes to casting directors. In this case, she used it for a message to us.

"Dear Fay & Bonnie,

You said to tell you when I'm in a TV show. Well, I have a nice-size role in a somewhat shocking skit on a program you'd never watch if I didn't send you this card. The show's demographics are for non-intellectual men of 18-30. Filming was quite an experience. It's *The Man Show*, July 21 on the Comedy Channel."

The Man Show??? Yes, I'd say it's exactly the kind of show I'd be expected to miss.

Early Wednesday evening I checked to make sure I could even get the Comedy Channel. Lucky me, I tuned in just in time to hear "Later tonight! *The Man Show*! The finest display of arrested development going!"

Then, they flashed a clip of a young man cozying up to my former acting colleague—a very dignified, middle-aged woman—with the agitated announcer hollering, "Need some fuuuun in your life? Go on a date with Mom!"

Oy. I could hardly wait for 10:30.

And speaking of Moms, while I was biding my time 'til *The Man Show*, I logged onto a wonderful gay and lesbian message board where my son-the-actor types back and forth with cyber-friends all over the globe.

After lurking on the board for a while last week, eavesdropping on several different conversation threads, everything from sports bras, tattoos, Petula Clark lyrics to JFK, I posted a note myself, asking folks why they converge there.

"It's a meeting of the minds, a communal graffitti board &

debate forum. And, yes, I passionately believe in the good stuff that can happen when good people communicate."

"I can't think of a taboo subject, and the amazingly rational discussion of abortion a month or so ago confirmed my belief in the goodness, the intelligence, the caring of all members herein."

"I'm here as one of the conditions of my parole. Okay, I'm lying."

Like my son says, "much of what we discuss there has nothing to do with sexuality or gender roles. But there's just something about that queer perspective."

Just the fact that it's an accessible queer perspective cheers me up. We had nothing like this when I was struggling to meet people and come out. Hell, I was sure I was the only gay woman on earth except the already-dead Gertrude Stein and those few lonely souls I'd heard about who met in dark, scummy bars. Now, of course, I recognize our wonderfully huge gay community and its history, rich in achievement and enjoyment all through the ages. But who knew??? Back in the 70s and early 80s you didn't get TV role models, you didn't get positive press. You got lesbian potlucks and liked it.

These days, people struggling with their identity, those just getting to know the gay community and those who need a link from their small towns and small-minded families have this and other marvelous cyberplaces to go.

One message said, "I have friends (gay and straight) all over the world. I've laughed and cried with people whose faces I could not pick out in a crowded room. The town in which I live is tiny, but the world in which I live is gigantic and as close as the keyboard."

For people not lucky enough to live in a diverse community like Rehoboth, the Internet is the missing link. And if the folks on this particular message board don't mind a lesbian mom lurking around and providing a stray comment now and then, I'm delighted to have the chance to participate.

But on Wednesday night, I traded communication central for Comedy Central.

Bonnie and I microwaved popcorn and sat down for THE MAN SHOW.

Oh. My. God. From the opening seconds featuring nearly naked girls (Let's hear it for the Juggies!") to the skit called "Drunks Say the Darnedest Things" with live, in-person, actual barfing, Bonnie and I sat gape-jawed and stunned. Then came an "infomercial" for flesh colored wedding rings ("for the best of both worlds") and "Household Hints from Adult Film Stars" with a bimbo rubbing red wine off a wet t-shirt. I was not amused.

Finally, we got to my poor thespian friend, playing a woman on a date with her gooney adult son—dining out, whirling around a dance floor, attending an amusement park, getting drunk and then, goon-boy and mom...going to bed together and...yech!!!!! What does he think, come Emmy time he'll be recognized for best actor in a compromising position?

"That's the most disgusting thing I've ever seen," said Bonnie.

I was too stricken to talk. Appalled as I was by the theme, I was even more aghast that hundreds of studio audience imbeciles roared with laughter and cheered at this colossal pile of unfunny poop. A.K.A. *The Moron Show.*

And I didn't tape it! With no evidence, how could I circulate a video of this offensive, sophomoric heterosexual menace through the halls of Congress? Damn! I would have had the perfect tool to counter those wingnuts circulating film of gay pride parades. Just imagine. For every gay person outraged at being broad-brushed as evil by films of a few nearly naked gay people having a little too much fun at parades, we could have all the diverse and wonderful straight people we know branded evil heterosexual louts by sending out copies of *The Man Show.*

Heck, we could use the identical "Protect Our Children" diatribes that usually accompany the parade films. I bet it wouldn't take five minutes for the ignorant masses to realize what bright gay and straight people have known for eons: *The Man Show* doesn't represent the entire heterosexual orientation any more than a few naughty boys in leather or tough girls on Harleys represent our side. Duh....

But it sure would be fun trying to make that point. I'm going to float the idea to the online message board and hope some young filmmakers want to give it a try. *The Man Show* could do more for gay equality than all the lobbying in the world.

And I'll help circulate the video. The only thing I refuse to do, with apologies to my friend in L.A. is ever watch it again. The Juggies and goons will have to survive without this mother. ▼

August 1999

I stared at the computer screen and mumbled obscenities. I'd already spent the better part of a day trying to diagnose a conflict between my hard drive and my printer and frankly, Scarlet, I no longer gave a damn.

On days like these I agree with my father who, at age 80, refuses to be in the same room with a computer. "They were supposed to make our lives easier. Everybody I know with a computer has nothing but trouble. Who needs it."

He may be right. It's hard to love your PC when your monitor is flashing "fatal error." Do I call the techie or the coroner? I tried Feng Shui and moved the computer to a different spot in the room for more fortunate energy and blessings. The damn thing still didn't work so I scrawled a document in long-hand.

Interestingly, that night Ted Koppel had a whole show on technology—charting man's genetic quest to go faster and faster. His examples were as exasperating as they were fascinating. Like who really needs the five seconds we got back changing from rotary to touch tone dialing? And are we better off with an expensive plastic spout on the orange juice container when it only took a second or two to claw open the cardboard flap?

And, fresh in my mind, is "what damn good is a pentium computer when your day's work is trapped inside, forcing you back to a Papermate pen."

In the end, Koppel concluded that man is biologically programmed to speed up. Like we didn't know this from watching teenagers in Isuzus peel away from a traffic light.

Heck, if man is driven to speed up, this particular woman is driven to slow down. If they stopped the world, I wouldn't get off, but I'd like to call delay of game.

Which is why I've been practicing Sussification. It's the ancient art of adapting to life in Sussex County, Delaware. The guiding principle of Sussification is to chill out in the face of deadlines, traffic and waiting for the electrician to show up. While there are many relaxation techniques and poses, my current favorite is on a barstool swilling a Cosmo. It puts me back in balance.

When we went to get our driver's licenses recently, there were Sussification disciples everywhere. One government worker (oxymoron alert!!) thought nothing of shrieking questions to me across a crowded room. I loved it when she screamed "Weight???," listened for my quiet response and then hollered "Couldn't hear you!"

To my credit, when I got finished shouting that great big number back to her, I practiced my new Sussification steps and did not leap over the counter and choke her.

Yes, thanks to my new regimen I've put my personal quest for speed on hold and I'm trying to chill out. Here's a thought: If Yoga is practiced at an Ashram, is a Sussification temple a single-wide?

To those of us balancing our lives locally, it may have been 100-degrees and frantic on Route One last weekend (I did love the liquor store sign reading "Drink Plenty of Fluids") but at Poodle Beach there was a nice breeze and great company. My kind of mosh pit.

Anyway, there I was at the beach, amid a bevy of lesbians of a certain age, when the conversation turned, as it often does, to…um, I forget where this was going…oh yes, to memory. Or lack of it.

I reported *USA Today's* disturbing news that stress causes your brain to shrink, resulting in memory loss. Honey I Shrunk My Brain. I'd refer you to the article, but I forget which day I read it.

"What we need are Gingko Biloba Margaritas," suggested a tribe member.

Sounds good to me. I've already attributed the fact that I can no longer remember all the lyrics to *Hot Town Summer in the City* to the stress of driving into DC one night last month. The traffic on Pennsylvania Avenue almost killed me. I could feel my brain shrinking. By comparison, a Saturday afternoon trip around here is massage therapy.

At the beach, calm and peace reign as I chant my Sussification mantra "oh well, whatever" whenever, say, my new puppy eats a sandal. Hey, who cares if the folks who promised to fix my kitchen floor skipped town. And it's entirely possible that the plumber will get back with the estimate within the twentieth century.

This new philosophy is working so well I'm beginning to think about politics calmly. In fact, I went to a wonderful Human Rights Campaign reception recently, and got to meet one of my personal heroes, Barbara Gittings—a pioneer of our gay equality movement. She was introduced to the group as a woman who really opened the doors for us. Not skipping a beat, she looked around the room teeming with energetic, interesting women and added "And look who's coming through those doors now!" It was a wonderful moment.

And one that surely feeds our brains instead of shrinking them.

You know, I'm becoming such a high priestess of Sussification that I'm considering buying a gazing ball for my back yard. According to a catalogue description, these decorative lawn ornaments, all the rage in the Victorian era, were used to attract fairies. From the number of gazing balls on my street alone and the demographics of the neighborhood, they seem to work.

Ah, Sussex County. One day on the sand, a friend scanned the crowd, leaned over to me and said, "If you'd told me in 1960 that I'd be sitting on a beach with thousands of other homosexuals, I would have been...well...very happy!"

Well, I am very happy. I've traded lots of stress away, and I'm working on the rest. Now if I could only figure out this computer nonsense. I just got an error message saying, "You've made changes to Normal.doc." Well I should hope so. ▼

November 1999
FAY JACOBS, THIS IS YOUR LIFE

First let me say Mea Culpa. I'm sorry. I realize now that I've failed miserably in my obligation to keep my loyal readers fully informed. What we had here was a failure to communicate. Three times during Rehoboth's October Pet Parade, fairly irate readers, none of whom I'd ever actually met before, stood before us, hands on hips, indignantly saying, "You didn't tell us you got a second dog!"

Well, with my humble apologies, I now announce (belatedly to be sure) the arrival of Paddy, the second Miniature Schnauzer to move into Schnauzerhaven. He joins his older half-brother Moxie, rounding out our brand new family. Which all goes to prove what a difference a year makes for pets and people. Whew. Halloween night marked the first anniversary of the passing of our beloved Max.

In the Jewish tradition, family and friends gather a year after the death of a loved one for a ceremony called an unveiling. It's a great comfort to be together again a year later, grief in perspective, to unveil the cemetery monument. Then you go pig out on lox and bagels. I'm not sure if I'm the first to have hosted a canine unveiling, but I figured a loved one is a loved one and why not.

And, as always accompanies these kinds of things, came reflection. Here we are, on the cusp of Y2K, with champagne and survival supplies at the ready. I can't believe we're here. Not in Rehoboth, not in 1999.

As I got dressed for Halloween costume parties around town, I remembered the first time I ever thought about the turn of the century. It was 1961, when my best friend and I, decked out in Roy Rogers holsters and cowboy hats (and we had no idea of our future orientation?) sat counting the decades 'til 2000 on our fingers (which, by the way, is still how I do my checkbook). Holy Dale Evans, we'd be an ancient 51!!!!

I don't have a clear picture of the drooling old biddy I imagined at the time, but you can bet I didn't conure a 51-year-old lesbian, dressed for Halloween as Tinky Winky. Reality rocks.

No crystal ball ever foretold this Big Apple native, happily partnered, overwhelmingly Schnauzered and living in the small town equivalent of Gayberry RFD.

But I can tell you exactly how I got here, based on my own personal Cliff Notes—my life on a single page. It arrived in the mail, compliments of an anal-retentive pal who's had the same address book since the Kent State shootings. She photocopied the "Fay page" for me. The antique address book entries are in bold. I've added an accompanying travelogue.

Fay @ American U. Dorm - Theatre major; insane crushes on leading ladies, but no idea an alternative future is possible. Dating male law student. Why am I miserable?

Fay & Bobby in Bethesda - Oy. Still lusting after Dolly Levi & Hedda Gabler but married, just to pacify the folks, to that accordion player. Start visiting fabulous disco 70s gay bars with the community theatre crowd, me as the token straight. Yeah, right.

Fay @ Mary Jane's - Bless the friend who takes me in after the divorce. Too scared to explore alternatives, but watching a lot of tennis and Jody Foster movies.

Fay in Annapolis - Final heterosexual adventures fail. Tell the folks I broke up with the butcher, the baker, the candlestick maker.

Fay @ Mary Jane's Again - One toe out of the closet, the 1980s era of lesbian potlucks and furtive bookstore visits begins. Folks are clueless.

Fay @ _____ - Okay, edited for propriety. Suffice it to say that when I told the folks I broke up with the Jewish banker, I kept it gender neutral.

Fay @ Bonnie's in Baltimore - About time. Folks still clueless. Learn to love hard shell crabs and the Orioles, hon. Fay very, very happy.

Fay & Bonnie's Townhouse - Got a Schnauzer, got a Subaru. Come clean with the folks. "Well...this is 1982," they say, bravely. The rest of the family doesn't miss a beat, asking "So, is she Jewish?"

F & B, new house in Md. - March on Washington '87 & '93. Life is good. Gay 90s. Vacations to Rehoboth begin. After 14 years, folks start sending us anniversary cards, just like they send to the other kids.

F-Hosp. Rm, 625-B - Do you believe the address book commemorates the farewell to my uterus?

F & B on boat - Summer weekends on Rehoboth Bay, writing for Letters, and experiencing a totally gay friendly environment. What can be better?

F & B in Reho - Better is buying our Maryland Ave. condo so we can be here winter weekends, too!

F & B @ mini-condo - Better yet is selling that hole in the water into which we throw money and buying the world's smallest condo to weekend on land year round.

F & B @ Mort's - At Dad's in Sarasota, February '99. Float the idea of quitting my job, uprooting Bonnie's business, downsizing and moving full-time to the beach. By now, nothing surprises the folks.

F & B Reho house - We did it! Moved to Rehoboth!

Move again and this address book is trash! warns the antique collector. No problem. After one long schlep for mankind, the eagle has finally landed. I'm here to stay. Write it in ink.

Since this is my last column of the century (now that's intense) I get to wish you all a happy new Millennium. And I promise that there are no more closeted Schnauzer puppies I haven't outed.

Like Dorian Gray's aging painting in the attic, somewhere out there, there must be a wrinkly 51-year-old hetero woman, gagging through her accordion player's zillionth rendition of the Beer Barrel Polka.

As for me, give me Tinky Winky and downtown Rehoboth. See you for Valentine's Day, and don't let the Y2K bugs bite. ▼

February 2000

Well, we're still here. Our computers didn't turn into two-slot toasters and nobody blew anything up. Well, no terrorists, anyway. Of course, with the world-wide pyrotechnics displays, maybe we missed it. Do you think there's a coven of hapless terrorists holed up in some 4th world country, pissed that nobody noticed their explosion at the Eiffel Tower? I hope so.

Always up for a party, I set the alarm for 4:45 a.m. on December 31 so we could start toasting with the folks down under on Millennium Island. Groggy from sleep, Bonnie stared at the TV as native people danced the hula to welcome the next century.

"Hmm...fat people with short arms. Fay, I think we've found your clan."

And you thought she was so nice. Only my own dawn-induced coma and her claiming the Snickers defense, saved her.

By late afternoon, we'd already celebrated New Years Eve in nine countries and time zones, making Peter Jennings my first male New Years Eve date since 1978. Back in our own time zone, my clever friends rented a bus for the big night, arranging a multi-house progressive pig out. The gang consisted of about two dozen women and our playwright son Eric. He'll either write a hilarious show about Keanu Reeves trapped on a runaway bus with a gang of menopausal lesbians alternately opening and shutting the windows, or wind up on a psychiatrist's couch talking about it.

So the hooting, hollering, hot flashing All-Girl (almost) Magical Mystery Tour careened through Rehoboth, tooting horns, spinning noisemakers and resting assured that if the world came to an end at midnight Eastern Standard Time, we'd all be together.

Heck, since the roly-poly natives made it to the 21st Century without incident some fifteen hours before, all that was left for us to do was eat, drink and be gay. Piece of cake. And a piece of everything else ever cooked, baked, shaken or stirred.

From their strategic position on the beach, the bus brigade rang in the New Year, made sure the ocean was Y2K compliant, and headed to Chez Bonnie & Fay for an I-Survived-the-20th-Century Breakfast. Dom Perignon and bagels ain't bad.

But once we crossed over to the next millennium, life did not slow down.

Okay, I'm going to answer the big question, the one all our friends back in Maryland ask; the one folks who just weekend here ask; the one thing people mulling a move to Rehoboth really want to know: "What do you do at the beach all winter?"

Do???? Why do I have a feeling they picture us camped on the sand, swaddled in goose down, waiting for boardwalk junk food to re-open?

"Aren't you bored?" they ask.

Bored? People cautioned us that things would slow down here in the winter. Really?? When? I'm busier than a lesbian at a barn raising.

Okay, it's true. There are many fewer activities here than say, Washington, D.C., but in Rehoboth, we do them all. Back there, I always meant to go to the film festivals, fundraisers, museums, and concerts, and work for the food bank, but somehow I never made it. Here, you can see 12 independent films, do a Breast Cancer benefit, read names on World AIDS Day, buy holiday crafts at the Art League, sing karaoke, have 50 cent tacos, and still have time for the laundry.

Of course, this year we had to get ready for our era's War of the Worlds humiliation: Y2K. Our parents may have mistaken Orson Well's radio script for a Martian attack, but we're the ones up to our butts in flashlight batteries and water jugs. Future generations will guffaw. But wasn't it great having an excuse to lay in a stash of Snickers?

With temperatures spiking near 70, the boardwalk was as crowded in January as September. Even when the thermometer did take a dive, life didn't stop spinning. Bonnie and I took the opportunity to stay indoors, paint, and arrange the closets. It was heavenly.

One night, as we sat watching the tube, even I wondered if the dreaded slowdown had finally befallen us.

"Are we old fogies, staying home in front of the fireplace and HBO? Would we be at the Kennedy Center or Nordstrom or Dupont Circle?"

"Fay, it's eleven degrees out."

So it was. And in typical Sussex County fashion, the weathercaster was saying "Snow is on the way. Stay tuned for winter storm information. Some areas of the peninsula may get up to...an inch!"

That's the beach for you. But truth be told, I figured on more down time myself. By now I was sure I'd have four spare columns in the computer. No such luck. In fact, things have been so busy, I looked out the window this morning and cheered. Snow was falling and there must have been, well, nigh on to three-quarters of an inch of the stuff on the driveway behind my four-wheel drive Subaru Outback.

Whoopee! Snowed in. And there's still a stash of Y2K Snickers. I just love the beach.

Author's note: Serves me right for trying to get this done before deadline...now it's the following Tuesday and we're up to our butts in ice and snow. We really are snowed in. I had to use the Y2K battery stash for my flashlight when our electric cut off...and those Snickers are goners. But even an ice storm at the beach is better than a good day anywhere...hey, I may love it here, but I'm not that nuts. Pass the ice scraper....▼

April 2000

Good news! Scientists have discovered that sharks don't like lunching on humans as much as had been believed. The bad news is when they do get a craving, it's for plump people. Not only was this bulletin disturbing, but I heard it immediately following a tragic afternoon of trying on bathing suits. That's it, I'm shark bait.

Is there a name for the kind of denial where, after a winter of parties and half-price pizza, you ignore all mirrors and suffer abject shock come April when your clothes don't fit? What would that be? Reflection Deficit Disorder? Clinical Dimension?

Whatever it is, I've got it.

And here I am, a woman with the motto "Life's uncertain, eat dessert first" living where you can't walk two paces in any direction without running into a Funnel Cake. After exactly one year in a town with legendary pizza, beach fries, and schnitzel sandwiches, I'm at the top of Orca's food pyramid.

Okay, it's not fair to blame the shape I'm in (round) on Rehoboth's goody glut. My long-term relationship with the bathroom scale has been rocky at best. I've tried every diet ever invented and they all work fine. Really. Scarsdale, Weight Watchers, the cantaloupe diet, that 80s rage The Cambridge Diet, you name it. I can lose lots of weight on all of them. Unfortunately, I don't, because I invariably fall off the wagon and onto the buffet table.

The only real success I ever enjoyed was during the Phen-Fen diet pill craze. Those things were great. Two pills a day and bingo! Better living through brain chemistry. In three months I shed thirty-five pounds, and a lifetime of excess guilt. It was terrific.

But next thing I knew, doctors started shrieking that our heart valves were becoming applesauce and wham, the government confiscated my Phen-Fen. Luckily, the only permanent medical damage I suffered was blowing back up into a Women's World shopper.

Then I tried a new drug I shall not name. You've seen the ads. Gaggles of substantial people troll the beach, tryst with spouses and eat what the announcer euphemistically calls a sensible meal. I think a sensible meal is an entire meatloaf, which is probably skewed thinking.

But have you heard the disgusting disclaimer? I won't repeat it verbatim on the chance you're reading this with lunch, but let's just say that the warning has to do with a teeny little medical side effect which causes your digestive system to drain like a Humvee with an oil leak.

Frankly, it's sadistic. There's nothing in the drug to help you say no to a side of fries, but you're expected to go cold turkey on fat grams to avoid this pesky little side effect. Duh. If I could go cold turkey on fat grams, who'd need their expensive wonder drug? I think it's a cruel hoax invented by the Kaopectate people. When you think about it, this drug works by figuratively scaring the poop out of you and then, if you stray, getting literal. Next!

Which brings me back to my original subject. Even if being shark bait is a far-fetched possibility, I do have to get back into last season's clothes. So, I'm turning to the e-word. Exercise.

Here, too, I have a checkered past. I'm just the kind of customer health club accountants love. I'd eagerly join up, go for a few glorious weeks, and thereafter get all my exercise just writing the monthly check to the spa.

Years ago I joined a trendy city gym to try to lower my cholesterol. After one week in a spandex outfit best viewed on Calista Flockhart, and being snubbed by buffed bodies with attitude, all I lowered was my self-esteem. At Slimnastics I hung out at the back of the room, hugging the mirrored wall for security. I loved finding out it was a one way mirror for thin folks in the sauna to watch my sorry butt.

Water aerobics was worse. Wading was nice, but when the instructor told us to hoist ourselves onto the side of the pool and bark like seals I wasn't waiting around for them to bounce a rubber ball on my nose and toss me a fish.

A glutton for food *and* punishment, I eventually bought a life-time gym membership, meaning I could drop out this year, next year, and every one after that, in perpetuity. But moving to Rehoboth turned my Maryland lifetime membership into packing paper.

So I bought a cheap treadmill. Getting it out of the car and into the house—now that was exercise. Advertised to fold up and practically disappear, it looked dainty in Sears. In my bedroom it could have had Leo DeCaprio hanging off its bow.

But for now, I seem to be using it. Every morning the dogs watch me walk my twenty minutes. And, until scientists invent something that makes celery taste like fried chicken, sharks prefer low-fat swimmers, or diet pills that won't turn us into new life forms, I'm logging the miles.

And it's a good thing. Bonnie and I just had our 18th anniversary and my sister, bless her heart, finally realized it's not just a phase. Along with a lovely card, she sent us an entire New York cheesecake. I'm sitting here staring at the thing and already I can hear the theme from *Jaws*. I'm going to get a fork. Da Dum...Da Dum....▼

April 2000

We're queer, we're here and our feet hurt. Bonnie and I got back to Rehoboth Beach late last night from the Millennium March on Washington. I'm trying to figure out how to tell you about all the remarkable things we experienced. So please indulge me. It's best if I just blurt.

With Bonnie having attended the 1979 march, and both of us marching in 1987 and 1993, there was so much that was familiar and oh so much that was different.

Heading to Washington, busses jammed the road, including several lumbering coaches with rainbow flags slapped on their butts. At Dupont Circle, a giant rainbow flag billowed over a luxury hotel, right next to the U.S. flag. The streets around Dupont Circle teemed with gay people. Restaurants overflowed with queers from every state in the nation; on the street, conversations erupted, people met, hugged, laughed and hollered. Blocks and blocks of pedestrians reveled in a spontaneous combustion of goodwill toward men, women, and transgendered people.

On Saturday, the city closed off a hunk of Pennsylvania Avenue for a giant street fair with food and merchandise vendors as far at the eye could see. I've been in D.C. over 30 years and had never, ever seen anything like it. Police cars flew rainbow flags; vendors hawked T-shirts, bumper stickers, jewelry, kabobs, hot dogs, ice cream, Internet access, magazines, the gamut of capitalism.

Favorite bumper sticker: Focus on your own damn family. Best T-shirt: Black, with the Blair Witch logo and the words Queer Bitch Project. Favorite placard: Respect is not an agenda.

Sunday morning dawned, another gorgeous sunny day ("God must love gay people," somebody said, "Look at this weather!") and we hopped the Metro along with throngs of gays, family and friends. If you've never been on an early morning

Metro ride, with both station and subway car filled to the gills with coffee-crazed gay, lesbian, bi, trans marchers and their gay-friendly colleagues, you've missed the commute of your life.

Once the queer-filled trains converged at the Smithsonian station, the riders joined thousands of other folks assembling for the March. I wish I could tell you about every second: the energy, creativity, and comedy.

Cheers for Vermont's contingent and their just-passed civil union legislation; college groups, high school groups, church after church after synagogue, after ministers and rabbis and parents and children and PFLAG groups and more parents. Then came a bunch of happy dads and cheering kids with the sign Men With Strollers. Next up, the gay pilots, the gay flight attendants (hell, they could have supported an entire march by themselves); gay doctors organizations; Amnesty international; gay legislators; transgender activists, senior citizens, military veterans, gay teachers groups, and more, more, more.

Stepping to the sidelines, we cheered and applauded the PFLAG parents until our hands stung. The parents marched along, shouting "we love you" to the crowd as arms stretched out from the side lines to the marchers, just to shake their hands.

With humor and seriousness, the crowd marched for equality and respect. From the laughter at campy drag queens and gutsy bare breasted womyn, to the choke of emotion for the parents with the sign, "We loved our gay son just the way he was" and his photo and the dates of his short life, the parade wound on.

We mourned for the throngs who marched in '79, '87 or '93 and were no longer with us, felled by the plague. Then we bounced back, cheering twice as hard in their place. Groups marched chanting "Hey, Hey, Ho, Ho, Homophobia's got to go" "Going to the Chapel and We're Gonna Get Married."

And the signs! Tinky Winky Made Me Do It; We're Proud of our Straight Parents; Four Out of Five Cats Prefer Lesbians; Protect All Our Families, and on and on.

Some people pranced, some danced, others rolled their chairs or slowed for their partners walking with canes; children skipped, carriages rolled and some of us dropped out and in, making our way down the Mall, grumbling, limping and laughing that we were too damn old to be marching after all these years.

With the Washington Monument looming behind and the Capitol steps welcoming ahead it was never more clear that bigotry and a denial of our human rights was just plain un-American.

After the marching was done, came the rally and speeches. From fiery rhetoric (DC's Eleanor Holmes Norton—you GO girl!!) to touching pleas for human justice (Matt Shephard's parents), most called for political action. Tammy Baldwin, the openly gay Congresswoman from Wisconsin had a compelling plan. "You want a world where you can put a picture of your partner on your desk? Put it there and you will have such a world; want a world where you can take your spouse to the company picnic? Take her and you will have such a world. Create this world by coming out!" Idealistic? In many cases, yes. But lots of us here in Rehoboth live just that way and she's right. We've created that world.

The difference from prior marches? While there's still plenty of wonderful diversity within diversity, there was far less spectacle. Where once the Park Police wore riot gear and rubber gloves, this time they strolled their steeds through the crowds, chatting and visiting. And the most notable difference? Everybody and his gay brother had a cell phone. The Mall was one big wireless ad. You'd hear a ring and thousands of marchers would clutch for their pockets. ("Hello, Fay's pants....") We want equality and free air time!

Well, one thing hasn't changed. The reporters and camera people trampled over 98 percent of the crowd to get photos and sound bites from only the most scandalously dressed drag queens and leather girls. At least the press is consistent.

So how many of us marched? *The Washington Post* guessed 300,000. The organizers figured 750,000, so it's a safe bet there were at least a half a million marchers and 100,000 cell phones.

Oh, and from what I could see, there were only about three or four sad-sack clusters of folks shaking Bibles and hollering for us to repent. And frankly, lots of the marchers kept asking them to pose for pictures, thereby confusing the heck out of them.

And all this happened to music by Melissa Etheridge, the Metropolitan Community Church Choir, and brass bands.

As the day ended and the crowd fanned out through town, we really *were* everywhere. Bonnie and I hobbled back to the Metro escalator, and I turned for a last look at the Mall. The last placard I saw said it best, "We All Matter."

We've come a long way, baby; we've still got a long way to go; which way to the Podiatrist? ▼

May 2000

Now that a million moms in sensible shoes marched on the Capitol to support gun control, we may be seeing a re-energized era in democracy. If grass-roots lobbying is back, how about a new American Revolution—one against the mighty HMOs (slogan: **H**ave **M**ore **O**perations).

Maybe it's because my move to Rehoboth put me into the HMO system for the very first time, or maybe it's just my advanced age (My sister just informed me that my old elementary school is now the town Historical Society. Nice.), but I'm fed up with health maintenance organizations.

I remember when HMOs first appeared on the scene as a choice. They were a lot cheaper than regular insurance and offered scads of preventative care coverage. Now, the only thing they prevent you from is seeing a doctor. Not only have HMOs morphed into regular insurance, but they cost more than our old insurance ever did.

I'm particularly ticked off today because I just returned from some routine blood tests to measure my donut to vegetable ratio, and I'm exhausted. Not from the tests, but from the staggering effort it took just to find out where I was supposed to go to give blood.

The prescription ordered tests at a place up the road. I get to the lab and they tell me my HMO doesn't play on their team. It's 7:30 in the morning, I haven't had breakfast, I'm ready to open a vein and nobody will tell me where to go. "Look it up in your HMO List of Providers," says the clerk.

I go back to the car, where, by sheer dumb luck, my provider list is still on the back seat with some junk mail. My book says I can go to Lab Corp ten minutes away. Bleary-eyed and hungry as hell, I wend my way to the next lab. After standing in a long line of people checking in for their mandatory drug tests and other humiliations, I hand over my insurance card and the receptionist tells me that Lab Corp no longer takes my particularly odious HMO. She saw the whites of my eyes quiver and said, "Wait a minute, I'll find where you should go."

Wouldn't it just be easier to use leeches to harvest my blood? Finally, I pull up to Transylvania Express, or whatever this blood collection depot is called, get the deed done and stagger into Wawa for caffeine.

As frustrating as the experience was, at least I wasn't sick at the time. Dealing with an HMO when you feel lousy is just sadism.

Once last winter, after a sleepless night of coughing, I called the doctor to refill my cough medicine prescription. Since HMOs rule that doctors must see patients every seven minutes to be profitable, my doctor was busy sprinting from examining room to examining room making her quota, and couldn't come to the phone.

When I finally got through, the doctor agreed I needed more cough syrup, but told me that since the stuff was a narcotic, she couldn't just call it in to the pharmacy. I had to pick up the prescription in person. Right. Tell the person with Bronchitis to cough their way to the primary care outpost, spreading a swath of infection and good cheer. I gathered up the written word and hacked and horkled my way to the drug store.

"Sorry," said the pharmacist, "your HMO won't approve it. It's too soon."

Excuuuse me????

"They won't approve a refill for another two days. The directions said two teaspoons at night and they calculate how many nights that covers and won't refill it until that time," explained the weary pharmacist.

Well here's the thing. Originally, the doctor prescribed it only at night since it would make me too sleepy to go to work. Once I was too sick to go to work anyway, the doctor told me to take the medicine in the daytime, too. Did the HMO clerk have this information on which to base her decision? Was this all-powerful HMO Pooh-Bah phone operator clairvoyant enough to have seen me hacking away all night?

Are they afraid I'm going to sell this stuff on the street? Have they ever tasted it? And did you see the size of the bottle? There's more controlled substance in a Starbucks Cappuccino.

Now, mind you, the big bad HMO doesn't say I can't have it; they just say they won't pay for it. Suffice it to say I forked over the price of a ritzy dinner for two for the two ounces of orange swill and went home to guzzle my stash.

These days, when I have nightmares, they're about HMOs denying coverage.

I remember when Bonnie went to that very expensive high tech sleep clinic, resulting in her diagnosis of sleep apnea. Fine, the HMO paid for all the tests, the overnight stay, the round the clock monitoring and the apple juice and danish in the morning. Trouble was, after her doctor prescribed a machine to keep her from asphyxiating in the night, the HMO refused to pay for it.

Sight unseen, not to mention without benefit of hearing the gurgling sounds she can make at night, they decided she didn't need the machine bad enough for them to pay for it. I wish them the living hell of watching her try to obtain a good night's sleep.

Needless to say, we forked over the $1900 for this thing they call durable medical equipment. At that price it sure as hell better be durable.

The one thing HMOs *can* do efficiently is bill you. In fact, it appears to be nearly impossible to resign from an HMO. I changed policies at the end of December and I'm still getting bills from my old HMO threatening to cancel my coverage because I haven't paid my bill. Duh, what did they do with the three (3) letters I wrote canceling my policy? Even though I know that my coverage is in place with my new stinking HMO, it's still disconcerting to receive these ominous threats from the old stinky one.

And just try to be self-employed and get coverage. It practically took an Act of Congress for Bonnie and her former business partner to get a policy. She had to provide more ID and paperwork than if she'd been applying for the Witness Protection Program. But just try and take somebody OFF the policy.

We canceled the partnership when said partner skipped town last fall, and then canned the insurance policy immediately thereafter. For all we know, the jerk really is in the Witness Protection program, but in January they were still billing us for his insurance and still sending his Viagra to wherever he was hiding out.

It's enough to make you crazy. Which, by the way, you better not be, because finding a therapist who takes your insurance is much, much harder than healing thyself.

I feel sorry for the beleaguered doctors and their staffs. I've walked into medical offices where everybody's running around shouting orders and running for equipment. A patient gone code blue? No, they can't find the right referral forms and the fax is on the fritz. These days, if the office gets high tech medical equipment it's a new copier.

And the poor pharmacist. It's a pitiful night when they have to tell me they're sorry that my full vial of Prilosec fell in the sink with the Woolite but I'm not due for a refill until July. It's enough to give you a belly ache.

That's that. I'm doomed to indigestion for the rest of the summer. I'm ready to march on Washington again. Hey, Hey, Ho, Ho, HMOs have gotta go....▼

June 2000

For the last month, I've has been camping out in various hospital rooms keeping my ailing spouse company. It started with a fall she took while painting our rental condo, and turned into a frightening and complicated medical mystery.

From a relatively simple knee injury, Bonnie developed scary, life-threatening blood clots in her lungs, spleen and kidney. It was a frantic, terrifying few days in the Emergency Room and Intensive Care Unit. She's recovering now, although she's lost the use of one kidney. And it's been suggested that the vitriolic screed I recently penned about the evils of HMOs might have contributed to this mess. It makes as much sense as anything else.

And as I sit in her flower and card filled Annapolis hospital room, *Letters* deadline hovering ominously and laptop computer screen staring me in the face, I've decided to go ahead and write this column—despite the fact that we have yet to find out why Bonnie turned into embolism central, let alone any suggestion of what to do about it or when she might come home.

Suffice it to say that she's feeling much better, starting to hobble up and down the halls, and is getting so bored we're thinking of keeping her in bed with bungee cords. Unfortunately, her team of very smart, very competent, and even prestigious doctors, including several top blood and kidney specialists cannot figure out exactly what happened. I've always told her she's one of a kind, but I really didn't mean relative to her hematology.

At any rate, more important than the diagnosis is the fact that the docs have yet to get Miss Bonnie's blood thin enough to ensure that she won't be throwing more blood clots when they let her loose. I say let's keep her here until they're sure they have a handle on this thing.

But in the meantime, there are some things I want to say and some things too important NOT to say.

First, if something like this had to happen, I'm glad it occurred when we were part of the Rehoboth community. I can't tell you how much it meant to both of us to have the support of our friends and family of affinity. That means you guys, our wonderful buddies, lots of *Letters* readers, and the folks at our favorite shops and restaurants—although it does give one pause when the most stunning floral arrangements come from drinking establishments....

Everyone has been just terrific, and the sincerity of the offers of help, and all manner of assistance, has floored us. And made us feel so lucky to be part of that can-do Create a More Positive Rehoboth community.

But the most important message I have concerns a piece of paper and peace of mind. It's called a Medical Power of Attorney. Bonnie and I have always had our legal paperwork handy. They are the documents that show, in lieu of a marriage certificate, that we are life partners and next of kin. Having that piece of paper means that there's no question that I'm the person the doctors consult, I'm the person with permission to visit Bonnie's room at all hours, and, frankly, that our relationship deserves recognition on an equal footing with married patients and kin.

Recently, Vanessa Redgrave did an HBO special where she played the long-time spouse of a woman who was hospitalized and their relationship was denied by hospital staff and her lover's family. To me, that was a horror story worse than anything Stephen King has ever penned.

When our own nightmare began, our legal paperwork (Medical Power of Attorney, Living Will, Durable Power of Attorney, etc.) was just back from our Delaware attorney's office, having been redone since our move from Maryland. It was completed but not signed and notarized.

In a scenario that is not yet, but may someday be funny, we had to call a notary public to the hospital emergency room to get the patient's signature. There was Bonnie, hooked up to oxygen, morphine, and goodness knows what else and we're asking her to sign on the dotted line. It was a tough sell getting her to believe I wasn't coercing her to change the will. Seriously, the last minute legal mumbo jumbo added to her stress, but we really needed the signature so the hospital would know we were married. Not to mention that I'd be able to write checks from her business account to pay bills.

I have to say, that even without the signed paperwork, Rehoboth's hospital staff was, overall, sensitive to our situation. On a couple of occasions, though, I had to speak out. One of Bonnie's doctors kept saying, "Well, your friend is very sick," and "your friend this, and your friend that..." Finally, I had to say, as nicely as possible, "She's not just my friend, she's my partner."

When the hospital chaplain visited (now there's a scary thing, too) and started with the "your friend" routine, I really had to set the record straight (so to speak). While everyone was as nice as can be, I think some sensitivity training is still in order for the hospital.

One thing is true, though. At the hospital, when we saw other gay people in the elevators, delivering food trays, or working on staff—and there were many—they were very friendly and warm to us.

Once Bonnie left Rehoboth and checked in at Annapolis, it was a little different. We made our relationship clear to the doctors and staff from the very beginning. Bonnie always starts with, "we're partners of 18 years" hoping that the longevity adds credibility. While we've been warmly received (everything from "Oh..." and dropped eyes, to "Really? What's your secret for a such a long relationship?"), it's clear that they are not used to such openness here.

In fact, we've spied lots of folks who made our gaydar twirl, but eye contact is usually avoided. The arrival of hordes of our visiting friends is probably good for this hospital's growth and development.

But the subject of being out is very important to this situation, too. I know that many, many people feel they cannot afford to be out of the closet at their jobs and with their employers. I'm so lucky that my employer and co-workers know my situation and have been nothing but supportive. I cannot imagine the unspeakable horror of going through a time like this while trying to keep your reason for absences and emotional turmoil a secret.

As I said, everyone's situation is different. And there are surely some cases where honesty may not be the safest policy. But I beg you all to assess your situation carefully and make sure its not internalized homophobia keeping you in the closet. Being open and honest may just save your sanity some day.

So that's the message. And please, please, whatever you do, consult an attorney and take care of the legal work needed to protect you, your partner, your possessions and your peace of mind.

In the meantime, I hope Bonnie will be recuperating at home shortly. Until then, thanks for all the kind messages, support, flowers and care packages. And, by the way, the dogs are at the breeder's home, happy to be visiting their biological parents. Thanks to all of you who inquired.

Before now, we were always pretty sure we knew who our friends were, but it's times like this when you really find out. We are truly blessed. We love you all. ▼

July 2000

Saturday, July 8, 2 p.m. We thought we'd be home weeks ago. It's now July 8 and Bonnie is still incarcerated, but we are starting to see a light at the end of the laparoscope. For all you *ER* and *Chicago Hope* fans, here's the scoop: Following a week in the hospital at Beebe and three weeks in Annapolis, we may have the answer to the seemingly age-old question of what's up with Bonnie's platelets. Apparently she has an elevated Homocystene (or something) level, which could have, although nobody can say for sure, led her to infarct (a vaguely scatological sounding word, loosely translated to "turned into toast") one kidney and her spleen. In the ensuing weeks, the doctors, in an effort to stay one step ahead of the HMO, took my girlfriend apart, one piece at a time, trying to find the culprit. As a result, she glows in the dark from drinking radioactive goo for CT scans and marrow biopsies, with the doctors having kept her uterus and ovaries as souvenirs (don't ask).

As we await parole, the medical team concurs that Bonnie could have a blood disease called Hyperhomocystenanemia. Hell, we've always known that Bonnie was a hyperhomo. Apparently it's now official. If she's got it, this disease is a one in a million thing—we couldn't have won Powerball?

But we're relieved to find out that the condition is controllable by medication, blood thinners and diet. Wendy's and Popeyes are in for a recession. And of course, no sharp objects for those on blood thinners. The yard sale for the power tools will begin shortly. Bonnie's convinced that I'm enjoying this part of the fallout.

Since we've been doing this hospital routine for over a month now, some things are clear. Mainly, if you sit in a chair next to a patient long enough, you will ossify and develop kennel cough.

Bonnie's been here so long the sixth floor nurses have made

her their mascot. And we're all afraid the HMO will have snipers posted downstairs when we finally leave.

And we've been worried about the dogs. During one of Bonnie's very few teary moments, she told my parents she feared the dogs would forget her. My folks assured her that their dog always gave them the same jubilant greeting and never knew whether they'd been gone for a six week vacation or just out with the trash. That made us both feel much, much better. But I'm sure our two are, as we speak, plotting their revenge. I never liked our carpets anyway.

Another lesson learned is that truth can be stranger than fiction. In an ironic twist, our friend Dorothy, at whose home I've been staying on Kent Island, had a severe intestinal ailment two weeks ago and also wound up in this hospital for surgery. In a move that would have been called contrived if it had happened in a sitcom, we managed to get Dorothy assigned as Bonnie's roommate. While it was bad that Bonnie and Dorothy had to be here, it was good that they were here together to cause laughter and mischief in the self-proclaimed Lesbian Ward.

Miraculously, amid the horrors, there were some amusing moments in quarantine. Along with wonderful cards, flowers and balloons sent to Bonnie, one well-wisher provided a gift item that looked like a pager. Push it's button, it growls "F**K You" or "A**hole!" That little gem may have been responsible for the transfer of Bonnie's first roommate.

But it was the morphine incident that really rocked the hospital. Following surgery, a seriously delirious Bonnie suddenly woke, reached out, grabbed the person nearest the bed and gushed, "I love you Faysie!!! I love you!!" Unfortunately, I was across the room at the time. Reach out and touch someone, indeed. It took two years off that nurse's life.

And our buddies on the other side of the room would want you to know they got the biggest kick out of watching a red-faced, mortified me try to keep our drugged out patient from spilling more beans. I stood by, trying to keep her mouth filled with soothing ice chips, a thermometer or whatever else I had in my arsenal, but to no avail. "Faysie, I missed you! Come here!" the wild-eyed one demanded. By this time, Dorothy was trying not to split her stitches and a variety of onlookers burst out laughing with every fresh declaration of morphined madness. "Are you laughing at me???" Bonnie would ask, eyes rolling back into her head. Us, laughing? We were howling.

Finally, at a moment when, for the first time in weeks, the hospital corridor was completely quiet, Bonnie rejected all my efforts to button her lip and shouted, "Does anybody care if I'm queer???"

As it turned out, no. Despite the post-op ruckus, a regular pride parade of visitors (some smuggling small dogs in backpacks), and lots of commotion, I think we provided a real eye-opener for some of the nurses and technicians. We made new friends, and, I think, put a good foot forward for diversity.

Here comes the doctor for a pow-wow. Over and Out.

Saturday, 4 p.m. and packing: Out, indeed! We're sprung! The freedom riders are heading to Rehoboth.

Sunday, July 9, 9 p.m.: It's fantastic to be home. The patient is doing great and she's thrilled to be in clothes that meet in the back; the dogs greeted us as if we'd just taken a really long trash run, and the four of us have been curled up on the sofa. Friends have called or stopped by all day, and we're holed up and catching our breath.

I know that real life will start to intrude by tomorrow, with plans for Bonnie's recuperation, continuing doctors appointments and all the emotional and logistical ramifications of this unexpected six-week ordeal. But for now, we're so happy to be back home, back at CAMP, back at the beach, and back among friends. That's all we need to make the rest more than manageable. Cheers to you all from Schnauzerhaven in Food Lion Estates. There really is no place like home.▼

August 2000

I accidentally caught a glimpse of that reality TV show *Big Brother* last night. Ohmygod. This has got to be the stupidest, most annoying, harebrained ratings grabber yet. Since *Survivor*, of course. What are these things and why is America watching? One perfectly sensible friend of mine sat glued to the TV watching a *Big Brother* participant stare into the one-way bathroom mirror and be videotaped brushing his tongue. EEEWWWW.

In case you've been watching more sophisticated and educational shows like *Hollywood Squares*, let me fill you in. On *Survivor*, a squad of diverse, fame-and-fortune seeking exhibitionists get stranded on a desert island along with hundreds of producers, video cameras, sound engineers and catering trucks. Only the survivors have to forage food for themselves on the island and survive by eating bugs, rats and the occasional frond. Then, amid bickering, rat-eating and back-stabbing, they gather around the campfire, sing *Puff the Magic Dragon* and decide which person is the most annoying and should be sent home to the city. Frankly, this is not a new concept. I played this game in the 1960s at summer camp.

On *Big Brother*, it's the same idea, only the cadre of obnoxious people are stranded inside a badly decorated house, have to survive on what's in the fridge and have their every waking and sleeping moment videotaped. As the housemates sit around deciding which of the annoying people is so super-annoying that they should be banished, teary-eyed participants admit their fear of being bounced with phrases like "I wanted to make my parents proud." Too late, bunky.

Meanwhile, oh-so-serious anchor persons interview the parents and spouses of the prospective losers as if they were Jack the Ripper or Yasser Arafat. Then, relationship counselors tell the audience at home exactly what kind of neurosis the banishee has that made the person ripe for expulsion. Has the CBS brass lost their minds entirely? That flipping sound you hear is the late great Edward R. Morrow, spinning in his grave.

I particularly liked when the aforementioned relationship counselor described a video moment when Jordon confides in slut-puppy Jamie. Good grief, she's confiding in him and six million viewers. It's absurd. Apparently, sometime in September, when the next to last occupant has been evicted, the sole housemate left standing will walk away with $500,000. A half a million isn't enough to live with those scuzzballs and their live chickens (really, they have chickens.)

Can you imagine if they produced the show with all gay men and called it *Big Sister*? First off, they'd have to make sure the house was stocked with politically correct Vodka, fabulous window treatments and a fully-equipped kitchen, right down to lemon zesters and pie weights. Those boys would be so busy partying and entertaining, they'd never have time to vote anybody out. In fact, it could become the biggest circuit party of all time. Quick, tell CBS.

Conversely, a house full of gay girls would find the housemates, their cats, and their dogs holding interminable tribal councils to decide who would be banished. Actually, in our version the girls could send half their number to the boys' house to fix all the broken stuff while the boys deport six sous chefs to cook a decent meal and bring some feng shui to the girl's quarters.

Frankly, if CBS wants a pilot combining *Big Brother* and *Survivor* all they have to do is come to my house. With Bonnie confined to quarters recuperating from her various arterial adventures and the dogs just back from a month in the country, our own dysfunctional family could be a ratings grabber. It's banal enough. I mean all the elements are here.

We've been surviving by foraging for food. While Bonnie was hospitalized, a band of short order cooks dropped by the house and stashed stuff in our freezer. Every night at dinner time we play a version of "I wonder who left this stuff and what do we do with it?" Sometimes it takes three or four phone inquiries before we find the matching chef and re-heating instructions for the mystery meat. But let me tell you, there have been some damn fine meals come out of that Tupperware. Down the road we're going to have a reverse Tupperware party, where people show up to claim and burp their kitchenware.

As for the diverse types confined to the house, they are us. We've got some serious role reversal going on. While the traditionally outdoorsy Bonnie rests up on the sofa, I've made my first-ever trek to the backyard shed where the lawnmower lives. Not that I actually used the mower. That's way too scary. But I did show a saintly friend where it was located and ran after her with a plastic bag for the clippings.

One time we failed to secure the clipping bag properly and gave ourselves an enormous mulch shower. Covered as I was with grass shards, it really wasn't a tragedy when I learned my second lesson of the day: turn the sprinkler off before you move it. Not even the rat-munching survivor cast contained somebody as pathetic looking as I was by the time I returned to the house.

I guess people are aware of my temporary need for a yard-work support group, because along with many offers of help, I received one clipping from the Hammacher-Schlemmer catalogue featuring a robot lawn mower. I wouldn't even have to go near the thing.

Alternately, it was Bonnie cautioning, "Take your filthy shoes off!" Bizarre. Not only that, but she was quickly getting into my house business. She actually managed to find our telephone book, figure out our friends' last names and make her very first independent phone calls. The hell she stirred in our social calendar is only now being unraveled.

As for our tribal council, Alpha-dog Moxie narrowly escaped being voted out of the house for a recent pillow chewing indiscretion.

But my favorite comparison between this spate of reality programming and our own reality is the viewer advisory. Before *Big Brother* there's a warning that goes like this:

"*Big Brother* is not scripted, but is a result of the participants reactions to their environment and interactions with each other on a day-to-day basis. Life is full of surprises, as anyone will tell you...It's important to realize that the unexpected may happen; ...and, you may be exposed to incidents, language or other situations you may find objectionable."

Hello. I think that's a viewer advisory for life don't you? Oh, Big Brother. We're all Survivors. I could use the $500,000. But tell CBS they can keep the live chickens.▼

August 2000

For those of you following Fay & Bonnie's not-so-excellent adventure with Bonnie's hospital stay and Fay's forced introduction to lawn implements, here's the latest: Bonnie's feeling much better and for the last several weeks angelic friends have saved Fay from an embarrassing and dangerous display of weed whacking ignorance.

Two incidents illustrate the above. First, Bonnie is feeling so well that she begged for and received permission to drive. This has been a relief for me, as my driving has always been a source of irritation, if not actually horror, for my spouse. She is never stoic about it, either. In fact, all the endoscopys in the world revealed less about Bonnie's emergency medical condition than her willingness to let me drive her to the emergency room while she sat quietly and gratefully in the front seat. Get this girl into ICU immediately.

But, as her health returned, so did her uncontrollable urge to comment on my ability to drive and, what's worse, assist me with faux-braking and color commentary. Oh, good—an extra passenger side air bag. The girl needed to regain control.

To wit, the first day she drove herself to physical therapy in Georgetown she returned with a souvenir Uniform Traffic Complaint and Summons (74 in a 55 mile per hour zone). The cop wasn't dumb enough to fall for her claim that the knee brace made her lead footed. Neither was I. She's baaaack!!

As for my own reprieve from Lawn Maintenance 101, our house was the scene of an intervention two weeks ago. A hearty band of women with tool belts and men with hamburger rolls and condiments, descended on a Friday evening and got down to business.

The girls put the finishing touches on Bonnie's deck, pulled nine weeks' worth of weeds, mowed, mulched and weed-whacked themselves into a frenzy. Meanwhile a small but creative band of royalty (that would be the queens and princesses) took kitchen refuge and whipped up a feast. By the time we were all outside working and feasting it looked like a scene from an Amish barnraising (minus Kelly McGillis, drat) or *Seven Brides for Seven Brothers* (or would that be seven brides *and* seven brothers?).

Meanwhile, Bonnie reclined on a chaise on the deck, field marshalling the troops and being very, very grateful for the work party. We both feel way beyond grateful and blessed by the help and all manner of assistance by our friends and their friends during our summer of adversity. If our quest for a CAMP Rehoboth community center (with or without walls) is true to its vision as the heart of the community, then my backyard included the left ventricle on Friday night. Sorry for such sincerity, I've been addled by generosity.

So with yard work and grabbing a few days at the beach between monsoons, we're catching up with a summer we almost missed. On some days, while I'm at work, friends have been accompanying our convalescent to the beach. Those handicapped-accessible beach wheel chairs have been great. And after several days in the sun, people are telling Bonnie how happy they are to see her looking so great. Then they look at me and say, "Of course you're looking pretty haggard." Nice.

Perhaps it was the time I spent in front of the TV checking out the bait-and-switch fest that was the Republican Convention. I wouldn't say that their party is talking out of both sides of Dubya's mouth, but there they were, spotlighting a speech by an openly gay Republican congressman and half of Dubya's own Texas delegation was down on their knees praying for his sodomizing soul.

Meanwhile, the Republican-backing American Family Council, was calling for Rep. Kolbe's arrest for that same sodomy thing. Huh? And there was lesbian daughter Mary Cheney bravely grinning and applauding her Dad's nomination for Veep. Does she know what the party platform says about gays? And where was her long-time girlfriend stashed? It's going to be interesting to watch how the party deals with the Cheney daughter that Jerry Falwell just called "errant." Let's see if blood really is thicker than orientation.

And now, on the cusp of the Democratic Convention, there's even more remarkable news. In a historic first, Senator Lieberman is on the ticket. I'm surprised and curious to see the electorate's reaction.

Personally, if a member of the tribe can be on the national ticket, I feel compelled to take a stand locally. I'm going fishing tomorrow—not a typically Jewish hobby. But then it's been a week of historic firsts. And my girl and I are determined to make up for the summer days we missed. I'll let you know if I catch anything besides hell for letting you all know about that speeding ticket. ▼

September 2000

It was inevitable. Like day following night, Black and Decker attracting lesbians, bears pooping in the woods, Bonnie got herself a big, shiny riding lawnmower.

The thing is asleep in the garage as I write, and I'm trying to reconstruct the series of events that led to my capitulation in the mower wars. I'd held out as long as I could, but in the final analysis my futile argument for not having one of those things was mowed and mulched asunder. I blinked first.

The final chapter in my tractorless life dawned last Saturday, after a month of monsoons. I don't know if this is the wettest summer on record, but we're starting to mildew and my leaky car is a terrarium on wheels. Weather.com has said, "Scattered thunderstorms, some severe, appear likely across the mid-Atlantic today...." continuously since July. And exactly what is a 50 percent chance of rain? It might and it might not? Or it's definitely going to rain half the day? But I digress....

The grass was as high as an elephant's eye and clearly something had to be done. Renting a goat squad was not an option, nor was, as Blanche DuBois would say, relying on the kindness of strangers. Ever since Bonnie's been sporting that big fancy knee brace, our friends, relatives and houseguests have been pitching in to mow our half-acre field of dreams. As grateful as we've been, I began to feel we were teetering over the abyss into taking advantage. But trust me, when I told Bonnie it might be time for us to shift for ourselves, I did not mean on a riding mower.

Unfortunately, her crafty mind made the leap. Then she was able to illustrate the amount of money we'd actually save over the next decade by not paying a lawn service. You gotta give the girl credit. She'd borrowed a page from my own Bloomingdales playbook.

While our houseguests watched, Bonnie headed out the door. My friend Kathy consoled me, but then her husband Ross, who'd secretly love a riding mower of his own, headed off to join Bonnie in our family truck. They were on a quest for a previously owned yard machine.

They returned with a large ugly mower in the truck bed and a rent-a-ramp to get the thing down onto our lawn. It was repulsive, with a ripped seat and rusty gears, not to mention the remnants of somebody else's lawn hanging all over its bottom.

"But it was cheap," said Bonnie.

Off she went for a test drive. She and Ross got it started, but sparks immediately spit from the side, followed by a black cloud of smoke from the engine.

"What's black smoke mean?" I asked Kathy.

"We haven't elected a Pope."

After a few more explosions and gear-stripping audibles, Bonnie and Ross pushed the offending conveyance back up the rent-a-ramp into the truck and out of our lives. Actually, in a case of impressive timing, the guys across the street saw the mower exiting stage left and announced they'd just bought a riding mower themselves, which we were welcome to borrow. In fact, in an effort to practice their skills, they offered to mow our lawn while we returned the used heap of junk. Fabu. Life was good again.

We came back to find our half-acre mowed magnificently, leaving us only two tasks: trimming and raking up grass shards. I chose raking over weed whacking since last time I traveled the north forty to the tune of "buzz, buzz OW...buzz, buzz OW...buzz, buzz OW....

Instead, I volunteered to bend over and stuff clippings into plastic bags. I became a living tableau of that nasty lawn ornament of the old lady bending over, butt in the air, hosiery around the ankles. The Maltese Hiney. Don't bend over in the garden granny, you know them taters got eyes. It was not a pretty picture. But I was happy. We had a neighborhood lawn mowing coalition and I wouldn't have to own my own farm equipment.

I should be so lucky. Bonnie tapped me on the shoulder, pointed at our neighbor and his mower and said "Look." He sat spit-shining and buffing the thing like it was a '39 Studebaker. I half expected him to lead it into the garage, give it a bag of oats and kiss it goodnight.

"I can't borrow his mower," Bonnie moaned, "I'll get it dirty."

She was right. The pressure to support his mower in the style to which it would become accustomed would be way too much to bear.

By breakfast the next morning, figuring I was doomed anyway, I made my pitch. "If we're going to get a mower, it should be a mulching mower so nobody (mainly me) would have to bend over and pick up grassy schmutz." That was all Bonnie needed. She grabbed my hand and dragged me off to Lowe's.

Procrastinating has its rewards. If we'd bought a riding mower at the beginning of the season when Bonnie first started campaigning, it would have cost us more. By late August we found a reconditioned machine with a two-year warranty and a nice price tag. Huzzah.

Back at home, Bonnie and Ross spent the rest of the afternoon playing like giddy kids at a Go-Kart park. I've never seen two adults have more fun with something with a motor (don't go there.) They were in lawn-care heaven.

Meanwhile, Kathy and I sat on the deck drinking margaritas, noting the absolute parity between gay and straight unions, and wondering why on earth riding mowers need headlights.

So Bonnie got her mulching dream machine, I don't have to rake clippings, and Old Landing Road traffic has been spared the distraction of my butt waving in the air.

Is that the end of the story? I don't think so. I'm certain Bonnie will want accessories and I don't mean pearls and purses. We're talking baggers and snow plow blades.

So now I own a truck *and* a tractor. They are going to revoke my princess card. Not only that, but it's 8:30 at night and riding mower headlights are shining in the window at me from across the street. I went to tell Bonnie about it and found her in the garage visiting our new family member.

Mow quickly into the good night. ▼

October 2000

While you know how thrilled we were to move to cosmopolitan Rehoboth Beach, it took us a while to realize that we'd actually moved to the state of Delaware. Things I'd never even imagined in my other life go on here.

We just went to the Annual Bridgeville Apple Scrapple Festival. Apples I've had, but scrapple is a horse of another color. In fact, I hope it's not horse.

I'm sure it surprises no one that prior to Saturday I was a scrapple virgin. Yes, I've heard Bonnie's tales of farmer Granny frying scrapple, but thus far I'd avoided having to sample any myself. Frankly, you know something's up when you ask normally glib people what scrapple is and they stutter. "Um, I can't really say. Pig mush, maybe?"

So there I was, along with the 40,000 people descending on little Bridgeville, Delaware, standing in line for a scrapple sandwich. Well, it wasn't the most disgusting thing I've ever tasted. Bonnie insisted it should have been crispier. I was negotiating it nicely until I looked up and saw the 40-foot scrapple company sign listing the ingredients as pig's snouts and lard.

At about the same time, the Hog Calling Contest began and grown men and women started wailing Suuu-eeeee, Suuu-eeeee, which was roughly the same sound I was making trying to spit out my pig snout sandwich. Wisely, Bonnie grabbed my arm and steered me toward a vendor hawking kosher hot dogs (which, if dissected, are probably the Hebrew National version of snouts and lard).

In between the hog calling and scrapple scarfing there was the scrapple carving contest. Scrapple sculptors had fashioned everything from a three little pigs tableau to a lovely woman's torso. Actually, raw scrapple is a pretty good carving medium—although as the day got warmer, the stuff started to droop and that torso aged twenty years. I think the winners should have been honored not so much for what they carved, but that they were willing to put their hands in that stuff.

Sadly, we were due at our next Delaware event by early evening, so we had to cut short the Bridgeville adventure to get ready for the chicken and dumpling dinner at the Lewes Grange.

Once again, I was in virgin territory. The Grange has something to do with farmers, and I don't. Unless you count Bonnie, who is descended from farmers.

"Haven't you ever had slippery dumplings?" asked a member of our party. No, can't say as I have.

Six of us converged on the Lewes Grange building at 6 p.m., paid our seven dollars each and got right down to piling our plates with slippery dumplings, thick white gravy, potatoes, green beans and chicken.

For the record, what I thought was going to be exotic foreign food was essentially the same noodles my grandmother served with beef brisket. We were stuffed to the dumplings in just under twenty minutes and back out on the street again before anyone could lobby us to change our political or sexual orientation.

But my favorite Delaware tradition so far is the yard sale. We hosted a three-family rummage event recently. When a friend told me to put the words "Early birds will be shot!" in my ad, I was clueless and failed to heed her advice. I learned.

The night before the sale, we started stickering the merchandise. Frighteningly, at K-Mart I'd found an actual product called "Garage Sale Dots" and it occurred to me that we were amateurs in a professional sport.

Two hours into putting twenty-five cent stickers on stuff that cost a week's salary in 1978, I wanted to quit. I mean how do you put a price tag on old Steve & Edie albums? The first gift my ex-lover gave me? The amazing Ginzu knife??

For a fleeting moment our crew started coveting each other's trash but then got a grip and banned swapping.

By 6 a.m. our crew re-assembled to sip caffeine. We lounged over donuts and then, by 7 a.m. leisurely walked into the garage and pushed the button to raise the door. Then, we saw them—a throng of glassy-eyed beings, inching toward our driveway like a scene from Night of the Living Dead.

"We're not open until 8," I hollered, waving them off. While most of the creatures waited in their cars, a few angrily peeled away, shouting, "We won't be back!" I did not see this as a negative.

As we frantically set up shop, the crowd at the foot of our driveway grew larger and scarier. Shoppers snorted and jockeyed for position, preparing to break from the gate.

By 7:45 I understood the need for weapons. In fact, unarmed and incredulous, we couldn't hold them off and our position was overrun 15 minutes early. "Um…Okay!" I shouted to the advancing army.

"You've never done this before, have you?" croaked a woman leading the charge.

"No, " I admitted. "Be kind."

Shoppers broke from the pack and raced to pick though our mountains of crap; prospectors rifled the debris like a crab picking contest.

"Does this vacuum suck?" squawked a wizened old woman.

All this stuff sucks, that's why we're getting rid of it, I thought, but assured her that the old Hoover sucked great. The frenzy continued, with people driving by, pointing and shouting, "How much??" I didn't know if they meant the merchandise or me.

Dollars, dimes and quarters flew as people scarfed up our junk. I sold a bent chandelier for $7 and some goofball came along and bid $9 to the guy who'd just bought it. Of course, the stylish stuff had to be marked down. The really ugly, useless stuff sold full price. We could have sold ice cubes to Eskimos. In fact, the guy who bought the rusty freezer looked vaguely Alaskan-American to me.

After the initial rush ebbed, the six of us looked at each other, exhaled and were stunned to discover it was only 8:17. We thought we'd been on the sales floor at Macy's for hours. Medic!

All morning, cars clogged our local transportation grid. I

couldn't believe the wad of bills accumulating in my pocket. Junk dwindled so fast that at one point I ran back into the house to restock. Heck, I never liked that toaster anyway.

One by one the excess lawn chairs, rocking chairs and footstools disappeared, leaving us to play musical chair with the lone remaining seat—an exercise bike. After that went, we just shuffled around, pockets so weighty with quarters, we couldn't have bent to sit anyway.

Incredulously, at the crack of noon, the hordes retreated and there was nothing left but a small rubble pile.

"Toto, we're not in Kansas anymore," said one of our merchants. No, we're in Delaware and I love it. But hold the pork snouts. ▼

November 2000

It must have been tough. One minute you're declared the winner and then, horrors, in a stunning reversal, you're not. I can just imagine how the contenders felt, both sides having snatched possible defeat from the jaws of victory. Everyone's in an uproar over it, legal challenges have been filed, and there's no telling how it will all come out. It's enough to give you gas. Actually, it's all about gas.

Naturally, you suspect I'm jabbering about the Bush/Gore election here, but despite television's proliferation of gaseous commentators and the national waiting game to find out who's the leader of the free world, I'm actually talking about the Punkin' Chunkin' Festival.

If you're not familiar with the event, it's Sussex County's answer to...hmm...I can't think of a festival quite as déclassé as this one. Suffice it to say that the Chunkin' contest, where teams compete to see how far they can shoot a pumpkin, makes County Fair crowds seem positively sophisticated. But the fact that just two days before November 7, the folks at Chunkin' gave us a peek at the way we'd be undeciding our presidential race seems a little spooky.

It's been reported that one pumpkin artillery team was hailed the winner and then the decision was reversed and another team of pumpkin punchers was crowned victorious. Apparently a New Jersey team shot their gourd with helium gas, instead of standard issue air. And a dispute rages on.

So too, does our national arithmetic test. Now there's a new word in our lexicon. Chad. It's that little paper fleck that gets punched out of a paper ballot. And here's a somber-faced Peter Jennings, explaining that the judges are debating the eligibility of swinging chads (partially attached), pregnant chads (sounds like an oxymoron, but it's a ballot with a bulging chad) and other funky chads. Frankly, I think the judges ducking helium propelled pumpkins had it easier.

Staying glued to TV for the endless ballot counting and legal maneuvering is sickening. It's a good thing Edward R. Morrow is dead because five minutes of contemporary TV news would kill him. Tabloid journalism is alive and well on the network news.

First it was "Two die in highway crash, film at eleven." At least the first sentence was news. Presumably the second part was to attract viewers who were sorry they couldn't actually enjoy the highway carnage in person.

When the lure of mere film paled in the ratings, promotion managers tried questions. "Judge rules in murder case. Will accused go free? Verdict at 11." They know the news, but won't tell us. That's vicious. If they have enough information to put together a teaser, they know enough to tell us the story right then and there. Period.

Recent media blabfests focused on hideous school violence. So what does the network do? After talking in solicitous, hushed tones about the stress youngsters face after these incidents, they stick a microphone in front of a ten-year-old and ask him to describe the horrific images he sees when he closes his eyes.

"How frightened are you? Do you think you'll ever put this tragedy behind you?" "Are you having trouble sleeping?" I'm against violence, except for the producer who put that report together.

And while I'm on a rant, I hate those special "crisis logos" TV stations use. Reeboks need logos; Wars do not. Are journalists afraid we'll be bored just watching Brokaw read the news? Isn't a shot of a bloody mangled car or a grainy security camera hold-up scene good enough? Now we have to have some graphic designer's concept of big stories. News logos set a new low standard for infotainment.

Racing for ratings, TV stations waited about three seconds into this latest mess to design "Election in Crisis" logos. Of course, how sensational do we get before news is science fiction? Or are we already there?

When a story breaks, that's news. When there's no more

news to report, stations and newspapers should just shut up. Instead, they keep the story alive by interviewing self-described "experts" pontificating about what it will mean if we should actually hear something new.

Meanwhile, economic news gets 40 seconds, tobacco legislation is a blip, and there's a tiny story about the Federal budget and tax revisions with no explanation whatever. But we sure as hell know more than we ever, ever wanted to know about Monica Lewinsky, O.J. Simpson and other tabloid superstars.

Amidst all the election result speculation last week I heard an NPR report that the Antarctic continental shelf is cracking, melting, and in danger of sending out icebergs that could one day sink civilization like the mighty Titanic.

We'll still be hearing about Florida's pregnant chads when they come through with bullhorns telling us to evacuate Delaware because Nebraska is going to be beachfront.

So I'm turning off the TV. I figure somebody will tell me if our country selects a president. In the meantime I'm off to the Rehoboth Beach Independent Film Festival. I've picked out eleven movies to see in four days, which will be my personal best. I have friends who have earmarked nineteen films to see. They will surely win the coveted Preparation H Award.

Next up will be the Rehoboth Hometown Christmas Parade. I always love that one. Every emergency vehicle in the county shows up, along with trash trucks decorated with reindeer antlers, and a bevy of twinkling tractors and farm vehicles rolling through town. It's not Macy's, but it's ours.

So from our house to yours, enjoy your Thanksgiving, savor the holidays, and have a happy, healthy new year. See you for 2001, the (Presidential) Race Odyssey. I'm sure we'll have a new leader by then. Won't we?▼

February 2001

Okay, Dubya has now been sworn in. Along with the official and unofficial swearing, if we've heard one thing over the past few months since our national electile dysfunction, it's that it's a time for healing. We agree. We've begun with things that soothe.

First, ostensibly to help heal Bonnie's knee injury, we ordered a new bathtub with whirlpool jets. Our original tub, when filled to its brim, would not cover Calista Flockhart much less one of us.

So the plumbers came, pulled out the teeny tub and set the new one in place. Then, the two butch plumbers, wearing dangerously low-riding blue jeans, explained that we needed to build a frame for the tub that extended at least six extra inches so "you have room to put the candles and wine glasses." Oh???

"Yeah," said the second plumber, "this should be the last thing you girls do each day so you can really relax and enjoy it." It was a wonderfully surreal moment.

Unfortunately, when the two most sensitive plumbers in history turned the motor on to test the whirlpool, water spewed all over the floor, the plumbers and our hopes of a candlelit evening.

"O.K." said the chief plumber, "while we arrange for replacement parts from the manufacturer, you can fill the tub, but don't use the jets."

That only sounded easy. First off, the faucet wasn't installed, so water just dribbled out of the copper pipe. At this rate we'd have a bath for the 2004 inaugural (Go Hillary!).

Eager to get to the candles and wine, we grabbed our spaghetti pot and lobster steamer from the kitchen, started filling them with hot water from the sink and dumping them overboard into the tub. There hasn't been so much running with pots of boiling water since Butterfly McQueen began birthing babies in *Gone With The Wind*.

By the time the tub was one third full, we uncorked the Merlot and figured that our ample body displacement would make up the difference. Just after we hopped in, the faucet's dribble turned icy cold.

Then *we* became uncorked. We sat in 8 inches of water, realizing that our water heater had just hollered Uncle. Not only didn't the tub's plumbing work, but when it did get repaired we wouldn't have enough hot water in the house to fill it. Great, our bargain spa needed a new water heater. Talk about taking a bath.

In the meantime, we hastily clinked glasses and climbed out of the tub—not as easy as we'd imagined either. Hauling ourselves up from the depths wasn't pretty. I now understand the value of grab bars, if not ejection seats.

Hence, the next part of our quest for healing involved striving for more flexibility. We signed up for yoga class.

I've always suspected that yoga was way too California-wear-some-flowers-in-your-hair for me. I just couldn't see myself quieting my brain or my mouth long enough to practice anything involving relaxation and patience. But alas, I was persuaded to go to a complimentary class.

Skeptical and scared of displaying my physical and mental inflexibility, I diffidently followed my mate into the studio —a room bathed in soft light and arranged with a dozen mats on the floor. Very kindergarten nap time.

As Yogameister Susan started her melodically soft-spoken instructions, I found myself going with the flow and coming as close to total relaxation as I'd ever imagined I could achieve.

So we signed up for a semester. Ours is the gentle yoga class, which is a polite way of saying it's for the elasticity challenged. We each have our own particular infirmities, with some of us just suffering from too much Ben & Jerry's Chunky Monkey.

But yoga eschews judgment at every turn. At our next class I found out that nothing is a problem. If somebody can't stretch far enough to achieve a specific position, a dowel in hand can bridge the gap. And you can roll blankets under any body part you want for comfort. Can't reach far enough around your own thunder thighs to pull your knees to your chest? There's a canvas belt available to help. I appreciated the assist, but I'm sure I looked like a piece of furniture cinched into place on a Bekins Van. Of course, I shouldn't have been thinking about how I looked, since I was supposed to be concentrating on my breathing and letting my brain and internal organs relax.

You know, it is possible to relax too much. Under the heading of "that's okay, it's supposed to happen," certain yoga positions can, how shall I put this, cause...um...flatulence. I think everybody in our class, at one time or another, has produced an audible emission. I find myself watching what I eat for lunch on yoga days. I don't think that praying you'll get through the hour without breaking wind is the kind of meditation we're encouraged to practice.

Anyway, when we did some bending movements, I was surprised to hear my instructor say I was very flexible. And not just my jaw, which I knew was in shape from blabbing. Apparently my waist and shoulders weren't as unyielding as I'd thought, either. Gee, next time Bonnie and I are having a "discussion," and I'm accused of being inflexible, I will have a retort.

This yoga stuff really is impressive. We've learned to be in the moment, concentrate on our breathing and try to calm the adrenalin rush of our daily lives. After stretching, comes quiet time, when Miss Susan reads to us. We all lie on our mats, surrounded by our blankies, dowels and belts, and, if we'd like, little black beanbag masks to block the light from our eyes. I know I'm supposed to be resting my mind, but I did wonder if, with all our innocent apparatus lying about, we looked like some kind of S&M cultists.

But the truth is, our yoga sessions are fun, good exercise and very, very soothing for both body and soul. Which is a good thing. Because the bathtub is still a construction site. And we've spent weeks trying to select tile. Hmmmm, now we've got a bad case of selectile dysfunction (sorry).

Bidding a fond farewell to tiling, we're off to yoga class to cleanse our minds of home improvement. I just love when Susan ends her class with the soothing mantra "Be in the moment, Go in peace, Take it with you." I usually take it with me right to

Tijuana Taxi because Wednesday is half price fajita night and there's a whole week for Beano before the next class.

Between the calm of yoga and our plumbers' prophecy of wine, women and song, I can feel myself healing already. Be in the moment, you-all. ▼

July 2001

It didn't take the June 20 *Delaware Coast Press* headline, "Gay Households Increase in Delaware" to tell us anything we didn't already know. Just check out Lowe's Hardware on Saturday morning, with pairs of boys buying vertical blinds and lesbians in line for potting soil, and you have a great snapshot of the recent census.

But, if your taste runs to statistics instead of anecdotal evidence, the recently released 2000 census figures contain lots of goodies.

According to the government, since 1990, the number of Delaware households with same-sex couples increased by more than 700 percent to 1,868 households. And of course, that's only those gay couples who felt comfortable sharing their marital status with Uncle Sam. Heaven knows how many others there actually are. Look for the rainbow stickers on cars parked at Giant and Food Lion and you'll get a pretty astounding idea. I bet there are 1,800 couples just in our own county.

And while Delaware and Vermont were the first states to have their same-sex stats released, the national numbers seem to be bearing out our Delaware trend.

In fact, a *Washington Post* article last week noted that not only were the numbers up for same-sex households, but the geographic breadth was startling. "They appear in all 105 counties in Kansas," said the *Post*. Now I don't think it's unusual to find queer households in every Kansas County; what I find unusual is that people are now willing to go on record about it. It's great. The catch phrase "Toto, I don't think we're in Kansas anymore" may not have the same connotation from now on.

Of course, another thing that the statisticians trumpeted is that gay male couples are more concentrated in cities, while women are putting down their roots in the suburbs. It took a team of census-takers to figure this out? Stereotypically speaking, gals love spreading mulch and guys want to decorate that urban penthouse. Who didn't know this? Well, it's nice having our lives validated by the numbers, anyway.

Although, since the census was only counting "unmarried partners," all of our single team members are still invisible as far as government figures go. If tabulators stood in the middle of Baltimore Avenue last week their abacuses would have been spinning.

As I read all about the census results, I loved some of the backpedaling done by the statisticians. One Associated Press article said, "Census specialists caution against drawing sweeping conclusions from the data released. For example, some people who consider themselves unmarried partners may in fact be elderly relatives living together, or two men or two women sharing a residence out of convenience."

Yeah, right. That kind of rhetoric may have worked in Boston in 1912, but these days, I'm pretty sure that people who checked "unmarried partners" knew exactly what they were doing. Other choices on the census form were "housemate," "boarder," and "other non-relative." Choosing "unmarried partner" was deliberate.

Like the gay activists and demographers that have been weighing in on the results, I don't think there are actually any more of us than there were before. I think we're just getting awfully tired of being invisible.

Sociology Professor Dwight Fee, from Middlebury College in Vermont, is quoted in *Time* magazine saying "Gay life is simply more visible in the culture now. Comedian Chris Rock is out there saying 'Everybody has a gay cousin.'"

And *Will & Grace* on prime time TV comes to Kansas as well as New York.

Which is not to say that there's less homophobia and danger in lots of places. It's just that gay people are starting to realize that being out is the only thing that's going to show how many of us there are—and how little straight folks have to fear. Out and Proud is not just a banner on a Pride float, it's a lifestyle that works.

187

Of course, that's easy to say in Rehoboth. It's tough to try it in, say, Lewiston, Idaho. But news on that front is improving, too. Upon returning from a family visit to that part of the world, one young man reported that he heard not a single "fag" joke, and his relatives, seeing him enjoying his toddling nephews, suggested, "You could always adopt." Pretty cool.

Actually, last weekend I was in upstate New York, feeling pretty invisible myself. Visiting Seneca Lake, home of those fabulous suffragettes (almost ALL of whom were happily ensconced in same-sex couplehood—and don't let any marriages of convenience fool you), I was surprised to see so few of us. At our hotel, there were no other beans to be found (You know, lez beans, like human beans). On the way home on the New York Thruway, a car passed and folks waved. I couldn't figure out what for, until I saw their rainbow sticker. Heck, if we waved at every car with a rainbow sticker in Rehoboth, we'd have no time to drive.

So living here in a gay-friendly ghetto is probably lots different from being in the hinterlands. But that doesn't mean we don't have work to do here, either.

And while all the national stats aren't released yet, it's a good guess that the numbers of same-sex unmarried partners nationwide is going to be a hard number to ignore. The census bureau estimated in 1998 that there were approximately 1,674,000 same sex couples in the United States. If the new numbers increase the same eightfold over 1990 numbers, and reflect only those who are willing to go on record, can you imagine how many of us there really are? That, ladies and gentlemen, is clout.

So let's start here at home. How many times am I going to have to fill out paperwork at a doctor's or dentist's office that gives me the choice of "Married, Single or Divorced?"

I've said it before. I can honestly check all three. I consider myself married, the government considers me single, and then there was that divorce from the accordion player. So who am I, if not "partnered" with Bonnie????

We have to start demanding a "partnered" category so we can stop being the invisible patients. Certainly, with the census backing up our numbers, we can ask our local hospital and doctor's offices to allow for the diversity within their practices.

Okay, that's my first salvo in the visibility war. In the meantime, settle down and be counted.▼

July 2001

Apparently, Rehoboth Beach used to have rustic cottages you could tour. Real summer places, with skimpy outdoor shower faucets, plank floors caked with sand, and furniture capable of surviving wet, mildewy towels. My family called them bungalows.

Well, for over 50 years, the Rehoboth Art League has been hosting its wonderful Cottage Tour and, just like everything else in life, evolution has had its impact. These days it's definitely not your grandmother's summer cottage tour.

You can debate whether change is good or bad all you want, but nowadays the Art League's Cottage Tour is part decorator showcase, part art appreciation and part eat-your-heart-out-that-you-didn't-buy-property-in-Rehoboth-when-it-was-affordable day.

At the League's most recent Cottage Tour the throngs tromping through the residences were as entertaining as the tour itself.

While it's very generous of the hosts to open their homes for the benefit of charity, I wonder if they had any idea of the kind of scrutiny they'd face. To the Art League's credit, there were little signs everywhere reminding people not to touch things since they were the host's personal belongings.

But let's face it, the cottage tour is a nosy person's dream come true. You get to check out the decor and personal effects of people you don't even know. Or some you do know. What better fun than to peer into other people's living rooms, dens, bedrooms, and closets.

And speaking of closets, some of the cottage owners, by letting the troops in for the tour, made a point of coming out of them. I loved the house with the framed National Coming Out Day poster in a guest room and copies of *Letters* casually displayed in visible places.

More fun still, in one living room there was a dramatic portrait of the homeowners.

Two grey-haired ladies entered behind me.

"Look at the lovely piano, and that wonderful paint...my word, that's two men."

"Oh, dear."

Enraptured, they stared, inert, at the painting until I thought their little straw handbags, not to mention their teeth, would clatter to the floor. It begs the question of exactly where in Rehoboth they've been.

As the ladies toddled off, their little white stack heels clacking on the hardwood, they made a point of looking at all the personal photos in the rooms—confirming what they saw in oil downstairs. The pair seemed to suffer no ill effects from the initial shock, and I actually think they enjoyed a sort of naughty pleasure as they looked around.

At another rainbow abode, the homeowner was upstairs, gleefully showing enthralled visitors a Barbra Streisand video on his high definition TV. This caused a significant backup, much like Saturday beach traffic. "Turn off the TV," instructed the downstairs docent, "we've got to get things moving again!"

The home, overflowing with movie memorabilia and Tom Cruise posters had dozens of people convinced that the owner knew Tom personally. "Why else would he have his pictures all over the place?" they demanded of the docents. Why, indeed.

For the record, the tour was equally divided between straight and gay households, as well as straight and gay cottage tourists. And all of the homes were magnificent in their own ways. It's interesting to note that by looking at the bookshelves you couldn't always tell a book owner's orientation by the book covers.

Sure, there were lots of fine art books and intriguing design tomes, but houses on both teams had John Grisham hardbacks and other popular fiction. A non-gay household had the latest Judy Garland bio. Go figure.

I loved the cottage with the requisite outdoor shower for sand reclamation. This rustic outdoor shower had two separate stalls, a dressing area complete with mirrors and hand lotion, and enough room for a seated attendant collecting tips, if they so chose.

With throngs of people tromping through the homes (1,400 over two days), the charity-minded proprietors all chose different ways to wait out the busybody invitational—hosting in the kitchen, offering refreshments; hiding in the kitchen, hoping to remain anonymous; or taking refuge at the beach, and reappearing only when it was safe to come out of the water.

For the most part, the cottage-peekers were very well-behaved, ooh-ing and ahhhh-ing at the properties, décor, art, and statuary. The docent army, schooled by the homeowners, could point out particularly wonderful pieces of art or fill visitors in on the history or idiosyncrasies of each home.

Imagine if I showed off my miniature manse on next year's tour. The crowd, after cutting their way through dust bunny jungle, would be greeted by a docent.

"On your right, please notice the gouge in the carpet, gnawed by the dog. Over here, you have the stunning Ethan Allen bedroom suite, with the foot of the armoire hacked into a teething ring by the dog. As we head to the diminutive sun porch, please note the striations in the screens, clawed by the...."

One of the best things about the real tour, of course, is the printed program, with a drawing and complete description of each residence. It includes comments like "built in the 20s by...folk art and artistry seen in every nook...energy flows with the open design...nestled in a picturesque landscape...etc.

I can see my write-up. "Welcome to Schnauzerhaven. Dating from 1997, this shoddily built tract-house opens to a backyard view of an adjacent barbed wire fence and trailer storage lot. The house is nestled amid small, recently-planted shrubs struggling to survive dog pee. The great room features a high ceiling fan that nobody can reach to dust, while the furniture dates back to twentieth century Ikea."

Okay, so you won't be seeing my "cottage" on the tour next year. You just have to make do with those impeccable in-town places and their lovely and unique art collections, distinctive architecture, and generous owners.

So until next year, keep this image with you. It was my favorite. Two ladies walk into a gargantuan walk-in closet in one home. In a hushed, slow and almost reverential tone, one woman says to the other:

"Hmmmm...pants...on...the...right...pants...on...the... left...I've never been in a gay couple's closet before. This is so interesting."

Ain't it now.▼

August 2001

Before you flip the page, saying, "She's writing about the damn dogs again," I beg your patience. This is not really a story about the dogs. It's about fragile human connections, cruel fate, and unconditional love.

Okay, this first part is about the damn dogs. My house has been in an uproar since last summer when Bonnie's illness led to a household fight over alpha dog status. Historically, Bonnie was always the boss, while the pack consisted of Moxie, Paddy, and me (please note my placement in that list).

However, according to our latest canine trainer, with Bonnie hospitalized a good part of last summer, then spending weeks on the sofa, Moxie felt the need to protect her and take over as Alpha Dog.

Unfortunately, it was a position he felt responsible to assume but insufficiently courageous to handle. His false bravado translated into irrational, hysterical barking at anything outside, near the front door, or entering the house. That included the riding mower, mailman, trash truck, vacuum cleaner, and any intrepid visitors who got past the gauntlet.

Prior to this new Moxie Braveheart, we actually needed a doorbell. In fact, we got a cool electronic device to sit atop the doorbell and respond to every door chime by amplifying and relaying the sound to other rooms.

Well now, with Moxie's frantic early warning system, the hair-trigger electronic chime responds not only to the doorbell but to Moxie's bark, so all day long, between the barking and chiming, you don't know if you're at Westminster Cathedral or Kennel Club.

Paddy, already a little neurotic, hides in the closet, sniffing Doctor Scholl's foot powder. His addiction escalated to gnawing leather, and one day I came home to discover that he'd munched one each of four pairs of shoes. My shrieking set Moxie and the door chime off and we all nearly lost our minds.

Then the phone rang.

Now I don't know if it's the same in your life, but I've started to view the new millennium as Reality, Part II. Part One was The Epidemic. Many of us had loved ones we lost to AIDS for a premature taste of life's cruelties. We often heard, "We're too young to be at our contemporary's funerals."

Well now we're at a stage where bad news and illnesses are creeping back and are slightly more age appropriate. When our contemporaries talk about various aches, pains and conditions, it can be just good-natured kvetching.

But kidding aside, life is starting to feel increasingly fragile.

This time the phone call was about my college roommate. A victim of the hideously cruel Huntington's disease, she now needs round the clock care in a nursing home. With Huntington's, your motor and mental skills all deteriorate—but you don't die. It's devastating.

When I called the nursing home, I was thrilled to hear that while Lesley's voice was slowed, speech somewhat slurred, her memory and sense of humor seemed pretty intact.

Lesley and I have been part of each other's lives pretty regularly since we were 18. I spent some of her honeymoon with her in France, after wiring funds so she and her new, now ex, husband could pay their Monte Carlo casino bill. Following my divorce, she, in turn, took me to Provincetown, sat me down on a bench and told me to take a great big look around. Without that push, I might still be in the closet.

Long a vegan (one serious vegetarian) and animal welfare advocate, Lesley sat around in plastic shoes, putting up with my carnivorous ways—provided I agreed to put up tomatoes with her. If not for her, I'd never ever have been near a farm or mason jar. And she'd have missed several plays and a boat trip.

"Are you going to bring the dogs to see me?" she haltingly, hopefully, asked when I called. "Please...."

So despite the recent household reign of terrier, we scheduled a road trip. Reclaiming her authority, Alpha Bonnie seatbelted the rest of the pack into the car and we took off. Eight long hours, two pee-breaks and several rawhide chews later (no, I did not. I gnawed cheese doodles instead), we arrived on the shores of Lake Seneca in Geneva, New York.

Miraculously, we'd found a Ramada that welcomed pets, checked in, and headed for the nursing home.

The smile on Lesley's face as the fuzzy grey Schnauzers burst into her room was worth its weight in kibble. Up on Lesley's bed the pups jumped, dispensing kisses and unconditional love.

Obviously my dogs felt no obligation to protect us, the nursing home, its occupants or visitors, since my pooches became perfect little angels. As we took Lesley down the hall for a haircut, Moxie perched on her lap in the wheelchair, regal as a prince. Paddy, the royal footman, heeled alongside the carriage.

All along our route, patients looked at our entourage, with smiles and sparkles in their eyes, waving, talking, and sometimes merely grunting to the dogs. People who seemed mired in lonely silence only minutes before reached out to pet and pamper my dogs. I cried more than once.

I'm not going to pretend that the weekend was easy. Seeing this once beautiful, dynamic woman dependent on aides and confined to a tiny, waning life was tough to handle. But given the circumstances, the weekend was far better than we could have expected.

There was an outdoor bar with live music along the lake at the hotel, where Bonnie and I sat, in the cool evening air (with the dogs!) listening to a chanteuse and sipping Smirnoff. It was all very European.

On Saturday we spent a long day back at the nursing home, our dogs adorning Lesley's bed like the New York Public Library's lions. When conversation was too tough, or cheeriness hard to sustain, Moxie and Paddy rescued us with their antics.

By Sunday morning, after emotional farewells (and a quick check to make sure all the nursing home residents still had all their shoes), we humans were emotionally spent—and the dogs were just plain spent. It was a long ride home, with time to discuss life's cruelties and the need to make every single day count.

The dogs, of course, know a thing or two about stopping to sniff the roses. While we suffered beach traffic, they awoke only for shards of hot dog and a potty break outside Philly.

This afternoon I was preparing a package with a portrait of the pooches to mail to Lesley for her room, when friends rang the doorbell. Moxie went off like the hound of the Baskervilles, the door chime did the Bells of St. Mary's, and Paddy raced to the foyer with half a Reebok in his choppers.

And you know, I didn't care. ▼

August 2001

"We're on a five-year plan." I hear that a lot from gay and lesbian couples who weekend in Rehoboth and are contemplating a move to full-time. That's when I usually laugh and remember that Bonnie and I were on a five-year plan that turned to a five-minute plan when I got a job offer.

People ask "What's it like to live in Rehoboth 24/7?" Fantastic. Not that there aren't adjustments when you move to a place where you used to vacation.

So for you 5-year planners and those who might be inspired, here's my take on it:

1. After years of weekending here, leaving chores, bills and responsible adult life back in Maryland, it's a shock when all that stuff comes with you. Fighting with the HMO…what is that doing here????? **Rule #1:** *Spend your weekends like you did before*—at the beach, boardwalk, whatever. Relegate chores to the time you used to spend commuting. And you can worship on Sunday morning at Our Lady of Lowes. The trade-off is that delicious 4 p.m. Tuesday trip to the beach, running into your friends everywhere, and morning coffee with buddies you meet at the post office. Spoiled? Only in a fabulous way.

2. Gayberry RFD has all the charm and aggravation of any small town (but much better food). While it's a joy to mingle with neighbors, shopkeepers and town movers and shakers, gossip travels faster than a boogey-boarder stung by a sea nettle. Whoever said a lie can travel half way 'round the world before the truth has its shoes on was smart. **Rule #2:** *Don't assume what you hear—good or bad—is true.* We try to check out the mouths of the involved horses. If you hear your money ain't good enough at your once-favorite watering hole, or a certain shop or organization has a bug up its butt about gay people, check it out yourself. There's guaranteed to be less black and white and more gray than you thought, and you might encourage positive

change. It sounds naïve, but it works.

Of course, don't expect to play hooky from work undetected. Here, everybody knows everybody else's business. But that's as good as it is bad. If you need help, everybody knows and rallies.

3. We do more here, even in the winter, than we ever did in the metropolis. **Rule # 3:** *Plan to stay busy!* Everything's five minutes away. You can brunch, swim, beach, shop, hit happy hour, cook dinner (okay, go out to dinner) and still catch a movie. If you're not old like me you can do even more. I can see two movies in the time I used to spend in line for tickets for one. It took moving to a hamlet to get me into yoga, independent films, auctions, new playwrights, winery tours and drinking beer where I know the brewer. I don't have time to miss Broadway, being the neighborhood's token lesbians or entire mornings in commuter traffic.

4. Pick up the phone! **Rule #4:** *Anybody who says they haven't gotten into "the community" hasn't tried.* If Rehoboth is cliquey, there's a clique for everybody. We've got sub-cultures within sub-cultures. Among our larger gay community there's a whole contingent of antique fanatics, animal welfare activists, people in book clubs, disabled gays, golf-obsessed girls, lipstick lesbians, hearing-impaired people, S&M devotees, people who love Enya (why???), artists' collectives, musicians, karaoke queens and more. There are even gay Republicans. I've seen people move here knowing no one, and after a phone call or two they are up to their armpits volunteering, attending free support groups which produce social connections and advising the next arrivals on how to get involved.

Corollary to Rule #4 is **Rule #4A:** *Just show up.* It annoys me when I hear people surmise that our local non-profits are exclusive clubs. Phooey. I know several volunteers whose major qualification, in addition to being energetic and interested, is that they just showed up. Stop whining and get off your butt. You can send me ugly e-mail if you want. I don't care.

5. I'm fearless here. Even if you never realized you were nervous about people peering over your shoulder at ATMs and

strangers' footsteps gaining on you from behind on Capitol Hill or in downtown Philadelphia, you'll feel the total absence of that fear in Rehoboth. Not only can you luxuriate over a romantic dinner with your sweetie at all the local eateries, and have your same-genderness seem positively ho-hum, but your car radio is safe in the street while you're doing it. **Rule #5:** *Relax and enjoy yourself.* Even if you never felt threatened by street crime or gay bashing "back home," the absence of it here is palpable.

The worst crime I've been party to was the discovery of a squatter in my condo one winter. I never saw the culprit, but there were T-shirts left behind and a great deal of toilet paper missing. Squatter, indeed.

6. Pack the piggy bank. **Rule #6:** *Don't believe the myth "it costs less to live here."* Ha! Okay, taxes are lower and you won't need corporate drag anymore. But you're not going to switch from dining out on Chilean Sea Bass to staying home with Rice-a-Roni. If you lived like Will or Grace before, you won't be Fred or Ethel Mertz here. And we certainly can't look to the gay-bashing Salvation Army any more for help. But you can maximize your buck, especially off-season. With half-price noodle nights and diner dinners, our restaurants cater to locals. You can stuff yourself on the cheap all winter and live off the fat when the prices go back up in June. There are locals nights at the movies and a staggering number of free activities like gallery openings, film previews, the boardwalk exercise track, and free band concerts.

And that's a good thing, because **Rule #6a** is: *Don't plan on making much money here.* Congrats to those of you retiring here, but for us working stiffs, unless you telecommute to corporate headquarters, become a gastroenterologist or reach the zillion dollar real estate club, you'll need overdraft protection. Careers in Rehoboth mean more fun, more free time, more job satisfaction, less commute, less clothes, less stress, and less money. But the trade-off works for me.

7. And finally, **Rule # 7:** *Never underestimate the value of zip-loc bags.* This is the beach. It's wet. There's salt spray in the air. Put a towel outside to dry and it gets wetter; Put metal hang-

ers in the closet and your clothes rust; put chips in a bowl fifteen minutes before company comes and you'll understand the origins of Limp Biskit. Not only do we need safe sex around here, but latex protection is a good idea for an open bag of Doritos. On the other hand, when the ocean breeze comes along, there's absolutely nothing like it.

All in all, besides asking Bonnie out for an iced-tea in 1982, moving to Rehoboth is the best decision I ever made. Of course, we could use a good dry cleaners, gourmet Chinese food and a shoemaker. But then we'd really be spoiled.

So, what are you all waiting for???? Call the movers....▼

September 2001

I don't think that any person who is privileged, as I am, to see their words published on a regular basis, could go back to the everyday business of writing without covering last week's tragic terrorist attacks and loss of life. I know I can't.

As our global, national, and local communities unite in horror over the World Trade Center and Pentagon events, and as our hearts go out to the people killed and the families forever altered, the kinships we have, whether biological or by affinity, are what get us through.

As I sit typing, the wall above the computer monitor sports a poster-sized photo I once took of the Trade Center towers. Formerly a symbol of my I Love New York hometown pride, it's now a much more moving tribute.

Like everyone else, for me, this last week has been steeped in disbelief, anger, fear, and the need to connect and re-connect with those we love. Bonnie and I were scheduled to dine with a group of friends on that awful Tuesday night, and we phoned to see if it was still "on."

"We might as well all watch this unfold together," said our prospective hostess.

So that's what we did—gather with one of our special families, and experience the awfulness of the events together. The hello hugs were longer, the conversations more serious, and the realization that our community of Rehoboth friends will be there in good times and bad was a comfort to us all.

Over the succeeding days I watched TV until I could no longer stand to see those incessant reruns of the planes diving into the skyscrapers and people running, like Indiana Jones, from the ball of billowing black smoke chasing them.

By Friday, I had to be in an Annapolis recording studio preparing the music for a show I'm rehearsing. By happenstance it showcases the music of the 1940s, including the inspiring tunes of World War II. Both the pianist and I had tears rolling down our faces as he played *The White Cliffs of Dover* followed by strains of *Rule Britannia*. The London Blitz wasn't just "over there" anymore.

On Saturday, our trio of performers rehearsed the show in one members' living room. The gorgeous afternoon, prompting wide open windows to savor this first crisp fall day, sent our sentimental journey of Glenn Miller's *In the Mood* wafting all over the neighborhood.

When we got to our first act finale, and the second verse of *God Bless America*, I glanced out the window and saw that the man across the street had stopped mowing his lawn, and stood, head bowed and listening. It took my breath away. Fortunately, next up was the Andrews Sisters' music and we could be silly again.

As Bonnie and I drove back to Rehoboth on Sunday night, along roads dotted with American flags flying from homes, businesses and vehicles, I was moved by the number of signs announcing prayers for the victims and the simple message "God Bless America."

More than once, radio commentators talked about the coming together of all Americans in this crisis—we were no longer Democrat or Republican, gay or straight, black or white—we were Americans.

Back at my computer, sadness turned to fury when my friend Kathy sent me an e-mail. "Fay—Like most of us, I had wondered what prompted the attack on the World Trade Towers. But after reading this I finally understand. Turns out it's our fault (or yours, but I'm counting myself in with the Pagans).—K"

She attached a September 15 article by Dan Thomasson of the Scripps Howard News Service.

"WASHINGTON—*One religious fanatic is pretty much like another when it comes to using the Bible or the Koran to justify the most unimaginable barbarisms. If there was much doubt about this, two of America's champion evangelical zealots—Jerry Falwell and Pat Robertson—put it to rest with an extraordinary example of insensitivity and bad taste.*

Both voiced the belief that the deaths of thousands of Americans at the hands of terrorists was inspired by God as a way of getting even with those who condone feminism, homosexuality, abortion rights and any number of civil liberties the two have no use for.

"God continues to lift the curtain and allow the enemies of America to give us probably what we deserve," Falwell said during a television appearance on Robertson's 700 Club, a Christian Broadcast Network showcase of right-wing religious dogma with an audience of millions.

"The abortionists have got to bear some burden for this because God will not be mocked," he was quoted as saying. "I really believe that the pagans and the abortionists and the feminists and the gays and lesbians who are actively trying to make that an alternative lifestyle...all of them who have tried to secularize American—I point the finger in their face and say, 'You helped this happen.'"

Omigod. I stared at the vicious words of Falwell and Robertson and wanted to scream.

I looked at Friday's *Washington Blade*. The front page announced that among the terrorist's victims was David Charlebois, the openly gay co-pilot of American Airlines Flight 77 and businessman Mark Bingham, who may have been among the men who overpowered the hijackers on the plane that crashed in Pennsylvania.

In addition, Father Mychal Judge, the gay chaplain of the New York Fire Department died in the rubble of the World Trade Towers, as well as two gay men and their adopted child who were aboard one of the hijacked planes.

As details filter out, it's clear that there were gay heroes and gay victims, as well as feminists, pro-choice advocates and any number of so-called pagans with secular views among the firefighters, police officers, health care workers, and, of course, hundreds of hardworking people who were able to flee the towers...and those who are still entombed there.

But it certainly didn't matter on September 11 whether they were gay or not or what lifestyle views they held. They were Americans, as we all are now, no matter how the despicable Falwell and Robertson want to impugn and splinter us.

So it's a week later. And just like the stock market, government, schools, and outlet malls, we all have to absorb the shock and, considering ourselves fortunate, return to our lives—shaken, profoundly sad, and more worried perhaps, but back to the business of living.

I realized this when, after days of watching the tragic stories on TV, something made me laugh. A good belly laugh. And though I felt guilty having a side-splitting I-gotta-pee laugh even as Peter Jennings was somberly droning on, I realized that sooner or later we have to stop obsessing about the lunatic terrorists and get back to our garden variety lunatics.

But how, when everything else seems awfully trivial? I had started writing a column on September 9. Between Congressman Gary Condit and the missing intern, and Anne Heche, ex girlfriend to Ellen DeGeneres, going certifiably nuts in the desert, I had plenty of material. I'll get to it next time. For now, God Bless us all, everyone.▼

October 2001

In answering our nation's call to go back about our business after Sept. 11, Bonnie and I did our best by land and sea.

As former power boaters, we're slightly shocked to find ourselves sailors now. The call of the waves beckoned to Bonnie when a new acquaintance asked her to go sailing on a rented catamaran. She loved it, and now we're really in cold water.

Mirroring our community's reputation for instant pairing off ("What's a lesbian bring on a second date? A U-Haul"), we bought a boat with our new friends on our second sailing date.

Said boat is a two-decade old Hobie 16, which, to my cabin cruiser enthusiast's eye isn't even a boat. It's two canoes held together by a trampoline. Picture Tom Hanks in *Castaway*. And it has an enormous mast and boom just waiting to make inadvertent contact with my head when the wind changes. But my girlfriend loves it.

Bonnie and her new co-captain set out for their first sail on a gorgeous September day. "Okay, girls," I said, "you'd better really enjoy this day because you know what they say: the two best days in a boater's life are the day you buy it and the day you sell it."

Punishment for that quip won me an invitation aboard. "Come on," Bonnie said to me, and her co-captain's equally reluctant partner, "the four of us should really take the first voyage together."

So our quartet climbed aboard this tiny raft with a sail and set out, in a whoosh of wind, across Rehoboth Bay. Have you ever been on a Hobie? The damn thing travels like a bat out of hell. I was so surprised by the speed of the craft, it took me a few minutes to realize that not only didn't the thing have an engine, but our captains courageous didn't even have an oar on board for emergencies. If the wind died we'd be up Love Creek without a paddle.

And it's a good thing the water was warm after a long hot summer. The canvas raft we indelicately sprawled across had water spouts spurting through its middle like old faithful. My god, the thing was a 16 foot bidet. We were a traveling wet T-shirt contest.

Every few minutes our captains would tell their intrepid passengers to shift positions lest we be swept overboard by the boom. Ah, memories of my being sent to the bow on our former boat-home to help raise the engine off a sand bar. My life as ballast, part two.

As we sailed along, enjoying the gorgeous weather and trying to normalize our lives, I can't say we weren't a little jumpy at the sound of aircraft overhead and helicopters buzzing the beach. Were they just normal training flights from Dover and typical Coast Guard flyovers?

We beached our craft, ending our maiden voyage with success, and hurried back to our lives. Over at the Art League, that Stage Door Canteen revue I was directing turned out to be an emotional experience. Opening night coincided with the day the U.S. launched air strikes against Afghanistan. When the performers closed the first act with God Bless America, half the cast and most of the audience couldn't keep tears from rolling down their cheeks. What followed, was a spontaneous sing-a-long. It was the most emotional, memorable theatrical moment I ever experienced.

Back at the 24-hour news stations, we heard New York Mayor Rudy Giuliani encouraging tourists to flock to the Big Apple to help New York's damaged economy. Now there was a Yankee Doodle Dandy idea.

Actually, we'd had theatre tickets for the following weekend for some time, but the idea that we'd be doing our patriotic duty by seeing shows, eating pastrami, and shopping made me positively giddy.

On our way up the Jersey Turnpike, where you would have seen the Twin Towers appear in the distance, a strange quiet overtook us. We couldn't fathom that they were missing.

We gazed to the right as we entered the Lincoln Tunnel and noticed the Empire State Building, shining in the afternoon sun, once again the tallest structure in town. It looked magnificent. But downtown, there was a murky, cloudy haze over the Wall Street area, and we couldn't bear to look at the empty skyline.

Out of the tunnel and onto Broadway however, it was clear that the Mayor and citizens of New York were going on with the show. Hastily posted signs shouted "I love NY Theatre," "Thank You Mayor Giuliani from the grateful citizens of New York," and "God Bless America." John Lennon's "Imagine all the people living in peace" was posted in two story letters.

At the very moment we ventured from our car to the street, a gathering of hundreds of Broadway celebrities stood right in front of us making a commercial to encourage folks to come to New York. Performers, police, cabbies, and tourists melded into one big family. It gave us goosebumps.

Determined to do our bit for America, Bonnie and I took full advantage of the plentiful half-price tickets, saw three shows, dined at the Stage Deli and gleefully shopped 'til we dropped—all to help the city get back on its feet, of course.

We saw a production of *Kiss Me Kate* and cheered the cast that took a 25 percent pay cut just to keep the show alive, and then donated another 25 percent of their salary to a fund for the WTC victims. At the play *The Allergist's Wife*, Valerie Harper spoke directly to the audience at the curtain call, humbly thanking us for coming to the show.

On Sunday, we dined with a friend who'd been helping cater food to the rescue workers and families at Ground Zero downtown. Her heartbreaking stories brought the horror back loud and clear, but also gave us a second-hand glimpse into the heroism, compassion, and awesome generosity of people coming together in a crisis.

All the way home to Delaware we talked about the enormity of the New York tragedy and the bounty of generosity it unleashed. Right here in Rehoboth, the most magnificent outpouring of charity produced several awesome events.

Of course, three weeks into the aftermath of September 11, crass commercialism and little ironies are creeping back into our lives. I love the rampant flag-flying and patriotism, but I really wouldn't think badly of a business that had to take down their patriotic message and go back to regular advertising. As it is, we're seeing a lot of muddled "God Bless America Try our New Chicken Sandwich." Or "United We Stand Free Sundaes with Every Fajita."

God Bless America, land that I love.▼

March 2002

"Do you want to take a ride up towards Wilmington, have some dinner and, uh, deliver some cats?" Until the cats part it sounded appealing.

Somehow my spouse had been recruited to save four cats and a dog from death row at our local shelter by transporting them to an animal rescue volunteer, who would then place them in loving homes.

Ah, animal rescue. I may have sold my pick-up, but I can keep my lesbian club card current with animal rescue credits.

"Well, where are we taking them?" I asked, realizing my question implied consent.

"Up near the Delaware Memorial Bridge," she said. The word "near" might have been a red flag.

"Okay. But do you know *exactly* who we are meeting, where and when?"

"Sure."

I shoulda asked more questions.

Like lion tamers, we stuffed four squirming, snarling, hissing felines into two small cat carriers and put them into our Subaru Outback (animal rescue + owning a Subaru = extra Lezzie club points).

Whitey, the blind terrier, was placed in a slightly larger cage. I met Whitey when Bonnie lifted him out of his crate so I could line it with one of our large beach towels. He emitted a blood-curdling scream along with a stream of poop pellets he'd doubtless been saving up since Thanksgiving. As I leapt back to avoid the flying BMs I got a good look at the dog—at least I think it was a dog. Is there a muskrat terrier? They must have unplugged his tail from an electric socket to bring him to us. Every shaggy hair on his body stood at attention.

Once we hosed the driveway and got ugly Whitey back in his crate, we headed up Route One. From the cargo hold came a series of low, rumbling growls, then random spitting, which led to a hiss, then another, followed by a scream, reaching a crescendo with an ear-splitting screech fest. I haven't heard such a good cat fight since Crystal and Alexis slugged it out on *Dynasty*. Finally, it got so bad I let out an Alfred Hitchcock scream myself just to startle them all and regain some control. Luckily, Bonnie didn't drive off into a ditch.

So the meow mix tried another tactic. On a feline count of ten they sent bodily fluids out of every orifice they owned. My god, they were peeing and coughing up hairballs in unison back there. Just to breathe, I wound up hanging my head out the window like a cocker spaniel.

With our ears turning to icicles, our traveling menagerie was still just twenty minutes up the road. I asked Bonnie exactly where in Wilmington we were going and it turned out we were going to New Jersey. To be exact, between exit two and three on the turnpike, which is a lot closer to Manhattan than Rehoboth. Aside from the time involved in transporting these orphans across state lines, I calculated the cost in gas and tolls and wanted to spit up a hairball myself.

Just then our cell phone rang. It was the rescue lady letting us know she'd be two hours late to the rendezvous site.

"It's okay," said Bonnie. "We can have dinner."

Like I had an appetite.

So we headed off road to find food and fresh air. By this time I was getting used to the low level growling and occasional spitting from the rear of the car and thankful there'd been a cease fire in the alimentary canal warfare. Of course, once my own cat allergies kicked in, I started making pretty ugly guttural noises myself.

Between sneezes I choked down some fast food (there's never slow food around when you need to kill time) and we proceeded to the appointed rest stop—arriving at least an hour and a half before the cat and dog deal was scheduled to come down.

Have you ever loitered at a rest stop? Of course not. Normal people just rush in on their way somewhere else for a quick pee and a chili dog. So there we were, leisurely checking out the lovely gift shop—a veritable cornucopia of packaged gummy bears and tabloids. Did you know that folks actually manufacture Jersey Turnpike souvenirs? We dropped $31 for commemorative mugs, several magazines ("The truth! Who's gay and who's not in Hollywood!!!") and a bag of Twizzlers.

Back at the car, the cargo bed was eerily quiet. Were Hogan's Heroes planning something? Actually the troops were all asleep. So Bonnie and I sat, reading by dome light, about the lesbian affairs that purportedly wrecked Drew Barrymore's marriage. Tsk. Tsk.

At one point, I started having trouble reading and thought my eyes were going. Why was the dome light flickering?

"You don't have the lights on, do you?" I asked Bonnie, just as the car's battery wheezed its last and plunged us into total darkness. Great. I wandered off toward the service area to find a jump start.

Although we were in the actual rest stop parking lot, less than 50 yards from the gas pumps, they had to send an official Turnpike truck, from the other side of the highway, to give us a jump. Naturally, Gomer the gas jockey had to charge us the extortionist price for a turnpike rescue. Is this any way to treat missionaries on the underground railroad?

Finally the tardy animal rescue lady showed up at the...hell, I've forgotten the name of the service area. Monica Lewinsky Service Area? (lip service?) Pee Wee Herman Service Area (just self-service? Oh, stop it, Fay), her small car packed, like a Rubic's Cube, with a dozen cages.

Retrieving the wild kingdom from our car and passing it off to hers involved a lot of scratching and screaming. And that was just me. To be consistent, when Whitey was sprung for transfer, he once again propelled himself with a poop stream. But it was Jersey girl's problem now.

And so we bid a fond farewell to our furry charges and headed for home—keeping ourselves awake humming "Born Free." We got back to Rehoboth at midnight.

For the record, there aren't enough little scented evergreen trees to hang from my car's rear view mirror to mask the souvenir smells. But I look at it this way.

Tolls: $7.00

Dinner and souvenirs: $37.00

Jump Start: $17.00

Saving Whitey's life: priceless. ▼

March 2002

According to etiquette books, a proper twentieth anniversary gift is china or occasional furniture. Twenty years and you get a gift-wrapped end table?

As I write this, Bonnie and I will hit the 20-year mark tomorrow, and frankly, we've got all the Mikasa and Ethan Allen we need. In fact, we often sit, feet up on the occasional furniture, amazed we ever met at all. That we wound up dancing together on a windy March night two decades ago was an absolute fluke. I'm about to tell the story, so if you mind my getting a little mushy, bail now.

I was over 30 and not long out of the closet. An acquaintance mentioned a women's dance in Baltimore at the Glass Pavilion at Johns Hopkins University. My vintage '82 internalized homophobia led me to ask "What moron books a gay dance in a glass room?" I wasn't sure I wanted to go.

Fear of flaunting wasn't the only thing that could have kept me home that night. Despite 16 years in D.C., Baltimore remained a mystery. I needed a tour guide. Moreover, it was unseasonably freezing out. I still don't know what made me grab my Rand McNally and mittens, and head North.

Meanwhile, Bonnie might not have made it there either. Her date, a horsewoman, was riding the afternoon hunt, and asked Bonnie to meet her at Hopkins. Did Bonnie really want to go by herself? It could have gone either way.

The dance started at 9 and, after riding my own frenzied hunt to Baltimore, I arrived at a pathologically early 9:01. Yes, the ballroom was glass. Purple balloons and lesbians were visible from the parking lot. I started to get the vapors.

Inside the nearly empty hall, I took one good earful of the all-woman "new age" band tuning up and almost fled. Women began arriving, mostly in pairs. Finally, I saw the couple that lured me there. With no energy for games, I cut to the chase.

"Know any singles here?"

My friends exchanged glances and pointed across the room to Bonnie.

"I'm looking for somebody who isn't screwed up," I said.

They still pointed to Bonnie—an attractive, nicely dressed woman eyeing the door.

I marched over to introduce myself, but sadly I have no memory of the conversation. The sounds of the band tuning up turned out to be the actual new age women's music and it was deafeningly awful.

We tried to dance, but after two tortured minutes without a detectable beat, I hollered the quintessential "Let's go someplace where we can talk" and we fled to the coat check. With that the horsewoman arrived, minus fox and hounds, but standing an aggressive six feet tall. I started to sweat.

"We're just leaving," Bonnie said, slightly apologetically. To her credit, the mistress of the hunt shrugged and said, "I should have known better than to leave somebody as good-looking as you here by yourself." I couldn't have agreed more.

So we headed to Mitchell's, an infamous Baltimore women's bar. Against tradition, March was going out like the same lion it was when it roared in. Wind sent twigs, leaves and city trash swirling around Bonnie's teeny Chevette as we drove past Baltimore Harbor and into Little Italy. We hit every traffic light on yellow, with Bonnie hollering "catch you next time" as we sailed through. By the fifth amber light it was a duet.

The bar was dark, smoky and as noisy as the dance, only we recognized the music. After two hours of *Bad Girls*, *I Will Survive* and *Gloria* we retreated to the car and reversed directions. "Catch you next time" we shouted, as ambers faded to red.

Back at Hopkins, we huddled in the 'Vette (we wished), finally speaking below a scream and started discovering our differences. Bonnie was into softball and camping; the only diamonds I saw were at Bloomingdales. As for camping, I refused to sleep anyplace with turf between my bed and bath. My accent screamed Noo Yawk; Miss Baltimore said, "I love gewin' downy ocean, dewnt yew?" It took me ten minutes to figure out she meant a trip to the beach.

I'd never had a soft shell crab; she'd never had a knish. She owned a dental lab; I was dental-phobic. I directed plays; she'd seen *Hello, Dolly* once. Bonnie built things and wired whole buildings; I couldn't stop my new VCR from flashing 12:00.

It got worse and we just laughed. Me: obsessively early; She: generally late; my Manhattan clan loved museums, contemporary furniture and worked in advertising; her people hailed from the Virginia hills, decorated early American, and farmed. She was D.A.R. eligible, I was Ellis Island. And forget about religion.

Amid howling winds in the deserted parking lot, opposites attracted. So we exchanged numbers and promised to call. By early April we were an item. By the following November we'd bought a home together.

Somehow, our different lives meshed, as we practiced the high art of compromise. I direct shows and Bonnie does tech. We get everywhere exactly on time, rushing Bonnie and panicking Fay. She gets me to the dentist by heading toward the outlets, then diverting. And I got her to trade camping for boating—it still involved ice coolers and bug spray, but there's carpet between berth and bath.

And every December we try not to burn down the Christmas tree with the Hanukkah candles. Sure, we occasionally scream "Princess!!!" or "Hillbilly!!!" at each other, but overall it works out very well.

And I have only one tiny regret. Collectibles.

Way back in 1983 I bought a Christmas ornament with a cute little seal on it because my mate loves seals. I was too stupid to notice the phrase "Second in a Series" on the box. In 1985, I bought a similar "Frosty Friend" with a penguin on it. To my horror, I realized I was collecting and felt compelled to buy the "collectible" every year from then on, waiting and praying for the words "Last in a Series" to appear. So far, no dice. I must have been AWOL in '96 and '98, because somehow I missed those.

Well, with our anniversary coming up, I wondered how I

could round out my set, since Frosty Friends Collectibles (phony marketing ploy that it is) began production the year Bonnie and I met. So a friend introduced me to eBay. When I looked online for my missing ornaments, I was flabbergasted. Hundreds of people were embroiled in chaotic bidding wars for those hunks of Hallmark plastic. Get a grip, folks. These aren't DaVinci.

According to the descriptions ("Original box, never opened, mint condition, blah, blah") the cardboard packing is worth as much as the plastic geegaws. Just before last Christmas, the '82 and '84 editions were in auction battles topping $200 with "just 12 minutes to go!" I may be nostalgic, but I'm not nuts.

Then, after Christmas, we were able to acquire the late '90s editions for $27 and $29 each. It was outrageous for cheesy plastic snow scenes and arctic animals, but also somehow satisfying. In February, a friend found the '84 Frosty Friend (with a missing box, alas) for just over $40 and I bit—leaving only the elusive 1982 ornament out of my grasp.

So that's it. Bonnie and I are celebrating twenty great years. We hope to make it legal whenever we actually get our civil rights, meaning we'll be lucky to have the ceremony at the nursing home.

And while tomorrow we celebrate, tonight I have to check out eBay. God knows, after 20 years, Bonnie and I have everything we need, but a cheap '82 Frosty Friend would be lovely.

Happy Anniversary, Bon. As I write, the '82 hunk of junk is up to $337.50 and I ain't goin' there. And if I ever again even glance at something that could possibly become a collectible, shoot me. ▼

April 2002

Texas should change its slogan from Lone Star State to Waste Not, Want Not.

I dragged Bonnie along to Ft. Worth recently for a conference I attended. We arrived in Cowtown (its nickname) to find 100,000 beer swilling, boot wearing, silver belt-buckle clad cowboys in full Nascar regalia on the street in the center of town. It was race weekend. I could have just stayed in Delaware.

After checking in at our hotel—decorated with lone star logos on the carpets, bedspreads, sheets, soaps, beer and butter—we headed out to a bar that had saddles for barstools, to drink Buffalo Butt Beer under an actual fuzzy buffalo butt on the wall.

We escaped to the street, where not only isn't it against the law to walk around with that proverbial "open container," it's encouraged. Outdoor vendors hawk chewing tobacco samples. You could just spit. And people do. Besides, where I come from leather and Levi-clad cowboys strutting their stuff and swaggering into a bar are going to one of our own, not some Honky Tonk to pick up girls with big hair. Texas is weird.

OD'd on liquored up guys in stupid hats, we hopped a bus to the hotel. Two Willy Nelsons, a mean-looking tattooed dude, and a straggly-haired woman devoid of teeth shared the ride. "You gals sisters?" asked the toothless one. The eyes of Texas were upon us, so we looked at each other and, in unison, said, "Yup."

By the time we saw the Marriott again we were in lesbian withdrawal and took to the Multiplex to see *Kissing Jessica Stein*. It's about two single gals, fed up with the men they're dating, who decide to explore alternatives. It had the potential to be hugely insulting and terrible, but was instead refreshingly honest, hilarious and plausible. (Hooray!)

But the fact remains we were in Texas in an empty theatre

except for a trio of 14-year-old girls, a straight middle-aged couple (the higher the hair, the closer to heaven), a blatantly heterosexual young couple flaunting it in public, and two lone women on opposite sides of the theatre who probably should have been sitting together. I prepared for jeering.

Well dang it, if everyone didn't respond respectfully and enthusiastically, improving my opinion of Texas. After all, Molly Ivins and Ann Richards live there, too.

The next day Bonnie and I hit the Stockyards area with its faux General Stores filled with Georgia O'Keefe animal skulls, expensive cowboy hats, and every kind of tooled leather boot imaginable. There was also the unimaginable, like a change purse made from a bull scrotum (Waste not, want not). I bought this "Saco de Toro" or Bullie ("Congratulations, you are the proud owner of an original Bullie—an actual scrotum of the proud, virile beast that once roamed the range and....") for a friend who'd warned me of such Texas oddities.

Next, we waited along the street with the rest of the gullible touristas for the promised "afternoon cattle drive along the actual site of the Chisholm Trail!" I didn't expect Clint Eastwood and a thundering herd, but what I got was three pathetic geezers in chaps on old grey mares helping twelve geriatric longhorns wobble down the street.

Frankly, the cattle drivers were extraneous. The bulls were self-propelled. None of the bulls wanted a pair of long horns anywhere near their saco de toros, so they just kept moving.

All this machismo made us hungry, so we headed for our choice of anything we wanted for dinner as long as it was meat. We tried Risky's Barbecue, but knew not how risky. After ordering Steak and Calf Fries for Two, the waiter asked, "What kind of potato do you want with that?"

This confused me. "I just ordered calf fries," I said.

"You don't know what those are, do you?" the waiter said, knowingly.

"No, I guess I don't," I responded.

"Cattle nuts."

Now there's no way to receive this news graciously. Suddenly I was in *Survivor: Texas*. My jaw dropped and I muttered, "Waste not, want not," which the waiter took to mean bring 'em on. Our unfortunate experience proves that after enough Buffalo Butt Beer, and with enough batter on the fried jewels, it's possible to take a tiny taste of just about anything.

We rinsed our mouths out with ice cream and headed for the Cowtown Rodeo. Now I admit to a long-held desire to see a rodeo. It stems from my repressed childhood when, like lots of other women of my persuasion, I ran around with plastic six guns and a Roy Rogers lunch box—no matter how much my parents wanted me to emulate Dale Evans instead. So forty-five years later I'm at a rodeo.

It started badly. One of the horses in the arena waited until the guest artist warbling the National Anthem got to "so gallantly streaming" and peed like the racehorse he was.

I'd heard that animal rights advocates hate rodeo culture and I saw why. It was fun watching violently bucking broncos and bulls bounce cowboys into the dirt until I asked Bonnie what motivates the animals to behave so badly. Turns out the poor bastards have some kind of cinch around their privates until they manage to buck it and the rider off.

No wonder they're cranky. Can you believe it, we're talking about scrotums again. Although I don't know why I was so upset about the bull's bullie being cinched, when I'd just sampled his cousin's nuts at supper. I was beginning to despise Texas.

It must be said, though, that while the cowboys tortured their mounts, the cowgirls, dressed in silky outfits with fringe, just raced horses around barrels. Girls are so sensible.

We had two more days of seminars and sights, visiting Billy Bob's—the World's Largest Honky Tonk, the Ft. Worth Woman's Club, where until 1999 there was a deed restriction against women wearing pants, and the Buckboard Museum. Okay, there were also some fabulous fajitas.

On our last night in town, as we faced yet another slab of USDA Prime, our waiter surreptitiously leaned over and whispered, "Are you family?" We gave the secret nod and he became our best buddy. When settling the bill, in addition to his 20 percent, I gave him another tip: "Lose Texas, come to Rehoboth."

In a bullie-for-you epilogue, back at our Rehoboth ranch Bonnie went to show somebody our Bullie purse purchase. She headed to the den to retrieve it, returning ashen faced, trying not to scream with laughter. "What, What??!!" I begged, as she howled until she couldn't breathe.

It turns out that treating our Schnauzers to those little freeze-dried pigs ears and hoofs from the pet store resulted in their having a taste for, um…organic treats. Git along little doggie! There was nothing left of the Bullie but the tag. Like I said…Waste not, want not.

Nuts. ▼

May 2002

No, I'm not writing about cattle parts again.

Living in Rehoboth is a trip. Not a road trip, like I used to take every weekend before I moved here, but a 1960s vernacular "what a trip, man" kind of trip. As a three-year local, I feel like I've never lived anywhere else. Okay, natives, I hear you sneering.

But much as I love my adopted hometown, there's weird stuff here—like last night's lead story on the 11 p.m. news: "Firefighters work together to save a horse caught in a chicken-house fire in Pittstown."

Don't get me wrong, I'm happy for the horse. But they never got to the hard-hitting facts, like what the horse was doing in the chicken coop in the first place, or why it was news that the Pittsville firefighters worked together. Oh yeah, the second story of the night was "Israel responds to suicide bombing with historic vote and movement of troops...." Priorities????

Of course, I've come to love the Farm Animal of the Day segment on *Good Morning Delmarva*. Yesterday it was a hog named Helen, who I think got a pizza for the honor.

Then there's the weather. It's spooky to see the crawl at the bottom of the TV screen warning of an impending twister. Last week they actually told folks in Ocean City to head for a basement or interior room. While O.C. and R.B. are miles apart culturally, we're really not all that far away as the cows fly. Come to think of it, I'd like the weather a lot better if Helen Hunt came here to track tornadoes.

As often as our weathercasters are wrong, every time there's a tornado warning anywhere on Delmarva I head for the closet, if you'll excuse the expression. But on the up side, last Wednesday meteorologist Tammy warned of thick fog and torrential downpours, advising us to allow extra time to get to work.

I added a minute.

For twenty years I commuted an hour each way. Now, when

there's traffic, it takes 11 minutes. Off-peak, it's five. So I just don't get our friends in the neighboring town of Lewes saying "you're going all the way into Rehoboth for dinner?" That would be a five to seven minute ride.

And it works both ways. People look at me like I've got two heads if I announce I'm off to Lewes for a 5 p.m. art opening. "But you'll never get back," they say. What am I, Ernest Shackleton leaving for Antarctica? Not to worry. I have lead dogs.

There are other weirdities. One day at my office I heard a rhythmic screeching sound, like somebody sawing through a metal dumpster. It got louder and louder and I finally looked up to see a pair of seagulls having sex on the roof of the Convention Center. When it quieted down I expected to see one of them smoking a cigarette.

The weird thing is working in a town quiet enough for this kind of behavior to be audible. I'm sure big city pigeons are just as busy propagating the species, but their love-making is drowned out by screeching taxi cabs. Around here, the honks are just short beeps by people waving at every third car or pedestrian because it's somebody they know.

And I devour the local papers—especially the published lists of marriage licenses, building permits, and divorces. From my personal experience with home improvement, I think the three lists are correlated. People get married, they try to renovate a bathroom and, if they are not skilled in communication and first aid, pfffft, they move to the divorce column.

Along with all the weird things I love about Rehoboth life, I still occasionally find a need for consciousness-raising.

I joined Weight Watchers after Christmas, along with tons (literally) of other folks stuffed with excess yams. The program works; I'm a big fan. But that's the problem, I want to be a smaller fan.

But let's face it. Weight Watcher meetings are not our kind of girls' nights out. We venture out of cloistered Rehoboth into a world of Sussex County moms, grandmoms, young marrieds and singles—heterosexual almost one and all. It's culture shock.

The half-dozen lesbians in the room huddle in one row, each of us experiencing the oddity of minority status again. At the first few meetings, the instructor punctuated her discussion with phrases like "now girls, when you go home to your husbands...," or "ladies, your husbands will love this recipe, too," or, my personal favorite, the question "Who's husband lets her...."

Hell hath no fury like a lesbian hungry. I took the instructor aside and gently asked her to remember that our meeting was within chewing distance of Rehoboth and husbands weren't the only kind of spouses at home. Actually, I thought the few men in the program should have spoken out, too.

"You could just refer to our 'partners or mates,'" I encouraged. "That would suit everyone."

Our instructor responded well, although she insisted on using the tongue-twisting phrase "husband, wife or significant other" some twelve or thirteen times a session. The class went from a half hour to forty-five minutes. But we were represented.

But far and away the most perfect example of why I love this town, more than anywhere else I've been, happened last night. A group of us locals (natives, stop sneering...) were dining at the new Thai Restaurant downtown.

We'd lingered over cocktails at one couple's home and gotten to the restaurant later than expected. We were just finishing up our Pad Thai and Curry when I looked at my watch and realized it was seven minutes to the season finale on *The West Wing* and none of us had set a VCR. Crisis!

Let me tell you, we stuck one person with the check (thanks, bunky) and five of us leapt from our seats, ran out to the street, hopped in our cars and raced off in three different directions. We all got home in time to see "previously on *The West Wing*...."

Followed by "Golf cart vandalized, bench seat stolen, details at 11."

You can take the girl out of the city AND you can take the city out of the girl. ▼

June 2002

As I lay frying on the beach at North Shores this week, looking around at the hundreds, if not thousands of women around me, I closed my eyes and reflected about how I came to this place. Figuratively.

I was a seriously late bloomer. It wasn't until my 40s that I developed the nerve and passion for speaking out publicly. I can say it was a very different time, with very different issues, twenty-something years ago. But truth is, I was asleep at the switch.

I wasn't even an activist in the 60s, when everybody and their dog was smoking dope and distrusting anyone over 30. Oh sure, I wore tie-dye and love beads, marching to protest the Kent State shootings, but I'm reasonably sure I just didn't want to be left back in the dorm. As a theatre major, the hippie clothes and Birkenstocks were costume, not commitment.

I'm ashamed to confess that while my friends lobbied for a woman's right to choose, animal welfare and the ERA, I memorized Broadway musicals and hung out at Bloomingdale's. I cared, but was never motivated enough to put down my charge card and defend a damn thing.

I wasn't even vocal about gay rights. I was divorced and 30 when I finally came out as a lesbian. Family and friends, so relieved to see me happy for once, adjusted without missing a beat. So blind was I, the early 1980s and Reaganism actually seemed like an era of good feeling between America and gays. I was truly delusional. I heard my friends' horror stories about the past and thanked my lucky stars it was 1982.

Then it was 1984 and AIDS hysteria hit. Amid the press barrage and tabloid trash I watched homophobia rear its head and bellow—it seemed—at me. Friends who'd grown up with bigotry and fought for Gay Pride were prepared for the ugliness. They fought back; they handled it. Not me. I just got miserably depressed.

Finally, Bonnie had had enough of my moping and told me to get angry, fight back, and get even. I started reading gay history and devouring anything about us in the press. I'd clip stories and highlight quotes I liked, and those I didn't. From the very back of the closet, and under a ridiculous pen name, I fired off letters to editors complaining about biased coverage, unwarranted sensationalism and false stereotypes. Venting my anger by mail felt great. Reading my published words in places like *People* magazine and *The Baltimore Sun* to balance the bigots' letters felt even better.

Although I never invented boyfriends at the office, I stayed very private. But one day in 1986 I heard one faggot joke too many and my mouth took on a life of its own. My nose was peeking out from the closet and I'd traded lesbian invisibility to make the point.

Teetering on the brink of full disclosure, I was outed at an early 90s (Gay Nineties?) office staff meeting. My boss and five other department heads—all married—sat discussing whose spouses would attend an upcoming conference reception.

"Hey, what about you, Fay? You and Bonnie never have to go to these things," said a cohort.

"Yeah," said another, "how come you two don't have to go?"

Before I could stutter an answer, my boss piped up. "That's true, we'll see you both Friday, as well, right?"

It took me a minute to process the fact that not only weren't they shocked I was queer, they were truly pissed that I'd had a free pass from odious meetings because of it. Fortunately, Bonnie was a good sport about going to office crap from then on.

I began to discuss my social life, in light generalities, with selected colleagues. And my real name replaced the pen name on letters and essays to local publications. That is, other than my own publication. As editor of a community newspaper, I lived a weird schizophrenic existence, writing out and proud letters and essays for the *Washington Blade* and other publications, while staying nauseatingly closeted on my own pages. Not only was it dishonest, but it was hell on my writing. Just try and tell a first person story like I do in this column without referring to the person who accompanies you on all your adventures. It made for constipated copy.

When I started writing for *Letters*, it was like being struck by fairy dust. Everything's honest. You say what you mean. You mean what you say. It emboldened me.

When I finally moved to Rehoboth, the only thing I knew about my future was that my personal and work life would be inseparable. I would never again be closeted for a job, and never stop being honest about my life. At my Rehoboth job interview I was asked, point blank, if I would continue writing for *Letters* once I'd moved to town and accepted the job being discussed. They hoped I'd tell them that I'd quit writing. I know that I almost lost the job offer because my answer was "yes, I will still be writing." I stuck to my guns and I hope that my employers are, if not glad, no longer uncomfortable.

So my evolution as an activist is going pretty well.

In fact, at dinner with friends the other night somebody pulled out the new *Damron Women's Travel Guide*. We were having all sorts of fun looking up gay venues in other cities when I said "Let's see what it says about Rehoboth."

You know that old saying "He's so gay that when you look up the word in the dictionary you see his picture?" Well Bonnie and I looked up Gay Rehoboth in *Damron's* and found our pictures. Literally. There we were, frolicking on the beach in a CAMP Rehoboth ad. How gay is she? Well, when you read The Best Lesbian Guide to the USA you see her picture. Now that's OUT.

From where I sit now, literally, basking in the sun and surrounded by a huge slice of lesbiandom, a good sprinkling of their offspring and plenty of their canine friends; and figuratively, saying anything I want to say, out loud and in print to whoever wants to know, my evolution seems pretty, well, complete.

My only regret is that when I lost all that internal homophobia it didn't take a few dozen pounds with it. ▼

June 2002

No matter how lovely the wedding, I have mixed emotions. While contemporary commitment ceremonies can involve bridal or groomal registry, dressing your friends like Ken and Barbie, and making a huge todoodle, I'm wistful that it just wasn't an option two decades ago. Even today, there's that pesky little problem of the state not recognizing our spouses with trifles like health insurance, social security and inheritance rights.

Soapbox aside, Bonnie and I recently went to Northern Virginia for my best friend's daughter's wedding. No, not the Julia Roberts film.

And *we* think we have traffic. Driving the Washington Beltway was like lapping at Dover Downs. If it wasn't too late it would have been enough to make me go prematurely gray.

Arriving surprisingly alive, we did the wedding service thing, gushed over the truly lovely bride and headed for the reception. If Christopher Guest made a movie spoofing weddings (*Mazel Tov!*) like he did with dog shows (*Best in Show*) his cast would include the characters at our table. Everybody was pretty talkative until they deduced they were sitting with lesbians. When we got back from the buffet we discovered that everybody else had found seats elsewhere. Eeeewww....

My friend's son introduced us to the wedding party as Aunt Fay and Aunt Bonnie. I suddenly pictured myself as a decrepit brandy-nipping spinster with an ear horn. Two actual spinster great aunts, who remembered me from eleventh grade, assumed that Bonnie was my sister from New York. I would have tried to clear up the faux pas but neither could hear well enough to absorb news that complex.

Finally, the mother of the bride stopped by our table. After exchanging hugs, congratulations, and lamentations about how we got this old, I laughed and said, "This is quite odd for us. We're the only gay people here."

"You're wrong," she said, pointing to an angelic blond crew cut person in black slacks, a maroon silk shirt and tie, who I'd (wrongly) assumed was a 17-year-old nephew.

Nope, it was 20-year-old niece Jennie, here from Germany for the wedding. "Her girlfriend couldn't come," said the mother of the bride, matter-of-factly, making me very, very proud.

"Well," said Bonnie, "we need to meet Jennie."

Jennie lived in the U.S. until age 12, so language wasn't a problem. Her life back home, however, is a problem. In her small town the only gay bar is for guys and gay life is closeted. She and her girlfriend want to move to the states soon, but for now, life is pretty tough for a Hilary-Swank-Boys-Don't-Cry butch lesbian.

Hours earlier, on the way to the wedding, Bonnie and I had remembered it was D.C. Pride Weekend, but nixed the idea of taking these old bones downtown. "Been there, done that." All of a sudden, with a youngster in tow it seemed like a fabulous idea. As the wedding wound down, we asked Jennie about a field trip and her eyes lit up. Offering our goodbyes, we exited to the DJ spinning *I Will Survive.* Yes!

At the Vienna, VA Metro stop, a gaggle of young women wearing rainbow colored leis around their necks headed back to their car. "Where's the fun, tonight, girls," I hollered. "Everywhere!" they shouted back, coming over to the car to hand us a *City Paper.*

Jennie was in shock. "I can't believe it. They spoke to you. It's so open here," she said, furtively staring at the women.

We hopped the train and headed to D.C.'s Dupont Circle. Bonnie and I stifled yawns and pretended this was normal for us, rather than the hour we usually sleep through *LIVE! It's Saturday Night!*

We exited the subway onto one of the world's longest and tallest escalators—which, judging by the number of gay people on it, must have seemed to Jennie like the stairway to paradise. "Oh, I can look, but not touch," she said, a nod to her girlfriend back home. "To be in awe" is overused, but Jennie was in gargantuan awe.

At the circle, it looked like the whole world was gay. Rainbow flags flew on hotel flagpoles and in store windows. Stacks of Pride Guides welcomed triple the number of gay men and lesbians usually found sitting by the fountain. The gorgeous spring night and crowds of gay people made you want to celebrate. I was impressed, so I can imagine what Jennie thought. We took pains to remind her that this was Pride Week, and not always like this, but I don't think she believed us.

We strolled amid throngs of people and Jennie didn't know where to look first. Plopping our butts at an outdoor café, we positioned Jennie facing the street so she could see a zillion gay couples go by holding hands. Her eyes got as big as the saucers under our java.

The entire gamut of gaydom passed by—from crew cuts, tattoos, leather pants, chain belts and pierced eyebrows (boys and girls) to wild summer sun dresses, high heels, and lots of perfume (also boys and girls). The real kick was the number of middle-of-the-road every-day same sex couples, indistinguishable from the middle-of-the-road every-day opposite sex couples loitering with Chai Tea. For Jen, it was an eye-opener. By this time, my lids required double espresso.

Badlands dance club on P Street hosted the official women's dance. Despite the hour, there was still a huge line to get in. Fearful of missing the last train to suburbia we made do with walking the line, gazing at the diversity. That was just fine with Jennie. I think she was on out and proud overload as it was. Just being in the midst of the celebration, without alcohol, pounding music or even talking to anyone, seemed to be affirmation enough.

I remember how absolutely medicinal that could be after conquering the self-loathing, and fighting your way out of the closet. Heck, even now there was something really exciting to me about so many young women out for a great time. It was also really exciting still being vertical at 1 a.m.

Heading back to the Metro, both men and women tried to catch Jennie's eye, with many, I'm sure, wondering which team she played on. I would have loved to ask about her transgendered identity and more about her life at home. But such seriousness could wait.

For now we just laughed, talked a little bit about Rehoboth, and retraced our steps to the burbs—where the Father of the Bride was waiting up.

And we'll never know if he was waiting up to make sure Jennie was home safe from a field trip with those wild and crazy lesbian aunts, or if he was worried about the survival of the fuddy-duddy escorts. I hope it was a little of both. ▼

July 2002

We're running a B&B. Well that's not exactly true. We don't serve B. Most of the things in our refrigerator are science projects in carry-out containers. So we just run a B. Although that's not really it either. We're actually running a B&D.

Bed and Dog.

As anybody with a beach house knows, build it (or buy it) and they will come. A lot. Visitors are a fact of life. I'm absolutely not complaining. We love our guests.

When Schnauzerhaven first opened, I tried to be Martha Stewart, with matching sheets and towels. Three years later, folks are lucky to get a top sheet. And as long as we're investigating Miss Martha, I want to know who makes those crappy Martha Stewart pillows. You sleep with them one night, and bingo, the things shrivel up and get lumpy like cotton candy in a Nor'Easter. (What am I talking about here? Just asking...).

Frankly, I've had to institute a two-night minimum at our B&D because it just isn't worth changing the linens for one night. One time I mistakenly made the bed with a sheet we'd used as a drop cloth. My guests got Rustoleum butt.

Another morning I found one of my frequent overnighters completely re-doing the linen closet. I know she was selfishly seeking a towel that hadn't been used with flea and tick soap, but I thanked her profusely anyway. The linen closet was neat for a week, encompassing two more guest cycles, before it degenerated again.

Our bathrooms are fully stocked with little toiletries pilfered from our last visits to major hotel chains and every once in a while we squeegee the tub-surround to make sure we're not growing truffles in the soap dish (although I guess the dogs would sniff them out).

It's easy to tell there's a problem with the accommodations when you find somebody snoozing on the living room sofa in the morning. That's how I discovered the den sleep sofa was descended from a Transylvanian Torture Rack. ("We have spacious rooms, including the Dracula Suite, complete with its own..."). I finally donated it to two of our regulars who just bought their own Rehoboth lodge. It's their torture rack now and I have a new futon for guests.

Have you seen our driveway? Most nights it looks like a used car lot. Guests leave their keys in a pile on the dining room table, fraternity house style, so nobody gets blocked in. Bonnie, of course, can turn her Tracker sideways on a dime and ride over the lawn so she's not late for Sunday prayer at Our Lady of Lowe's.

And of course, there's the dog thing. Everybody and their dog shows up. One weekend we had six people and five dogs in our 1450 square foot bungalow. That's a lotta barking. And that was just the people.

We had three Schnauzers (our two plus a visitor), a 3 lb. Maltese and a three-ton Great Dane. Ever see a Great Dane puppy loose in a living room? It leaps tall coffee tables in a single bound, usually taking most of the tchotchkes off the table with it. Our male guests spent the weekend shielding their privates from the Dane's whipping tail.

Our B&D brochure should read: "The circa 1999 inn is located on half an acre of parched landscaping nestled in a private residential neighborhood between Food Lion and Wal*Mart. We have full service bathrooms, although dogs like to come in and watch. We serve a complimentary breakfast provided you pick up bagels the night before. For a full breakfast, The Crystal is just down the road. We have free issues of *Letters* and Cable TV featuring Animal Planet. The Terrier Lounge is open nightly, serving fresh water and Milk Bone biscuits; a companion cocktail lounge has a fully stocked bar, with margaritas and cosmos served on the pre-fab sunroom veranda. Check-in is whenever, provided the dogs let you in the house. Express check out happens when you've had enough. There's a spacious lawn for outdoor activities, but guests should watch for, er...land mines. This is a non-smoking facility unless the hosts try to cook the occasional breakfast. Then there's plenty of smoke. Nearby attractions include Poodle Beach, North Shores, and the Wash & Wag Dog Salon. It is a clothing optional establishment—for the dogs."

It's all very civilized. Of course, when family members check in, our stress level rises. Why is it, no matter how old you are, your parents imminent arrival makes you feel like a pre-teen?

This last visit I was all set: dog slobber wiped off the sliding glass doors, and green Swiss cheese culled from the fridge. An hour before the New Yorkers were to arrive my living room came under attack by an army of ants advancing across the windowsills and into the great room. Honey, I shrunk the extras from *Braveheart.*

I screeched out to Food Lion and stood, comatose, before the exterminating products. My God, if I buy Ant & Roach killer they'll think we have roaches. Ant and Insect Bomb? Pest and Wasp Killer? They don't have Dad-Is-Due-and-You-Live-in-an-Ant-Hill Spray.

When I got home, Bonnie was washing the houseplants because in looking for ants she found something called Aphids. I don't know what they are but I don't want my father to know I have them.

My parents and I survived the visit. The ants did not.

The strangest thing is happening, though. Here at the B&D we are losing a lot of our repeat visitors. I've been assured that it's not our spotty hospitality. In the past several months, three couples who regularly lodge with us have just bought their own Rehoboth places. And a fourth couple has been poring over financial statements to see if they can afford to check out of Schnauzerhaven and into their own summer retreat. I hope they understand they'll be going into the hospitality business.

Meanwhile, B&D life goes on, with no shortage of guests and no shortage of fun. But I want everybody to know that our establishment does not put little chocolates on the pillows. If guests see little brown things there, they probably ought to worry.▼

July 2002

When the week starts with the son of Ted Williams threatening to turn the baseball icon into a Popsicle, where can it go but up?

In case you missed it, the daughter of baseball great Ted Williams is suing to keep her half-brother from putting the former slugger in deep freeze—a process called Cryogenics. The kid figures science will eventually cure old age, they can wake dad, clone his DNA and produce pennant winners. Or something like that.

In the meantime, with the *Ted Williams on Ice* controversy all over *Entertainment Tonight*, you'd think they were touting Disney on Ice, which, is kinda funny now that I've mentioned it, because rumor has had it for years that Walt himself was flash frozen for posterity. I happen to have inside information from a VIP at Forest Lawn Cemetery in L.A. that Walt is indeed in the earth and not in an ice cube tray somewhere.

Be that as it may, to freeze or not to freeze Ted is still page one. Which is amusing, given the rest of the news. Love the stock market. You need Dramamine just to watch CNBC. After an internal audit of my personal finances, I've pretty well resigned myself to funding my 80s with a paper route.

And I'm trying to figure out why the words "special prosecutor" haven't been revived for our Prez & Veep's insider trading and failure to report stock deals. Somebody reported that W's failure to let the SEC know about transactions was "not a federal offense." Does this mean that a lowly blow job was a federal offense?

While I found things that Bill and the bimbos did federally offensive, let's get real. Politicos with runaway zippers are vastly more interesting than, say, CEO's raping and pillaging our 401(k)'s, but where are the calls for hearings and public hangings?

If journalists revealed as much detail about insider trading and inflated stock prices as we got about Monica Lewinsky's damn dry cleaning, we might actually protect investors. There's a concept.

You think I'm hot under the collar? I can't help it. Hot Flash! Hormone Replacement Therapy gives women every single disease it was supposed to prevent! If we didn't have strokes just hearing that news, we can now look forward to them. Do we throw away our estrogen, fry eggs on our foreheads, and sprout macramé on our chins?

An entire nation of my peers, 13.5 million women to be exact, will have to decide whether to chuck their age-defying Fountain of Youth pills and get used to a humiliating array of symptoms. We'll be wracked with insomnia, night sweats, hot flashes and, my personal favorite, violent mood swings. Even if nature didn't provide the mood swings, this medical science double cross would have.

And what about homeopathic remedies like Soy and Black Cohash? It sounds like a Humphrey Bogart film noir—*The Case of the Black Cohash*. I'm convinced we should just go out and start randomly eating twigs and leaves. Even doctors I know are shaking their heads.

Okay, let's review. We've got millions of irritable females, up all night worrying about morphing into Mammy Yokum, with perspiration on body parts that should be dry and dehydration of parts that should be moist. We're mad as hell and we're not going to take it any more.

I say we harness the energy and sic this army of pissed off, moody women on big business. Faced with clammy, crazed, middle aged women with goatees who've been up all night sweating over annual reports, CEOs will spill the goods and beg for mercy. We'll find out who cooked which books faster than you can grill a Steak-Um with a hot flash.

Following the triumphant corporate crackdown, we head out West, dousing the forest fires with our night sweats and bestowing cantankerousness on the estrogen fueled cheeriness of Britney Spears and the Olsen Twins ("Just you wait!!! You'll shrivel up some day, too!").

Then we deploy Troop Menopause to the Middle East to occupy all disputed territories until everybody plays nice. Two weeks into this Feminist Jihad, as both Arabs and Jews are being driven crazy adjusting their thermostats and staying one step ahead of the violent mood swings you'll have them begging to come to the peace table.

Find Bin Laden? No problem. Although I still don't understand why the covert operations of the entire free world cannot find a six-foot tall terrorist in a bathrobe, tethered to a dialysis machine. Even so, we'll just go in and smoke him out with the steam coming out our ears. After all, thirteen million women just learned their hormones were being revoked, their health was at risk and, oops, medical science used them for guinea pigs.

I can hear Martha Stewart's lawyer now. The Twinkie Defense has been replaced by the Prem-Pro Defense. "Your honor, they took away my Estrogen and I can't remember a thing!"

And we should infiltrate religious congregations where elders have been shuttling pedophile priests around faster than you can say *Where's Waldo*. Okay, millions of bad-tempered women are telling you to stop it right now, pay the victims enough to get counseling and instead of running a villain protection program, put them in jail where they belong. Fix this, or else. Be afraid, be very afraid!!!!!

That's it. We start a brand new acronym. Like MADD and GLADD, we have WIMMAN—Women in Menopause Marching Against Noxiousness. Our motto: Don't sweat the small stuff. Our mascot: the Purple Flash. Imagine the stuff we can fix. The possibilities are endless.

Of course, we'll have to do our work fast. One minute we'll be fiery crones on a mission, the next we'll be shivering and weeping in the corner, apologizing for living. Frankly, it's enough to make me very irritable. Although, as I tell my mate, "don't like this mood? Wait a minute." ▼

August 2002

It started with a conversation about gay pride. A request had come from upstate to hold a gay pride parade here. Frankly, I don't think we need one. The way we live our lives here every single day is much more significant than a parade.

As many of us know, pride parades were born of brave individuals having the courage to come out as gay in often hostile, unsafe environments. It was the combination of the safety in numbers theory and that marvelous gay male sensibility that produced flamboyant floats, parades and headlines. Oh yeah, those courageous dykes often did lots of the organizing, provided security, and led the way on their motorcycles.

Those early parades gave millions of people the courage to face their true orientation bravely, honestly, and healthily. To this day, pride parades in conservative states and communities continue to validate and motivate people to come out and live their lives truthfully, with confidence. And big city parades are giant, well-organized, expensive celebrations in themselves.

While there has been great progress and we have TV's *Will & Grace*, it still takes bravery to come out in a majority of cities and towns. Across the nation gays and lesbians still fight discrimination, and fear for their families, jobs, and lives. But at least here in Rehoboth, we have come a long way, baby. For Delaware, a true pride parade would be most valuable outside of Rehoboth Beach.

Why? In a single summer weekend, Rehoboth had the following pride parade:

On Friday night a political fundraiser was held at the home of two delightful and generous gay men. The candidate was a straight man promising not only to support anti-discrimination legislation for Delaware but to fight strenuously for it. The crowd, split evenly between gays and non-gays, mixed and mingled and pressed the candidate on quality of life issues large and small. In this candidate's campaign, equal rights for all voters is a given.

Afterward Bonnie and I went to dinner with a heterosexual friend who lamented that it would be much easier to meet a mate here in this area if she were of a different orientation. We all made lots of those "sorry, it's not a choice" jokes. But her comments said a lot about the size of our community here and its welcoming nature.

Also on Friday, *Letters* published answers to questions posed to the three candidates for City Commissioner. Here too, refreshingly, equality for all was an absolute given. In fact, one of the candidates responded "don't vote for me just because I am gay, but because I will...."

Following the night of politics, I spent Saturday rehearsing for the CAMP Rehoboth Follies. During the day, (and for the preceding weeks) I had the pleasure of working with eight lesbians putting together an amateur skit for the event.

Having worked with all sorts of divas in my theatrical career I'm happy to say this was one exceptionally cooperative, if not experienced, bunch. Of course, everybody had their own ideas and wanted to process all the directions and make sure everybody was happy. Women's Collective Meets Community Theatre. Directing them was like herding cats.

Our cast was delighted with the reception they got from the approximately 1000 cheering audience members (straight and gay) at Convention Hall that evening. As one of only two groups of women among the men's drag acts, we were thrilled to take part. Our gals spoofed lesbian stereotypes, had power tools for props, and sang "Nothin' Like a Dame."

"Oooh, you lesbians are so cool, and you do have a sense of humor!" said one young man with washboard abs. "I need to meet me some lesbians," said another. So we had another kind of pride—pride that Rehoboth's gay men and gay women were celebrating together.

Even the very straight sound technicians got with the program and found themselves offering their votes for best skit.

Two straight women friends of mine from D.C. came to the Follies, and hooted and hollered along with the crowd. "We've never been to such an outrageous show and had so much fun in our lives!" they said, and I think they meant it. The cheers, laughs, mega trashy humor and community pride just rocked that Convention Center.

At 11 p.m. when the curtain came down, the audience and performers (many of the boys still in high heels, high hair and phony tits) spilled out onto Rehoboth Avenue, heading for home or around town for a nightcap. It was an impromptu gay pride parade all its own.

By the next morning, when our heads cleared (oh, did I mention the cash bars at Follies, dispensing vodka etc. all evening? It was all for charity, hon....) we wound up at one of our gay friendliest restaurants for brunch. As our party walked in, people at several tables recognized some of our divas and commented on their performance. Most tables included both gay and straight diners, and everyone was jabbering about the Follies.

Do we need a gay pride parade here in Rehoboth? I think not.▼

August 2002

I sat around from 8 a.m. to 4 p.m. the other day waiting for the cable person to show up. He or she never did. As I stewed, I fantasized about all the wrongs I'd right if I had the chance.

1. We'd tell the cable crew we'd be home some time between noon and four, and then hit the beach, leaving them sitting in their sweltering truck on my driveway, staring at their watches.

2. I'd re-record my answering machine.

If this is a credit card offer, press 1

If you are calling from a long distance phone company, press 2

If you are a telemarketer trying to sell me something I don't need, press 3

If you're calling to solicit donations for my alma mater you must be kidding.

And after having them press a dozen numbers, followed by the go pound sand sign, I'd program the phone to revert to dial tone. Buh-bye. Oh, and if a telemarketer asks "Is your husband home?" he or she would simply be zapped with an incapacitating electric shock.

3. Every time I had to go to the bathroom in the middle of the night, or thought I heard a strange sound, I'd be sure to wake the dogs, make them go outside (sometimes in the rain) and then make them wait patiently for me to be ready to go back to bed.

4. I'd tell the HMO "I'm sorry, that charge is over my personal customary and reasonable amount, so I'm only paying $20, and $10 of it is your co-pay. As for the mammogram, my having breasts is a pre-existing condition so I'm not paying you every year to look at them.

5. I would tell the folks building our garage that we'd write them a check on Monday, then say my pen hadn't been delivered, so they'd have to wait until Tuesday, and then on Tuesday

I wouldn't show up at all, and then on Wednesday I'd remember I was out of checks and....

6. Instead of Anna Nicole Smith or the exemplary Osborne family on reality TV, we'd get the real life of Jodie Foster and her family.

7. Rehoboth locals would have cars equipped like James Bond to bulldoze over tourists' mini-vans blocking our intersections. And, for good measure, we'd spray tacks out our exhaust systems directly in front of their SUVs. (Oh, is it ever August...)

8. There'd be the same number of hot dogs in a package as there are hot dog rolls.

9. Only Lesbians wanting offspring would menstruate monthly and the rest of us could do it only once a year like other large mammals.

10. Diane Sawyer and Katie Couric would be forbidden to feature three-month long wedding profiles, contests to pick the most fabulous love story, or other such alienating twaddle, until they agreed to feature at least one gay couple in each group.

11. Jerry Falwell and Pat Robertson would have to apologize for besmirching the reputations of all lesbians, since we aren't even *mentioned* in the *Bible*.

12. Stress would induce dramatic weight loss, clear up your complexion, lower your cholesterol and give you an edge with Publisher's Clearing House.

13. Maitre d's seeing two women coming into a restaurant together on a Saturday night would immediately lead them to a prime table (Yeah, like that would ever happen).

14. Emergency Rooms that make you wait five hours would be mandated to be called Waiting Rooms. And Trauma Centers could retain the name only if they treated trauma rather than dispensing it.

15. Instead of sending Americans to Kosovo to monitor elections, they'd send Eastern Europeans to Florida to monitor elections.

16. Grown-ups could open child proof containers.

17. Anyone sending you glitter or confetti in an envelope

would have to come to your house and vacuum it up; ditto for businesses that pack things in Styrofoam peanuts.

18. Bottled water and tofu would be horrible for your health and Belvedere Vodka and Funnel Cake would be hailed as miracle cures.

19. Only candidates who support the Delaware HB99 Anti-Discrimination bill would be elected this fall.

And finally, if I had my way, headlines would read...

20. Heterosexual serial killer arrested in California; Heterosexual priests settle with families of molested girls, Openly heterosexual elected; Heterosexuals quaffing green beer parade through town on March 17...you get the idea. ▼

October 2002

My father calls it the organ recital. You know, when everybody sits around complaining about ailments. Frankly I try not to bore people with that sort of thing since we're all starting to leak at the seams from one thing or another these days.

But over the past two weeks several medical oddities surfaced and I thought I'd share them with you. If sitting around in person kvetching is a recital, I guess I'm publishing the sheet music. It's Tin Pain Alley. (ba-da-bing)

First, the doctor called me intolerant. I've been called a lot of things in my time, but intolerant was never one of them. But then I never expressed a prejudice like this before either. All of a sudden, I'm anti-dairy. Lactose intolerant, and it's a bitch.

Me, who never met a frozen custard she didn't like; me, who's equally happy with a bowl of Cheerios and milk as a gourmet dinner; me, who lives for crème brulee.

So I opened negotiations with my stomach, offering to trade half and half for skim and a future draft choice. Even that watery stuff caused trouble. I was stuck with the disgusting powdery non-dairy creamer, and for a while I saw no point in going on.

My doctor gave me a prescription for one of those remedies advertised on TV. And if I might digress here, what the hell are drug companies doing advertising prescription drugs in the first place? Call me old fashioned, but shouldn't that be the doctor's call? Why should I go to a doctor asking for the drug I saw advertised by showing us a dog doing Tai Chi or people standing on mountains to cure their throat lesions? It's not like Madison Avenue is trying to convince me to buy soup. They're pushing me to buy something I'd be arrested for getting without a prescription. Does this bother anybody else?

And while I'm off the topic, how about those second generation drugs, like Sneezinex that replaces the older Sneezatin. The original drug didn't stop my allergies and the new one won't either. From what I hear, it's just a drug company ploy to keep making money once the generic of the original drug is released. Why is the public so gullible?

Okay, so I gladly stayed away from cottage cheese and skim milk, which wasn't really the problem, and grudgingly skipped the ice cream, which was. One day, sitting at my desk, eating my dairy-free lunch, I looked down and discovered a couple of little black spots on the hem of my khaki pants.

That darn stray cat I'd let into the office for a drink of water the day before must have had fleas. I walked to the convenience store, purchased some over-the-counter flea spray, gave my office a little shot and went home.

Back at the ranch, Bonnie gleefully told the dogs not to get near me because I had fleas. She rushed to apply prophylactic flea soap to the boys and threatened to wash me with it as well.

Overnight, in Rehoboth's own *Monsters, Inc.*, the fleas propagated their entire species in my place of employment. By morning, when I walked in the door, literally thousands of little black spots attached themselves to me, my clothes, my desk chair, etc.

In the time it took me to call an exterminator, open my e-mail, get my phone messages and flee the flea circus, the attack on my person was akin to the first forty-five minutes of *Saving Private Ryan*.

If you're wondering if I'd sat down in my desk chair, let me assure you I had. Benadryl spray was schpritzed head to toe, including, as Noel Coward once said, right up to Trafalgar Square.

I had flea bites down my shirt, up my pants, in my ears, it was disgusting. I didn't know whether to go to the dermatologist or the vet. And I couldn't even soothe my agony with a scoop of chocolate mint chip, which made me both intolerant and grumpy.

Fast forward, several days later. The exterminator had thousands of notches to add to his bombers' nose cone and my bites began to disappear. Except for a peculiar-looking one in the plunging neckline of my shirt. Hmmm, now that I looked at it in the mirror, it didn't look like a fleabite at all. This odd red blemish looked, well, more sinister.

Now here's a sentence you don't often hear: "It's a good thing you had fleas."

But that's what my dermatologist said as she did a biopsy of my non-fleabite.

Turns out that waaay back in my 20s or 30s I'd probably gotten waaaay too much sun in a low cut bathing suit and there it was—a small skin cancer that required attention.

Gee, since the biopsy was just a little scrape, I figured the trip back to the doctor to remove the thing was no big deal. Okay, I was delusional. Turns out the dermatologist gave me a local anesthetic and hoped I wouldn't notice that she and her team were using what appeared to be a front-end loader to make an incision on my chest. The damn thing took ten stitches to close. Who knew I was going to have a quasi-lumpectomy?

So there I was with stitches in my cleavage. If you bump your head or hurt your arm you're allowed to favor the injury. What could I do, walk around saying the Pledge of Allegiance?

Well, this whole organ recital thing finally came full circle on our drive home from the dermatologist. I decided to write about these events since the disgusting attack of the flea circus seemed, after all, to have some higher purpose. I could warn sun worshippers to use sunscreen or at least check for things that don't look like flea bites.

But the really odd part of this medical mystery happened as I had my hand to my chest, giving the impression I was doing a Mea Culpa. I already felt queasy from the minor surgery, so I figured that having a good old-fashioned milk shake to make myself feel better couldn't hurt. The hell with intolerance.

Funny thing was, I was just fine. The next morning, I snuck milk in my coffee. No problem. By nightfall I had my face in a half-gallon of Cherry Garcia. My lactose intolerance must have been mere temporary indigestion. I can be a dairy queen again. That's a good thing. So is being careful about too much sun. Go get checked out, please. ▼

March 2003

You can tell a winter night in Rehoboth. We were watching sports at our favorite bar. No, not football. We were watching the Dog Agility Trials on Animal Planet.

There we were, a bar-stool cheering section hollering, "Go, Sparky!," "Atta Boy, Rufus!"

We had everyone rooting for the four-legged critters, even our vaunted bar tender. "Hey, this is great," said one patron. "I was in a sports bar the other night and every TV had football or basketball. I guessed it would be dangerous to ask if they could change to House & Garden's *Trading Spaces.*"

Smart move. I could just imagine.

But as much as I like the dog shows, the rest of TV is a sludge pool lately. I should sue *CSI* for loss of consortium.

That's right, after two decades, my mate and I no longer watch the same television programs. It's not that I don't like mysteries and documentaries. It's just that somebody replaced *Murder She Wrote* with Murder She Showed Us in Disgusting Detail.

With the highest rated shows being *Crime Scene Investigation* and *Law and Order,* guts and gore have completely engulfed television. Luckily, it's not smellovision, but that's gotta be next.

Used to be, when you saw a little leg on TV it was the Rockettes or the Miss America Pageant. Now you get some pathologist holding up an actual little leg. It's disgusting.

Take *CSI.* I love the idea of forensic pathology. I loved it when Jack Klugman's *Quincy* was on the tube, explaining how some barely detectable poison killed the guy everybody hated.

But he *explained* it. Now the pathologists show it to you in living, pumping color. And not just under a microscope. There's always a big, full-screen zoom of an excavated corpse with identifiable organs. For this I need a 32-inch screen?

And if it's realistic, that's one thing, but *CSI* and some of the other shows now go in for special effects and futuristic travels through the esophagus of life. *St. Elsewhere* meets *Star Wars*.

And I love the *TV Guide* descriptions: "Horatio examines a torso found in the stomach of a tiger shark." Um…what else is on?

I was watching The Learning Channel the other day and they were showing me stuff I didn't need to learn. I mean there are lots of topics good to know, like how to escape a sinking car or survive a smoky fire, even if I'm lucky enough never to need the knowledge. But there is absolutely NO WAY I'll ever accidentally participate in an 18-hour heart-lung transplant. Exactly who is the learning channel trying to teach? Interns are sleeping.

And with the "if it bleeds it leads" TV news mentality, we're not spared platelets at six o'clock either. Why should I invest in a new large screen plasma TV when all I'm able to watch is large screen plasma?

All this is just a preface to tell you that my spouse loves to watch this stuff. I try to stick it out and watch what she watches, but it always reaches a point where it gets way too disgusting and I have to leave the room. Not only am I thoroughly grossed out, but I never find out who dunnit.

Of course, sometimes these shows might be valuable. I can waltz through the TV room on the way to the kitchen for popcorn and accidentally become witness to an amputation or hysterectomy. An inadvertent glimpse of somebody's oozing vital organ is one of very few things that can make me lose my appetite. For me, *CSI* can be minus 23 Weight Watcher points.

Channel surf and it doesn't get any better. Yesterday, over on Animal Planet, I caught a big slobby sow (or was that was Anna Nicole Smith on E!?) birthing a dozen slippery, gooey piglets. "Here ya go, Louise," says the vet, "let me see your teats. Yessir, they're squirting pretty good. You're due any second. Here they come!" Waaaay too much information.

Was that me squealing or the three little pigs? I huffed and I puffed and I managed to keep my lunch down.

This isn't Reality TV, it's Fluid TV. If ESPN is all Sports all the time, and CNN is all News all the time, then the rest of the hundred channels are all mucous all the time.

I want to know how this bloody craze got started. And how to stop it. Even HBO's *Six Feet Under*, as ghoulish (and as fabulous) as it is, can't resist the temptation to give embalming lessons. I'm not squeamish about dead people. I'm squeamish about seeing the telltale signs of why they turned into dead people.

Okay, say this guts and gore craze is here to stay. Taken to a logical conclusion, the great ratings for entrail TV will inspire other perfectly lovely programs to get on the blood bath wagon. What's next, Food Network kitchen accidents? The implications for HGTV's power tools are horrific. Network executives could insist that Katie and Matt undergo on-air root canals. Would Diane Sawyer and Barbara Walters be so eager to sign million dollar contracts if live electrolysis were part of their must-see TV deals?

Hey now. How about real bullets on those political cross fires? There have been days I've wanted to start shooting myself. The possibilities are endlessly disturbing.

Even Sponge Bob Square Pants is liable to drown and we'll get to see his little cartoon self, tossing his cookies after CPR.

So I'm thinking of a class action suit to try to bring some class back to the action. TV needs a transfusion. I'm going to sue the networks for loss of consortium not to mention their loss of blood. Just like that old Faye Dunaway movie *Network*, I want to scream at the TV, I'm angry and I don't want to watch it anymore!!!!!

It's like my favorite line from the old Broadway comedy *Butterflies Are Free*. After coming back from a contemporary play, a mother tells her son she's disturbed by the violent content.

"But Mom," says the son, "those things are all part of life."

"Yes," she says, "so is diarrhea, but I don't classify it as entertainment."

Amen. ▼

March 2003

By now, those of you who pass my house regularly on the evac-
uation route out of town may have noticed we added a garage.
The construction wasn't without its adventures, but the final result
is great. Especially for the blizzard of '03.

But while having a garage to house two cars plus an assortment of tools, holiday ornaments and schmutz has its good
points, there's been at least one drawback.

My friends keep accosting me with the rant, "You are NEVER
home! Where have you been? We keep driving by and there's
NEVER anybody there!"

Okay, pals, think about it. We are not skiing in Aspen; not out
every night slurping Cosmos; and certainly not wintering in the
tropics. We simply parked the chariots in the garage. Duh.

I can't tell you how many otherwise intelligent people didn't
connect those dots.

That being said, we did sneak off to Florida for a week in
February and had a grand time visiting friends and family.

Amid lots of fun came a story that's too good to keep to myself.

My friend Ronni and I have known each other since the days
when anti-war activists took to the streets and...hmmm. Okay,
that time 30 years ago.

Unlike me, Ronni has a passion for exercise. Having been an
enthusiastic but not particularly fast marathon runner, she always
joked that her autobiography should be called *I Finished Ahead
of the Clean-up Truck.*

Now that we're older, and new generations of students are
out running and protesting, Ronni has traded marathons for brisk
dog walking. Last month when we visited her in Ft. Lauderdale,
she set out early one morning to take her Jack Russell Terrier
Rufus for a morning jog.

After quite a long time, she and Rufus returned, the both of
them looking rather shell shocked.

"What happened?" I asked.

"Well, we were coming back from our walk, when I saw this guy on the beach and he started running toward us. I couldn't figure out what he was doing, and next thing I knew he came up to us, ripped my fanny pack right off me and jumped into a waiting car."

She was giving me this horrid news, but seemed oddly bemused. Shock, I thought.

"Oh my god!" I said. "You could have been hurt, and he stole your purse, omigod!!!!"

"Think about it, Fay," said Ronni, "we were coming back from our walk. I'm a responsible citizen, what do you think was in the fanny pack?"

"He stole a bag of dog poop?"

She started to laugh. "Exactly. There was a ziploc bag full of it," Ronni says.

Now I'm laughing like a lunatic.

"Wait, there's more. I was standing there, wondering what to do, when this car comes up and a man leans out the window saying 'Lady, you just had your purse stolen, right? Well, I saw the guy get into the car and I chased him.'"

"I think 'oh, no,'" says Ronni.

"But he got away," says the stranger.

"I think 'oh, good,'" says Ronni.

The stranger says "But don't worry, I called the police and reported it."

Ronni tells me she thanked the guy and sent him on his way.

From there, Ronni and Rufus walked back to their condo. Rounding the corner, Ronni sees a whole squad of police cars converged up the street and figures something awful has happened.

"Excuse me," she says to a female officer, "I don't want to bother you, but I wanted to report that my fanny pack was just stolen."

With a look of relief and then glee, the officer shouts to her colleagues, "We got the victim!!!"

"We're really glad we found you," the officer explains, "because we caught the guy and recovered your purse. Now can you identify the contents of the purse?"

"Um, er...three keys...." says Ronni.

"Yup, the keys were there. Anything else?"

Ronni tries to gauge whether the officer is putting her on. No, she seems serious.

"Well, there was a plastic bag with..." Ronni looks down at Rufus and up at the officer. "Dog poop."

The officer starts to laugh, barely being able to spit out "No, we didn't recover any dog poop." Both victim and cop picture the hapless thief inspecting his booty and dumping the offending package in disgust.

"And I thought I was having a bad day," the officer says, looking at the police car where the poop snatcher sat, sullen and handcuffed.

"You are going to press charges, aren't you?" she asks Ronni, "since we went to a lot of trouble to catch him and besides, this was a serious crime, you could have been hurt."

The upshot was that Ronni had to go over and I.D. the guy and fill out a report telling the whole truth and nothing but.

A couple of days later, Ronnie found out that the hapless poop perp had already been arrested once for a drug offense. He was about to be put under house arrest for the doody heist and with the state having a three strikes law, it was only a matter of time before he broke out to score again.

The judge figures he'll wind up doing fifteen to life for stealing a bag of shit. *Les Miserables*, indeed. Jean Valjean may have been arrested for stealing a loaf of bread, but nobody's writing an opera for this doofus. Can't you just picture him in the yard at the big house with his fellow inmates asking him what he's in for?

And we thought we were tough on this sort of thing on the Rehoboth Boardwalk.

In Florida, if you doodo the crime, you doodo the time. ▼

April 2003

I happen to know, really well, two women who left their husbands to run off with their high school sweeties. Let's hear it for Classmates.com.

Apparently, the Internet really is a great way to reach out and eventually get to touch someone.

I was incredulous the first time I heard a story like that, taken aback by the second one, and now I'm just sitting around wondering who'll be next. That both of my friends who linked up (no pun intended) with their former beaus were straight probably gave me a false sense of vicariousness to this phenomenon.

Then one day I was leafing through *Damron's*, that wonderful gay travel guide, looking for New York accommodations, when I came across a B&B in the Chelsea section of the city. It had a website and I surfed over to it.

What follows is the e-mail exchange in its entirety. Only some names have been changed to protect the clueless.

Hello—I was browsing *Damron* looking for NYC accommodations when I came across (name of inn). I checked out your web site and got a surprise because I recognized the innkeeper's name (he who shall remain nameless).

Are you the (first name) who was my senior prom date in 1965? Rhodes School, Waldorf Astoria and then a post prom ride to Bear Mountain state park????

If so, we should have known we were both gay. Nobody else hates camping and likes Broadway THAT much.

I live in Rehoboth Beach (Gayberry RFD) with my partner of 21 years (Bonnie) and will definitely have to check out (name of inn) when we head for New York! If you have *Damron's Women*, our photos are in the CAMP Rehoboth ad under Rehoboth Beach. We're the two with dark hair on the right, front.

Cheers—Fay (Rubenstein) Jacobs

Dear Fay—Okay, I'm stunned (and my office staff is driving me crazy, insisting that you became a lesbian after you dated me!) and here's what I remember:

We were introduced by our mutual friend (name omitted to protect the yente), while you were both attending the Rhodes school (your family had class, she was just pretentious), and your other best friend was Mary Ellen (who starred in *Sound of Music* on Broadway) and you starred in *Outward Bound* in high school (you were pretty good, but what a bad play!), and we used to make out furiously in your parents' living room while they were out (Robert Goulet and Carol Lawrence lived in your W. 54th St. building, and so did the drunken Elaine Stritch, talk about your lesbian) and I hoped you'd never want to go further (which you didn't for a while), and we went to the Top of the Sixes for your prom, and you had a Corvette which you were still too young to drive, and our trip to Bear Mountain, and your visit to my home in Brooklyn (and making out in my parents' bed, which really freaked me out), and my telling you that we could never marry because my mother had the same name (!!!), and your going away to be drama counselor at summer camp and coming back and wanting to have more serious sex (God help me), which probably was the final wedge in our relationship. I still have photos of us dressed for your prom tucked away in my memory box (pretty scary).

How's that for recall????

And it's been 36 years since we last spoke!! And how cool to hear from you; I don't know if I have the *Damron Womens Guide*, but I'll check to see you. And it would be great if you and your lover would come to NYC and stay here; I'll make you a great deal. Much more to tell you, but time for dinner, and hope you'll write again and tell me how you got here from there over the last 35 (!!!) years.

Love, (HE WHO SHALL REMAIN NAMELESS)

Dear (HE WHO SHALL REMAIN NAMELESS)

Oy! Where to start!!!!!

First off, every man I ever dated (except the man I married, which is a whole other embarrassing story) turned out to be gay, so it had to be me that was the culprit, okay?

I'm glad you remember it was (Blankety-Blank) who introduced us, cause I'd lost that bit of info to the ages. I have no idea what happened to her, but you're right, she was pretentious.

As for Drama Club (I've heard it called Gay Head Start, you know), you were right about *Outward Bound* being a perfectly awful play. However, you were being too polite about my performance, as I'm a dreadful actress and you knew it even then. That's why I became a director. I foolishly tried to make my living that way for a while, but I have come to my senses.

Now to some appalling ancient miscommunication: Yes, we used to make out in my parents living room, where Goulet & Lawrence lived next door and Elaine Stritch dieseled to and fro. But, silly boy, it was I who prayed we'd never go farther than kissing; I was petrified and bizarrely disinterested. We sure could have saved ourselves years of angst if we'd just discussed it then.

And yes, I remember Top of the Sixes Restaurant, and Bear Mountain prom night. I actually do have the photos, 36 years later. However, I've totally repressed the Brooklyn make-out session in your parents bed (gawwwd!!!) and, contrary to your tragic misinterpretation, all I wanted to do when I got back from summer camp was go to more Broadway shows with you. So you had it all wrong!

What have I been up to? In college I majored in theatre and communications, watched all my friends get married, figured it was mandatory, married a freakin' professional accordion player (stop laughing), got divorced six endless years later, met my partner Bonnie 21 years ago, and then four years ago we chucked everything to move to Rehoboth Beach. I work in tourism & PR, and write a column for our local gay publication. You can check me out at www.camprehoboth.com.

By the way, that old Corvette croaked in 1973. I now drive the official lesbian car, the Subaru Outback.

We'd love to come to NYC and stay at your place sometime.

What a hoot that would be. Thanks so much for writing, even with those seriously skewed memories. With all the stories you hear about people reconnecting through the internet and running off with their high school sweethearts, we can both rest assured it won't happen here.

Cheers—Fay▼

June 2003

I'm in a love-hate relationship.

Everywhere we go, there's tension. I'm scared the relationship will fall apart. I've sought professional help from One Hour Photo so often I wish they took Blue Cross. I love/hate my digital camera.

I was a little dykette when I got my first Brownie Starflash. I've been through Instamatics, flash cubes, strobes, 35 millimeter, single-lens reflex, Polaroid, and point and shoot.

Taking pictures was simple. You plopped film in the Kodak, took pictures and left them at the drug store, waiting expectantly, sometimes for a week, to see if the photos "came out."

Well, since those days, almost everyone I know has come out but that doesn't help the evolving state of photography. Going digital seems like a good idea, but so did Phen-Fen.

Truthfully, I like taking digital photos. I shoot multiple shots until I get one with everybody's eyes open. I also love dumping pictures which, if they accidentally got published in this column could get me sued or at least disinvited to parties.

But the real negative is the fact that there are no negatives. A hundred years from now historians won't have a clue. Most people take digital pictures, send them to friends over the Internet, store the pictures on their hard drive and never even print them. What happens when the Dell detonates? Will a whole nation wander around in a daze like tornado survivors, having lost their wedding pictures? Yeah, yeah, we're supposed to be backing things up. But you know how THAT goes.

I'm the kind of person who believes if you don't have a picture of it, it didn't happen. Today, you can hold Matthew Brady's Civil War photos and negatives in your hand and see history. Where will our negatives be? In the bowels of some computer in a landfill at Mt.Trashmore? I'm telling you, there will be no evidence of us.

Now this truly makes me nuts because my secret obsession is photo albums. Bonnie will tell you, one time when we thought our house was on fire she practically herniated herself running down the stairs with a dozen leaden photo albums in her arms. Our fire drill is Women, Dogs and Albums first. I'm such a photo album lunatic that years after everyone else was sliding pictures into plastic album sleeves, I was still licking little black photo corners. When the company making them went under I had to detox from picture corner glue and there wasn't even a support group for me.

So I have a long history of understanding things like aperture, back lighting and red eye reduction. So why don't I get the pixel thing? Yeah, I know they are tiny bits of data that form a digital picture and they come in big bunches called mega-pixels. The more megas you have, the sharper the picture, the more expensive the camera.

What I don't get is why my 5 Mega-Pixel state-of-the-art camera, which cost as much as my sofa, can't deliver a picture as clear as those cardboard and plastic single use cameras from the drugstore.

The first time I printed an 8x10 from my new Olympus, everybody looked like Doris Day in those movies where she was filmed through a gauze-covered lens to make her look as young as Rock Hudson. Besides that, for some reason the flash ricochets, making everybody wearing glasses look like Tinkerbell landed on their frames. Animal eyes are particularly vulnerable. I can't get a Schnauzer shot without my boys looking like the poster children from *Night of the Living Dead*.

But as worried as I am about blurry photos and the lack of a permanent negative collection, I'm more bereft by the devastating psychological toll of going digital. I used to rush from vacation directly to the camera shop, and eat lunch next door while my umpteen rolls of film got processed. Vacation budgets included big bucks for the après trip picture glut. I didn't care what it cost because the thrill of ripping open those envelopes and seeing what you'd been doing for the past week was absolutely exhilarating.

Well, there's something far less satisfying about having already seen your pictures and then thinking about paying somebody to print stuff you've had hanging around in the camera for ten days. Just like that, the thrill is gone.

Hoping to reclaim the excitement I decided to try printing the pictures at home. My speedy printer managed to turn one-hour photo back into one-week photo with just the click of a button.

And the cost is staggering. Know why printers are absurdly cheap now? Because they practically give you the hardware and software, but make you pay through the nose for the wetware—ink. After just two or three 5x7s and right in the middle of cropping somebody's thighs out of a family portrait, my computer starts flashing "cartridge almost out of ink." And if you've ever stood in the aisle at Staples trying to figure out which cartridge goes with your printer then you know the fresh hell I'm talking about.

Of course glossy paper isn't cheap either. Between paper, ink and the time it takes to print the pictures, I could go on vacation again.

So for me, the answer was to bring my camera to the nice folks at the photo shop for digital printing. But unlike regular one-hour equipment that prints from that antiquated stuff called film, new digital machines are merely big, stupid computers with slots for your camera's memory chip. The machine had a slot that accepted Memory Sticks, Magic Memory Cards, digi-chips, cow chips, and pop tarts, but it didn't take the memory chip from my hot-shot camera.

I had to ask the local photo shop to order, at best, some kind of exotic adapter for my chip, or at worst, a whole new $20,000 machine so they can print me and Bonnie standing in front of stuff. It's humbling, to say the least.

So there you have it. I love playing with the camera. It's excellent for e-mail pictures and snapshots. It's fun at parties. But I hate how much it costs and what an ordeal it is to print the photos. While I love pressing the delete button after a goofer shot, I hate worrying that my hard drive will crash and take all of 2003 with it. And I detest making back-ups of my back-ups.

So as far as I'm concerned, digital is fun for now, but the second I head off for a major vacation or an important family occasion I'm stopping by the drug store for a cellophane-wrapped $7.95 disposable Kodak Fun-Saver.

It's the least I can do for posterity. ▼

June 2003

We're becoming a civilization with attention deficit disorder and I blame CNN. And MSNBC, CBS, NBC, ABC, QVC, and every other network and local affiliate with the possible exception of Nickelodeon.

I'm talking about that infuriating and relentless news crawl that's been on the bottom of our televisions since 9/11. Exactly how much simultaneous information do we need?

In a time of national crisis, having breaking news at eyeball level was innovative and informative. Now it's just irritating.

Turn on the set and you see a reporter, with film of beautiful downtown Baghdad in the background. It's interesting, but you can't process the words or the scene because the bottom of the screen is screaming about FBI warnings, debunked diets, sports finals and Eminem's rank on the music charts. With time, temperature, and weather graphics for city after city scrolling in one corner, and the NBC Peacock or CBS Eye blinking in the other, where the heck are we supposed to look? Chiropractors all over the country are seeing people for video whiplash.

One news channel reserves the upper left hand corner for really frightening stuff like flood or tornado warnings. Confusingly, another channel uses the same corner of the screen for network logos. Turn on the set and you see a logo of crossed palm trees and, depending which channel you're watching, it's either film from Saudi Arabia state television or a gale warning in Pensacola.

Sometimes the juxtaposition is entertaining. A reporter blabs about the President's tax cut and the bottom crawl acknowledges the anniversary of the day the Hindenburg Blimp blew up. I didn't know which story hawked a bigger disaster.

The thing about these news tickers is that the fronts and backs of sentences are forever being lopped off by station breaks. You come back from a commercial and see "...found alive in the wreckage." Who? It sounds like a living hell. It takes another twenty minutes staring at the bottom of the screen to find out it was a box of worms from a science experiment aboard the space shuttle. Yuck.

You glance away from the talking head in the middle of the screen for just a second and see the words "hoping to avoid the worst meltdown since..." And bang, we're right back at a commercial. Worst meltdown since Chernobyl? 3 Mile Island? No, I had to sit through a whole hour of headline news, which by the way, repeats more often than that, to find out somebody was accused of having the worst meltdown in NBA history. Foul.

At one point a blurb announced a class in make-up application taught by drag queens. Now this is something I would have liked to know more about, but it's like a phantom headline. No newspaper, magazine, Internet site or evening news ever breathes another word about it. I think interns make this stuff up and type it onto the AP wire.

And speaking of drag queens, that's who I thought the phrase "taking off their horsehair wigs and elaborate gowns" was referencing, but no, an interminable time later I discovered that the crawl was about British jurists contemplating changing their traditional garb.

I loved the CNN piece about an Asian city under threat from the SARS virus. A shortage of disposable face masks prompted women to use brassieres instead. Go ahead, picture it. Not only was the picture worth many thousand words, but the simultaneous news crawl happened to be about zany new fashion trends. Coincidence?

Actually, it might not have been a coincidence, since some stations enhance their incredible shrinking commentator's words with a news ticker about the same subject—giving you additional useless facts and figures about the story in progress. Other stations just crawl completely random factoids just to distract you. It's cruel and unusual punishment.

Often, the shorthand needed to put complex stories into news crawl form breeds confusion. "Senator Kerry accuses President

Bush of waging a war based on questionable intelligence." Okay, maybe that's not confusing at all.

Following are some of the news items I managed to see either the beginnings or endings of, but never found out another word:

"...but over brushing of teeth is harmful."

"100K angry bees sting truck driver in..."

"...beating her with an iron skillet."

And my personal favorite, "...when sour neighbor busts lemonade stand."

Quick cuts and splices may be fine for the MTV generation, but just trying to read the damn thing gives me a headache.

Apparently, I'm not alone, because I found a web site petition online called "Stop the News Crawl!" I signed it, although I imagine its fate will merely be fifteen seconds of fame some day on the bottom of my screen.

The final humiliation comes closer to home. Since every Sussex County morning is fog bound, the regular cluttered mess of a screen is reduced to a third its size so the local station can run school delays. My favorite is the curious crawl, "John the Baptist two hours late."

During the school delay marathon my 27-inch television screen is reduced to the size of the set I watched *Howdy Doody* on in 1955. Boy I'm glad I didn't buy that 54" $8,000 flat screen plasma TV so I could watch a 13" screen surrounded by a flashing list of every charter school on the Eastern Shore.

Frankly, now that all news is breaking news, including, this morning, a crawl announcing the box office receipts for *Dumb and Dumberer*, what will happen when we actually have a national emergency? I guess they'll just break in with, gasp, a full screen of some newsperson talking directly to viewers. The novelty will be absolutely riveting. Shock and awe. ▼

July 2003

In the interest of full disclosure, let me say that I recently hit the speed limit birthday. Double nickels, that is, not the I-95 limit, and certainly not the three digits-plus on the Autobahn.

And when you write a first person column, incorporating the amusing antics of others, you have to tell on yourself sometimes, too.

So the truth is, I'm older than I ever imagined I'd be. I bought my first home in 1975, and I can remember staring in disbelief at the mortgage paper noting loan payoff in 2004. It seemed unimaginably distant.

Since then, of course, I got rid of both that house and that spouse. However, it is now perilously close to 2004, and there'll be a Wawa on Mars by the time I pay off my current digs.

I'm in the pharmacy now more than the liquor store, and have a slew of minor age-related ailments (okay, maybe they're jalapeno and stress related) but I still feel a lot younger than my driver's license admits. Am I deluded or, as some magazines suggest, is 55 the new 35? Okay, 45????

As my birthday approached, I found myself doing things unbecoming a woman my age, and I liked it. For instance, America Online now has a roster of sounds you can adopt to announce your online presence. If you instant message, your signature sound accompanies your comment.

My adopted son-the-comedian told me about this stuff and helped me select my audio John Hancock. We auditioned a symphony of instruments ending up with the most disgusting of barnyard calls. He'd type "hi" with a bleat and I'd answer with a burp. He'd boing and I'd bray.

We'd gotten to the protracted electronic flatulence when I was laughing too hard to continue. I told him we had to stop because my stomach hurt, but I'd forgotten to change the sound and my message came with a loud fart. Is this any way for a woman who would have gray hair if she didn't dye it to behave?????

One night a party of six sat at my dining room table playing Trivial Pursuit, and having more fun than I can ever remember overhearing when my parents had dinner guests. The only way we remembered our age was from the questions in my two-decade old edition of the game.

"What presidential assassin is due for parole in 1986?" (Yipes! Is he out?????)

"What's the capitol of West Germany?" (um, where IS West Germany???")

"What is the Soviet Union's ruling political body called?" (Defunct?)

Ashamed as we were to admit it, we did know that the answer to "What musician's license plate is 'A1ANA2' ?" was Lawrence Welk. But hey, some of us have at least heard of Britney Spears.

The most amusing antique question was "What U.S. President declared 'the White House had no involvement what-ever in this particular incident?'" Geez, what president didn't? From Iran-Contragate to Zippergate and now Iraqgate, that card's sadly contemporary.

I really tried to eschew my age for my June journey to the DC Pride festival. Subtitled "How Old People Go to Pride," the day started with checklists. My friend Joan and I made sure we had sweaters for a chill, water for our medications, Elmer's Glue-like SPF45 sunscreen, and inhalers for going to dinner in DC where they don't have Delaware's smoking ban.

We left Rehoboth twice, departing with glorious abandon, but turning around three miles up Route One because we couldn't remember if we'd let the dogs back into the house or pressed the button to put the garage door down. We had, but I felt like I was channeling my grandmother.

Once we got to the DC 'burbs we hopped the Metro to the City. Would we know where to go when we got off the train? No problem. Exiting, we were swept up in a roiling sea of young, pierced, tattooed, baby-carrying gay people flowing toward the fest.

Carried by the tide, we witnessed the most incredible diversity of people—diversity within diversity. It was a multi-cultural, multi-ethnic, multi-age mix with as many little old ladies like us as there were gaybies, trannies, drag queens, drag kings, dykes on bikes, leathermen, and all manner of gay families.

We did, of course, rush through dinner at that smoky Dupont Circle bar so we could get back on the Metro and back to our cars and back to Rehoboth without turning into pumpkins.

But my most age-related revelation came last Saturday at the Stonewall Democrats Fundraiser, where Congressman Barney Frank spoke to the crowd with hilarious, yet very moving, stories.

As we stood under the trees in the vast backyard of a home along Silver Lake, Barney Frank reminded the nearly 300 people that although gay rights have come a long way in twenty or thirty years, we shouldn't be expected to feel grateful; we should fight for and expect full equality. He told a story of a soldier shot in the neck during World War I, who was told he was lucky to have survived. Yes, he said, but I'm not as lucky as those people who have never been shot in the neck.

Amen. This incipient geezer wants freedom from discrimination and recognition of her long-term relationship (inheritance rights, medical power of attorney, pensions, partner insurance) and all those other things married couples who have never been shot in the neck take for granted.

I don't give a hoot whether they call it marriage or not, but I want equality before I'm too old to dance at my civil union. ▼

August 2003

I was absolutely not going to write about gay marriage. Everybody else has been yammering about it for weeks. But a confluence of events left me no choice.

First, I got a call from the *News Journal* asking me what I thought about the whole gay marriage debate. I said something very bland about wanting equal legal rights but not caring whether it was called marriage or not. They quoted me verbatim. Only they added "said Fay Jacobs, gay activist."

Yipes! When did that happen? I don't consider myself a gay activist. I'm a columnist who happens to be gay. And I write about my life and things that are important to me.

So am I a gay activist? If so, I'm also a theatre activist and a Schnauzer activist (Paw Power!). Actually, I'm less a Gay activist than a Fay activist. I speak for me. I mean what's gay about ranting and raving about TV commercials, yoga class or rescuing cats? Okay, the cat thing might be borderline.

Half-smarting and half-proud of the pigeon holing, I went about my business, which happened to be planning an Alaska vacation. Owing to my vast ignorance of geography (If you get a blue question at Trivial Pursuit, don't look at me) it was weeks into vacation research before I realized our departure city was not Vancouver, USA.

I'm going to Canada? Lots of the current vituperation over gay marriage in this country has been stoked by our progressive Northern neighbor. Hmmmmmm.

"Hey Bonnie, want to get married in Vancouver before we leave for the cruise?"

"Sure. I'd love to."

Time out. Before I continue, let me weigh in on gay marriage.

1. If gay marriage had been legal, we would have married in 1982.

2. Since my religion (and lots others) already unite gay people in synagogues and churches, is a religion banning gay marriage suddenly our national religion?

3. Why is this a religious issue, when marriage is a civil rite, as in ceremony, performed as a legal contract between individuals and the state?

4. And where was I when the separation of church and state went missing?

That having been said, my innocent question to my girlfriend suddenly became a snowball rolling down the glacier face.

It took just a little over sixty seconds to find the Gay Vancouver web site and click onto the flashing Gay Marriage link. There, I learned exactly how to get the marriage license (walk into an insurance office), what kind of I.D. we needed (just a Passport will do), and how to arrange for a gay-friendly marriage commissioner to do the deed. It turns out that the license office is four blocks from our hotel and a commissioner lives nearby. A few e-mails later, the whole thing's arranged.

At that point, we alerted our travel buddies, Robert and Larry, to our plans and they decided to take the leap too. Now it's to be a double wedding.

"Okay," I said, "let's keep this quiet until we get home. We'll surprise everybody."

Yeah, right. One whispered comment to a friend led to another and we had to call our whole address book and tell them, lest they take umbrage at being out of the loop.

As for our families, not only are they pleased, but they're glowing. My father is sincerely thrilled about the wedding, and also, I suspect, that he doesn't have to pay for it. There's a Jewish mother in Florida announcing her son's plans to the whole canasta group.

My sister, who's sweet, but not always up on current events, accused me of eloping so she couldn't be there. Uh, Gwen, same-sex marriage is not legal in the U.S. "Oh, I forgot," she said. "Well, you're the only one." I replied.

Telling our family and friends was wonderful and we are all lucky to have so many people really happy for us. But I certainly had no intention of publishing our plans until that cute and hilarious columnist Marc Acito pre-empted us in the last issue of *Letters*.

Right in the middle of wedding planning I opened *Letters* to read that Marc and his boyfriend crossed into Canada from the state of Washington to be hitched. Congratulations, Marc and Floyd!

But when Marc was planning his wedding I bet the commissioner had heard of Washington State. The first person I talked to actually sounded like that joke "Dela-Where????" I had to explain I was calling from a small, but important state on the east coast of the United States.

"Oh, is it near North Carolina?" he asked. The two of us could use a good atlas.

So what with Marc bringing the subject up, and the rest of the world's news focused more on gay marriage than Iraq or the Terminator, it felt right to join the conversation.

Our quartet will leave for Vancouver on Thursday, August 21. Our rehearsal dinner will be airline food. The wedding is set for Friday morning. We get on the cruise ship for our honeymoon that afternoon. It remains to be seen if we raise our hands when the Captain asks newlyweds to identify themselves. After all, we don't want to add to reports of hundreds of passengers coming down with the vapors on a cruise ship.

As for tradition, we'll be taking SOMETHING OLD: Us!!! SOMETHING NEW: the latest copy of *Letters* to pose with it at our wedding; SOMETHING BORROWED: yeah, like the whole trip from MasterCard; and SOMETHING BLUE: hmmm...My varicose veins? The Planter's Peanuts bag from the flight? Me, when I think that I have to leave my own country in order to celebrate something so important and joyous.

Somebody call to see if we qualify for the *Guinness Book of Records* for the world's longest engagement.

We'll report more when we return. In the meantime, I am not an activist. I'm a bride. Or is that Bonnie?▼

September 2003
WE DID, WE DID.

It must have happened, I read it in *The Washington Post*. There it was, right smack in the middle of the Weddings page on September 10, 2003, photo and all.

Vancouver Nuptials for
Bonnie Quesenberry and Fay Jacobs

Fay Jacobs and Bonnie Quesenberry were married August 22nd in a civil ceremony at Le Soleil Hotel in Vancouver, British Columbia. Marriage Commissioner Karen Ell officiated. Ms. Jacobs, a graduate of American University, Washington, D.C., is executive director for Rehoboth Beach Main Street, a non-profit organization in Rehoboth Beach, DE. From 1982 to 1999, she worked as director of communications for Montgomery Village Foundation. Her parents are Mort Rubenstein and the late Shirley Rubenstein. Her father and stepmother, Joan Windell Rubenstein reside in Somers, NY. Ms. Quesenberry, a Baltimore native owned and operated Quesenberry Dental Lab in the area for more than 20 years, where she was affiliated with Johns Hopkins Hospital among other clients. In 1999, she relocated the lab to Delaware. She is also an accomplished designer of hand-made gold jewelry . Her parents are Natalie and Ray Quesenberry of Frederick, MD, formerly of Baltimore. The couple has been together for 21 years.

And, I might add, as soon as we were pronounced wife and wife, Canada did not fall into the sea. Actually, getting the announcement in *The Post* was more difficult than getting married. At first they wanted to publish it under "Celebrations" since they called it a civil union.

"Oh no," I said, "We have a marriage license from Canada."

"Okay then," said the clerk, "fax it to me and we'll run it with weddings!"

As for the wedding itself, Fay and Bonnie, and Bob and Larry, arrived in Vancouver, BC on the evening of August 21.

Awaiting us were two bride's bouquets and two groom's boutonnières sent to our hotel by our adorable son-the-actor. We all had jitters.

On Friday morning at 8 we walked a few blocks to the insurance office where marriage licenses are bestowed. "Oh, yes, come right back here," said the clerk, whereupon the boys sat at one desk and the girls another. "Oh, I see," said the clerk, without judgment. In fact, she apologized as she crossed out the word groom on our application and hand-wrote a second "bride." She added, "the new paperwork hasn't come yet."

With shaky signatures we signed on the dotted lines, paid our license fee and, clutching our marriage licenses (!) walked back to the hotel.

"We're getting married at 10 a.m., is it possible to use this back lobby of the hotel for the ceremony?" we asked the cute, blond, earring-wearing boy-toy concierge. He loved the idea, and told us he'd try to keep people from loitering and throwing their luggage back there.

Marriage Commissioner Karen Ell was waiting for our call and we asked her to meet us in the lobby at 10. "My husband will join me, to take pictures if you'd like," she said. We liked.

They arrived, all smiles, and following a flurry of signatures, Bob and Larry indicated that Bonnie and I should go first. At this point I have to say that my memory gets a little foggy. All I know is that instead of the sterile civil ceremony I expected, it was an incredibly sweet and personal few minutes. We stood looking at each other, glancing at our stalwart witnesses, repeating after Karen, smiling, fidgeting with the rings, and soaking up every minute of the event. I certainly remember savoring the words as I repeated after the Marriage Commissioner "I solemnly declare that I do not know of any lawful impediment why I, Fay, may not be joined in matrimony to Bonnie." Emphasis on lawful.

The brides kissed and made way for the second part of the daily double. Near the end of Bob and Larry's ceremony—a ceremony different from, and equally lovely as ours—a tear ran down Robert's cheek, followed by Larry misting up; then Bonnie went and I followed. One of the best photos shows us all falling apart. Even Karen the Commissioner started to sniffle.

The lobby formalities concluded, several heterosexual couples came up to congratulate us, and Bonnie and I tossed our bouquets to two little girls who were there with their parents. Gee, I wonder if they will grow up to marry lesbians?

We did notice that the handsome young bellhop who had stopped work to watch the ceremony grinned from ear to ear as he went back to work.

We ended the morning with a champagne brunch reception for four at a lovely restaurant along Vancouver's English Bay. Our friendly concierge had made the reservations and sent us congratulatory canapés.

It was a splendid and surprisingly lovely affair—and our only regret is that our friends and family could not have been there to share it with us.

I know I'm not doing my usual complement of whining and snarling, and I apologize for the mush. But we're Sadie, Sadie Married Ladies now and we can't stop smiling. ▼

A NOTE ABOUT THE AUTHOR

Fay Jacobs, a native New Yorker, spent 30 years in the Washington, DC area working in journalism, theatre and public relations. She has contributed feature stories and columns to such publications as *The Baltimore Sun*, *Chesapeake Bay Magazine*, *Washington Blade*, *The Wilmington News Journal*, *Delaware Beach Life*, and more.

Since 1995 she has been a regular columnist for *Letters from CAMP Rehoboth*, and won the national 1997 Vice Versa Award for excellence. Her writing is also included in the 1998 Alyson Publications' anthology *Beginnings*.

She and Bonnie, her partner of 22 years, relocated to Rehoboth Beach, DE in 1999. They have two Miniature Schnauzers and a riding lawn mower.

A NOTE ABOUT THE PUBLISHER

A&M Books was established in 1995 by Anyda Marchant and Muriel Crawford. It is now the publisher of the fourteen Sarah Aldridge novels, the first eleven of which were originally published by the Naiad Press. The Naiad Press was incorporated in 1974 by Marchant and Crawford as a Delaware Corporation, along with Barbara Grier and Donna J. McBride as shareholders. Marchant and Crawford sold their interest in the Naiad Press to Grier and McBride in 1995. All of the Sarah Aldridge novels are still available through A&M Books, including the latest Aldridge novel *O, Mistress Mine*. A&M Books is pleased to present this collection of the essays of Fay Jacobs under its imprint.

THE SARAH ALDRIDGE NOVELS
NOW AVAILABLE EXCLUSIVELY FROM A&M BOOKS

The Latecomer $6.95
Tottie $6.95
Cytherea's Breath $6.95
All True Lovers $8.95
The Nesting Place $7.95
Madame Aurora $7.95
Misfortune's Friend $7.95
Magdalena $9.95
Keep To Me Stranger $9.95
A Flight of Angels $9.95
Michaela $10.95
Amantha $10.95
Nina in the Wilderness $11.95
O, Mistress Mine $15.00

P.O. Box 283
Rehoboth Beach, DE 19971
1-800-489-7662